WordPerfect Office™:
The Complete Reference

WordPerfect Office™:
The Complete Reference

Kristy Clason and David Hansen

Osborne **McGraw-Hill**

Berkeley New York St. Louis San Francisco
Auckland Bogotá Hamburg London Madrid
Mexico City Milan Montreal New Delhi Panama City
Paris São Paulo Singapore Sydney
Tokyo Toronto

Osborne **McGraw-Hill**
2600 Tenth Street
Berkeley, California 94710
U.S.A.

Osborne **McGraw-Hill** offers software for sale. For information on translations and book distributors outside of the U.S.A., please write to Osborne **McGraw-Hill** at the above address.

WordPerfect Office is a trademark of the WordPerfect Corporation.

WordPerfect Office™: The Complete Reference

1234567890 DOC 99876543210

ISBN 0-07-881667-X

CONTENTS AT A GLANCE

Program Templates

Using Appointment Calendar *(continued)*

Using Appointment Calendar *(continued)*

Using Appointment Calendar *(continued)*

Using Calculator *(continued)*

Using Editor *(continued)*

Using Editor *(continued)*

Using Editor *(continued)*

Using File Manager *(continued)*

Using File Manager *(continued)*

Using Mail *(continued)*

Using Mail *(continued)*

Using Notebook *(continued)*

Using Notebook *(continued)*

NINE

Using Scheduler 431

Using Scheduler *(continued)*

Using Shell *(continued)*

ELEVEN

Using Notify, Repeat Performance, and TSR Manager

Predefined Macros *(continued)*

Program Templates

ACKNOWLEDGEMENTS

First and most importantly we wish to thank our families, for without them this book would not be possible. To Chris, for his unending support, encouragement, and love. To Angie, Devin, and Loryn for their patience and long suffering.

We are also grateful for all those at Osborne/McGraw Hill who have worked with us on this book. Thanks go to Roger Stewart for his wisdom and guiding hand, Laurie Beaulieu for her patience and knowledge, Janis Paris for her attention to detail, and the many others editors and designers who have spent long hours working on this book.

Many thanks to our technical editor, E. A. Glazener for his thorough review of the book and his insightful suggestions. Our thanks also go to Steve Dyson for his confidence and friendship.

WordPerfect Office™ is a complete office automation software package. With the increased popularity of WordPerfect, there is a need for other desktop programs that are compatible with this powerful word processor and that will add other capabilities to meet your computer needs. WordPerfect Office shares many of the standard WordPerfect keystrokes and functions which makes learning and using the WordPerfect Office programs much easier. Whether your office is in a business environment with hundreds of users, or in a home with just a few users, the seven desktop programs that come with WordPerfect Office will help you perform and automate many of your daily tasks. WordPerfect Office is also used as a means of integrating and sharing information between programs, users, and other communication systems. The power of WordPerfect Office can be as simple as performing a basic arithmetic calculation with the Calculator program or as complicated as sending a Mail message to a user across the country using one of the WordPerfect Connections gateways.

About This Book

This book is for all users of WordPerfect Office, whether you are just learning the basics of the programs, or are a veteran user of the program and want to know how to use the more advanced features of the programs. This book is also for system administrators responsible for setting up and maintaining the WordPerfect Office system. The book is specifically organized to meet the needs of all users with step-by-step instructions, practical examples, and informative technical material.

After reading this book you will be able to use all the desktop programs that come with the WordPerfect Office package. The examples and hints discussed in each chapter will help you customize the programs and utilities to meet your individual or system needs.

INTRODUCTION

How This Book Is Organized

Each chapter begins with the basic fundamentals of the subject at hand. As the chapter progresses the concepts build upon previous material and become more advanced. This approach makes the book excellent for both first-time and advanced users.

Part I contains two chapters. The first chapter introduces you to the components and capabilities of WordPerfect Office. The second chapter gives step-by-step instructions for installing Office and gives valuable information regarding the setup of Office.

Part II includes Chapters 3 through 11 and is a reference section giving detailed information about all the WordPerfect Office desktop programs and utilities. Each of these chapters is divided into two sections. The first section contains step-by-step instructions for using the program along with detailed examples for many features. This section is ideal for those who want all the information about a feature along with examples. The second section of each chapter is an alphabetical list of all the functions and features contained in the program. This section is designed to be a quick reference guide for those who do not need a comprehensive explanation. This section lists the function or feature, followed by the keystrokes, and if necessary a reference to a section in the first part of the chapter that gives more detailed information.

Part III is a system administration guide consisting of three chapters. These chapters are useful for both system administrators and Office LAN users. Chapter 12 gives a definition of terms used with WordPerfect Office LAN as well as requirements and recommendations for installing WordPerfect Office LAN on a single file server on a network. Also included are step-by-step instructions for completing the installation. Chapter 13 gives steps and suggestions for maintaining your WordPerfect Office system on the network. This chapter will help you fully utilize the performance of WordPerfect Office LAN. Chapter 14 gives you steps and suggestions for expanding your WordPerfect Office system to multiple file servers and for how to use gateways.

Seven appendix sections are included at the end of the book. Appendix A contains all the instructions needed to set up individual users on the network when installing WordPerfect Office LAN. Appendix B contains a list of all the ASCII characters. Appendix C is a list of all the WordPerfect character sets. Appendix D is a comprehensive list and description of all the files used with WordPerfect Office. Appendix E lists and describes the predefined macros that are shipped with Word-Perfect Office. Appendix F is a complete description of all the advanced macro commands that are available for use with Shell and Editor macros. The back of the book includes program templates for all of the programs shipped with WordPerfect Office.

Conventions Used in This Book

To help you fully utilize the step-by-step instructions and examples in this book, conventions are used to simplify the input of information.

- All keys that appear on the keyboard (ENTER, TAB, HOME, F1) are printed in small caps.

- All menu choices that are numbers or letters appear bolded and, if applicable, both the number and the mnemonic are listed (Press **2** or **O** for Options). The sample screens do not display the bolded options as they do on your monitor.

- Any text or options that should be typed are printed in boldface (Type **install** or press **1** for Go To DOS).

- When the word "Enter" precedes an instruction, press the ENTER key after typing the necessary information (Enter the default directory).

- Any keys that are separated by a hyphen inform you that the keys should be pressed together (SHIFT-F8).

- Keys separated by a command indicate that the first key should be pressed and released and then the second key pressed and released (HOME, 9).

- Text that is italicized indicates that the information displayed is a variable. Many times startup options allow you to enter many different things in combination with the same option as shown here, /D-*pathname*.

LAN

- A LAN icon, shown here in the left margin, is used to indicate that the information following pertains only to Office LAN users. This lets Office PC users skip information that does not apply to them.

No matter what your needs are, this book contains all the information you will need to effectively use WordPerfect Office. This book was written to help you, the user, increase your efficiency and productivity through the use of WordPerfect Office.

If you are a first-time user, the simple, step-by-step instructions make this book easy to use. You will also appreciate the way each chapter begins with the basic fundamentals of the subject at hand. If you are a more advanced user, the sophisticated applications will intrigue you. The functions and features at the end of each desktop program chapter in Part II will be helpful as a quick reference to keystrokes for every function. If you are a system administrator, Part III was written especially for you. This guide helps you set up and maintain your WordPerfect Office system in the most timely and effective manner. The appendixes will provide you with valuable time-saving presentations of ASCII and other special characters, program file lists, and macro commands.

WordPerfect Office: The Complete Reference is for every user of WordPerfect Office. As the title suggests, there are no other sources necessary for learning everything you need to know about WordPerfect Office—this is the complete reference.

WordPerfect Office Basics

Introduction to WordPerfect Office 3.0
Getting Started

P
A
R
T

O
N
E

Introduction to WordPerfect Office 3.0

WordPerfect Office PC
WordPerfect Office LAN
WordPerfect Connections

WordPerfect Office 3.0 is an office-automation software package designed to improve the integration (sharing of information) of WordPerfect and non-WordPerfect products, as well as provide quality programs to increase overall office productivity. WordPerfect Office 3.0 is available for personal computers (PCs), local area networks (LANs), and wide area networks (WANs). Each Office package allows users to fully utilize their system's individual capabilities.

WordPerfect Office PC

The PC package runs on a stand-alone machine (one machine without connections to any other computers) or on individual stations on a network (on a local drive of a computer on a network). The PC package includes six desktop programs: Appointment Calendar, Calculator, Editor, File Manager, Notebook, and Shell.

Appointment Calendar is a time and task organizer that lets you create memos, appointments, and to-do items for each day of the week.

Calculator includes financial, statistical, programming, and scientific capabilities.

Editor is an advanced macro editor, a sophisticated program editor, and a simple text editor. (*Macros* are a series of keystrokes or commands that are recorded for later use.) Editor uses the WordPerfect 5.1 advanced macro language.

Notebook is an information organizer and storehouse, similar to a small database. Notebook files may be used as secondary merge files with WordPerfect 4.2, 5.0, and 5.1.

File Manager is an easy-to-use advanced file-management program. File Manager features include Double Directory display, Directory Tree display, Directory Name Search, Find File, and Word Search.

The Shell program organizes your programs through a menu system, which allows increased integration and movement between all WordPerfect and non-WordPerfect programs.

For detailed information on all the desktop programs, see the corresponding chapters in Part Two, "Reference Section," of this book.

WordPerfect Office LAN

The LAN version of Office directly supports the following networks:

Novell Netware	IBM LAN Network
AT&T StarGroup	DEC PCSA
TOPS	3Com 3+ OPEN
3Com 3+	10Net
Banyan	Nokia PC-Net
LANtastic	Banyan Street Talk

WordPerfect Office LAN includes all the programs listed in the preceding section with the addition of the Mail and Scheduler programs. Mail lets you send messages to all users on a LAN network. Multiple security and priority levels may be attached to individual messages to let users know the importance of a message. On-screen notification of incoming messages is available. The Scheduler program works with the Calendar program in scheduling events. Scheduler uses information from users' calendars to display free and busy times. For more information on Mail and Scheduler, see Chapters 7 and 9.

WordPerfect Connections

The WordPerfect Connections package addresses the needs of users on a wide area network. This package includes the necessary files for installing the connection server. The *connection server* facilitates communication across multiple file servers and/or across multiple gateways with Mail and Scheduler. A *file server* is the computer that organizes and directs all the files on a local area network. Each local network has a file server. With the connection server, users attached to one file server can send messages to users attached to a different file server. *Gateways* are the means to convert or transport mail and scheduled items to other file servers, foreign mail systems (mail systems other than WordPerfect Office), and across different platforms (machines that use the same operating system) such as the Macintosh. The WordPerfect Connections package gives Office users a comprehensive office-automation package that communicates across many platforms. For more information on the Office Connections package, see Chapter 14.

WordPerfect Office is designed to address your individual and system needs with the PC package, the LAN package, and/or the WordPerfect Connections package.

Getting Started

Each package of WordPerfect Office 3.0 provides the user with an installation program (Install) to simplify the initial setup or update of Office. The Install program for Office PC takes you through the steps of creating an Office directory, installing the Office files, and editing the CONFIG.SYS and AUTOEXEC.BAT files. This chapter explains how to set up and install Office PC.

If you are an Office LAN user, see Appendix A, "LAN User Installation," for help on performing a LAN-user setup. Instructions for system administrators installing Office LAN are contained in Chapter 12, "Single Host Installation."

System Requirements

In order to run Office 3.0, your computer must meet certain requirements. The initial part of this chapter explains Office 3.0's memory and DOS (disk operating system) requirements. This chapter also provides recommendations to help you more fully utilize Office 3.0's capabilities.

WordPerfect Office PC runs under the same memory requirements as WordPerfect. You must use DOS version 2.1 or later. Table 2-1 outlines minimum system requirements, along with recommendations to enhance the performance of Office 3.0.

The minimum requirements are the same for Office LAN except you must use DOS version 3.0 or later. If you are using Office LAN and have questions about the setup of your computer, then contact your system administrator.

	Minimum Requirements	Recommended Configuration
DOS Version	2.1	3.0 or later*
Amount of Base Memory	384K	640K
Mass Storage Device	Dual floppy disk drives	Hard disk

*Office LAN requires DOS 3.0 or later

Table 2-1.   System Requirements for Office 3.0

System Setup

When you turn on, or boot up, your computer, it automatically loads a copy of the DOS instruction set into memory. DOS then looks for two files on the system disk used to boot up your machine, CONFIG.SYS and AUTOEXEC.BAT. These files are located on a floppy disk if your computer only has floppy disk drives or on the root directory of the hard disk if you have a hard drive system. From the CONFIG.SYS file, the computer gets information about any special system requirements you want installed. The AUTOEXEC.BAT file is made up of a series of DOS commands to be performed on startup. While you could enter these commands one at a time on the DOS command line, they are more conveniently placed in the AUTOEXEC.BAT file for automatic execution.

CONFIG.SYS

The CONFIG.SYS file contains information on how to configure your system. It tells DOS how to allocate its own resources—such as how many files may be open at one time—and how many memory buffers it should create. During installation of Office PC, Install will ask if it should check the CONFIG.SYS file. If you answer Yes, Install looks for the instruction

```
FILES=40
```

which tells DOS to allow for up to 40 files to be opened at a time. If the current FILES command in the CONFIG.SYS is less than 40, a new FILES command (containing 40) is added to the CONFIG.SYS.

If you don't currently have a CONFIG.SYS file, then your system is configured according to the default DOS settings. If you tell Install to check CONFIG.SYS and the file does not exist, Install creates a CONFIG.SYS file and inserts the FILES instruction.

AUTOEXEC.BAT

Another file that DOS looks for on startup is the AUTOEXEC.BAT file. The AUTOEXEC.BAT file includes specific DOS commands to be automatically executed every time you start up the computer.

During the installation of Office PC, Install asks whether to check the AUTOEXEC.BAT file for three specific commands. If you answer Yes, Install edits AUTOEXEC.BAT and adds the necessary commands.

The first command Install looks for is a PATH command containing the Office program directory. The PATH command tells DOS which directories to search through for files it can't find in the current directory. This lets you run all Office programs without having to specify the full path to the file.

The second command is the instruction to install the alarm module for Calendar, CL/I. The alarm module is a terminate-and-stay-resident (TSR) module that notifies you of appointments in Calendar. If CL/I is not added to the AUTOEXEC.BAT file, your alarms will not work. For more information on alarms and notification, see "Alarms" in Chapter 3, "Using Appointment Calendar."

The third command Install looks for is the command to load Shell. Shell is a program manager that allows you to specify startup options, default directories, and file names for any program and start them from a program menu. For a more complete explanation of Shell, see Chapter 10, "Using Shell."

If you do not currently have an AUTOEXEC.BAT file, Install creates one and inserts the three necessary commands. An AUTOEXEC.BAT file created by Install contains the following commands:

```
PATH=C:\office30
C:\office30\cl/i
C:\office30\shell
```

Installation

As noted previously, the installation program for Office PC takes you through the steps of creating an Office directory, installing the Office files, and editing the CONFIG.SYS and AUTOEXEC.BAT files. Throughout the installation process there are built-in break points, or places where you can safely exit Install without the risk of leaving an incomplete *program module*. A program module consists of the executable file, help files, and data files needed to correctly run a single program.

Running the Install Program

To run the Install program, insert the floppy disk labeled Office PC1 into a floppy drive and switch to that drive by entering the drive letter followed by a colon, usually **A:**, then type

    install

and press ENTER. Your monitor displays the title screen with an option to continue or exit. Type **Y** to proceed. A menu appears outlining the different types of installations available, as shown in Figure 2-1. While all of the options copy the programs to a specified target directory, the Basic Installation option does this without stopping between programs, making it ideal for a first-time setup. The other installation options ask if you want to install each program before continuing. This allows you to install selected programs without performing a complete installation.

If you select Basic Installation, Install then asks where you want the files installed, as illustrated in Figure 2-2. If you select anything other than Basic Installation, you are asked for the *source directory* (where the files should be installed from) as well as the *target directory* (where you want them installed to). You can install Office PC to a set of floppy disks by specifying a floppy drive as the target directory. If the target directory does not exist, Install creates it for you.

After completing your selections and pressing 3 to proceed, Install prompts you to input your personal customer registration number. If

```
Office PC Installation Options                    Installation Problems?
                                                      (800)321-3253

1 - Basic Installation           Install all Office 3.0 file groups.

2 - Custom Installation          Install user-selected Office 3.0 file groups.

3 - Update from Library 2.0      Install user-selected Office 3.0 file groups
                                 and convert Library 2.0 system files.

4 - Update Office 3.0            Do not change existing Office 3.0
                                 directories; install Office 3.0 update file
                                 groups (i.e., interim release installation).

5 - Notes on Office LAN 3.0




Selection: 1                                              (F7 Exit)
```

Figure 2-1.   Installation options

you enter your registration number here, all the Office programs display it on their main help screens. You can then easily locate your registration number when working with WordPerfect Customer Support. Entering this number is optional, and Install continues when you press ENTER.

Once you've entered the registration number or pressed ENTER, Install begins copying files. The files on the Office disks are in a compressed format to minimize disk space, which makes it impossible to run any programs from the Office disks without first running Install to restore the files to their normal format. During this process, if you selected Basic Installation (and are using 5-1/4″ disks), you will only receive a prompt to insert disks 2, 3, and 4. If you selected one of the other installation types, Install gives you the choice to install or bypass each Office program module individually.

After completing the installation of the main Office programs, Install checks for any existing *template files* (such as SHELL.FIL or CALENDAR.FIL). Template files are information files used by the

---

```
Office PC 3.0 Directory Structure (Basic)          Installation Problems?
                                                       (800)321-3253

   Installing from C:\TEMP1\

   Install Office 3.0 Files To
                            will be created
1 - Hard Drive (directory path): C:\OFFICE30\

2 - Floppy Disk (drive letter):


3 - Install All Office 3.0 File Groups
```

```
            ┌──────────────────────────────────────────────┐
            │ NOTE:  If you do not want to use the suggested │
            │        directory, select Hard Drive (1) and enter a │
            │        new directory, or select Floppy Disk (2) and │
            │        and enter a drive letter.  If the directory │
            │        you specify does not already exist, it will │
            │        be created.  When you are ready to continue, │
            │        select option 3.                        │
            └──────────────────────────────────────────────┘
```

```
Selection: 3                                          (F7 Exit)
```

Figure 2-2.   Directory Structure menu for Basic Installation

Office programs; other WordPerfect programs may use them as well. If you are performing an update or are reinstalling and want the template files installed, Install copies them to the Office directory with a .NEW extension. This prevents Install from destroying any template files that may already be present.

The next step is to edit the CONFIG.SYS and AUTOEXEC.BAT files as discussed earlier in this chapter. Install prompts you before making any changes to these files and lets you choose whether or not to allow the changes.

The final step in the installation is to install Repeat Performance, a keyboard-enhancement product. Repeat Performance increases cursor speed, expands keyboard input buffer, and changes the tone of your beep, as well as performing many other useful functions. If you so specify, Install copies the Repeat Performance files to the Office directory and runs the RPINSTAL program. RPINSTAL then edits CONFIG.SYS for you according to the parameters you set for Repeat

Performance. For more information on Repeat Performance, see Chapter 11, "Using Notify, Repeat Performance, and TSR Manager."

The installation of Office 3.0 is now complete. If you made any changes to CONFIG.SYS or AUTOEXEC.BAT, you'll need to reboot your computer so it can set up according to the new configuration. After rebooting your computer, the Office Shell menu should display, as shown in Figure 2-3. The Shell menu for Office LAN users will also have listings for the Mail and Scheduler programs. Programs that come with Office are displayed on the left; other WordPerfect products (sold separately by WordPerfect Corporation) are displayed on the right. This menu is designed to help you get started. You may want to edit it to fit your individual needs. For more information on editing and customizing your Shell menu, see Chapter 10, "Using Shell." If the Shell menu does not appear, the SHELL command was not added to your AUTOEXEC-.BAT file. To answer questions about Shell or any of the other Office programs, refer to the chapter on that program in Part Two, "Reference Section."

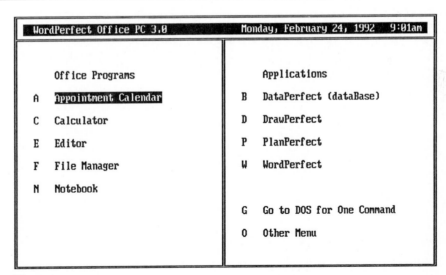

Figure 2-3.   Startup Shell menu for Office PC

Reference Section

Using Appointment Calendar
Using Calculator
Using Editor
Using File Manager
Using Mail
Using Notebook
Using Scheduler
Using Shell
Using Notify, Repeat Performance, and TSR Manager

**P
A
R
T

T
W
O**

Using Appointment Calendar

The Appointment Calendar lets you keep track of daily, monthly, and yearly calendar items, all in one program. You can set an appointment for today as well as one for next year. Keeping track of daily memos, appointments, and to-do items is easy and practical. With the Appointment Calendar, all these items are stored in one central location—your Calendar file.

The Calendar is divided into four main windows as shown in Figure 3-1: the main Calendar window, the Memo window, the Appointments window, and the To-Do List window. The TAB key moves you from window to window. The main Calendar window displays a monthly calendar on the left with the current date bolded. The other three windows display information for whichever date you are on in the main Calendar window. If there is more information in the Memo, Appointments, or To-Do List window than can display on screen, the Zoom feature enlarges the window. The top line displays in reverse video and lists the name of the Calendar file, the current date, and the current time.

With the Memo window you can enter any special information for the day, such as birthdays, paydays, or holidays.

The Appointments window helps you keep track of daily appointments by displaying each appointment and giving you the option of setting an alarm. With an alarm set, Calendar notifies you of your upcoming appointment ten minutes before the appointment. The notification is a beep along with a window that pops up displaying the appointment description and time. You do not have to be in the Calendar program to receive this notification; it can appear in any program.

The To-Do List window helps you keep track of daily to-do items. To-do items are prioritized alphanumerically, giving you great flexibility

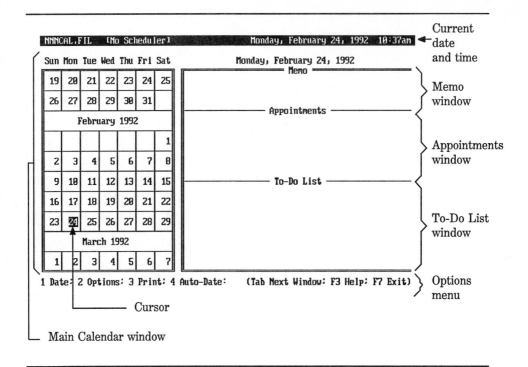

Figure 3-1.   Main Calendar screen

in assigning priorities to specific items. Marking a to-do item with an asterisk indicates that you have completed it. Any unmarked items are automatically carried over to the next day so you do not have to reenter them.

The Date feature lets you figure the number of days between two dates, move to a specific date, and move a certain number of days forward or backward from the current date. These options display at the bottom of the main Calendar screen after choosing **1** for Date from the main Calendar window.

Using the Print feature you can have a hard copy of your Calendar information. The printed information can then be inserted in a planner or other paper task organizer for use when away from your computer. Calendar information can also be saved to a merge file and then used as a secondary merge file in WordPerfect.

You can save specific Calendar information to the Shell Clipboard and use it in other programs. This is especially useful if you want to use information already entered in Calendar in a WordPerfect document. You can save the information to the Clipboard and retrieve it directly into your document. With the Clipboard feature, the sharing of information between programs is simple. Information from other programs can also be saved to the Clipboard and retrieved into Calendar.

LAN If you are on a network and using the WordPerfect Office Scheduler program, Calendar helps you keep track of scheduled items and reports available times to the Scheduler. If you keep your Calendar up-to-date, people using the Scheduler program will know when you are available for an event. When an event is scheduled, the event is automatically added to your Calendar.

The Appointment Calendar is a timely and organized way of storing and viewing almost any type of information. With the Appointment Calendar, time and task organization is at your fingertips.

Starting Calendar

To start Calendar from the Shell menu, press the letter next to the Appointment Calendar entry—the default letter is **A**. To start Calendar from DOS type **cl**. The first time you start Calendar a blank calendar appears as shown in Figure 3-1.

Default Calendar Files

When you first start Calendar, it retrieves the default Calendar file. This default file is CALENDAR.FIL if you are using Office PC, or *XXX*CAL.FIL if you are using the LAN version of Office, where *XXX* is your File ID. Although these are the default calendar files, you can create new calendar files. See "Creating New Calendar Files" later in this chapter.

Moving Around In Calendar

As already noted, when you first enter Calendar the cursor is in the main Calendar window and the current date appears in reverse video and bolded. With certain cursor key combinations you can quickly move to past or future dates to view information or to enter new information. The date the cursor is on appears above the Memo window. The current date is always displayed in the main header at the top of the Calendar screen. While in the main Calendar window, the following keystrokes move you to different dates:

PGDN/PGUP	Next/Previous Day
LEFT ARROW/RIGHT ARROW	Next/Previous Day
DOWN ARROW/UP ARROW	Next/Previous Week
SCREEN UP/SCREEN DOWN (+ and − on numeric keypad)	Next/Previous Month
HOME, PGDN/PGUP	Next/Previous Year
HOME, RIGHT ARROW/LEFT ARROW	Last/First Day of Week
HOME, DOWN ARROW/UP ARROW	Last/First Day of Month
HOME, HOME, DOWN ARROW/UP ARROW	Last/First Day of Year

You can also move to a different date while entering or editing information in the Memo, Appointments, or To-Do List windows without exiting back to the main Calendar window. The following keystrokes move you to different dates while in these windows:

PGDN/PGUP	Next/Previous Day
HOME, PGDN/PGUP	Next/Previous Year

Using the Date Feature to Move Around In Calendar

Along with the cursor keys listed in the preceding section you can also use the Date feature to move to a specific date or move a certain number of days forward or backward.

Go to Date or CTRL-HOME

If you know the date you want to move to, you can use the Go to Date feature to quickly move to the date instead of using the cursor keys. To use Go to Date:

1. Press **1** or **D** for Date from the main Calendar screen.

2. Press **1** or **G** for Go to Date, and the following prompt appears with the current date displayed:

`Enter date (mm/dd/yyyy): 12/3/90`

   If you are not in the main Calendar screen or if you want to use a short cut, you can press CTRL-HOME to display the same prompt.

3. Enter the date to which you want to move.

The cursor moves to the new date and the date appears underlined or in reverse video in the main Calendar window.
   You can change the format of entering dates with the Date/Time Formats options (SHIFT-F5), as discussed in "Using Calendar's Date/Time Format" later in this chapter. When entering dates you do not have to include the entire date. To enter partial dates type nothing and separate the different date items with a /. The / represents the current date item.

Today's Date	Date Entered	Result
2/24/92	//93	2/24/93
7/24/91	/23/	7/23/91
12/24/93	1//94	1/24/94

When entering a date you can separate the numbers with the following characters:

Comma	8,9,90
Space	10 27 93
Dash	2-22-91
Slash	10/23/92

Move Days

If you do not know the specific date you want to move to but you do know how many days backward or forward it is from a date, you can use the Move Days feature. Before using Move Days make sure the cursor is on the date you want as the starting date. To use Move Days:

1. Press **1** or **D** for Date from the main Calendar screen.

2. Press **2** or **M** for Move Days.

3. Enter the number of days to move or type a minus (−) and then the number to move backward from the date the cursor is on.

After you've entered the number, the cursor moves to the new date, which appears in reverse video. You might want to use Move Days to determine the date of a meeting that must occur 15 days from today.

Using Calendar's Memo Feature

The Memo window is the top window on the right side of the main Calendar screen. Use the Memo window to enter and display any pertinent information for the day. Some examples of what kind of information you may want to enter in the Memo window are paydays, holidays, birthdays, or thoughts for the day. There is no limit to the type of information you can enter in the Memo window.

Creating a Calendar Memo

To add a memo to your Calendar:

1. From the main Calendar window press TAB once to move to the Memo window.

2. Type in the memo.

As soon as you begin typing the memo, the window opens as shown in Figure 3-2. After typing 40 to 45 characters, Calendar automatically wraps the next word to the following line. You can create a new line by pressing ENTER. The Memo window can hold a maximum of 255 bytes of information, approximately 255 characters. If you enter too much information, the error message "Edit Buffer Full, insertions ignored" appears at the bottom of the screen. The *edit buffer* is where Calendar holds information. At this point Calendar does not allow you to enter any more information. To make a particular part of a memo more noticeable you can use the Bold (F6) or Underline (F8) key.

Editing and Deleting a Memo

If you need to edit an existing memo, move to the Memo window. Use the arrow keys to move the cursor to the desired location and make the necessary changes. If you need to delete a memo:

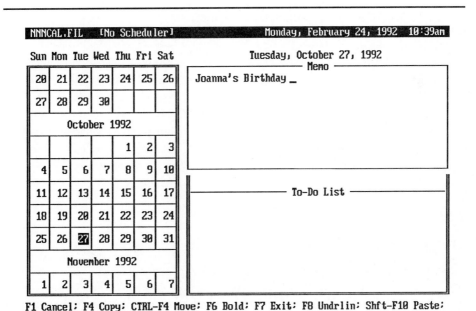

Figure 3-2.   Open Memo window

1. Press TAB once to move to the Memo window. Make sure the cursor is resting on the first word of the memo.

2. Press CTRL-PGDN.

3. Type **Y** for Yes to delete the entire memo.

Calendar considers the entire contents of the Memo window as one memo, even though you may have several different entries in the window. If you do not want to delete everything in the Memo window you may use the following cursor keys to delete selected portions of the memo:

BACKSPACE	Deletes character to the left of the cursor
DEL	Deletes character at cursor
CTRL-BACKSPACE	Deletes one word at a time
CTRL-END	Deletes from cursor to the end of the line

Using Calendar's Appointment Feature

The Appointments window is the middle window on the main Calendar screen. The Appointments window is an advanced appointment book for keeping track of meetings, interviews, classes, lunches, places to be, conferences, and so on. With Calendar's Appointments window you are not limited to one or two lines for the appointment description as you usually are with desktop calendars. And, as noted, you can set a reminder alarm that sounds ten minutes before an appointment.

Adding an Appointment

To add an appointment to your Calendar:

1. Press TAB twice to move to the Appointments window.

2. Press INS. The Appointments window opens and the cursor moves to the Time line as shown in Figure 3-3.

3. Type in the beginning time of the appointment.

4. Press TAB to move to Ending Time (the ending time is optional; press ENTER to move directly to the description window).

5. Type the ending time of the appointment.

6. Press TAB to move to the description window.

7. Type a description of the appointment.

When adding an appointment you have the option of pressing INS or simply typing in the beginning time. You do not have to press INS to add an appointment. In either case, the window automatically opens and the cursor is on the beginning time.

Once an appointment is added to the Appointments window a bullet appears next to the date in the main Calendar window. This helps you know when you have Calendar information for a specific day without having to go to that day and view the information. Any time there is a memo, appointment, or to-do item for a given day a bullet appears.

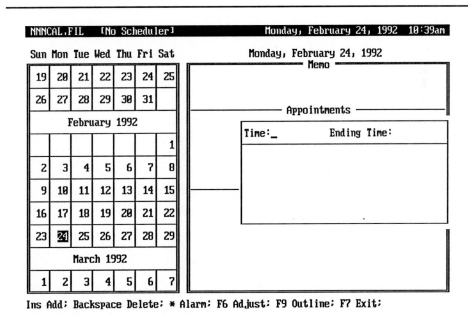

Figure 3-3.   Open Appointments window

The Appointments window displays the beginning and ending time (if entered), along with the description. A single line connects the beginning and ending times of an appointment as shown here:

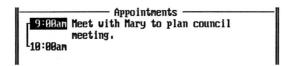

If your screen does not display the connecting line, you have changed the default Appointment Overlap Display to No in the Appointment/ To-Do Options menu (SHIFT-F8, 3, 4).

If your appointments overlap, a double line appears at the point when the second appointment overlaps with the first:

```
┌──────────── Appointments ────────────┐
┌ 8:00am Board Meeting
│ 9:00am Review Committee Meeting
├10:00am
└12:00n
```

You must enter an ending time for an appointment in order to have the double line appear. The double-line display helps you quickly note conflicts in your schedule.

The Appointments window can hold a maximum of 255 characters of information for each appointment. If you enter too much information the error message "Edit Buffer Full, insertions ignored" appears at the bottom of the screen. At this point Calendar does not allow you to enter any more information. You may use the Bold (F6) and Underline (F8) keys when entering the appointment description. You cannot use Bold and Underline when entering the appointment times. Calendar automatically bolds the beginning time of the next appointment of the day.

Editing an Appointment

After entering an appointment you may change the description or add more information to it.

1. Press TAB twice to move to the Appointments window.

2. Use the UP ARROW or DOWN ARROW key to highlight the appointment you want to edit.

3. Press ENTER and make the desired changes or simply begin typing the new text.

Once you press ENTER (or any key) the Appointments window opens and the cursor rests at the beginning of the description.

Adjusting an Appointment

The Appointment Calendar has an a Adjust feature that automatically opens the Appointments window and places the cursor on the beginning time. This feature is useful to quickly change the time of an appointment. To adjust or change the time of an appointment:

1. Press TAB twice to move to the Appointments window.

2. Use the UP ARROW or DOWN ARROW key to highlight the appointment you want to adjust.

3. Press F6 for Adjust; the cursor rests on the beginning time of the appointment.

4. Enter the new beginning time.

5. Press TAB to move to the ending time or press ENTER to move to the description.

6. Enter a new ending time and/or edit the appointment description.

The only difference between editing an appointment and adjusting an appointment is the location of the cursor when the Appointments window first opens. When you edit an appointment the cursor rests on the appointment description when the Appointments window opens. When you adjust an appointment the cursor rests on the beginning time of the appointment. You may change the description of an appointment after pressing Adjust (F6) or change the time of an appointment after pressing ENTER.

Deleting an Appointment

If an appointment is canceled or you are unable to attend an appointment, you can delete the appointment from the Calendar. To delete a future or past appointment:

1. Press TAB twice to move to the Appointments window.

2. Use the UP ARROW or DOWN ARROW key to highlight the appointment you want to delete.

3. Press DEL or BACKSPACE.

Once you delete an appointment, Calendar removes it from the Appointments window. If you deleted an appointment and then want to restore it follow these steps:

1. From the Appointments window, press Cancel (F1). A prompt will appear at the bottom of the screen as shown here:

```
Undelete 12:00n  Lunch with Chris 1 Restore; 2 Previous: 0
```

2. Press **1** or **R** to restore the most recently deleted appointment or press **2** or **P** to see the previous deletion.

Calendar stores the two most recent deletions in the *restore buffer*. The restore buffer is a temporary holding place for deleted items. Once you exit Calendar the restore buffer is cleared and your deletions become permanent.

You can also use the Undelete feature as a short cut to move an appointment to a new location.

1. Delete the appointment.

2. Move the cursor to the new date and/or time.

3. Press F1 for Cancel.

4. Press **1** or **R** to restore the appointment in the new location. This would be especially useful if the appointment had been rescheduled.

You can delete all appointments for a single day by pressing CTRL-BACKSPACE while in the Appointments window. Calendar does not save these deletions in the restore buffer.

LAN If you are using the WordPerfect Office Scheduler program, you can delete appointments added by Scheduler. After pressing BACKSPACE or DEL, you are prompted to delete the event or to delete and reply. If you choose to delete the event, it is immediately removed from the Calendar. If you choose to delete and reply, Calendar prompts you for a reason for rejection. The deletion and reason, if specified, are reported back to the organizer of the scheduled event. If you delete appointments entered by Scheduler, Calendar does not store them in the restore buffer.

Changing Appointment Options

You can change the way appointments display in Calendar through the Appointments/To-Do Options screen. Calendar displays the Appointment options with the To-Do options. The To-Do options will be covered in "Changing To-Do List Options" later in this chapter. To change the Appointment options:

1. Press SHIFT-F1 or SHIFT-F8, or from the main Calendar screen you can also press **2** or **O** for the Setup Options menu as shown in Figure 3-4.

2. Press **3** or **T** for Appointments/To-Do options. The options shown in Figure 3-5 appear with the default values listed.

3. Select an option and make the desired changes.

Options

The following Appointment options are found on the Appointments/To-Do Options screen.

Appointment Outline   The Appointment Outline options let you change the beginning and ending times of the outline as well as the time interval of the outline.

```
Setup Options

        1 - Date/Time Formats

        2 - Alarms

        3 - Appointments/To-Do

        4 - Archive/Delete/Backup

        5 - Colors

        6 - File Format

        7 - Scheduler File Paths




Selection: 0
```

Figure 3-4.   Setup Options screen

```
Appointments/To-Do Options

    Appointment Outline
        1 - Beginning Time:  8:00am
        2 - Ending Time:  5:00pm
        3 - Time Interval (in minutes): 60

    4 - Appointment Overlap Display: Yes

    5 - Single Line Display (Memo, Appts, To-Do): No

    6 - Auto-Alarm Mode (Appts): No

    7 - Auto-Mark mode (To-Do): No

    8 - Unique Priorities (To-Do): Yes




Selection: 0
```

Figure 3-5.   Appointments/To-Do Options screen

Appointment Overlap Display   With Appointment Overlap Display set to Yes, Calendar connects the beginning and ending times of your appointments with a single line. All conflicting appointments display a double line. If this option is set to No, beginning and ending times will display without connecting lines.

Single Line Display   This option applies to all Calendar windows (Memo, Appointments, and To-Do List). If set to Yes, appointments only display one line of the appointment description. You may view the other information by highlighting the appointment and pressing ENTER.

Auto-Alarm Mode   If set to Yes, Calendar automatically sets an alarm for every new appointment. Once you add the appointment a musical note appears to the left of the appointment time. Calendar will also automatically set alarms for appointments added with the Auto-Date feature and appointments added by Scheduler. If Auto-Alarm mode is set to No, you must manually set alarms for each appointment. To manually set an alarm, highlight the appointment and type an asterisk.

Creating an Appointment Outline

With Appointment Outline, Calendar inserts an outline of daily appointment times. You can change the beginning and ending times and the time between appointments, thus making the Appointments window a customized daily planner. Once an appointment outline is displayed, you can easily enter your daily appointments without having to enter a time for each appointment.

To create an appointment outline:

1. Press TAB twice to move to the Appointments window.

2. Press F9 for Outline. Calendar displays a list of appointment times as shown here:

```
╓─────────── Appointments ───────────╖
║    8:00am                           ║
║    9:00am                           ║
║   10:00am                           ║
║   11:00am                           ║
║   12:00n                            ║
║    1:00pm                           ║
║    2:00pm                           ║
║    3:00pm                           ║
║    4:00pm                           ║
║    5:00pm                           ║
```

3. Use the UP ARROW or DOWN ARROW key to highlight the desired appointment time.

4. Type the appointment description. Once you begin typing, the Appointments window opens.

5. If you need to enter an ending time press SHIFT-TAB.

6. Type the ending time.

7. Press F7 twice to return to the main Calendar screen.

The default range for the time outline is 8:00 a.m. to 5:00 p.m. The default interval between times is 60 minutes. If your normal business hours differ from these settings you can change them in the Appointment/To-Do Options menu (SHIFT-F8, 3). You can also change the time interval to fit your needs. For example, if your appointments are scheduled for every 30 minutes, change the time interval to 30. The time interval must be entered in minutes and can range from 1 to 60. If you enter an invalid time, Calendar ignores the entry and restores the previous setting.

If you press Outline, and appointments already exist for that day, the appointments will be inserted in their correct location in the outline.

Setting an Alarm for an Appointment

If you want Calendar to remind you of upcoming appointments, you can set an alarm. When the alarm goes off you hear a beep and then a box appears on the screen listing the time and description of the appointment. (As noted previously, you do not have to be in Calendar to see and hear the alarm; the alarm will sound in any program.) Alarms help you to avoid missing appointments because you were busy with another project. Alarms can be useful if you have several appointments one after another. If your appointment is not near by, you can increase the number of minutes before the appointment for which you want the alarm to ring (the alarm default is set to ring 10 minutes before an appointment and every 30 seconds thereafter until you turn it off) to give you enough time to get to your appointment. To set an alarm for a single appointment:

1. Highlight the appointment for which you want to set an alarm.

2. Type an asterisk (*). A musical note appears to the left of the appointment time indicating the alarm is set as shown here:

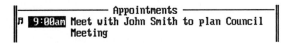

If you want Calendar to sound an alarm for every appointment you enter, you can do so by turning the Auto-Alarm option on. To turn on the Auto-Alarm option:

1. Press SHIFT-F1 or SHIFT-F8, or from the main Calendar screen you can also press **2** or **O** for Options.

2. Press **3** or **T** for Appointments/To-Do options.

3. Press **6** or **A** for Auto-Alarm Mode (Appts).

4. Type **Y** for Yes.

5. Press F7 twice to return to the main Calendar screen.

When Auto-Alarm is on, all appointments have the musical note to the left of the appointment time as shown here:

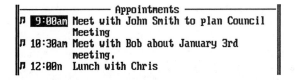

To turn off an alarm press ALT-SPACEBAR if you are using Office PC or CTRL-ENTER if you are using Office LAN. Once you turn off the alarm, it does not sound or display a message across the screen. If you do not turn off the alarm, it continues to display the appointment title every 30 seconds without the beep.

If you are using Office PC you must include the CL/I command in your AUTOEXEC.BAT file or execute it before starting Shell in order for alarms to be installed. The CL/I command installs the alarm handler, which makes on-screen notification possible within any product. If you are in a graphics mode when the notification displays, you might not see the message.

LAN If you are running Office LAN you must run the Notify program along with CL/I. For information about the Notify program, see Chapter 11, "Using Notify, Repeat Performance, and TSR Manager."

Calendar does not limit the number of alarms you can set, but there are two limitations to the number that may be installed for a current day. The maximum number that can be installed at one time is 20. The other limitation involves the actual size of the appointments. When CL/I installs the alarms it places a memory limit of 600 bytes for Calendar alarms. The alarm itself only takes up 3 bytes. However, one appointment description and alarm could take up to 255 bytes. If you have several lengthy appointment descriptions for one day, you may reach the memory limit for installing alarms.

Changing Alarm Options

The Alarm options let you set the number of minutes before an appointment the alarm will sound and the number of seconds to pause between each alarm display. To change the current Alarm options:

1. Press SHIFT-F1 or SHIFT-F8, or from the main Calendar screen you can also press **2** or **O** for Options.

2. Press **2** or **A** for Alarms.

3. Press **1** or **M** for Minutes Before Appointment to Start Alarm.

4. Enter the number of minutes.

5. Press **2** or **S** for Seconds to Pause Between Each Alarm.

6. Enter the number of seconds.

7. Press F7 twice to return the main Calendar screen.

You can set the Minutes Before Appointment to Start Alarm option from 0 to 60. If you set it to 0 the alarm will sound at the appointment time. The Seconds to Pause Between Each Alarm can be set from 5 to 60 seconds.

Using Calendar's To-Do List Feature

The To-Do List window is the bottom window on the main Calendar screen. The To-Do List helps you organize and prioritize daily tasks. Here is an example of a To-Do List window with possible to-do items:

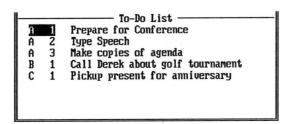

```
|------------------------- To-Do List ------------------------||
| ▓ 1   Prepare for Conference                                 |
| A  2   Type Speech                                           |
| A  3   Make copies of agenda                                 |
| B  1   Call Derek about golf tournament                      |
| C  1   Pickup present for anniversary                        |
|                                                              |
|                                                              |
```

You can enter several to-do items for a single day. When you assign priorities to your to-do items, Calendar lists the items in order of importance with the most important items listed at the top. If your priorities change, you can simply adjust the priority of the to-do item without reentering the entire item.

Calendar also has a "haunting" way of never letting you forget about uncompleted to-do items. If you do not mark a to-do item as completed, Calendar automatically adds it to your next day's To-Do List and continues to do so until you mark it as complete.

Creating a To-Do Item

To add a to-do item to your Calendar:

1. Press TAB three times or SHIFT-TAB once to move to the To-Do List window.

2. Press INS. The To-Do List window opens and the cursor moves to the Priority line as shown in Figure 3-6.

3. Type in the priority.

4. Press TAB or ENTER to move to the description window.

5. Type a description of the to-do item.

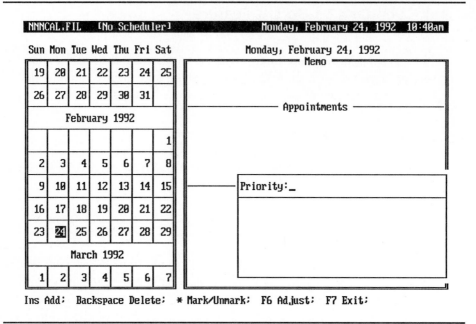

Figure 3-6.   Priority line in To-Do List screen

When adding a to-do item you do not have to press INS. You can simply type in the priority.

Calendar automatically sorts the priorities and puts them in the correct order. You can assign priorities by a letter, number, or both. To-do items assigned only a number hold the highest priority. To-do items assigned both a letter and a number are prioritized by letter first, then number. Here is an example of the way Calendar prioritizes to-do items:

```
┌──────────────── To-Do List ────────────────┐
║     1    Compute Monthly Sales              ║
║   A 1    Review new applications            ║
║   A 2    Check status of employee files     ║
║   B 1    Call Brooks about conference       ║
║                                             ║
║                                             ║
║                                             ║
╚─────────────────────────────────────────────╝
```

The To-Do List window can hold a maximum of 255 characters of information for each to-do item. If you enter too much information the error message "Edit Buffer Full, insertions ignored" appears at the bottom of the screen. At this point Calendar will not allow you to enter any more information. You may use the Bold (F6) and Underline (F8) keys when entering to-do item descriptions to add emphasis. You cannot use Bold and Underline when entering the priority.

Editing a To-Do Item

Once you have entered a to-do item you may change or add information to the description. To edit a to-do item:

1. Press TAB three times or SHIFT-TAB once to move to the To-Do List window.

2. Use the UP ARROW or DOWN ARROW key to highlight the to-do item you want to edit.

3. Press ENTER and make the desired changes or simply begin typing the new text.

Once you press ENTER (or any key) the To-Do List window opens and the cursor rests at the beginning of the description.

Adjusting the Priority of a To-Do Item

If the priority of a to-do item changes, Calendar has a quick and easy way to adjust or change its priority. To adjust the priority:

1. Highlight the to-do item you want to edit.

2. Press F6 for Adjust.

3. Type in the new priority.

When pressing Adjust (F6) the cursor immediately moves to the Priority line. After adjusting a to-do item, Calendar automatically re-sorts the to-do list, so you don't have to reenter to-do items when changes are made.

The only difference between editing a to-do item and adjusting a to-do item is the location of the cursor when the To-Do List window first opens. When you edit a to-do item, the cursor rests on the to-do item description when the To-Do List window opens. When you adjust a to-do item, the cursor rests on the Priority line of the to-do item. You can change the description of a to-do item after pressing Adjust (F6), or you can change the priority of a to-do item after pressing ENTER to edit.

Deleting a To-Do Item

If a to-do item is no longer relevant or has been assigned to someone else, you can delete it from the To-Do List window. When an item is deleted, Calendar automatically updates the priorities of the other items. To delete future or past to-do items from your Calendar:

> 1. Press TAB three times or SHIFT-TAB once to move to the To-Do List window.
>
> 2. Use the UP ARROW or DOWN ARROW key to highlight the to-do item you want to delete.
>
> 3. Press DEL or BACKSPACE.

Once you have deleted a to-do item it is removed from the To-Do List window. If for some reason you need to restore the to-do item, follow these steps:

> 1. From the To-Do List window press Cancel (F1). A prompt appears at the bottom of the screen as shown here:

Undelete ▇▇ 1 Prepare Agenda 1 Restore; 2 Previous: 0

> 2. Press **1** or **R** to restore the most recently deleted to-do item or press **2** or **P** to see the previous deletion.

Calendar stores the two most recent deletions in the restore buffer. Once you exit Calendar the restore buffer is cleared and your deletions are permanent.

You can delete all to-do items for a single day by pressing CTRL-BACKSPACE while in the To-Do List window. These to-do items are not saved to the restore buffer.

Changing To-Do List Options

You may change the way to-do items display in Calendar through the Appointments/To-Do Options screen. The To-Do options are listed with the Appointment options.

1. Press SHIFT-F1 or SHIFT-F8, or from the main Calendar screen you can also press **2** or **O** for Options.

2. Press **3** or **T** for Appointments/To-Do options. The options shown in Figure 3-7 appear with the default values listed.

3. Select an option and make the desired changes.

Options

The following To-Do options are found on the Appointments/To-Do Options screen.

```
Appointments/To-Do Options

    Appointment Outline
        1 - Beginning Time:  8:00am
        2 - Ending Time:  5:00pm
        3 - Time Interval (in minutes): 60

    4 - Appointment Overlap Display: Yes

    5 - Single Line Display (Memo, Appts, To-Do): No

    6 - Auto-Alarm Mode (Appts): No

    7 - Auto-Mark mode (To-Do): No

    8 - Unique Priorities (To-Do): Yes




Selection: 0
```

Figure 3-7.   Default values for Appointments/To-Do options

Single Line Display   This option applies to all Calendar windows (Memo, Appointments, and To-Do List). If set to Yes, to-do items only display one line of the description. You may view the other information by highlighting the to-do item and pressing ENTER.

Auto-Mark Mode   When you complete a to-do item you should mark the item as done by typing an asterisk (*). After marking an item as done, a bullet appears to the left of the to-do item as shown here:

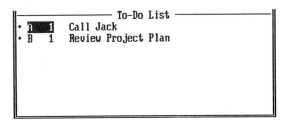

If you do not mark items as done, Calendar carries them over into the next day. With Auto-Mark mode set to Yes, to-do items are automatically marked as done when you enter them. This prevents completed to-do items from being accidentally carried over to the next day.

Unique Priorities   When you enter a to-do item, the first information you enter is the priority. By default, Calendar will not let you have more than one to-do item with the same priority. When you enter a priority that already exists, Calendar keeps the priority on the newest to-do item and adjusts the others accordingly. If you want Calendar to allow duplicate priorities change this option to No.

Using Calendar's Auto-Date Feature

The Auto-Date feature automatically inserts memos, appointments, and to-do items that occur on a regular basis. For example, if you have an appointment every Monday through Friday at the same time, you can enter an auto-date formula for the appointment, and Calendar automatically inserts the appointment for each day. With Auto-Date you do not have to enter the memo, appointment, or to-do item each time it occurs.

Adding an Auto-Date

To add an auto-date from the main Calendar window:

1. Press **4** or **A** for Auto-Date.

2. Press INS to move to the Auto-Date window.

3. Type in the auto-date formula (see "Creating Auto-Date Formulas" in this chapter).

4. Press TAB to move to the Memo, Appointments, or To-Do List window.

5. Type in the appropriate text.

6. Press F7 until you return to the main Calendar screen.

Invalid Auto-Dates

If you enter an auto-date formula that is incorrect, Calendar displays an error message at the bottom of the screen and marks the auto-date with an asterisk as shown in Figure 3-8. Calendar displays one of two error messages. These error messages help you to know what is incorrect in the formula.

Message	Meaning
Error: Invalid token	Calendar does not recognize one of the characters or symbols in the formula. The unrecognized character or symbol is displayed with the error.
Error: Syntax error	An operator has been entered in the wrong order. Calendar displays the operator along with the error message.

Auto-Dates and To-Do Items

If you have an auto-date for a to-do item that includes both past and future dates, make sure to mark the item as done with an asterisk. If

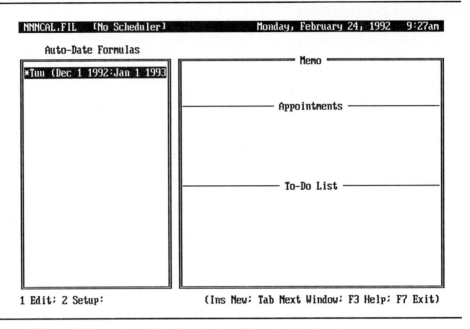

Figure 3-8. Asterisk indicating invalid auto-date formula

you do not mark the to-do item as done, Calendar will only insert it into the future dates. Marking a to-do item as done also prevents the to-do item from being carried over to the next day.

If you set Auto-Mark mode to Yes in the Appointments/To-Do Options, Calendar will only insert the to-do item in future dates.

Deleting and Editing Auto-Dates

If the description, dates, or times for an auto-date change after being entered you can edit or delete the auto-date. Any changes you make to the text of an auto-date memo, appointment, or to-do item are automatically changed in the main Calendar. If you delete an auto-date formula, Calendar also deletes any memos, appointments, or to-do items associated with the auto-date formula. To edit or delete an existing auto-date:

1. From the main Calendar screen press 4 or A for Auto-Date.

2. Use the UP ARROW or DOWN ARROW key to highlight the formula you want to edit.

3. Press **1** or **E** for Edit.

4. Make the desired changes in the formula, or press TAB to move to the Memo, Appointments, or To-Do List window and edit the text, or press DEL or BACKSPACE to delete the formula.

5. Press F7 until you return to the main Calendar screen.

Creating Auto-Date Formulas

The auto-date formula is what Calendar looks at to know on which dates you want specific memos, appointments, and to-do items added. Auto-date formulas consist of functions and operators that tell Calendar when to insert the memo, appointment, or to-do item.

Auto-Date Functions

Functions are the most global entries for auto-dates. Table 3-1 outlines the names and uses of auto-date functions.

Auto-Date Operators

An operator further limits or defines the days for which an auto-date is valid. Calendar uses operators in conjunction with auto-date functions.

Function	Definition	Example	Explanation
Day of the Week	Specifies one day of the week	fri	Friday
Day of the Month	Specifies one day of the month	5	Fifth day of the month
Day of the Year	Specifies one day of the year	245	245th day of the year
Month of the Year	Specifies all days in a month	Sept	September
Year	Specifies all days in a year	1992	The year 1992
Weekday of the Month	Specifies a particular day of the month	fri(last)	Last Friday of the month

Table 3-1.   Auto-Date Functions

Operators are much like mathematical functions and carry certain priorities. Table 3-2 outlines the Calendar operators by priority.

The following sections give an example of each of the operators and a brief explanation.

High Priority And

Example: fri dec

This formula tells Calendar to schedule all Fridays in December.

Positive/Negative Offset

Example: fri (last)-3

Priority	Operator	Name
1	space	High priority And
2	+ or plus	Positive Offset
2	− or minus	Negative Offset
3	: or to	Range
4	every...starting...	Every Starting
4	every...ending...	Every Ending
5	before	Before
5	on/before	On/Before
5	after	After
5	on/after	On/After
5	near	Near
5	on/near	On/Near
6	, or or	Or
6	! or not	Not
7	& or and	Low Priority And

Table 3-2.   Calendar Operators

This formula states the day must be the last Friday of the month minus three days.

Range

Example: tues:thur

This formula indicates every Tuesday through Thursday.

Every Starting/Every Ending

Example: every 7 starting May 1 1990 ending December 31 1990

This formula indicates every seventh day beginning May 1, 1990 and ending December 31, 1990. If you do not specify a beginning or ending date, Calendar uses the first or last date in the Calendar.

Before, On/Before, After, On/After, Near, and On/Near

Example: mon:fri on/near 15, mon:fri on/near last

This formula indicates the 15th and the last day of the month if they fall on a Monday through Friday; Friday if they fall on a Saturday; or Monday if they fall on a Sunday. This is a common payday schedule for many companies. You can enter a payday memo and the formula will insert it accordingly.

Or

Example: Dec 15 (sat or sun)

This formula indicates December 15th if it falls on a Saturday or Sunday. You can replace the Or operator with a comma (,).

Not

Example: Sept Mon:Fri !1:15

This formula indicates every Monday through Friday in September except the 1st through the 15th.

Low Priority And

Example: On/Before April 15 and Mon:Fri

This formula indicates a day on or before April 15th that must be a Monday, Tuesday, Wednesday, Thursday, or Friday. If April 15th is a Saturday or Sunday, Calendar inserts the items on Friday. With the Low Priority And, Calendar evaluates all other operators first and then evaluates the And.

Grouping Functions and Operators

If you are unsure about the order in which Calendar evaluates the operators in a formula, group them in parenthesis. Calendar evaluates the contents of parenthesis before any other operations.

Printing Your Calendar

At times you may need a hard copy of your Calendar information. You can use the Print feature to send specific Calendar information to a printer. Calendar prints the date along with the information in the Memo, Appointments, and To-Do List windows.

Note: WordPerfect Office includes several powerful macros that automate and enhance the printing of Calendar information. For information on these macros see Appendix E, "Predefined Macros."

To print your Calendar:

1. Press SHIFT-F7 for Print. The menu in Figure 3-9 appears.

2. Make the needed changes to options 2 through 6.

3. Press **1** or **P** to print the Calendar.

Options

The Print menu shown in Figure 3-9 offers the following options.

Print   As soon as you press **1** for Print, all information is sent to the printer. Calendar allows you to send only one print job at a time.

Format   You can choose between two print formats: Normal and Merge Output. Normal prints the information in text format to the printer as shown in Figure 3-10. Merge Output prints to a file in secondary merge format. Once in secondary merge format, the information can be used in a WordPerfect merge file (see "Using Calendar Information with WordPerfect" later in this chapter).

Options   Select Options (discussed in more detail shortly) to indicate how printed information should appear on the page and what information should be printed.

```
Print

    1 - Print
    2 - Format        Normal
    3 - Options
    4 - Hand-fed Forms  No
    5 - Device or File  LPT1
    6 - Select Printer  GENERIC

Control

    7 - Abort Print Job
    8 - Stop Printer
    9 - Send a Go to Printer




Selection: 0
```

Figure 3-9.   Print menu

```
Friday, January 4, 1991
  Payday!

  8:00am  New Employee Orientation; Meet at Reception Area
 12:00n   Lunch
  1:00pm
  3:00pm  Staff Meeting

      1   Compute Monthly Sales
  A   1   Review new applications
  A   2   Check status of employee files
  B   1   Call Brooks about conference
```

Figure 3-10.   Calendar information printed with Normal format

Hand-fed Forms   If your printer uses hand-fed forms or you want to send a go to the printer for each page, set this option to Yes. You would want to set this option to Yes if you were using special paper and had to insert each sheet individually. When hand-fed forms is set to Yes, the computer will beep when it is ready for the form to be inserted into the printer. After the beep, you must send a go to the printer by pressing SHIFT-F7, 9.

Device or File   Calendar gives you the following options for directing print output:

`Print Device: 1 LPT1; 2 LPT2; 3 LPT3; 4 Device or File: 1`

Choose the correct port or choose 4 and enter a device or filename. After selecting device or filename type **Y** if you are printing to a network printer. If you are printing to a network printer you can also use your own network redirection command to direct printer output. If you do use a redirection command to print to a network printer, type **N** for No to the network printer prompt.

Changing Print Options

With Calendar's Print Options menu you can specify margins, how far to indent the information, what merge format to use if you are printing to a file, how many days to print, what information to print, whether to print a day with no information, and the number of days to print per page. To change any of the preceding options:

1. Press SHIFT-F7 for Print.

2. Press 3 or O for Options. The menu in Figure 3-11 appears.

3. Select an option and make the desired changes. The options are described in the following section.

Options

Calendar stores the changes you make to the Print Options menu in the Calendar file, and they remain in effect until you change them again.

```
Page Size

        1 - Page Length (in lines):   66
        2 - Top Margin (in lines):    6
        3 - Bottom Margin (in lines): 6

        4 - Left Margin (column #):    10
        5 - Right Margin (column #):   74
        6 - Number of Col, to Indent: 2

Options

        0 - One Day Per Page: No
        E - Print Empty Days: No
        W - WP Merge Format:  WP 5.0
        D - Duration:         Week

Contents

        A - Appointments: Yes
        I - To-Do Items:  Yes
        M - Memos:        Yes


Selection: 0
```

Figure 3-11.   Print Options menu

Page Length   Enter the length of the current page. The default for an 11-inch page in a 10-point font is 66 lines. If you wanted to print on a legal-size piece of paper, you would change this to 72.

Top/Bottom Margin   Enter the number of lines from the top and bottom the text should print. Six lines equals 1 inch in a 10-point font.

Left/Right Margin   Enter the column position from the left and right edges. The default settings are 10 for the right and 74 for the left, which equals 1 inch for each in a 10-pitch (characters wide per inch) font. If you are going to insert the page into a binder of some sort you may want to increase the left margin.

Number of Columns to Indent   When printing Calendar information, use this option to indent the information under the date. Figure 3-12 shows the printed text indented five columns.

One Day per Page   If you want each day of Calendar information to print on a separate page set this option to Yes.

Print Empty Days   By default, Calendar does not print any text for days that do not contain information in the Memo, Appointments, or To-Do List window. If you want to print these days, set this option to Yes. The only information that prints is the date.

```
Friday, January 4, 1991
    Payday!

    8:00am  New Employee Orientation; Meet at Reception Area
   12:00n   Lunch
    1:00pm
    3:00pm  Staff Meeting

         1  Compute Monthly Sales
      A  1  Review new applications
      A  2  Check status of employee files
      B  1  Call Brooks about conference
```

Figure 3-12.   Calendar information printed with five-column indent

WP Merge Format   If you are printing information in merge format to disk you need to specify which merge format to use. See "Using Calendar Information with WordPerfect" later in this chapter for more information.

Duration   The Duration option lets you decide exactly how many days of information you want printed. You can select Today, Day, Week, Month, or Year. All of the options except for Today start printing from the day on which the cursor is resting.

Appointments, To-Do Items, Memos   The Contents options let you decide which information is included when you print. Select Yes or No for each option. For example, if you only want to print your appointments, set the Memos and To-Do items to No and Appointments to Yes.

Using Calendar Information with WordPerfect

The information you enter in the Memo, Appointments, and To-Do List windows can be printed to a WordPerfect merge file. You can then use this information as a secondary merge file or retrieve it into Notebook. To print to a merge file:

1. Press SHIFT-F7 for Print.
2. Press **2** or **F** for Format.
3. Press **2** or **M** for Merge.
4. Press **5** or **D** for Device or File.
5. Press **4** or **D** for Device or File.
6. Enter a name for the merged file.
7. Press **3** or **O** for Options.
8. Press **W** for WP Merge Format.
9. Press **1** for 5.0 (5.0 is compatible with 5.1) or press **2** for 4.2.
10. Press F7 to return to the Print menu.
11. Press **1** or **P** for Print.

Once the file is printed you can retrieve it into Notebook or Word-Perfect. The information saved in the file depends on the settings selected for the Contents options (SHIFT-F7, 3). A merge file might be helpful if you need to create an agenda for a meeting. You could simply print only the appointments of the particular day and use that information to merge with a predefined agenda form.

Along with printing to files, you can also save information to the Shell Clipboard and retrieve it into WordPerfect or any other program.

Archiving Calendar Files

If you are an active Calendar user, your Calendar file can get quite large, which tends to slow down the program's performance. If you use your Calendar as a record keeper, you will not want to delete your Calendar information. With the Auto-Archive feature, Calendar automatically archives (saves) old Calendar information to a file. You must specify the number of days before the file is archived. The name of the archive file is *.ARC where the * is the name of the current Calendar file. If you are running Office PC the name of the archived file is CALENDAR.ARC. If you are running Office LAN the archive file is *XXX*CAL.ARC, where *XXX* is your File ID. If you have created Calendars with different names, these filenames will differ. To turn on Auto-Archive:

1. Press SHIFT-F1 or SHIFT-F8, or from the main Calendar screen you can also press **2** or **O** for Options.

2. Press **4** or **B** for Archive/Delete/Backup.

3. Press **1** or **A** for Auto-Archive.

4. Type **Y** to turn on Auto-Archive.

5. Press **3** or **N** for Number of Days Before Archived and/or Deleted.

6. Enter the number of days old information should be before Calendar archives it.

When Auto-Archive is set to Yes, Auto-Delete is automatically set to Yes also. This means that when old Calendar information is archived, the information is also deleted from the current calendar file. This avoids having large working Calendar files.

Once the information is deleted from the working Calendar file you can only access it by retrieving the .ARC file. This is important to keep in mind when specifying the Number of Days Before Archived and/or Deleted. If you specify seven days (the default), for example, you will not be able to access information older than seven days from your working Calendar file. If you use your Calendar to refer back to previous memos, appointments, or to-do items, it is a good idea to set the Number of Days Before Archived and/or Deleted to a workable number. You can set the option from 1 to 365 days.

To view archived Calendar information you can retrieve the *.ARC file. The archive file is stored in the same directory as your working Calendar file. To retrieve the file:

1. Press F10 for Save to save the current Calendar file.

2. Press SHIFT-F10 for Retrieve and enter the filename. The "1 Replace; 2 Merge:1" prompt appears.

3. Press **1** or **R** to replace the existing file with the archive file.

Once you retrieve an *.ARC file, Calendar turns off the Auto-Archive options so the same information is not archived again. If you make any changes to the archive file you can save it with the same name or with a different name. To save the file, press Save (F10) and enter a filename.

Backing Up Calendar Files

Along with the Auto Archive-feature, Calendar can back up files automatically with the Timed Backup feature. The difference between archiving and backing up a Calendar file is that when you archive a file, the old information is deleted from the current Calendar file. When you back up a Calendar file, an exact duplicate of the file is made and then deleted when you exit the Calendar program properly. The Timed Backup feature helps avoid accidental loss of your current Calendar file due to computer or power failure. When Timed Backup is on, Calendar automatically backs up your Calendar file at regular intervals. To turn on Timed Backup:

1. Press SHIFT-F1 or SHIFT-F8, or from the main Calendar screen you can also press **2** or **O** for Options.

2. Press **4** or **B** for Archive/Delete/Backup.

3. Press **4** or **T** for Timed Backup.

4. Type **Y** to turn on Timed Backup.

5. Press **5** or **M** for Minutes Between Timed Backup.

6. Enter the number of minutes between each backup.

The default setting for Timed Backup is Yes and the default time is 30 minutes. Calendar only makes a backup file if you have made changes since the last time the file was backed up.

The name of the backup file is *.BK!, where the * is the name of the current Calendar file. If you are running Office PC the name of the backup file is CALENDAR.BK!. If you are running Office LAN the archive file is *XXX*CAL.BK!, where *XXX* is your File ID. If you have created custom calendars the names may differ. For example, if the name of your Calendar file is DWHCAL.FIL the name of the backup file is DWHCAL.BK!. Calendar stores the backup file in the same directory as your working Calendar file. If you exit Calendar normally with F7 the *.BK! files are deleted.

If you have had a power failure and need to retrieve a timed backup file:

1. Press Retrieve (SHIFT-F10) and enter the filename. The "1 Replace; 2 Merge:1" prompt appears.

2. Press **1** or **R** to replace the existing file with the backup file.

If there is information in the backup file that is not in your working Calendar file you will need to save the backup file.

1. Press F10 for Save and enter a filename. The filename should be the name of your working Calendar file.

2. Type **Y** to replace the old file.

Backing Up Files Through Update Calendar on Go to Shell

Calendar provides another means of backing up your Calendar file. With Update Calendar on Go to Shell, Calendar automatically saves any changes or additions to the Calendar file when you use the Go to Shell option or when you switch to another program and leave Calendar in memory if this option is set to Yes. This avoids the loss of new Calendar information if you have problems while out of Calendar. The default setting for this option is Yes. To turn on the option:

1. Press SHIFT-F1 or SHIFT-F8, or from the main Calendar screen you can also press **2** or **O** for Options.

2. Press **4** or **B** for Archive/Delete/Backup.

3. Press **6** or **U** for Update Calendar on Go to Shell.

4. Type **Y** for Yes.

If you use the Go to Shell feature or the Switch Program feature it's a good idea to keep this option set to Yes. If your machine locks up while you are in another program and Calendar is resident in memory, this option makes sure that all the information you entered or changed before going to Shell is saved.

Note: The Go to Shell feature does not save your Calendar information if you are leaving Calendar from a location that is only supported by the Shell's Allow Switch Anytime option. For more information on Allow Switch Anytime see Chapter 10, "Using Shell."

Using Calendar's Date/Time Formats

The Date/Time Formats options let you change the way the dates and times are displayed in Calendar, which day displays as the first day of the week, and the DOS date and time. To change any one of these options:

> 1. Press SHIFT-F1 or SHIFT-F8, or from the main Calendar screen you can also press **2** or **O** for Options.

> 2. Press **1** or **D** for Date/Time Formats. The options shown here appear.

> 1 Date Format; 2 Time Format; 3 Start Day of Week; 4 DOS Time; 5 DOS Date: 0

> 3. Select one of the options and make the desired changes.

Options

The following options are available on the Date/Time Formats screen.

Date Format   This option changes the way the date in the header on the main Calendar screen and the date above the Memo window appear. Here is an example that shows the date set to the default format.

> NNNCAL.FIL   [No Scheduler]   Monday, February 24, 1992 10:42am

You can alter the date format using any of the special date characters shown in Figure 3-13, along with any text, punctuation, or spaces. Calendar allows up to 29 characters for the date format.

Time Format   The Time Format determines the display of appointment times and the current time listed on the main Calendar screen. The % sign and $ sign are useful with time formats. The % sign pads numbers less than 10 with a leading zero. The $, which is the default value, pads numbers less than 10 with a space.

```
Number  Meaning
  1     Day of the month
  2     Month (number)
  3     Month (word)
  4     Year (all four digits)
  5     Year (last two digits)
  6     Day of the week (word)
  7     Hour (24 hour clock)
  8     Hour (12 hour clock)
  9     Minute
  0     am / pm
  #     Week (number)
  %     Pad numbers less than 10 with a leading zero, or
            Output only 3 letters for the month or day of the week
  $     Pad numbers less than 10 with a leading space

Examples: 3 1, 4  Wk # = January 15, 1991 Wk 3
          %6 %3 1, 4   = Tue Jan 15, 1991
          %2/%1/5 (6) = 01/15/91 (Tuesday)
          8:90         = 10:55am
```

Figure 3-13.   Date/Time Formats' options

These characters make the display of the Appointments window, as shown in Figure 3-14, as well as printed Calendar information more uniform.

Start Day of Week   You can change the day of the week that is listed first on the main Calendar screen. After selecting Start Day of Week, 3, from the Date/Time Formats menu, use the arrow keys to display the different days of the week. When the correct day is displayed press ENTER.

DOS Time   You can use DOS Time to change the DOS time setting of your computer.

DOS Date   You can use DOS Date to change the DOS date setting of your computer.

Creating New Calendar Files

When you first start Calendar there is only a default Calendar file. This file is CALENDAR.FIL if you are using Office PC, or *XXX*CAL.FIL if

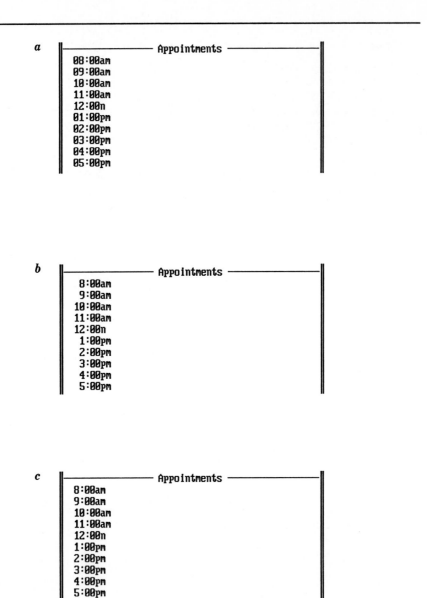

Figure 3-14. Appointment times comparing the use of % (a), $ (b), and nothing (c)

you are using Office LAN, where *XXX* is your File ID. There may be instances when one Calendar file is not enough to meet your needs. For example, you may want to have both a personal and a business Calendar file or you may want a Calendar file that only has information about a particular client. The following sections explain how to create new Calendar files.

Creating a Calendar File from an Existing Calendar File

You can create a new Calendar file from an existing Calendar file by saving the file with a new name.

1. With the cursor in the main Calendar screen press F10 for Save.

2. A "Calendar to save:" prompt appears at the bottom of the screen.

3. Enter the name of the new Calendar file.

This method of creating a Calendar file is useful if you need to duplicate information from an existing file.

Creating a Blank Calendar File

If you want a completely blank Calendar file you can create one by retrieving a nonexistent file into Calendar.

From the Shell Menu

1. From the main Shell menu press 4 for Setup.

2. Use the UP ARROW or DOWN ARROW key to highlight the Appointment Calendar entry on the Shell menu. You can also press the bolded letter that corresponds to the entry—the default is **A**.

3. Press **1** for Edit.

4. Press ENTER until the reverse video bar rests on Startup Options as shown in Figure 3-15.

```
                          Program Information

Menu Letter:             A

Menu Description:        Appointment Calendar

Menu Item Type:          Normal        Pause: NO

Default Directory:

Program Name:            cl.exe

Clipboard Filename:

Macros Names - End of Line: EOLA.SHM  Go to: GOSHELLA.SHM  Return: RTSHELLA.SHM

Startup Options:         ████████████████████████

Prompt for startup options?  NO      Swap Shell out?          NO

Start resident?          NO          Allow switch anytime?    YES

        Enter any startup options, switches, filenames, etc., if any.
        DO NOT enter the program name here again.
                                       (F7 = Exit, F3 = Help)
```

Figure 3-15.   Shell Program Information screen for Calendar

5. Enter the name of the new Calendar file.

6. Press F7 twice.

7. Use the UP ARROW or DOWN ARROW key to highlight the Appointment Calendar entry on the Shell menu.

8. Press ENTER.

When Calendar starts, "Error: File not found" appears at the bottom of the screen and a blank Calendar file appears. The "Error: File not found" message indicates that the file does not yet exist and must be created by Calendar. Once you exit the Calendar file, anything you added is saved to the new Calendar file. If you keep the new name on the Startup Options line, you will retrieve the new Calendar file each time you start the Appointment Calendar from the Shell.

From the DOS Command Line

From the DOS command line type **cl NEWCAL.FIL** (here, NEWCAL-.FIL is the name of a Calendar file that does not yet exist).

"Error: File not found" appears at the bottom of the screen, and a blank Calendar file appears. The "Error: File not found" message indicates that the file does not yet exist and must be created by Calendar. Once you exit the Calendar file anything you added is saved to the new Calendar file. To retrieve the file again you must specify the new name on the command line. If you do not specify the new name the default Calendar file is retrieved.

Retrieving a Calendar File

Once you have created a Calendar file you can retrieve it any time you are in the Calendar program. You can also retrieve other users' Calendar files if you are on a network. The Retrieve feature is especially useful to secretaries, for example, who keep track of different people's appointments. They can simply retrieve the other person's Calendar file and add an appointment or a to-do item. You can set a password on your Calendar so only those who know your password can retrieve it (see "Using Passwords with Your Calendar" later in this chapter). To retrieve an existing Calendar file:

1. Press SHIFT-F10 for Retrieve.

2. Enter the name of the Calendar file. The "1 Replace; 2 Merge:1" prompt appears.

3. Press **1** or **R** if you want to replace your existing file with the new file or press **2** or **M** if you want to merge the file with the existing file.

If you choose the Replace option all your Calendar information disappears and is replaced by the retrieved Calendar file. For this reason it is a good idea to save your original Calendar file before you retrieve another Calendar file. If you choose to merge the new file with the existing Calendar file, the information is merged on the screen. If the new file contains large memo, appointment, or to-do entries, and the existing file contains large memo, appointment, or to-do entries, information in the new file may be deleted. Make sure you exit without saving the merged file by pressing F1 for Cancel, or use F10 and save it with a different name so you do not overwrite your original Calendar file.

If a password has been set for the file you are trying to retrieve, Calendar prompts you to enter the password. If you do not know the password, an "Error: File is Locked" message appears at the bottom of the screen, and the file is not retrieved. If you receive this error message while in Calendar, press Cancel (F1) to return to the original Calendar file. If you receive this message when trying to enter Calendar, you are returned to the Shell menu or to DOS depending on where you were when you tried to start Calendar.

Using the Shell Clipboard and Go to Shell Features with Calendar

The Shell Clipboard is one of the main tools that all the WordPerfect Office programs use to integrate and share information. While in Calendar, the Shell Clipboard lets you save information from the Memo, Appointments, To-Do List, and Auto-Date Formulas windows and retrieve it to a different location in Calendar or to a different Shell-compatible program. You can also save information to the Clipboard from another program and retrieve it into Calendar. With the Go to Shell feature you can quickly return to DOS or the Shell menu without exiting a Calendar file.

Using Go to Shell

To return to the Shell menu or DOS:

1. Press CTRL-F1 for Shell.

2. Press **1** or **G** to return to the Shell menu or to go to DOS, if you are running Calendar from DOS.

The Go to Shell option lets you keep Calendar in memory while exiting to Shell. After exiting to Shell you can choose any option on the Shell menu. The Appointment Calendar entry displays an * to remind you that Calendar has been left in memory. Go to Shell is especially useful if you want to go to another program and retrieve the contents of the Clipboard and then return to Calendar.

Saving and Appending Memos, Appointments, To-Do Items, and Auto-Date Formulas to the Clipboard

To save or append information:

1. Move the cursor to the Memo, Appointments, To-Do List, or Auto-Date Formulas window.

2. Use the UP ARROW or DOWN ARROW key to highlight the appointment, to-do item, or auto-date formula you want to save or append.

Note: The entire Memo window is saved or appended to the Clipboard, so it's only necessary to position the cursor in the window.

3. Press CTRL-F1 for Shell.

4. Press **2** or **S** for Save to Clipboard or press **3** or **A** for Append to Clipboard.

When you save information to the Clipboard it overwrites any existing information in the Clipboard. Appending to the Clipboard adds the information to the end of any existing information.

Saving or Appending an Entire Day to the Clipboard

If you want to save all the information for one day to the Clipboard:

1. Move the cursor to the main Calendar screen.

2. Press CTRL-F1 for Shell.

3. Press **2** or **S** for Save to Clipboard or press **3** or **A** for Append to Clipboard.

Only information specified in the Print Options menu under Contents (SHIFT-F7, 3) is saved to the Clipboard.

Retrieving Text from the Clipboard

To retrieve information saved to the Clipboard in Calendar or in another program:

1. Move the cursor to the Memo, Appointments, To-Do List, or Auto-Date Formulas window.

2. Press ENTER to open the window for editing. If you are retrieving text into the Memo window you do not need to press ENTER.

3. Press CTRL-F1 for Shell.

4. Press **4** or **R** for Retrieve from Clipboard.

Calendar inserts the text at the cursor location.

The Clipboard feature allows a great deal of integration between Calendar and other Shell programs. For example, you can save a memo to the Clipboard, switch to Mail (CTRL-ALT-M), and retrieve the memo into the message box. Text saved to the Clipboard can also be retrieved into WordPerfect documents and vice versa.

Using Passwords with Your Calendar

Often information contained in a Calendar file is confidential. You can set a password for your Calendar file to help ensure that no one else can access your Calendar information. You can also remove passwords that have previously been set. To add a password:

1. Press SHIFT-F1 or SHIFT-F8, or from the main Calendar screen press **2** or **O** for Options.

2. Press **6** or **F** for File Format.

3. Press **3** or **A** to Add or Change a password.

4. Enter the password.

5. Enter the password again.

6. Press F7 for Exit to return to the main Calendar screen.

Adding a password to your Calendar file increases the confidentiality of the information within the file. If you are running Office PC the only way someone else can access your Calendar file is from your machine. If you do not have a password and are away from your machine, anyone will be able to start Calendar and view your Calendar information.

LAN If you are your running Office LAN, your system administrator may have already assigned a password to your Calendar file. If you do not have a password assigned, any user who has rights to the directory where your Calendar file is stored can retrieve it. The need for a password depends on the contents and confidentiality of your Calendar file.

Calendar allows 23 characters for a password. If you add a password, each time you start Calendar you must enter the password. If anyone else tries to retrieve your Calendar file they must also enter the password. If you forget your password or enter the wrong one, Calendar will not retrieve the Calendar file. If you forget your password there is no way to access your Calendar information.
To remove a password:

1. Press SHIFT-F1 or SHIFT-F8, or from the main Calendar screen you can also press **2** or **O** for Options.

2. Press **6** or **F** for File Format.

3. Press **4** or **R** to Remove Password.

Communicating with Scheduler

LAN If you are using Office LAN you may receive notification of Scheduler events while using your Calendar. When you receive notification of the events, you may accept, delete, or wait to respond to them. If you accept, the event is added to your Calendar as an appointment. If you delete the event, you are given the option to reply and enter a reason for deleting it. If you choose to wait to respond, Scheduler gives the event a pending status. The next time you enter Calendar the event displays again.

If you accept events while in the Scheduler program, they are automatically added to your Calendar Appointments window.

If you are not receiving events in Scheduler in your Calendar there are several things you can check.

- Make sure your Calendar file has the correct File ID. Scheduler will only communicate with Calendar files whose first three letters match your File ID. So if your File ID is KRC, your Calendar file must be KRCCAL.FIL.

- Make sure the path in the Scheduler File Paths screen is correct (SHIFT-F1, 7).

- Try using the Reset option in the Scheduler File Paths screen (SHIFT-F1, 7). When you reset the path all shared information between Scheduler and Calendar is deleted and reinserted.

Setting Scheduler File Paths

LAN If you are using Office LAN, you must tell Calendar where your Scheduler files are, in order for Calendar and Scheduler to communicate. To check this path and set additional paths if you have several Scheduler systems:

1. Press SHIFT-F1 or SHIFT-F8, or from the main Calendar screen you can also press **2** or **O** for Options.

2. Press **7** or **S** for Scheduler File Paths.

3. Press **1** for Insert and type in the path to another SCHAL directory, or highlight an existing path and press **2** or **M** for Move and enter a new path number, or press **3** or **D** for Delete to delete a path, or press **4** or **R** for Reset a Scheduler path.

4. Press F7 to return to the main Calendar screen.

You should always have a default Scheduler File Path. If you see the message "[Default path not defined]" you need to talk to your system administrator. The default or primary path is established when Office LAN is installed on the network.

The Reset option, 3, deletes all information from Calendar that has been sent through the path. Scheduler then resends all information to the Calendar. As the events are being inserted into Calendar the message "<Event inserted by Scheduler, press enter>" appears. You need to press ENTER on each event.

Adjust

Adjust allows you to quickly change the time of an appointment or the priority of a to-do item.

Keystrokes

To adjust an appointment time:

1. Highlight the appointment you want to edit.
2. Press F6 for Adjust.
3. Enter the new time.

To adjust the priority of a to-do item:

1. Highlight the to-do item you want to edit.
2. Press F6 for Adjust.
3. Enter the new priority.

Alarms

Calendar allows you to set alarms to notify you of upcoming appointments.

Keystrokes

1. Highlight the appointment you want to set an alarm for.

2. Type an asterisk (*). A musical note appears to the left of the appointment time indicating the alarm is set.

For more information on alarms see "Setting an Alarm for an Appointment" earlier in this chapter.

Appointments Window

The Appointments window is the middle window on the main Calendar screen. From the Appointments window you can add, view, and edit daily appointments in your Calendar.

Keystrokes

1. To add an appointment to your Calendar, press TAB twice to move to the Appointments window.

2. Press INS. The Appointments window opens and the cursor moves to the Time line.

3. Type in the beginning time of the appointment.

4. Press TAB to move to the ending time (the ending time is optional; press ENTER to move directly to the description window).

5. Type the ending time of the appointment.

6. Press TAB to move to the description window.

7. Type a description of the appointment.

For more information on appointments see "Using Calendar's Appointment Feature" earlier in this chapter.

Appointment Outline

With Appointment Outline, Calendar automatically inserts an outline of daily appointment times. Once an appointment outline is displayed you can easily enter your daily appointments at the times displayed.

Keystrokes

1. Press TAB twice to move to the Appointments window.

2. Press F9 for Outline. Calendar displays a list of appointment times.

3. Use the UP ARROW or DOWN ARROW key to highlight the desired appointment time.

4. Type the appointment description. Once you begin typing, the Appointments window opens.

5. If you need to enter an ending time press SHIFT-TAB.

6. Enter the ending time.

7. Press F7 twice to return to the main Calendar screen.

Auto-Archive

When Calendar information is a specified number of days old, Calendar automatically archives (saves) it when Auto-Archive is set to Yes.

Keystrokes

1. Press SHIFT-F1 or SHIFT-F8, or from the main Calendar screen you can also press **2** or **O** for Options.

2. Press **4** or **B** for Archive/Delete/Backup.

3. Press **1** or **A** for Auto-Archive.

4. Type **Y** to turn on Auto-Archive or type **N** to turn off Auto-Archive.

If you turn on Auto-Archive

5. Press **3** or **N** for Number of Days Before Archived and/or Deleted.

6. Enter the number of days old information should be before Calendar archives it.

See "Archiving Calendar Files" earlier in this chapter for additional information.

Auto-Alarms

Calendar can automatically set alarms for each new or adjusted appointment with the Auto-Alarm option.

Keystrokes

1. Press SHIFT-F1 or SHIFT-F8, or from the main Calendar screen you can also press **2** or **O** for Options.

2. Press **3** or **T** for Appointments/To-Do Options.

3. Press **6** or **A** for Auto-Alarm mode.

4. Type **Y** for Yes to turn on the Auto-Alarm mode or type **N** for No to turn off the Auto-Alarm mode.

See "Setting an Alarm for an Appointment" earlier in this chapter for more information.

Auto-Date

The Auto-Date function automatically inserts memos, appointments, and to-do items that occur on a regular basis.

Keystrokes

1. From the main Calendar screen press **4** or **A** for Auto-Date.

2. Press INS to move to the Auto-Date window.

3. Type in the auto-date formula.

4. Press TAB to move to the Memo, Appointments, or To-Do List window.

5. Type in the appropriate text.

6. Press F7 until you return to the main Calendar screen.

See "Using Calendar's Auto-Date Feature" earlier in this chapter for specific examples of auto-dates.

Auto-Delete

Auto-Delete allows you to delete old information from your Calendar file to avoid large working Calendar files. Large Calendar files slow down the speed of the Calendar program.

Keystrokes

1. Press SHIFT-F1 or SHIFT-F8, or from the main Calendar screen you can also press **2** or **O** for Options.

2. Press **4** or **B** Archive/Delete/Backup.

3. Press **2** or **D** for Auto-Delete.

4. Type **Y** to turn on Auto-Delete or type **N** to turn off Auto-Delete.

If you turn on Auto-Delete

5. Press **3** or **N** for Number of Days Before Archived and/or Deleted.

6. Type a number to indicate the number of days (from 1 to 365) before Calendar should delete the current Calendar file.

Auto-Delete is automatically turned on when Auto-Archive is on. However, you can use Auto-Delete without Auto-Archive.

Backup

To avoid accidental loss of your Calendar file due to computer or power failure, use the Backup feature to have Calendar automatically back up your Calendar file at regular intervals.

Keystrokes

1. Press SHIFT-F1 or SHIFT-F8, or from the main Calendar screen you can also press 2 or O for Options.

2. Press 4 or B for Archive/Delete/Backup.

3. Press 4 or T for Timed Backup.

4. Type Y to turn on Timed Backup or type N to turn off Timed Backup.

If you turn on Timed Backup

5. Press 5 or M for Minutes Between Timed Backup.

6. Enter the number of minutes between each backup.

Bold

You can bold memos, appointment descriptions, and to-do items in Calendar to make them more visible on the screen and when printed.

Keystrokes

To add bold:

1. Press TAB to move to the desired Calendar window.

2. Press F6 for Bold and type the word or words you want bolded.

3. Press F6 for Bold again to turn off boldfacing.

To delete bold:

1. Press TAB to move to the appropriate Calendar window.

2. Press CTRL-RIGHT ARROW for Word Right or CTRL-LEFT ARROW for Word Left until the cursor is on the first letter of the bolded word.

3. Press DEL. The "Delete Bold (Y/N)?N" prompt appears.

4. Type **Y** to delete the Bold codes.

Calendar File Format

With Calendar File Format options you specify in which format Calendar files are saved.

Keystrokes

1. Press SHIFT-F1 or SHIFT-F8, or press **2** for Options from the main Calendar screen.

2. Press **6** or **F** for File Format.

3. Press **1** for Calendar 1.1 or Earlier, or press **2** for Calendar 2.0/3.0.

Hints

The default Calendar file format is 2.0/3.0. WordPerfect Office 2.0 and 3.0 use the same Calendar file format. If you need to use your Calendar file in Office or Library 1.1 or earlier, change this option.

Cancel

Cancel backs you out of a Calendar menu or prompt. Cancel also lets you exit Calendar without saving any changes. Cancel restores deleted information in some parts of the program.

Keystrokes

Canceling out of Menus or Prompts

To back out of a menu or prompt, press Cancel (F1). Calendar returns you to the previous menu or screen.

Exiting Calendar Without Saving Changes

To exit Calendar without saving any of the information you added or edited:

1. Move the cursor to the main Calendar screen.

2. Press F1 for Cancel. The "Exit calendar without saving changes (Y/N)?N" prompt appears.

3. Type **Y** to exit without saving your changes or type **N** to remain in Calendar.

Clipboard

The Shell Clipboard is a temporary buffer to which you can save and append information and from which you can retrieve information. Calendar uses the Clipboard to save information from the Memo, Appointments, To-Do List, and Auto-Date Formulas windows and retrieve it to a different location in Calendar or to a different Shell-compatible program.

Keystrokes

To access the Shell Clipboard:

1. Press CTRL-F1 for Shell.

2. Select the desired option.

See "Using the Shell Clipboard and Go to Shell Features with Calendar" earlier in this chapter for specific information on using the Clipboard.

Copy

Copy lets you copy text from the Memo, Appointments, or To-Do List window and retrieve it to another location.

Keystrokes

1. Move the cursor to the Memo, Appointments, or To-Do List window.

2. Highlight the appointment or to-do item you want to copy. If you are copying text in the Memo window you do not need to move the cursor.

3. Press F4 for Copy.

4. Move the cursor to the exact location in the Memo, Appointments, or To-Do List window where you want the information copied.

5. Press SHIFT-F10 for Retrieve.

Hints

When you press Copy, Calendar saves this information to a temporary buffer. The buffer only holds one item (memo, appointment, to-do item, or formula) at a time. If you want to copy information from multiple windows, you must retrieve the information before you begin copying the next item. Information in the copy buffer is deleted when you exit Calendar. Calendar will also move text (see the "Move" section later in this chapter for more information).

Colors

If you have a color monitor, the Colors option lets you set colors for normal, bold, underline, and reverse video text. You can also choose how you want underline displayed on a single-color monitor. For monitors with Hercules cards and compatibles you can select the mode.

Keystrokes

1. Press SHIFT-F1 or SHIFT-F8, or from the main Calendar screen you can also press 2 or **O** for Options.

2. Press 5 or **C** for Colors. The following menu appears.

```
Color Setup

Monitor Characteristics: 0
    1 Color Monitor
    2 Single Color Monitor (eg. Black & White or Compaq)
    3 Hercules RamFont Card (InColor or Graphics Plus)
```

3. Choose the option that corresponds to your monitor and make the desired selections.

CTRL-HOME

CTRL-HOME lets you quickly move to another date while in Calendar.

Keystrokes

1. From the Memo, Appointments, or To-Do List window, or main Calendar screen press CTRL-HOME.

2. The following prompt appears at the bottom of the screen.

```
Enter date (mm/dd/yyyy): 12/3/90
```

3. Enter a new date in the format shown. The default format is mm/dd/yyyy which is month, day, year.

Date

The Date feature has three options that let you move to a specific date, move a certain number of days forward or backward, or figure the number of days between two dates.

Keystrokes

Go to Date

1. Press **1** or **D** for Date from the main Calendar screen.

2. Press **1** or **G** for Go to Date.

3. Enter the date to which you want to move.

You can also press CTRL-HOME to perform the Go to Date function from any Calendar window.

Move Days

1. Press **1** or **D** for Date from the main Calendar screen.

2. Press **2** or **M** for Move Days.

3. Enter the number of days to move or type a minus ($-$) and then the number to move backward from the date the cursor is on.

Date Difference

1. Use the cursor keys to move the cursor to the starting date.

2. Press **1** or **D** for Date from the main Calendar screen.

3. Press **3** or **D** for Date Difference.

4. Enter the ending date.

Date/Time Formats

The Date/Time Formats options let you change the way the dates and times are displayed in Calendar, which day displays as the first day of the week, and the DOS date and time.

Keystrokes

1. Press SHIFT-F1 or SHIFT-F8, or from the main Calendar screen you can also press **2** or **O** for Options.

2. Press **1** or **D** for Date/Time Formats.

3. Select one of the options and make the desired changes.

For more information on the Date/Time Formats options see "Using Calendar's Date/Time Formats" earlier in this chapter.

Exit

From any Calendar menu or prompt you can press Exit (F7) to take you back to the previous screen. Pressing Exit from the main Calendar screen exits you from the Calendar program without a prompt. When you exit Calendar with the Exit function, Calendar saves all information you added or modified to the current Calendar file. Pressing Exit while in the Memo, Appointments, or To-Do List window takes you back to the main Calendar window.

Help

The Help feature displays on-screen information about the Calendar features.

Keystrokes

1. Press F3 for Help from the main Calendar screen. Calendar displays the screen shown in Figure 3-16.

2. You can access information by typing one of the menu item letters to see information about the specific topic; pressing a function key to see information about the feature associated with that key; or pressing F3 for Help again to see the Calendar template, which is especially useful since WordPerfect Office does not come with a keyboard template for Calendar.

3. Press ENTER, SPACEBAR, or 0 to exit a help screen or ESC to return to the main help screen.

```
Help                                         CL 3.0  06/14/90
   File: C:\OFFICE30\CALENDAR.FIL


      Press any function key to get information about the use of the key.
      Press Help (F3) again to see a template for the function keys.
      Press the following letters to get information about specific topics:

      A - Movement in Calendar         N - Saving/Retrieving Calendars
      B - Entering Memos and Text      O - Starting/Exiting Calendar
      C - Entering Appts/Alarms        P - Startup Options
      D - Entering To-Do Lists         Q - Auto-Date Formula Entry
      E - Moving or Copying Text       R - Holiday Autodate Formulas
      F - Printing the Calendar        S - Date
      G - Date/Time Formats
      H - Alarm Options                Y - Customer Support
      I - Appt/To-Do Options           Z - Extended Character Set
      J - Auto Archive/Delete/Backup Options
      K - Set Colors
      L - File Export Format/Password
      M - Scheduler File Paths



   A-Z Topic: 0            (ESC Topics; Space Exit; Function Key Help for Key)
```

Figure 3-16.   Main Calendar help screen

Hints

The help screens are a valuable tool for accessing information about the Calendar program. You do not have to press Help (F3) from the main Calendar screen. Pressing Help from any Calendar menu displays information about the features associated with that screen. Calendar displays the keystrokes (if any) for the feature in the upper-right corner of the help screen as shown in Figure 3-17.

Insert

The INS key opens up the Appointments, To-Do List, or Auto-Date window so you can add a new entry.

```
Printing the Calendar                                           [Shift-F7]

     You can print memos, appointments and/or to-do items for selected days.
     From the main Calendar window, select Print (3) or press Print (Shift-F7)
     to display the following options:

     1  Print                Prints the specified information.
     2  Format               Select Normal or Merge.
     3  Options              Formats the printed page and indicates what
                             information should be printed.
                             Press 1 for more information.
     4  Hand-fed Forms       Specify Yes or No.
     5  Device or File       Select the proper device (or file) to print to.
     6  Select Printer       Select the proper printer definition.


     7  Abort Print Job  Cancels the current print job.
     8  Stop             Stops the printer without canceling the job.
     9  Send Go          Restarts a print job when stopped and/or sends next
                         page for hand-fed forms.



 1 More; A-Z Topic: 0       (ESC Topics; Space Exit; Function Key Help for Key)
```

Figure 3-17.   Printing the Calendar help screen

Keystrokes

1. From the Memo, Appointments, To-Do List, or Auto-Date window press INS.

2. Type in the information for the entry.

Memo Window

The Memo window is the top window on the right side of the main Calendar screen. From the Memo window you can add, view, and edit daily memos in your Calendar.

Keystrokes

1. To add a memo to your Calendar, press TAB once to move to the Memo window.

2. Type in the memo.

For more information on Memos see "Using Calendar's Memo Feature" earlier in this chapter.

Move

Move takes text from one location in Calendar and moves it to another location.

Keystrokes

1. Move the cursor to the Memo, Appointments, or To-Do List window.

2. Highlight the appointment or to-do item you want to move. If you are moving text in the Memo window you do not need to move the cursor.

3. Press CTRL-F4 for Move.

4. Move the cursor to the exact location in the Memo, Appointments, or To-Do List window where you want the information moved.

5. Press SHIFT-F10 for Retrieve.

Hints

When you press Move, Calendar deletes the text from the current location and saves it to a temporary buffer. The buffer only holds one item (memo, appointment, to-do item) at a time. If you want to move information from multiple windows, you must retrieve the information before you begin moving the next item. Calendar deletes information in the move buffer when you exit Calendar.

Options

Calendar's Setup Options menu lets you customize the default settings for your Calendar. When you change the options, the settings are stored in the Calendar file. You can change the display of the date and time format, set Alarm options, change the display of appointments and to-do items, turn on the Auto-Archive, Auto-Delete, and Backup, set colors, change the file format, set and remove passwords, and change Scheduler file path information.

Keystrokes

1. Press SHIFT-F1 or SHIFT-F8, or from the main Calendar screen you can also press **2** or **O** for Options. The options shown in Figure 3-18 appear.

2. Select an option and make the desired changes.

3. Press F7 for Exit until you return to the main Calendar screen.

Options

The following sections give a brief description of the options. For more detailed information see the sections for the individual title earlier in this chapter.

```
Setup Options

      1 - Date/Time Formats

      2 - Alarms

      3 - Appointments/To-Do

      4 - Archive/Delete/Backup

      5 - Colors

      6 - File Format

      7 - Scheduler File Paths




Selection: 0
```

Figure 3-18.   Setup Options screen

Date/Time Formats

The Date/Time Formats options let you change the way Calendar displays the dates and times, which day displays as the first day of the week, and the DOS date and time. You can also access this option with SHIFT-F5.

Alarms

You can change the following two Alarm options:

```
Alarm Options

      1 - Minutes Before Appointment to Start Alarm: 10

      2 - Seconds to Pause Between Each Alarm: 30
```

Appointments/To-Do

With this option you can change the settings shown in Figure 3-19 to fit your individual needs.

Archive/Delete/Backup

You can change the following settings with this option:

```
Archive/Delete/Backup Options

    1 - Auto-Archive: No

    2 - Auto-Delete: No

    3 - Number of Days Before Archived and/or Deleted: 7

    4 - Timed Backup: Yes

    5 - Minutes Between Timed Backups: 30

    6 - Update Calendar on Go to Shell: Yes
```

```
Appointments/To-Do Options

    Appointment Outline
        1 - Beginning Time: 8:00am
        2 - Ending Time: 5:00pm
        3 - Time Interval (in minutes): 60

    4 - Appointment Overlap Display: Yes

    5 - Single Line Display (Memo, Appts, To-Do): No

    6 - Auto-Alarm Mode (Appts): No

    7 - Auto-Mark mode (To-Do): No

    8 - Unique Priorities (To-Do): Yes




Selection: 0
```

Figure 3-19.   Appointments/To-Do Options menu

Colors

With the Colors option you can change the way Calendar displays boldface, underlining, and reverse video text.

File Format

The File Format option gives you the ability to change the format that Calendar files are saved in and to set and remove passwords.

Scheduler File Paths

LAN If you are using Office LAN you must have a path set up in order for Calendar and Scheduler to communicate.

Password

You can set a password for your Calendar file to help ensure that no one else accesses your Calendar information. You can also remove passwords that have previously been set.

Keystrokes

To add a password:

1. Press SHIFT-F1 or SHIFT-F8, or from the main Calendar screen you can also press **2** or **O** for Options.

2. Press **6** or **F** for File Format.

3. Press **3** or **A** to Add or Change a password.

4. Enter the password.

5. Enter the password again.

6. Press F7 twice to return to the main Calendar screen.

To remove a password:

    1. Press SHIFT-F1 or SHIFT-F8, or from the main Calendar screen you can also press **2** or **O** for Options.

    2. Press **6** or **F** for File Format.

    3. Press **4** or **R** to Remove Password.

Print

You can print the contents of your Calendar file to the printer or to a merge file. Calendar prints the date and the information in the Memo, Appointments, and To-Do List windows.

Keystrokes

    1. Press SHIFT-F7 for Print.

    2. Make the needed changes to options 2 through 6.

    3. Press **1** or **P** to print the Calendar.

For more information on printing in Calendar see "Printing Your Calendar" in the first section of this chapter.

Print Options

Print options let you customize how and what information Calendar prints.

Keystrokes

1. Press SHIFT-F7 for Print.

2. Press **2** or **O** for Options.

3. Select an option and make the desired changes.

See "Changing Print Options" earlier in this chapter for specific information on the Print options.

Printer Control

The Printer Control options in the Print menu help you manage print jobs while printing.

Keystrokes

1. Press SHIFT-F7 for Print.

2. Choose the desired option (7 through 9).

Options

The following Control options are available in the Print menu.

Abort Print Job   Abort Print Job immediately stops the printing process. If your printer jams or the wrong information is printing, use this option. The speed at which the print job is affected by this option is determined by the printer's buffer.

Stop Printer   Stop Printer temporarily stops the printing process. If you run out of paper or need to check the information that has printed before continuing, use this option.

Send a Go to Printer   After pressing Stop Printer, Send a Go to Printer resumes the printing process. You will also use this option if you set Hand-fed Forms to Yes on the Print menu.

Priorities

When entering to-do items you may set alphabetical and numerical priorities to help organize your list. For information on setting priorities see "Creating a To-Do Item" earlier in this chapter.

Retrieve

After using the Copy or Move feature, Retrieve or Paste (SHIFT-F10) inserts the text in the Memo, Appointments, or To-Do List window at the location of the cursor. See "Copy" or "Move" earlier in this chapter for more information.

Save

You can save Calendar files without exiting or create new Calendar files with the Save feature.

Keystrokes

1. From the main Calendar screen press F10 for Save.

2. Type the name you want the file saved under or press ENTER to save the file with the existing name.

Scheduler File Paths

LAN If you are using Office LAN you must have a path set up in order for Calendar and Scheduler to communicate.

Keystrokes

1. Press SHIFT-F1 or SHIFT-F8, or from the main Calendar screen you can also press **2** or **O** for Options.

2. Press **7** or **S** for Scheduler File Paths and choose one of the options.

For more information on communicating with your Scheduler see "Setting Scheduler File Paths" earlier in this chapter.

Screen

The Screen options manage various display functions, including rewrite, change colors, zoom window, and check Scheduler files (the last option applies to Office LAN users only).

Keystrokes

1. Press CTRL-F3 for Screen.

2. Select one of the options.

Options

The following Screen options are available.

Rewrite   Rewrite does exactly as its name states—it rewrites the screen. There may be times when you need to manually rewrite the screen with this option, for instance, if you receive a DOS error message that doesn't automatically clear.

Colors   You can change the ways colors display for color monitors. See "Colors" earlier in this chapter for more information.

Zoom Window   Many times there is more information in a window than can be seen on the normal screen. With the Zoom feature you can expand the size of the windows to view more information.

LAN **Check Scheduler Files**   Calendar automatically checks for incoming scheduled events at specified time intervals. With the Check Scheduler Files you can manually check to see if there are any pending events for you.

Search

Use the Search feature to find a specific word or word pattern in a memo, appointment, or to-do item.

Keystrokes

1. Press F2 for Forward Search or SHIFT-F2 for Reverse Search.
2. Type in the word or word pattern.
3. Press F2 for Search to begin the search.

Hints

If Calendar finds the word or word pattern it underlines the Memo window title, underlines the appointment time in the Appointments window, or underlines the priority in the To-Do List window. Search only finds one listing of the word per window. So if the word "letter" is found twice in the Memo window, Calendar only finds the first listing. To repeat the same search press F2 or SHIFT-F2 twice. Search will search from the cursor to the beginning or ending of the year and then ask you if you want to continue the search into the next year.

Shell

The Shell feature lets you exit to Shell without exiting Calendar, save and append text to the Shell Clipboard, and retrieve text from the Clipboard.

Keystrokes

1. Press CTRL-F1 for Shell.

2. Choose from the options shown here.

```
1 Go to shell; 2 Save to clipboard; 3 Append to clipboard: 0
```

For more information on the Shell options see "Using the Shell Clipboard and Go to Shell Features with Calendar" earlier in this chapter.

Startup Options

Startup options override certain default Calendar conditions on start-up. You may put startup options on the command line if you are starting Calendar from DOS or add the options to the Shell Program Information screen for Calendar.

The following is a list of all the startup options that you can use with Calendar.

LAN	/C	If starting Calendar from DOS or if you have set Calendar to start resident on the Shell menus, /C checks for new requests from Scheduler and starts Calendar if there are any new requests.
	/CM	Does the same as /C but only informs you of new Scheduler requests instead of taking you into Calendar.
	/CN	Does the same as /C but Calendar does not stay resident under Shell if no new items are found.
	/D-*path*	Lets you specify a directory for Calendar temporary files.
	d-%X	Allows you to run several Calendars from the same directory by giving the temporary file a unique name; *x* represents the number of the temporary file for this Calendar.
	/I	This option only works from DOS. /I installs the resident alarm handler; setting all current alarms without entering Calendar. This is often added to the AUTOEXEC.BAT batch file.
	/M-*macro*	This option only works if Calendar is started from SHELL. It invokes a Shell macro at the startup of Calendar.
	/NA	Disables bold and underline attributes for notification. The bold and underline may cause problems on some monitors.
	/NC	Tells Calendar not to check for items in Scheduler at startup.
	PH-*path*	Overrides the default path set by the system administrator to your Scheduler files.
	/SS-RW,CL	Overrides the automatic row and column settings.

/W-*xxx*   This option only works under Shell. It allows you to
                 specify a different value for the memory work space
                 for Calendar. By default, Calendar uses enough
                 memory to handle the current Calendar file.

TAB

The TAB key moves you from window to window on the main Calendar
screen and in the Auto-Date screen. Press TAB once to move to the
Memo window, twice to move to the Appointments window, and three
times to move to the To-Do List window. You can also use SHIFT-TAB to
move in the opposite direction.

Timed Backup

See "Backup" earlier in this chapter.

To-Do List

The To-Do List window is the bottom window on the main Calendar
screen. From the To-Do List window you can add, view, and edit daily
to-do items in your Calendar.

Keystrokes

1. To add a to-do item to your Calendar, press SHIFT-TAB to move to
the To-Do List window.

2. Press INS. The To-Do List window opens and the cursor moves to
the Priority line.

3. Type in the priority.

4. Press TAB to move to the description window.

5. Type a description of the to-do item.

For more information on to-do items see "Using Calendar's To-Do List Feature" in the first part of this chapter.

Underline

You can underline memos, appointment descriptions, and to-do items while in Calendar in order to make them more visible on screen and when printed.

Keystrokes

To add underline:

1. Press TAB to move to the desired Calendar window.

2. Press F8 for Underline and type the word or words you want underlined.

3. Press F8 again to turn off Underline.

To delete underline codes:

1. Press TAB to move to the appropriate Calendar window.

2. Press CTRL-RIGHT ARROW for Word Right or CTRL-LEFT ARROW for Word Left until the cursor is on the first letter of the underlined word.

3. Press DEL. The "Delete Underline (Y/N)?N" prompt appears.

4. Type **Y** to delete the Underline codes.

Hints

You can use underlining in memos, appointment descriptions, and to-do item descriptions. You cannot underline the appointment beginning or ending times or the to-do item priority.

To delete the Underline codes use the Word Right and Word Left commands. The Word Right (CTRL-RIGHT ARROW) and Word Left (CTRL-LEFT ARROW) commands move the cursor to the commands. Deleting the on code at the beginning of the text also deletes the off code at the end of the text.

If you have a color monitor you can change the on-screen color for Underline in the Setup Options menu (SHIFT-F1, 5, 1). See "Colors" in the "Functions and Features" section of this chapter for information on setting screen colors.

Update Calendar on Go to Shell

This option automatically saves your Calendar file when you Go to DOS (CTRL-F1, 1) or switch to another program and leave Calendar in resident memory.

Keystrokes

1. Press SHIFT-F1 or SHIFT-F8, or from the main Calendar screen you can also press 2 or O for Options.

2. Press 4 or B for Archive/Delete/Backup.

3. Press 6 or U for Update Calendar on Go to Shell.

4. Type Y for Yes or type N for No.

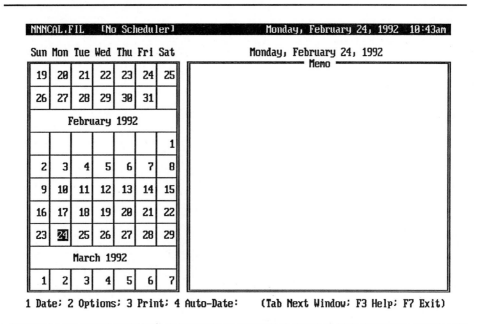

Figure 3-20.   Memo window in Zoom mode

Zoom

If you have more information in the Memo, Appointments, or To-Do List window than you can see, Zoom lets you enlarge the window to occupy the entire right side of the main Calendar screen as illustrated in Figure 3-20.

Keystrokes

1. Press CTRL-F3 for Screen.

2. Press **2** or **Z** for Zoom Windows.

3. Type **Y** for Yes to enlarge the windows or type **N** for No to return the windows to the normal size.

When Zoom is on each Calendar window enlarges as you move to it.

Using Calculator

FOUR

You can use Calculator for most of your everyday calculator needs. Beyond providing basic arithmetic functions, Calculator has four enhanced function menus to meet many special needs. It has a Scientific Functions menu that enables you to perform exponential, logarithmic, and trigonometric calculations. The Programmer Functions menu lists several common programming commands and operations. Calculator's Financial Functions menu lets you solve annuity, profit margin, and loan calculations. The Statistical Functions menu has data evaluation functions for both populations and samples.

In Calculator, you have the choice of four different number systems in which to perform calculations: decimal, hexadecimal, octal, and binary. You can even change number systems in the middle of a calculation. Calculator also gives you the choice of using fixed-point or exponential notation to display all decimal values.

Calculator's Tape feature simulates a paper tape that keeps track of the values you enter and the results of your calculations. This allows you to review intermediate steps leading to a final solution. The data on the Tape can be stored on disk for future reference, saved to Shell's Clipboard to be imported into another program if you are using Calculator under Shell, or printed. There is also a temporary Memory Register that is useful for storing intermediate values when performing long or complicated calculations.

Starting Calculator

To start Calculator from the Office Shell menu, press the letter listed next to the entry for Calculator. This default letter is C if you are using the standard Shell menu. The Shell menu display is replaced by Calculator's main screen as shown in Figure 4-1. To start Calculator from DOS, type **calc** and press ENTER on the DOS command line. If the directory for Calculator is one of the directories listed in your DOS path statement, you can enter this command from any directory.

Located at the top of all screens in Calculator is the ALT-Key menu. Using the ALT-Key menu from any screen you can change the number system Calculator uses and the display format for decimal numbers. With the Main menu on the left of the main Calculator screen, you can access on-screen help, the Tape Options menu, the Colors menu, and the Scientific, Programmer, Financial, and Statistical Functions menus. Selecting any of these menus causes the Main menu to display the commands specific to that menu.

To make the process of entering values in Calculator easier, Calculator automatically turns on the NUM LOCK key when you enter the program. With NUM LOCK on, any keystrokes made on the numeric keypad

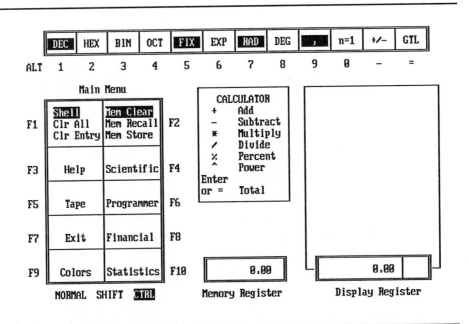

Figure 4-1.   Calculator's main screen

on the right side of most keyboards are entered as numbers and not as cursor movement keystrokes. If the NUM LOCK key was off when you started the program, Calculator turns it off again when you exit after use.

Exiting Calculator

To exit Calculator and return to the Shell menu or to the DOS command line, press F7 from Calculator's main screen. Calculator allows you to exit from any of the enhanced function screens by using the Quit function, CTRL-Q. Upon exiting, Calculator clears the contents of the Memory Register and the Tape.

Screen Display

In order to meet your Calculator needs, the main Calculator screen is divided into five parts, which are described in the following sections.

ALT-Key Menu

Located at the top of every screen in Calculator is the ALT-Key menu shown here:

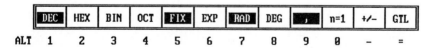

The ALT-Key menu outlines the setup options in Calculator. To help you identify the setup, the current default settings are highlighted. To select an option from the menu, press ALT-x where x is the number displayed beneath the option. For example, pressing ALT-3 changes Calculator to using binary numbers; ALT-= performs a Grand Total function.

Display Register

In the bottom-right corner of all Calculator screens is the Display Register as shown here:

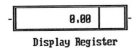

Display Register

The left section of the register is where Calculator shows all numeric values you enter and the results of all calculations. The Display Register displays up to 10 digits with room to the left for a negative sign. The right section of the display shows the functions you can perform. If the Tape feature is active, each time you select a function, Calculator copies the entire contents of the Display Register to the Tape.

Tape Display

Along the right side of the screen just above the Display Register is the Tape Display as shown here:

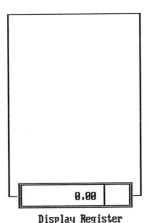

Display Register

With the Tape on, the Tape Display scrolls up, and the contents of the Display Register are moved to the bottom of the Tape Display each time you select a function. When the Tape is turned off, the Tape Display remains blank.

Function Key Menu

On the left side of all screens in Calculator is the Main menu or Function Key menu as shown here:

Main Menu

	Shell	Mem Clear	
F1	Clr All	Mem Recall	F2
	Clr Entry	Mem Store	
F3	Help	Scientific	F4
F5	Tape	Programmer	F6
F7	Exit	Financial	F8
F9	Colors	Statistics	F10

NORMAL   SHIFT   CTRL

It displays the commands assigned to each function key for the current screen. Keys F1 and F2 have the Shell, Clear, and Memory features associated with them on all screens; keys F3 through F10 have different operations for each of the screens in Calculator depending on the function menu you select.

Memory Register

In the bottom-center of all Calculator screens is the Memory Register as shown here:

Memory Register

It displays any value you place in the temporary memory buffer using Memory Store (F2). The Memory Register is a temporary buffer, and any contents are lost upon exiting Calculator. Like the Display Register, it can show up to 10 characters with space on the left for a negative sign.

Using the ALT-Key Menu

The ALT-Key menu, which is located at the top of every screen in Calculator, lists the options available in Calculator. The current default options are highlighted on the menu to help you identify how Calculator is set up. To select an option from the menu, press ALT-x where x is the number displayed beneath the option.

Options

Using the ALT-Key menu you can choose a number system, set the format for display and input, adjust the repeating variable, and perform the Grand Total function.

Number Systems   Calculator gives you the choice of four different number systems to use during calculations. The following list outlines the number systems available and the keys associated with each system.

Number System	Base	ALT-Key Combination
Decimal	10	ALT-1
Hexadecimal	16	ALT-2
Binary	2	ALT-3
Octal	8	ALT-4

While you can use any of the number systems in any function, octal, binary, and hexadecimal are normally reserved for the Programmer functions.

Decimal Display Format   In Calculator you have a choice of display formats for decimal numbers in the Display Register. You can select the Fixed Point Notation (FIX) mode by pressing ALT-5. Calculator asks you how many digits (from 0 to 8) to display to the right of the decimal point. If a calculation produces a number too large to display in fixed-point notation, Calculator automatically shows that number in exponential notation.

You can change the mode to Exponential Notation (EXP) by pressing ALT-6. Exponential or Scientific mode displays all numbers with an exponent offset with a plus (+) or minus (−) sign. When you select Exponential mode you still enter numbers in normal decimal notation, and Calculator converts the number to exponential notation when you select a function.

Trigonometry Display Format   When you use Calculator to perform trigonometric calculations, you can format the input and display in radians or degrees. You can select Radian mode (RAD) by pressing ALT-7. Calculator then expects all angles you enter to be in relation to pi (PI). You can change to Degree mode (DEG) by pressing ALT-8. Calculator cannot change an entry from radians to degrees, so you should never change modes after entering an angle value.

Comma Display Format   Using ALT-9 you can choose whether or not to display a thousands separator. When you press ALT-9, Calculator asks if you would like a separator displayed. If you enter No, Calculator removes the thousands separator from the display. If you want a separator displayed, Calculator asks if a comma or period should display as the decimal point. The other automatically becomes the thousands separator and is displayed on the ALT-Key menu. This option is for the display only. You should not put a thousands separator in any number you enter into Calculator.

Repeating Variable   Four of the Programmer functions available in Calculator (ROLn, RORn, SHLn, SHRn) have an attached variable that you can set with the ALT-Key menu. This variable tells Calculator how many times to repeat the function. You can set the repetition value by pressing ALT-0 and entering a number from 0 to 9.

Change Sign   Using ALT-MINUS you can change the sign of the current value in the Display Register. A positive number has no sign displayed in the Display Register. A negative value displays a negative sign (–) next to the left-most digit.

Grand Total   When you use the Grand Total function (ALT-=), Calculator finds the sum of all calculations performed since the last occurrence of a Clear All function. If you are using the Tape, Calculator records a Grand Total with a "T" next to the result. Calculator uses all Grand Totals when computing the next Grand Total until it encounters a Clear All function.

Using Calculator's Tape Feature

Using Calculator's Tape feature you can save the values you enter, the functions you perform, and the results of all calculations in the Display Register. You can save, print, or review the Tape with the Tape Options menu, which is accessed by pressing F5 from the main screen or CTRL-T from any screen in Calculator.

Options

The following options allow you to clear, save, print, and review the contents of the Tape.

On/Off   To turn the Tape on and off:

1. Press F5 or CTRL-T to display the Tape Options menu.

2. Enter **1** or **T** from the Tape Options menu.

3. Type **Y** to turn the Tape on or type **N** to turn the Tape off.

Calculator does not save any calculations to the Tape that you perform while the Tape is off.

Clear   To clear the contents of the Tape:

1. Press F5 or CTRL-T to display the Tape Options menu.

2. Press **2** or **C** from the Tape Options menu to clear the Tape.

This clears both the Tape Display and the buffer storing the Tape.

Print   To print the contents of the Tape:

1. Press F5 or CTRL-T to display the Tape Options menu.

2. Press **3** or **P** for Print.

3. Press **1** or **P** to print the Tape's contents.

To change the printer port or device:

1. Press F5 or CTRL-T to display the Tape options menu.

2. Press 3 or P for Print.

3. Press 2 or S for port or device.

4. You can press numbers 1 through 3 to select a port. You can also press 4 or D and enter a device or filename to which you want the contents of the Tape saved.

5. Press 1 or P to print the Tape's contents.

Save to a File   To save the contents of the Tape directly to a file:

1. Press F5 or CTRL-T to display the Tape Options menu.

2. Press 4 or F for File.

3. Type a filename and press ENTER. To save the file to a directory other than the default directory, enter the full path to the directory before the filename.

Save to the Clipboard   To save the contents of the Tape to Shell's Clipboard:

1. Press F5 or CTRL-T to display the Tape Options menu.

2. Press 5 or B for Clipboard.

Look   Using the Look option, you can review any calculations that are recorded on the Tape. To use the Look option:

1. Press F5 or CTRL-T to display the Tape Options menu as shown here:

`Tape: 1 T-Yes; 2 Clear; 3 Print; Save 4 File; 5 Clipboard; 6 Look; 7 Append: 8`

2. Press 6 or L to select the Look option.

The Tape will be reset to the start. A pointer displays along the right side of the Tape Display to indicate your current position on the Tape.

The UP ARROW and DOWN ARROW keys scroll the Tape up and down past the pointer in the Tape Display. F2 stores the current value at the Tape Display's pointer in the Memory Register. Pressing ENTER places the current value at the Tape Display's pointer into the Display Register. F7 exits the Look option.

Append   To append the contents of the Tape to the current contents of the Clipboard:

1. Press F5 or CTRL-T to display the Tape Options menu.

2. Press **7** or **A** for the Append option.

Calculator then appends the Tape to the Clipboard.

Setting Colors with a Shell Macro

Since Calculator does not store its setup options in a file when you exit, all settings you make in Calculator are temporary, including the color setting. Using Calculator under Shell, you can use the /M startup option to define a macro that will automatically set the colors each time you start Calculator. To define the macro, do the following from Calculator's main screen while running under Shell:

1. Press CTRL-SHIFT-F10 to begin defining the macro.

2. When a prompt appears at the bottom left corner of the display, enter a name for the macro; for example, type **CALCSTRT**.

3. Enter a description for the macro. A description is useful if you should ever need to edit the macro. However, this is not necessary for the macro to run, and you can press ENTER to continue.

4. A "*Starting shell macro*" prompt appears briefly. You are now in Macro Definition mode.

5. Press F9 to select Colors.

6. Use Colors menu to set up your display.

7. Press F7 to exit back to Calculator's main screen.

8. Press CTRL-SHIFT-F10 again to finish defining the macro.

To have Calculator call the macro automatically on startup, you need to edit the Shell Program Information screen for Calculator. From the Shell menu that lists Calculator:

1. Press 4 for Setup.

2. Move the cursor to the entry for Calculator and press 1 or ENTER to edit the Program Information screen for Calculator.

3. Move the cursor down to the Startup Options line.

4. Type **/m-** for macro, followed by the macro name; for example, type **/m-calcstrt**.

5. Press F7 twice to exit the Program Information screen and return to the Shell menu.

The next time you enter Calculator, Calculator executes the macro you defined and sets the colors automatically.

Basic Arithmetic Functions

In the center of the main Calculator screen is a listing of Calculator's basic arithmetic operators or functions. While these operators only display when you are in the main screen, they are available to you from any screen in Calculator. To use the arithmetic operators, enter the first value to be used in the calculation, then press the key for the function you want to perform. Type in the second value, and then press the equal sign ($=$) key or ENTER. Calculator then completes the calculation. For example, to add 2 and 2 use the following keystrokes:

1. Type 2. The number 2 then displays in the Display Register in the lower right corner of the screen.

2. Press +; the addition symbol displays in the operator section of the Display Register. With the Tape Display on, 2 is copied to the bottom line of the Tape Display as shown here:

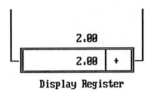

Display Register

3. Type **2** as the second value.

4. Press = or ENTER to complete the calculation. The Tape Display scrolls up and the second 2 and the plus sign (+) display beneath the first value. A line displays below the second value and the result is placed in the Tape Display beneath the line with an equal sign (=) next to it as shown here:

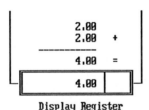

Display Register

You can also perform several calculations with the result of one calculation becoming a value used in the next. Calculator uses any existing contents of the Display Register as a value, unless you change or clear the display.

Calculating Loan Payments

Using the Financial Functions screen you can solve loan and payment calculations. If you wanted to find the monthly payments for a $12,000 loan at 11.5 percent annual interest over a 60-month period, you would do the following from the main screen:

1. Press F8 to enter the Financial Functions screen, which is shown in Figure 4-2.

2. Press ALT-1 to use decimal numbers.

3. Press ALT-5 for Fixed Decimal Display.

4. Type **2** to display two numbers after the decimal point.

5. Press SHIFT-F1 to clear all values.

6. Type **60** and press F3 to enter the number of payment periods for the loan.

7. Find the periodic interest rate by dividing the annual rate by 12. To perform this calculation, type **11.5** and press **/** to divide. Type **12** for the number of months and press **=** or ENTER. Assign the interest rate value by pressing F4.

8. Type **12000** and press F6 to enter the present value of the loan. Since the future value is 0 there is no need to enter it.

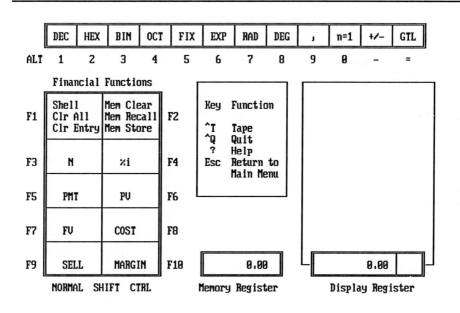

DEC	HEX	BIN	OCT	FIX	EXP	RAD	DEG	,	n=1	+/–	GTL

ALT   1   2   3   4   5   6   7   8   9   0   –   =

Financial Functions

	Shell F1 Clr All Clr Entry	Mem Clear Mem Recall F2 Mem Store		Key Function ^T Tape ^Q Quit ? Help Esc Return to Main Menu
F3	N	%i F4		
F5	PMT	PV F6		
F7	FV	COST F8		
F9	SELL	MARGIN F10	0.00	0.00

NORMAL   SHIFT   CTRL   Memory Register   Display Register

Figure 4-2.   The Financial Functions screen

9. Press SHIFT-F5 to solve for the payment amount. The monthly payment amount of $263.91 should show in the Display Register as shown here:

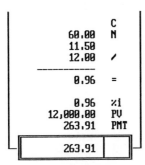

Display Register

You could also find a loan amount based on a given interest rate, payment amount, and number of payments. To find a loan amount requiring $250-a-month payments at an 11.5 percent annual interest rate over 60 months, enter the following from the main screen:

1. Press F8 to enter the Financial Functions screen.

2. Press ALT-1 to use decimal numbers.

3. Press ALT-5 for Fixed Decimal Display.

4. Enter **2** to display two numbers after the decimal point.

5. Press SHIFT-F1 to clear all values.

6. Type **60** and press F3 to enter the number of payment periods for the loan.

7. Find the interest rate per payment period by dividing the annual rate by 12. To perform this calculation type **11.5** and press / to divide. Type **12** for the number of months and press = or ENTER. Assign the interest rate value by pressing F4.

8. Type **250** and press F5 to assign the payment amount.

9. Press SHIFT-F6 to solve for the loan amount or present value. A loan amount of $11,367.46 will display in the Display Register.

Calculating Annuities

From Calculator's Financial Functions screen you can solve calculations involving annuities. For example, to find the value of $1000 after 5 years if invested at 10 percent annual interest compounded quarterly, perform the following steps from the main screen:

1. Press F8 to enter the Financial Functions screen.

2. Press ALT-1 to use decimal numbers.

3. Press ALT-5 for Fixed Decimal Display.

4. Enter 2 to display two numbers after the decimal point.

5. Press SHIFT-F1 to clear all values.

6. To find and assign the periodic interest rate, divide the annual rate by the number of periods. For this example type 10 and then press / to divide. Type 4 for the number of periods, and then press = or ENTER to calculate a rate of 2.5 percent. Press F4 to assign this value to the interest rate.

7. To enter the total number of periods, multiply the number of years by the number of periods per year. In this case, type 5 for the number of years and press * to multiply. Type 4 for the number of periods per year, and press = or ENTER to calculate 20 periods. Press F3 to assign the number of periods.

8. Type 1000 and press F6 to input the present value.

9. Press SHIFT-F7 to solve for the future value after 5 years. This solves for the future value and returns the amount of $1638.62 as shown here:

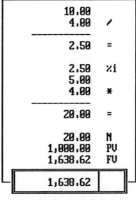

Display Register

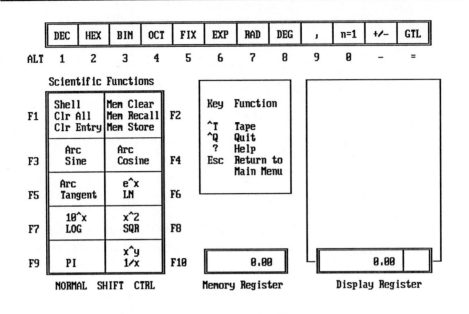

Figure 4-3.   The Scientific Functions screen

You can use Calculator to solve for present value (PV), future value (FV), or periods (N) in annuity calculations. Since Calculator cannot solve for the interest rate using the input in the examples above, it is important that you know the interest rate when solving any annuity problems.

Trigonometric Calculations

Using operations from the Scientific Functions screen you can solve trigonometric calculations in both Radian and Degree modes. To find the sine of a 45-degree angle, use the following keystrokes from the main screen:

1. Press F4 to enter the Scientific Functions screen, which is shown in Figure 4-3.

2. Press ALT-1 to use decimal numbers.

3. Press ALT-5 for Fixed Decimal Display.

4. Enter 2 to display two numbers after the decimal point.

5. Press ALT-8 to change to Degree mode.

6. Type 45 to input the angle in degrees.

7. Press F3 to calculate the sine.

The Display Register and Tape Register should look like this:

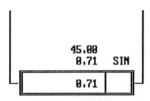

Display Register

Using the inverse trigonometric functions you can also solve for angles given a sine, cosine, or tangent value. To find the angle in radians that has a tangent of 1, do the following from the main screen:

1. Press F4 to enter the Scientific Functions screen.

2. Press ALT-1 to use decimal numbers.

3. Press ALT-5 for Fixed Decimal Display.

4. Enter 4 to display four numbers after the decimal point.

5. Press ALT-7 to change to Radian mode.

6. Type 1 in the Display Register.

7. Press SHIFT-F5 to perform the calculation. The arctangent is .7584 radians.

If you did the same calculation in Degree mode, the result would be a 45-degree angle. Since Calculator cannot convert between Radian and Degree modes in the middle of a calculation, you must be careful never to mix modes in the same operation.

Logarithmic Calculations

You can use the Scientific Functions screen to solve logarithmic and antilogarithmic calculations. These functions are available for both natural (base e) and common (base 10) calculations. To find the natural logarithm for 50, do the following from the main screen:

1. Press F4 to enter the Scientific Functions screen.

2. Press ALT-1 to use decimal numbers.

3. Press ALT-5 for Fixed Decimal Display.

4. Enter **2** to display two numbers after the decimal point.

5. Press SHIFT-F1 for Clear All.

6. Type **50** in the Display Register.

7. Press F6 to calculate the natural log. The result 3.91 shows in the Display Register:

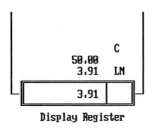

Display Register

Since Calculator can also perform common logarithm operations, you could use it to find the common antilog of a number. To find the common antilog of 4.77, do the following from the main screen:

1. Press F4 to enter the Scientific Functions screen.

2. Press ALT-1 to use decimal numbers.

3. Press ALT-5 for Fixed Decimal Display.

4. Enter **2** to display two numbers after the decimal point.

5. Press SHIFT-F1 for Clear All.

6. Type **4.77** into the Display Register.

7. Press SHIFT-F7 to calculate the common antilog. The Display Register shows the result 58,884.37.

The format in which these results are displayed depends on the options set with the ALT-Key menu. If you have changed the display format since entering Calculator, what actually displays may differ slightly from the preceding examples.

Exponential Calculations

In Calculator, you can change the display format for decimal numbers from fixed- or floating-point display to exponential notation. This allows you to work with numbers far larger than those that can fit in the Display Register in fixed-point notation. Select Exponential Notation by pressing ALT-6 from the ALT-Key menu. You may then enter a number in a fixed-point notation and Calculator converts it to exponential notation when you select a function.

If you need to enter a number that is too large for the Display Register, you can enter it in exponential notation. To enter a number in exponential notation you must first enter the exponent and then the number. For example, to enter 1.2345e6 do the following:

1. Press ALT-1 to use decimal numbers.

2. Press ALT-6 for Exponential Notation.

3. Type **10** and press SHIFT-6.

4. Type **6** and press *.

5. Type **1.2345** and press =.

The Tape and Display Register should look like this:

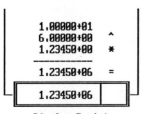

Display Register

This calculation first raises 10 to the correct power and then multiplies it by the number 1.2345. In exponential notation the number displays as 1.23450+06. You can then use the number in any calculation using decimal numbers. Calculator can work with results up to 10^{75}.

Converting to Different Number Systems

It is often necessary to change a number from one number system to another when using some of the Programmer functions. To translate the value 123 decimal into the hexadecimal number system, do the following from any screen:

1. Press ALT-1 to use decimal numbers.

2. Type the value to be converted, **123**.

3. Press ALT-2 to convert the contents of the Display Register to hexadecimal notation. The contents of the Display Register should be 7B. If you press ALT-1, the number converts back to decimal notation.

Analyzing Statistical Data

The operations Calculator provides on the Statistical Functions screen help you analyze a set of data representing an entire population or a sample from a population. To input the data, type each value followed by ENTER or =. After entering the information, use the function keys to select the operations you want Calculator to perform on the data.

For example, you give ten people a typing test to find the number of words per minute they can type and come up with the following scores: 85, 72, 71, 65, 64, 64, 63, 57, 49, 42. You can enter the results into Calculator and have it find the average, variance, and standard deviation. To do this, enter the following from the main screen:

1. Press F10 to enter the Statistical Functions screen, which is shown in Figure 4-4.

2. Press ALT-1 to use decimal numbers.

3. Press ALT-5 for Fixed Decimal Display.

4. Enter **2** to display two numbers after the decimal point.

5. Press SHIFT-F1 to clear all values.

6 Enter each score and press = or ENTER. Repeat this for each score.

7. After entering all the scores, press F6 to find the mean or average of the scores.

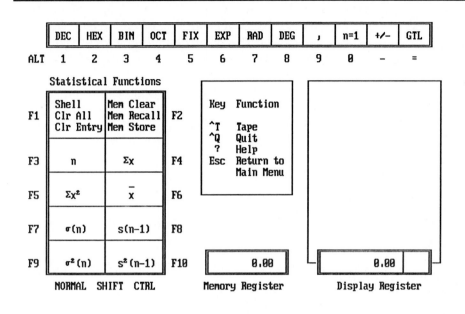

Figure 4-4.   The Statistical Functions screen

8. Press F9 to find the variance for a population.

9. Press F7 to calculate the standard deviation for a population.

When you are finished, the Tape and Display Register should look like this:

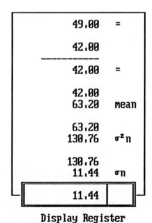

Display Register

If the scores were only random samples instead of a complete list of scores, you could use the variance and standard deviation for samples to complete the calculation. To do this, use the following keystrokes from the main screen:

1. Press F10 to enter the Statistical Functions screen.

2. Press ALT-1 to use decimal numbers.

3. Press ALT-5 for Fixed Decimal Display.

4. Enter 2 to display two numbers after the decimal point.

5. Press SHIFT-F1 to clear all values.

6. Enter each score and then press = or ENTER. Repeat this for each score.

7. After entering all the scores, press F6 to find the mean or average of the scores.

8. Press F10 to find the sample variance.

9. Press F8 to calculate the sample standard deviation.

Note: The calculation for the mean is not dependent on whether the data represents an entire population or a random sample.

Using an End-of-Line Macro

Using Calculator under Shell you can retrieve the contents of the Shell Clipboard and have Calculator automatically perform an arithmetic function on the contents using an End-of-Line (EOL*n*) macro. The EOL*n* macro is a Shell macro and must be named EOL*n*.SHM, where *n* is the letter on the Shell menu for Calculator. The SHM extension denotes that it is a Shell macro.

To use an EOL*n* macro, you must first define the macro and then set up the Shell Program Information screen. To define the macro with Calculator running under Shell:

1. Press CTRL-SHIFT-F10 to begin defining the macro.

2. Enter an EOL*n* name for the macro, where n is the letter on the Shell menu for Calculator.

3. Type a description for the macro or press ENTER to continue. A "* Starting shell macro*" prompt briefly displays and then all keystrokes are recorded for the macro.

4. Press the key associated with the arithmetic function you want Calculator to perform on the contents of the Clipboard. These will normally be +, −, *, and /, but you can use any of the arithmetic functions. Calculator inserts the functions after it reads in each value from the Clipboard.

5. Press CTRL-SHIFT-F10 again to finish defining the macro.

To set up Shell's Program Information screen for Calculator to use the EOL*n* macro:

1. Go to the Shell menu that lists Calculator.

2. Press **4** for Setup.

3. Press the Shell menu letter for Calculator or using the cursor keys, highlight the entry for Calculator.

4. Press **1** or ENTER to edit the Program Information screen.

5. Using the cursor keys, move down to the Macro Names line.

6. Type the letter that displays next to Calculator on the Shell menu.

7. Press F7 twice to exit the Program Information screen and return to the Shell menu.

With an EOL*n* macro defined, anytime you retrieve the Clipboard into Calculator the macro executes after each entry is retrieved. This is useful if you are importing numbers from a spreadsheet program and always want to perform certain calculations on the numbers.

ALT-**Key Menu**

Located at the top of every screen in Calculator is the ALT-Key menu shown here:

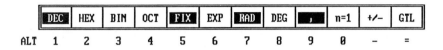

The current default options are highlighted on the menu to help you identify Calculator's setup.

Keystrokes

1. To select an option from the menu, press ALT-*x*, where *x* is the number displayed beneath the option.

For more information on the ALT-Key options, see "Using the ALT-Key Menu," earlier in this chapter.

AND Command

With the AND command, Calculator performs a logical bit-wise AND of the two values you input. For a bit to be set in the result, the corresponding bits in both values must set.

Keystrokes

1. From the Programmer Functions menu enter the first value.

2. Press F3 to select the AND command.

3. Enter the second value.

4. Press = or ENTER.

If you are using the Tape, Calculator records the values and the result. AND displays next to the second value, and = displays next to the result.

Arithmetic Functions

In the center of the main screen is a listing of Calculator's basic arithmetic functions. While these functions only display when you are in the main screen, you can use them from any screen in Calculator.

Available Functions and Keystrokes

The following list outlines Calculator's arithmetic functions and their associated keystrokes.

Function	Keystroke
Addition	+
Subtraction	−
Multiplication	*
Division	/
Percent	% (SHIFT-5)
Power	^ (SHIFT-6)
Total	= or ENTER

Clear All

The Clear All function clears the contents of the Display Register, erases any function present, and resets the Grand Total to 0.

Keystrokes

1. Press SHIFT-F1 from any screen to use the Clear All function. The Tape displays a C to indicate a Clear All was performed.

Clear Entry

You can clear the current contents of the Display Register using Clear Entry. This allows you to enter a new value at any point in a calculation without affecting the overall result.

Keystrokes

1. Press F1 from any Calculator screen to perform the Clear Entry function. This will have no effect on the Tape if you are using it to record calculations.

Colors

Each time you start Calculator, it uses the colors defined for the Shell menu. You can temporarily set colors for your Calculator screen. Since Calculator does not have a system or setup file to store permanent option settings, you must set these each time you enter Calculator.

Keystrokes

1. From the main screen, press F9 for Colors.

2. Select the option for your monitor.

3. Type **Y** or **N** to select or bypass fast text display.

4. Set up your display according to the type of monitor you have.

5. Press F7 to return to the main screen.

For information on creating a macro to automatically set up colors on startup, see "Setting Colors with a Shell Macro," in the first section of this chapter.

Complements

To help perform calculations using the Programmer functions, Calculator provides commands to find both the 1's and 2's complements of the current contents of the Display Register.

Keystrokes

To find the 1's complement of the contents of the Display Register:

1. Press F9 from the Programmer Functions screen.

To find the 2's complement of the contents of the Display Register:

1. Press SHIFT-F9.

If you are using the Tape, Calculator records the result on the Tape with either 1's or 2's displayed next to it.

Cosine

Calculator finds the cosine of any angle entered in either Radian or Degree mode. It can also perform the inverse function, arccosine, and output the result in either angle format.

Keystrokes

To find the cosine of an angle, enter the following from the Scientific Functions screen:

1. Enter the angle in either Radian or Degree mode.

2. Press F4 to find the cosine of the angle.

To find the arccosine of a value:

1. Enter the value in the Display Register.

2. Press SHIFT-F4 to find the arccosine of the angle.

If you are using the Tape, Calculator records the result on the Tape with the corresponding function next to it.

Cost

On the Financial Functions screen you can use the Cost function to either enter an item's cost or solve for the cost after entering the selling price and profit margin.

Keystrokes

To solve for the cost of an item, do the following from the Financial Functions screen:

1. Type the selling price in the Display Register.

2. Press F9 to assign the selling price.

3. Type the desired profit margin in the Display Register. Calculator assumes the profit margin is a percentage, so do not include a leading decimal point. For example, for a 10 percent profit margin, type **10**.

4. Press F10 to assign the profit margin.

5. Press SHIFT-F8 to solve for the required cost.

If you are using the Tape, Calculator records the results of both functions on the Tape with CST displayed next to it.

Exit

Calculator provides a normal Exit function from the main screen. You can also perform a Quick Exit from any screen in Calculator.

Keystrokes

To exit Calculator from the main screen:

1. Press F7.

To exit Calculator from any screen:

1. Press CTRL-Q.

Both types of exits clear the temporary color settings and erase the Tape.

Exponential Functions

From any screen in Calculator you can perform exponential calculations with the Exponential function (SHIFT-6 for ^). From the Scientific Functions screen you also have the option of using the x^y function (SHIFT-F10).

Keystrokes

To perform an Exponential function from any screen:

1. Enter the number to be raised to a power.
2. Press SHIFT-6 for ^.
3. Enter the power for the number.
4. Press = or ENTER.

To perform an Exponential function from the Scientific Functions screen:

1. Enter the number to be raised to a power.
2. Press SHIFT-F10 to select the Exponential function.
3. Enter the power for the number.
4. Press = or ENTER.

If you are using the Tape, Calculator records both Exponential functions on the Tape with ^ displayed next to the power and = next to the result.

Financial Functions

Calculator provides several financial functions to help you solve calculations involving interest rates, payment schedules, profit margins, and both present and future values.

Functions and Keystrokes

To access the Financial Functions screen, press F8 from the main screen. The following list outlines the Financial functions available and their corresponding keystrokes.

Function	Keystroke
Number of Periods (N)	F3
Interest Rate (%i)	F4
Payment (PMT)	F5
Present Value (PV)	F6
Future Value (FV)	F7
Cost (COST)	F8
Sell (SELL)	F9
Profit Margin (MARGIN)	F10

You can use each of these functions to enter information for a calculation or solve for a function by pressing the SHIFT key with the function. For example, to solve for a payment amount, press SHIFT-F5 after entering the required information.

Future Value

You can use the Future Value function either to assign a future account balance for other financial calculations, or solve for a future account balance.

Keystrokes

To assign an amount to the future value from the Financial Functions screen, enter the value in the Display Register and press F7. To solve for the future value, press SHIFT-F7 after entering all necessary information.

Help

Calculator provides an on-screen help menu. Help is screen sensitive, so pressing a key from the help screen displays information for that key on the current Calculator screen.

Keystrokes

1. To access Help from the main screen, press F3. From any other screen press ?.

2. With the help menu displaying on the screen, select any key or set of keystrokes that Calculator uses to display information about that function.

3. Press the spacebar to exit Calculator's help screen.

Logarithmic Functions

From the Scientific Functions screen, Calculator provides functions to solve both natural (base e) and common (base 10) logarithm and antilogarithm calculations.

Keystrokes

To perform any logarithm calculations from the Scientific Functions screen, enter the value and then select the correct keystrokes from the following list.

Function	Keystroke
LN (natural log)	F6
e^x (natural antilog)	SHIFT-F6
LOG (common log)	F7
10^x (common antilog)	SHIFT-F7

If you are using the Tape, Calculator records the results of these operations with the function displayed next to it.

Mean

From Calculator's Statistical Functions screen you can find the arithmetic mean, or average, for a set of data.

Keystrokes

1. Press SHIFT-F1 to clear the Display Register.

2. Enter each value individually.

3. After entering all data, press F6 to calculate the mean.

If you are using the Tape, Calculator records the result with "mean" displayed next to it.

Memory Clear

From any screen in Calculator you can clear the contents of the Memory Register without affecting the results of the current calculation.

Keystrokes

1. To clear the Memory Register, press CTRL-F2. This resets the contents to 0.

Memory Recall

Memory Recall retrieves the contents of the Memory Register into the Display Register for use in calculations. The Memory Register remains unchanged.

Keystrokes

1. Press SHIFT-F2 for Memory Recall.

Memory Store

You can store the current contents of the Display Register in the temporary Memory Register with Memory Store. This is convenient for completing long calculations with several intermediate steps.

Keystrokes

1. With the value displayed in the Display Register, press F2 for Memory Store.

MOD Command

The MOD command is only available from the Programmer Functions screen. MOD returns the integer remainder after dividing the first value you enter by the second value.

Keystrokes

1. Enter the dividend, or value to be divided.

2. Press F10 to select the MOD command.

3. Enter the divisor, or value to be divided by.

4. Press = or ENTER.

If you are using the Tape, Calculator records the result with MOD displayed next to the divisor or second value.

NOT Command

The NOT command performs the same operation as the 1's Complement function. It returns the bit-wise (bit-by-bit) inverse of a value you enter. The NOT command is only available from the Programmer Functions screen.

Keystrokes

1. Enter a value.

2. Press SHIFT-F3 to execute the NOT command.

If you are using the Tape, Calculator records the result with NOT displayed next to it.

OR/XOR Command

The OR and Exclusive OR (XOR) commands perform a bit-wise comparison on two values that you enter. With the OR command, the corresponding bit in the result is set if either or both of the variables have the same bit set. The result of an Exclusive OR command has a bit set if one and only one of the input values has the corresponding bit set. The OR/XOR command is only available from the Programmer Functions screen.

Keystrokes

1. Type in the first value.

2. Press F4 to select the OR command.

3. Type the second value.

4. Press = or ENTER.

To perform an XOR operation:

1. Enter the first value.

2. Press SHIFT-F4 to select the XOR command.

3. Enter the second value.

4. Press = or ENTER.

If you are using the Tape, Calculator records the result with the function displayed next to the second variable.

Payment

Using the Payment function on Calculator's Financial screen you can enter a payment amount to solve annuity and interest calculations.

Keystrokes

To solve annuity or interest calculations, enter the known values followed by the corresponding function key. After entering all of the known information, press SHIFT-x to solve for an unknown factor, where x is the function key for that factor. For more information on the Payment function, see "Calculating Loan Payments" earlier in this chapter.

Present Value

You can use the Present Value function either to indicate the principal value on a debt or a current balance on an account. The way Calculator interprets the present value depends on the other information that you input about the problem.

Keystrokes

To use the present value as the amount of a debt, you must perform a calculation using Payments (F5). However, if you assign a value to Future Value (F7) in an operation, Calculator assumes the present value to be an account balance instead of debt amount. Using SHIFT-F5 in either type of calculation solves for payment amount based on the rest of the information you input.

Profit Margin

Using Calculator's Financial Functions screen you can find the profit margin of a transaction. To solve for the profit margin it is necessary to have information on the cost and selling price for the item in the transaction. When entering a profit margin, the value is assumed to be a percentage.

Keystrokes

1. Type in the original cost and press F8.

2. Type in the selling price and press F9.

3. Press SHIFT-F10 to solve for the profit margin of the transaction.

If you are using the Tape, Calculator records the result with MAR displayed next to the result.

Programmer Functions

Calculator provides Programmer functions to help you solve calculations involving binary, octal, and hexadecimal numbers.

Keystrokes

To access the Programmer Functions screen, press F6 from the main screen. Table 4-1 outlines the functions available on the Programmer

Function	Keystroke
AND	F3
NOT	SHIFT-F3
OR	F4
Exclusive OR (XOR)	SHIFT-F4
Shift Left (SHL)	F5
Shift Left n times (SHLn)	SHIFT-F5
Shift Right (SHR)	F6
Shift Right n times (SHRn)	SHIFT-F6
Rotate Left (ROL)	F7
Rotate Left n times (ROLn)	SHIFT-F7
Rotate Right (ROR)	F8
Rotate Right n times (RORn)	SHIFT-F8
1's Complement (1's CMPL)	F9
2's Complement (2's CMPL)	SHIFT-F9
Module (MOD)	F10

Table 4-1.   Functions Available on the Programmer Screen and Their Corresponding Keystrokes

Function screen and their corresponding keystrokes. If you are using the Tape, Calculator records the result of any Programmer function with the function label next to it.

Reciprocals

By using the Reciprocal function, 1/x, on the Scientific Functions screen, Calculator finds the reciprocal of the value in the Display Register.

Keystrokes

1. Enter the value in the Display Register.

2. Press F10.

If you are using the Tape, Calculator records the reciprocal value with 1/x displayed next to it.

Rotate Commands

You can use the Rotate commands on the Programmer Functions screen to calculate the result of a Rotate Right or Rotate Left command for a 16-bit register. Using the ALT-Key menu to assign a value to the repeating variable n, you can also have these commands repeated up to nine times automatically. The Rotate Left and Rotate Right commands can only be accessed from the Programmer Functions screen.

Keystrokes

To use the Rotate Left command:

1. Enter the value in the Display Register.
2. Press F7 to execute the Rotate Left command.

To repeat the Rotate Left command n times:

1. Press ALT-0 to assign a value to the repeating variable.
2. Type a value from 0 to 9.
3. Enter the value in the Display Register.
4. Press SHIFT-F7 to execute the Rotate Left command n times.

To use the Rotate Right command:

1. Enter the value in the Display Register.
2. Press F8 to execute the Rotate Right command.

To repeat the Rotate Right command n times:

1. Press ALT-0 to assign a value to the repeating variable.
2. Type a value from 0 to 9.

3. Enter the value in the Display Register.

4. Press SHIFT-F8 to execute the Rotate Right command n times.

If you are using the Tape, Calculator records the result with ROL or ROR displayed next to it.

Scientific Functions

Calculator provides scientific functions to help you solve calculations involving logarithms, trigonometry, exponents, and reciprocals.

Keystrokes

To access the Scientific Functions screen, press F4 from the main screen. Table 4-2 outlines available functions on the Scientific Functions screen

Function	Keystroke
Sine	F3
Arcsine	SHIFT-F3
Cosine	F4
Arccosine	SHIFT-F4
Tangent	F5
Arctangent	SHIFT-F5
Natural Logarithm (LN)	F6
Natural Antilog (e^x)	SHIFT-F6
Common Logarithm (LOG)	F7
Common Antilog (10^x)	SHIFT-F7
Square Root (SQR)	F8
x^2	SHIFT-F8
Pi	F9
Reciprocal (1/x)	F10
Exponential (x^y)	SHIFT-F10

Table 4-2.   Functions Available on the Scientific Screen and Their Corresponding Keystrokes

and their corresponding keystrokes. If you're using the Tape, Calculator records the scientific function next to its corresponding values.

Sell

On the Financial Functions screen you can use the Sell function to either assign an item's selling price or solve for the selling price after entering the cost and profit margin.

Keystrokes

To assign the selling price of an item:

1. Type the value in the Display Register.

2. Press F9 to assign the value as the selling price.

To solve for the selling price of an item:

1. Type the cost in the Display Register.

2. Press F8 to assign the cost.

3. Type the desired profit margin in the Display Register.

4. Press F10 to assign the profit margin.

5. Press SHIFT-F9 to solve for the necessary selling price.

If you are using the Tape, Calculator records the results of both functions on the Tape with SEL displayed next to it.

Shell

Using Calculator under Shell gives you several advantages not found when running Calculator from the DOS command line. You can move between programs without exiting Calculator. You can also create and use Shell macros to help increase productivity on repetitive calculations. With the Shell Clipboard, a temporary memory buffer, information can be transferred between programs.

Keystrokes

Program Switch

To leave Calculator resident and go to Shell you can press CTRL-ALT-SPACEBAR. You can also use the Shell function from almost any screen in Calculator:

1. Press CTRL-F1.

2. Press **1** or **G** to select Go to Shell.

You can also switch to other programs listed on the same Shell menu by pressing CTRL-ALT-*x*, where *x* is the Shell menu letter or Shell option you want to change to.

Clipboard

To save or append the current contents of the Tape to the Clipboard:

1. Press F5 from the main screen or (CTRL-T) from any Calculator screen.

2. To replace the current contents of the Clipboard with the Tape, press **5** or **B**. To append the Tape to the contents of the Clipboard, press **7** or **A**.

To save or append the current contents of the Display Register to the Clipboard:

1. Press CTRL-F1 for the Shell options.

2. To replace the current contents of the Clipboard with the value in the Display Register, press **2** or **S**. To append the Display Register to the contents of the Clipboard, press **3** or **A**.

End of Line Macros

See "Using an End-of-Line Macro" earlier in this chapter.

Shift Commands

You can use the Shift commands on the Programmer Functions screen to calculate the result of a Shift Right or Shift Left command for a 16-bit register. Using the ALT-Key menu to assign a value to the repeating variable n, you can also have these commands repeated up to nine times automatically. The Shift Left and Shift Right commands can only be accessed from the Programmer Functions screen.

Keystrokes

To use the Shift Left command:

1. Type the value in the Display Register.
2. Press F5 to execute the Shift Left command.

To repeat the Shift Left command n times:

1. Press ALT-0 to assign a value to the repeating variable.
2. Type a value from 0 to 9.
3. Type the value in the Display Register.
4. Press SHIFT-F5 to execute the Shift Left command n times.

To use the Shift Right command:

1. Type the value in the Display Register.

2. Press F6 to execute the Shift Right command.

To repeat the Shift Right command n times:

1. Press ALT-0 to assign a value to the repeating variable.

2. Type a value from 0 to 9.

3. Type the value in the Display Register.

4. Press SHIFT-F6 to execute the Shift Right command n times.

If you are using the Tape, Calculator records the result with SHL or SHR displayed next to it.

Sine

Calculator finds the sine of any angle entered in either Radian or Degree mode. It can also perform the inverse function, arcsine, and output the result in either angle mode.

Keystrokes

To find the sine of an angle, enter the following from the Scientific Functions screen:

1. Enter the angle in either Radian or Degree mode.

2. Press F3 to find the sine of the angle.

To find the arcsine of a value:

1. Enter the value in the Display Register.

2. Press SHIFT-F3 to find the arcsine of the angle.

If you are using the Tape, Calculator records the result on the Tape with the corresponding function next to it.

Squares and Square Roots

From the Scientific screen, Calculator provides a function to square values. You can also perform the square root function.

Keystrokes

To square a value:

1. Enter the value.

2. Press SHIFT-F8 to square the value.

To find the square root of a number:

1. Enter the value.

2. Press F8 to find the square root of the value.

If you are using the Tape, Calculator records the result on the Tape with the corresponding function next to it.

Standard Deviation

Using Calculator's Statistical Functions screen you can find the standard deviation for a population or a sample set of data.

Keystrokes

To find the standard deviation for a population:

1. Press SHIFT-F1 to clear the Display Register.

2. Enter each value individually.

3. After entering all data, press F7 to calculate the standard deviation.

To find the standard deviation for a sample:

1. Press SHIFT-F1 to clear the Display Register.

2. Enter each value individually.

3. After entering all data, press F8 to calculate the standard deviation.

If you are using the Tape, Calculator records the result with the function displayed next to it.

Statistical Functions

Calculator provides several statistical operations to help you solve calculations for an arithmetic mean, standard deviation, and variance. You can use the standard deviation and variance functions for both population and sample calculations.

Keystrokes

To access the Statistical Functions screen, press F10 from the main screen. The following list outlines the statistical functions available and their corresponding keystrokes.

Function	Keystroke
Number of Data Entries (n)	F3
Sum of Data Entries (Σx)	F4
Sum of Data Entries Squared (Σx^2)	F5
Mean ($\bar{x}$)	F6
Standard Deviation for a Population σ(n)	F7
Standard Deviation for a Sample s(n$-$1)	F8
Variance for a Population σ^2(n)	F9
Variance for a Sample s^2(n$-$1)	F10

If you are using the Tape, Calculator records the function symbol next to the function result on the Tape.

Tangent

Calculator finds the tangent of any angle entered in either Radian or Degree mode. It can also perform the inverse function, arctangent, and output the result in either mode.

Keystrokes

To find the tangent of an angle from the Scientific Functions screen:

1. Enter the angle in either Radian or Degree mode.

2. Press F5 to find the tangent of the angle.

To find the arctangent of a value from the Scientific Functions screen:

1. Enter the value in the Display Register.

2. Press SHIFT-F5 to find the arctangent of the angle.

If you are using the Tape, Calculator records the result on the Tape with the corresponding function next to it.

Tape

Using the Tape option in Calculator you can save the values you enter, the functions you perform, and the results of all calculations in the Display Register. You can save, print, or review the Tape through the Tape Options menu.

Keystrokes

1. Press F5 from the main screen or CTRL-T from any screen to display the Tape Options menu.

2. Select an option.

For more information on the Tape options, see "Using Calculator's Tape Feature," earlier in this chapter.

Variance

Using Calculator's Statistical Functions screen you can find the variance for either a population or a sample of a population.

Keystrokes

To find the variance of a population:

1. Press SHIFT-F1 to clear the Display Register.

2. Enter each value individually.

3. After entering all data, press F9 to calculate the variance for a population.

To find the variance for a sample:

1. Press SHIFT-F1 to clear the Display Register.

2. Enter each value individually.

3. After entering all data, press F10 to calculate the sample variance.

If you are using the Tape, Calculator records the result with the function displayed next to it.

Using Editor

Editor is a multimode editing program that you can use to create and edit *DOS text files* and macros for WordPerfect products. A DOS text file is a file that does not have special formatting codes. Files created in WordPerfect are not DOS text files because they contain many different kinds of codes. A DOS text file is made up of the ASCII equivalents of the characters entered or displayed so DOS can recognize the characters saved in the file. A DOS batch file is one example of a DOS text file.

A macro is a file that contains keystrokes that are automatically invoked when you run the macro. Macros can contain macro commands, keystrokes, and text. Within Editor you can edit and create macro files for Editor, Shell, and other WordPerfect products. Editor is especially useful for editing and creating advanced macros for WordPerfect.

Editor provides several special editing commands to make the task of creating or editing files easier. Editor allows you to copy words, entire lines of text, and blocks of text to another place in the same file or to a different file. Copying text avoids having to input text over and over again. Along with copying text, Editor allows you to delete text. You can delete single characters, a word, an entire line, or a block of text. The commands for deleting text are similar to the commands used in Word-Perfect.

Editor allows you to edit up to nine files simultaneously. Multiple file editing allows you to switch between several files quickly and easily. With multiple files you can easily share information between several files.

Along with DOS Text mode and Macro mode, Editor has a Binary mode. With the Binary mode you can retrieve and edit files—including data files and executable files—in almost any format.

Editor is as simple or complex as your needs and abilities. It may be used by a novice for editing batch files or by a programmer for creating complicated macros and routines. Many of the basic functions you find in WordPerfect are also used in Editor.

Starting Editor

To start Editor from the Office Shell menu, press the letter listed next to the entry for Editor, usually **E**. After pressing the letter, the Shell menu is replaced by a blank Editor screen. To start Editor from DOS, type **ed** on the DOS command line and press ENTER.

When you enter Editor, the screen is blank except for the status information along the bottom of the screen as shown here:

DOS   File 1 Pg 1 Ln 1   Pos 1

This information is the *status line*. The three letters on the left side of the status line identify which editing mode Editor is using. On startup, Editor defaults to DOS Text mode and the status line displays DOS. If you retrieve a file with a format other than DOS text, such as a macro, Editor automatically changes to the correct editing mode. For example, if you retrieve a WordPerfect macro into Editor the editing mode changes to WPM as soon as the file is on screen as shown in Figure 5-1.

After retrieving a file, Editor displays the full path and the name of the file to the right of the mode indicator. The right side of the status line indicates which file number is currently on the editing screen and the position of the cursor in the file. The information displayed here depends on which editing mode you are working in. For more information on the different editing modes see "Changing Editing Modes" later in this chapter.

Retrieving with the Retrieve Command and List Files

There are several options for retrieving a file into Editor. If you know the full name of the file, as well as the directory in which it is located, you can use the Retrieve command (SHIFT-F10). For example, if you wanted to retrieve the AUTOEXEC.BAT file you could do the following from a blank screen:

1. Press SHIFT-F10 to retrieve the file. Editor displays the "File to be Retrieved:" prompt.

2. At the prompt, enter the path, if necessary, and type the name of the file, in this case **AUTOEXEC.BAT.** Press ENTER.

Editor then retrieves the file to the editing screen and you can edit it as you wish.

Another way to retrieve a file into Editor is to use the Retrieve option under List Files. To retrieve your AUTOEXEC.BAT file using List Files:

1. Press F5 for List Files.

2. Enter the drive and directory where your AUTOEXEC.BAT file is located.

3. Using the cursor keys, highlight your AUTOEXEC.BAT file.

4. Press **1** or **R** to retrieve the file.

```
{LABEL}Color~
        {ASSIGN}8~CGM/MCGA·Display~
        {PROMPT}{^P}{NTOK}40~{NTOK}15~Display·Detected:··{^R}{VARIABLE}8~{^Q}~
        {WAIT}50~

        {STATUS PROMPT}{^Q}{^R}CGA/MCGA·Display·Type~
        {IF}"{VAR 7}"="Check"~            {;}Do·we·want·to·create·a·checklist~
               {Switch}
               Display·Adapter·Type·Detected:··
               {Flush Right}{Flush Right}
               CGA/MCGA{Enter}{Enter}    {;}Print·Display·Type·Detected~
               {Switch}                  {;}Back·to·Doc·1~
        {END IF}

        {DISPLAY ON}
        {CALL}ColorAttr~
        {WAIT}80~
        {CALL}ViewDoc~
        {IF}"{VAR 7}"="Check"~
               {DISPLAY OFF}
               {BELL}
               {CHAR}6~{^Q}·{^R}
···Font·Test·Completed.··Please·Mark·Worksheet.··Press··ENTER·to·
WPM C:\OFF30\MACRO.WPM                    Mac 1 Ln 220      Pos 1
```

Figure 5-1.   WordPerfect macro on screen in WPM editing mode

Both of the retrieve methods allow you to combine existing files of the same format by retrieving them into the same editing screen. For example, if you have a batch file you want to add to the middle of the AUTOEXEC.BAT file, follow these steps:

1. Retrieve the first file, AUTOEXEC.BAT, into the editing screen.

2. Position the cursor where you want the second file to be inserted.

3. Retrieve the second file. If you use Retrieve under List Files, Editor asks for confirmation before it retrieves the second file.

Be careful to position the cursor exactly where you want each file to be inserted as it is retrieved.

A third way to retrieve a file is to tell Editor the name of a file to retrieve when starting Editor. If you are using Shell, list the filename on the Startup Options line of Editor's Program Information screen. If you are starting Editor from the DOS command line, enter **ed** and then the filename. For example, if you start Editor from DOS and want to retrieve your AUTOEXEC.BAT automatically, type **ed c:\autoexec.bat** on the DOS command line and press ENTER.

A title screen will briefly display, and then you'll see an editing screen containing your AUTOEXEC.BAT file.

Changing Editing Modes

In Editor, you can retrieve and edit files saved in several different formats. The most common format is DOS text, which is Editor's default format mode. You can edit files such as AUTOEXEC.BAT and CON-FIG.SYS in DOS text mode. Editor defaults to DOS Text mode on startup.

A second editing mode you can use is the Macro mode. The macro formats that you can use in Editor include macros for WordPerfect, PlanPerfect, DrawPerfect, Shell, and Editor. Each of these macros uses different commands, and Editor must have access to the .MRS, or macro resource file, that comes with each WordPerfect product to interpret the commands correctly.

Another mode that Editor uses is Binary mode. This mode allows you to retrieve and edit any type of file, including data or executable files. In Binary mode the contents of the files display as their ASCII equivalents.

To change the editing mode for the current editing screen:

1. Press CTRL-F5 for Text In/Out. This displays a menu of all the formats available, similar to the one shown here:

```
Text Editor Modes

     1 - DOS (ASCII/DOS Text)
     2 - BIN (Binary)

Macro Editor Modes

     3 - DR
     4 - ED
     5 - PL
     6 - SH
     7 - WP
```

2. Select the number of the desired editing mode.

3. Press ENTER to return to the editing screen with the new mode selected.

You cannot change from DOS Text mode or Binary mode to Macro mode when there is text on the editing screen. Editor requires that the screen be empty before the editing mode is changed.

The number of entries for macros listed when you press Text In/Out (CTRL-F5) depends on the number of .MRS files Editor can locate. The following list outlines the WordPerfect products that have macro resource files and the name of the .MRS file.

Product	.MRS Filename
WordPerfect 5.0 and later	WP.MRS
PlanPerfect 5.0 and later	PL.MRS
DrawPerfect 1.0 and later	DR.MRS
Shell 3.0	SH.MRS
Editor 3.0	ED.MRS

To ensure that Editor can locate all of your .MRS files, specify the directory in Editor where your .MRS files are located. Before specifying the directory, select or create a directory where all .MRS files will be located. Once you have selected or created a directory, copy all .MRS files into that directory. To set the path in Editor:

1. Press SHIFT-F1 for Setup.

2. Press **4** or **L** for Location of Files.

3. Press **2** or **M** for Macro/MRS Files.

4. Enter the correct path.

5. Press F7 twice to return to the main screen.

Editor checks this directory each time you press Text In/Out to determine to which .MRS files you have access. If this path is left blank, Editor searches the current default directory for the .MRS files.

Status Line Displays

Because of differences in the various editing modes, the file and position information shown on the status line changes for each mode.

DOS Text Mode Display   In DOS Text mode, the right side of the status line displays the file number, page number, line number, and column position for the current location of the cursor as shown here:

DOS   File 1 Pg 1 Ln 1   Pos 1

If you change the line numbering format (SHIFT-F1, 1, 3) from relative (line number per page) to absolute (line number in the entire document), the status line displays Abs for absolute line number, rather than Ln.

Binary Mode Display   In Binary mode, the position indicators are similar to those for DOS Text mode. However, since page numbering is not important for most files under Binary mode, the page number is omitted, leaving the file number, line number, and column position indicators as shown here:

BIN   File 1   Ln 1   Pos 1

Macro Mode Display   In Macro mode, Editor does not display a page number with the position indicators. Only the current macro number (similar to the file number in DOS Text mode), line number, and column position indicators display as shown here:

```
EDM                                          Mac 1  Ln 1      Pos 1
```

Using List Files

With the List Files (F5) feature, you can perform many common file-management functions without exiting to DOS. The List Files feature is similar to List Files in WordPerfect and has many of the basic commands and functions found in File Manager. For more information, see Chapter 6, "Using File Manager."

List Files displays the files and subdirectories contained in a given directory. From the List Files menu you can select one of the functions at the bottom of the menu as shown here:

```
1 Retrieve; 2 Del; 3 Move/Rename; 5 Hex; 6 Look;
7 Other Dir; 8 Copy; 9 Word Srch; F2 Name Search; 6
```

The function you select applies to the currently highlighted file in the file listing. If you have marked files with an asterisk, the function affects all marked files.

Retrieving a File

The Retrieve option on the List Files menu retrieves the currently highlighted file into the editing screen. Editor retrieves the file at the position where the cursor was before entering List Files. To retrieve a file:

1. Press F5 for List Files.

2. Press ENTER if the file you want to retrieve is in the displayed directory or type in the correct directory and press ENTER.

3. Use the cursor keys to highlight the file you want to retrieve.

4. Press **1** or **R** to retrieve the file.

Deleting a File

You can use the Delete command to delete a single highlighted file or all marked files. Be careful that you are deleting the correct files—not files you previously marked for another function. To delete a single file using List Files:

1. Press F5 for List Files.

2. Press ENTER if the file you want to delete is in the displayed directory or type in the correct directory and press ENTER.

3. Use the cursor keys to highlight the file you want to delete.

4. Press **2** or **D** to delete the file.

5. Type **Y** to delete the files.

To delete several files using List Files:

1. Press F5 for List Files.

2. Press ENTER if the files you want to delete are in the displayed directory or type in the correct directory and press ENTER.

3. Use the cursor keys to highlight the first file you want to delete.

4. Type an asterisk (*) to place a mark next to that file.

5. Repeat steps 3 and 4 until all the files you want to delete have an asterisk next to them.

6. Press **2** or **D** for Delete.

7. Type **Y** at the "Delete Marked Files? (Y/N)N" prompt.

The files are deleted and removed from the file listing.

Moving a File

You can use the Move/Rename function to move files to another directory and/or rename them. To move a single file to another directory:

1. Press F5 for List Files.

2. Press ENTER if the file you want to move is in the displayed directory or type in the correct directory and press ENTER.

3. Use the cursor keys to highlight the file you want to move. Editor displays the "Move/Rename This File To:" prompt.

4. Press **3** or **M** for Move/Rename.

5. Enter the name of the directory to which you want to move the file.

If you would like to move several files from one directory to another:

1. Press F5 for List Files.

2. Press ENTER if the file you want to move is in the displayed directory or type in the correct directory and press ENTER.

3. Use the cursor keys to highlight the first file you want to move.

4. Type an asterisk (*) to place a mark next to the file.

5. Repeat steps 3 and 4 until all the files you want to move are marked with an asterisk.

6. Press **3** or **M** for Move/Rename to move the marked files. Editor displays the "Move Marked Files? (Y/N)N" prompt.

7. Type **Y** to continue the move. Editor then displays the "Move All Marked Files to:" prompt.

8. Enter the name of the directory to which you want to move the files.

Renaming a File

The Move/Rename function also allows you to rename a single file without moving it to a new directory. If you would like to rename a file and leave it in its original directory:

1. Press F5 for List Files.

2. Press ENTER if the file you want to move is in the displayed directory or type in the correct directory and press ENTER.

3. Use the cursor keys to highlight the file you want to rename.

4. Press **3** or **M** for Move/Rename to rename the file. Editor displays the "Move/Rename This File To:" prompt.

5. Enter the new filename. As soon as you begin typing the old name disappears.

Editor replaces the original filename in the listing with the new filename. If marked files exist when you use the Move/Rename function, Editor only allows you to move the files.

Other Directory

While in List Files, Editor allows you to change to another directory and work with the files in that directory. The directory displayed when you press List Files (F5) is Editor's current default directory. This is the directory where Editor first searches for files and where Editor saves files if no other directory is specified. If you would like to change to another directory:

1. Press **7** or **O** for Other Directory.

2. Enter the path of the directory you want to display. Editor then displays the default filename pattern of *.*.

3. Press ENTER if you want to display all the files in the directory; if you only want certain files displayed, you can edit the filename pattern. For example, if you want only batch files displayed, change *.* to *.BAT. You can enter any DOS wildcard characters in the filename pattern.

After entering the filename pattern, Editor displays the new file listing.

Copy

You can use the Copy function in List Files to copy files from one directory or drive to another. To copy a single file to another directory:

1. Press F5 for List Files.

2. Press ENTER if the file you want to move is in the displayed directory or type in the correct directory and press ENTER.

3. Use the cursor keys to highlight the file you want to copy.

4. Press 8 or **C** for Copy to copy the file. Editor displays the "Copy This File To:" prompt.

5. Enter the path and/or filename to which you want the file copied.

If you would like to copy several files from the current directory to another directory:

1. Press F5 for List Files.

2. Press ENTER if the file you want to move is in the displayed directory or type in the correct directory and press ENTER.

3. Use the cursor keys to highlight the first file you want to copy.

4. Type an asterisk (*) to mark the file.

5. Repeat steps 3 and 4 until all the files you want to copy are marked with an asterisk.

6. Press 8 or **C** for Copy to copy the marked files. Editor displays the "Copy Marked Files? (Y/N)N" prompt.

7. Type **Y** to copy the files. Editor then asks for the directory to copy the files to by displaying the "Copy All Marked Files To:" prompt.

8. Enter the path to the directory where you want the files copied.

Saving a File and Exiting Editor

Editor provides you with two methods of saving the current contents of the editing screen. You can save a file as part of the exiting process or you can simply save the file and remain in Editor.

If you want to save a file as part of exiting Editor, press F7 to exit, and type **Y** when asked if the file should be saved. Using the AUTO-EXEC.BAT file as the example, you would

1. Press F7 to exit Editor.

2. Type **Y** when Editor asks if you want to save your file.

3. If AUTOEXEC.BAT is an existing file, the original name displays on the status line as shown here:

```
File to be Saved (1): C:\AUTOEXEC.BAT
```

4. Press ENTER to save the file under its original name or enter a new name. If you save the file to its original name or enter a name that already exists, Editor displays the "Replace *filename*? (Y/N)N" prompt.

5. Type **Y** to replace the file or type **N** if you don't want to replace the file. If you type **N**, Editor again asks you for a name for the file, and you can enter a different name.

After the save is complete, Editor displays the "Exit Editor? (Y/N)N" prompt. At this point you can type **Y** to exit Editor and return to the Shell menu or DOS. If you type **N**, you remain in Editor and the file is cleared from the editing screen. If you press Cancel (F1), Editor aborts the exit and the file remains on the editing screen.

Using the Save command (F10), saves the contents of the editing screen to disk and keeps the file on the editing screen. For example, if you have retrieved and edited your AUTOEXEC.BAT file and wish to save it you would:

1. Press F10 for Save. If the AUTOEXEC.BAT file already exists, the original name displays on the status line.

2. Press ENTER to save the file under its original name or enter a new name. If you save the file to its original name or enter a name that already exists, Editor displays the "Replace *filename*? (Y/N)N" prompt.

3. Type **Y** to replace the file or type **N** if you don't want to replace the file. If you type **N**, Editor again asks you for a name for the file and you can enter a different name.

After completing the save, the cursor returns to its previous position on the editing screen.

Backing Up Editor Files

To help protect against loss of information, Editor provides you with two different methods to back up your work: Timed Backup and Original Backup.

Using Timed Backup

When you are using Timed Backup, Editor regularly saves files to Editor's default directory. To turn on Timed Backup:

1. Press SHIFT-F1 for Setup.

2. Press **2** or **E** for Environment.

3. Press **1** or **B** for Backup.

4. Press **1** or **T** for Timed Backup.

5. Type **Y** to turn on Timed Backup.

6. Enter the number of minutes between backups.

7. Press F7 until you return to the editing screen.

The backup files are saved in the directory specified in the Setup menu. To set this directory:

1. Press SHIFT-F1 for Setup.

2. Press **4** or **L** for Location of Files.

3. Press **1** or **B** for Backup Directory.

4. Enter the name of the directory in which you want your backup files saved.

5. Press F7 until you return to the editing screen.

If you do not specify a path in the Location of Files option your files will be saved in one of two places. If you are running under Shell, they are saved in the directory specified under the Default Directory option on the Shell Program Information screen as shown in Figure 5-2. If you are running Editor from DOS, your backup files are saved in the directory from which you started Editor.

Editor names the backup files with an ED}ED.BK*n* format if you are using Office PC, or with an *XXX*}ED.BK*n* format if you are using Office LAN, where *XXX* is your File ID. In both cases the *n* is a number from 1 to 9 that corresponds to the number displayed next to File or

---

```
                            Program Information

   Menu Letter:             E

   Menu Description:        Editor

   Menu Item Type:          Normal          Pause: NO

➡  Default Directory:       c:\office30\ed_files

   Program Name:            ed.exe

   Clipboard  Filename:

   Macros Names - End of Line:  EOLE.SHM  Go to: GOSHELLE.SHM  Return: RTSHELLE.SHM

   Startup Options:

   Prompt for startup options?  NO      Swap Shell out?            NO

   Start resident?              NO      Allow switch anytime?      NO

        Enter the name of the program.  You may include the full path
        for the program if it is found in another directory.
                                          (F7 = Exit, F3 = Help)
```

Figure 5-2.   Shell Program Information screen with Default Directory specified

Mac on the status line at the bottom of the screen. Editor only backs up files currently displayed on screen; files are only backed up if you have edited them since the last backup occurred.

Retrieving a Timed Backup File

If you need to retrieve a timed backup file following a system failure, follow the steps below:

1. Press F5 for List Files.

2. Press ENTER if the directory containing your backup files displays or enter the directory where the backup files are located.

3. Use the cursor keys to highlight the backup file.

4. Press 3 or **M** for Move/Rename and enter a new filename.

If you leave a timed backup file in the default directory following a system failure, Editor will notify you that an existing backup file was found the first time it tries to perform a backup. You will then have the option to either rename the existing file or delete and replace the existing file.

Using Original Backup

The Original Backup feature protects you from overwriting existing files with the wrong file. With Original Backup, anytime you modify a file and try to save it to the original name, Editor first makes a copy of the original file and saves it with a .BK! extension. Editor saves this file in the same directory as the original file rather than automatically placing it in the default directory. To activate Original Backup:

1. Press SHIFT-F1 for Setup.

2. Press 2 or **E** for Environment.

3. Press 1 or **B** for Backup.

4. Press 2 or **O** for Original Backup.

5. Type **Y** to turn on Original Backup.

6. Press F7 until you return to the editing screen.

Retrieving an Original Backup File

If you discover you have replaced a file you need, you can retrieve an original backup file with the following steps:

1. Press F5 for List Files.

2. Press ENTER or enter the directory where the original file is located.

3. Highlight the original backup file (*XXXXXXXX*.BK!).

4. Press **3** or **M** for Move/Rename and enter a new filename.

It is important that you rename the original backup file with an extension other than .BK! to keep it from being replaced if it is retrieved and edited. Also, since Editor uses the .BK! extension for all files, be aware that any files that share the same name will be saved to the same backup file.

Copying Text and Commands

Editor gives you four different methods of copying text or macro commands in Editor. First, you can duplicate a word on the line above the cursor. Second, you can duplicate the entire line above the cursor. Third, you can copy any line in the file on the editing screen. Fourth, you can copy a block of text or commands.

Duplicating a Word

The Dup Word command (F6) copies the word in the line directly above the cursor to the current cursor position. Editor duplicates all characters in the word until it reaches a space, tab, or return. For example, if

Deleting Single Characters

The most common way to delete in Editor is to erase single characters. You can delete the character at the cursor by pressing the DEL key. You can also use the BACKSPACE key to delete the character to the left of the cursor and move the cursor back one space.

For example, if you are editing your AUTOEXEC.BAT file in Editor and you enter the PATH command incorrectly by typing **patth=c:\;c:\dos;c:\office**, you can correct it by deleting the extra "t" in "path." To do so:

1. Use the arrow keys to move the cursor beneath either "t."

2. Press DEL.

Editor deletes the extra "t" and the rest of the line shifts to the left one column. In Macro mode, BACKSPACE and DEL consider each macro command to be a single character.

Deleting a Word

In Editor, you can delete the word at the cursor using the Delete Word command (CTRL-BACKSPACE). In both DOS Text mode and Macro mode, a word is considered to be a character or group of characters with a space, tab, or return on both sides of it. In Macro mode, a macro command or string of spaces is not deleted when using Delete Word. This is different from Dup Word because Delete Word uses a tab or space to signal a word boundary. Since macro commands do not require a space between them for Editor to recognize them individually, Delete Word could delete entire strings of commands.

An example of using Delete Word would be to remove the word "Word" from the following line of text:

```
This is how the Delete Word command works.
```

1. Position the cursor on the word "Word."

2. Press CTRL-BACKSPACE.

Editor removes the word and shifts the remainder of the line to the left as shown here:

```
This is how the Delete command works.
```

Deleting a Line

Editor provides a Delete to End of Line command (CTRL-END), which deletes all text from the current cursor position to the end of the line. Editor leaves any return character at the end of the line so that any following text also stays in place. This allows you to edit the line before repositioning the return.

The Delete to End of Line command is useful anytime you need to remove an entire line of text, especially if there is text both before and after the line. For example, if you wanted to remove an entire command from your AUTOEXEC.BAT file you would:

1. Retrieve your AUTOEXEC.BAT file into the editing screen (see "Retrieving a File" earlier in this chapter).

2. Use the arrow keys to position the cursor at the beginning of the line you wish to delete.

3. Press CTRL-END to delete the line.

Since the Delete to End of Line command deletes from the current cursor position to the end of the line you can also delete part of a line by positioning the cursor where you want to begin the deletion and pressing CTRL-END.

Deleting a Page

Using the Delete to End of Page command (CTRL-PGDN) you can delete the contents of the current page from the cursor position to the next page break. Since this could amount to a very large section of text, Editor prompts you to confirm the deletion before it completes the command.

To delete a whole or partial page of text:

1. Use the arrow keys to position the cursor at the point where you want the page delete to begin.

2. Press CTRL-PGDN to delete to the end of the page. Editor displays the "Delete Remainder of Page? (Y/N)N" prompt.

3. Type **Y** to confirm the deletion or type **N** to cancel.

Remember that in Editor an entire document may be considered one page. Be sure to insert a page break (CTRL-ENTER) when performing a Delete to End of Page if you do not want the remainder of the document to be deleted.

Deleting a Block

Deleting sections of text larger than a few lines is easily done by defining a block of text and then deleting it. You can delete the block by pressing either the DEL or BACKSPACE key. Editor asks you to confirm the deletion before performing it.

To define a block of text and delete it:

1. Move the cursor to the beginning of the text you want to delete.

2. Press ALT-F4 to turn on Block. A "Block on" prompt blinks in the lower-left corner of the status line.

3. Use the cursor movement keys to move to where you want the block to end. The text or commands inside the block will be highlighted.

4. Press DEL or BACKSPACE to delete the block. Editor displays the "Delete Block? (Y/N)N" prompt.

5. Type **Y** to confirm the deletion or type **N** to cancel the deletion.

Editor deletes the contents of the block from the editing screen and the remaining text is repositioned at the cursor.

Restoring Deleted Text or Commands

To help recover text or commands lost by an accidental deletion, Editor stores the three most recent deletions in a buffer. You can use the

Cancel command (F1) to restore the last three deletions. The amount of text saved in these temporary buffers depends on the amount of memory and disk storage space your computer has available. If you try to delete more text than fits in the buffer, Editor asks if the text should be deleted without being saved. If you type **Y**, Editor deletes the specified text, which cannot then be restored. If you type **N**, Editor saves as much of the text as will fit into the temporary buffer. This text can be restored with the Cancel command. To restore the contents of the temporary buffer:

1. Use the arrow keys to position the cursor where you want the text restored.

2. Press F1 to restore a deletion. At the bottom of the screen, Editor displays the "Undelete 1 Restore; 2 Previous Deletion; 0" prompt. The most current deletion displays where the cursor is located.

3. Press **1** or **R** to restore the deletion as it appears or press **2** or **P** to show the next most recent deletion. Pressing **2** or **P** again shows the third deletion in the buffer. If you press **2** or **P** again, the display returns to the most recent deletion. Press **1** or **R** to restore any of the three deletions or press ENTER to exit Restore.

After a deletion is restored to the editing screen, it remains in the temporary buffer until it is replaced by other deletions.

Printing in Editor

In Editor you have the option of printing an entire file or a blocked portion of a file. In DOS Text mode you can also print a single page of a file. Editor lets you define a header to be printed at the top of each page and specify the number of lines to print per page. You can also specify that Editor print to a particular network printer.

Selecting a Print Device

Within Editor you can send print jobs to one of eight possible local ports or devices. In addition to the local devices, if you are using Office LAN you can tell Editor to print to a network device that you define (see "Printing on a Network" later in this section). To define a local port or device in Editor:

1. Press SHIFT-F7 to display the Print menu.

2. Press **4** or **S** to select a device.

3. To define an *LPT*, or parallel port, select a device number **1** through **4**; to define a *COM*, or serial port, select a device number **5** through **8**.

The device you select becomes the default printing device. Each time you print a file it is sent to this device.

Printing a File

When you press SHIFT-F7 to print in Editor, the contents of the editing screen are sent to the printer you previously defined. To print a file in Editor:

1. If necessary, select the correct printer device (as described in the previous section).

2. Retrieve the file into the editing window (see "Retrieving a File," earlier in this chapter).

3. Press SHIFT-F7 to print the file.

4. Press **1** or **F** for Full Document to print the entire file, or if the file is in DOS Text mode you can also press **2** or **P** for Page to print the page where the cursor is located.

Printing a Block

In addition to printing pages and files, Editor allows you to define a block for printing. To define and print a block from the editing screen:

1. If necessary, select the correct printer device.

2. Move the cursor to the position where the block should begin.

3. Press ALT-F4 to turn on Block. A "Block on" prompt blinks in the lower-left corner of the status line.

4. Use the cursor movement keys to move the cursor to the position where you want the block to end. The text or commands inside the block are highlighted.

5. Press SHIFT-F7 to print the block. Editor displays the "Print Block?(Y/N)N" prompt.

6. Type **Y** to print the block.

Editor prints the block of text to the device you defined and returns to the editing screen.

Setting Print Options

In Editor, you can set an option to determine the number of lines that are printed per page. You can also set the print format for any control characters to be printed.

To set the number of lines on a printed page:

1. Press SHIFT-F1 for Setup Options.

2. Press **3** or **I** for Initial Settings.

3. Press **2** or **P** for the Print Options menu.

4. Press **1** or **T** for Number of Text Lines per Page and enter a number or press **2** or **M** for Number of Macro Lines per Page and enter a number.

5. Press F7 until you return to the main editing screen.

The page breaks produced after setting the number of text or macro lines do not display on the editing screen. The only time you will see the page breaks is when Editor prints a file. If you want page breaks on the editing screen, you must insert them manually by pressing CTRL-ENTER.

Printing on a Network

Editor allows you to send output to a network printer. For example, to set up Editor to print on a Novell network, you must know the server and print queue that services the printer. When you have that information:

1. Press SHIFT-F7 for Print.

2. Select **4** or **S** to select a device.

3. From the Device menu, press **9** or **N** to define a network printer.

4. Enter the server name followed by a forward slash (/) and the print queue name. For example, to have Editor print to Printq_0 on the file server named Office, type **office/printq_0** and press ENTER.

Editor then redirects all print jobs to the network print queue you defined.

You can also use a network redirection command to direct local printer output to the network printer. For information on your specific redirection command contact your system administrator.

Defining a Page Header

When you print in Editor, a header is inserted at the top of every page similar to the one shown here:

Filename	Date	Pg#
↓	↓	↓
AUTOEXEC.BAT	February 24, 1992	Page 1

```
PATH=c:\office30
c:\office30\cl/i
c:\office30\shell
```

If you want to temporarily change the page header you can do so in the Options menu. This setting is temporary; when you exit Editor, the header you defined is not saved. To edit the page header:

1. Press SHIFT-F8 to enter Options.

2. Press **2** or **P** to select Page.

3. Insert the commands you want in the header. Editor provides special commands that insert the filename, date, and page number in the header as shown here:

```
Print Header Definition

Keystroke    Code     Inserts
Shift-F5     {Dat}    Date
Ctrl-Enter   {Pg#}    Page Number
F5           {Fil}    Filename

Example:
     {Fil}{Tab}{Tab}{Dat}{Tab}{Tab}Page {Pg#}{HRt}{HRt}
Output:
     FILENAME.EXT        12/7/91        Page 15
     <Blank Line>

Current Header: {Fil}<Tab><Tab>{Dat}<Tab><Tab>Page {Pg#}<HRt><HRt>
```

The page header you define is not specific to the file in the editing window. It is inserted at the top of every file Editor prints.

Creating a Macro

You can use Editor to create a macro for any WordPerfect product for which you have a correct macro resource, or .MRS, file. For example, you could create a macro for Editor that retrieves the AUTOEXEC-.BAT file and beeps once the file is retrieved. This macro requires the use of text, *keystroke commands,* and *macro commands.* Before you can begin creating this macro you must make certain the Editor macro resource file, ED.MRS, is in a directory where Editor can find it. For more information on setting up a default .MRS directory, see "Changing Editing Modes," earlier in the this chapter.

The first step in creating a macro is to change to the correct macro Editor mode using the Text In/Out command.

1. From a blank editing screen press CTRL-F5 for Text In/Out.

2. From the list of possible modes, press the number next to the entry for ED.

3. Press ENTER to select the macro Editor mode and return to the editing screen.

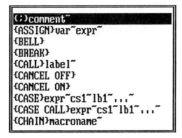

```
{;}comment~
{ASSIGN}var~expr~
{BELL}
{BREAK}
{CALL}label~
{CANCEL OFF}
{CANCEL ON}
{CASE}expr~cs1~lb1~...~
{CASE CALL}expr~cs1~lb1~...~
{CHAIN}macroname~
```

(Name Search; Enter or arrows to Exit)

Figure 5-3.   Macro Commands window

Editor provides an on-screen listing of all commands available for the current macro type. To access the macro commands list, press CTRL-PGUP. A window appears in the upper-right portion of the screen, and a listing of commands displays as shown in Figure 5-3. From this window you can use the arrow keys to scroll through the commands, or you can type the command name and Editor moves the cursor to the name. When you find the command you want to retrieve into the editing screen, press ENTER. The Macro Commands window then closes, and the command is retrieved into the editing screen where the cursor is positioned. For a listing of available macro commands, see Appendix F, "Advanced Macro Commands."

To begin creating the macro, first insert a comment about the macro to help you remember what it is used for. This line is ignored by Editor when it executes the macro. To insert the comment:

1. Press CTRL-PGUP to display the Macro Commands window. The first command on the list, {;}comment~, is for entering a comment.

2. Highlight {;}comment~ and press ENTER to select. The Macro Commands window closes, and {;} displays on the editing screen where the cursor was located.

3. Type in a descriptive comment about the macro for your personal reference. For this example, type **Retrieves C:\AUTOEXEC.BAT**.

4. Now type a tilde (~) to mark the end of the comment. The screen will look like the following:

```
{;}Retrieves·c:\autoexec.bat~
```

Any command that requires additional input, like text, to be completed must be marked at the end by a tilde. Commands that are made up of a single instruction do not require a tilde.

Now you can enter the command to retrieve the AUTOEXEC.BAT file. There are two different ways of entering the keystrokes. First, you can use the Value command (CTRL-V). When you press CTRL-V, a "Key:" prompt displays at the bottom of the screen. To continue the example in steps 1 through 4:

5. Position the cursor after the tilde.

6. Press CTRL-V; the next keystroke is entered into the macro at the current cursor position.

7. Press SHIFT-F10 and Editor inserts {Retrieve} into the macro as shown here:

```
{;}Retrieves·c:\autoexec.bat~{Retrieve}
```

You can also use the Functions command (CTRL-F10) to insert {Retrieve} (the Retrieve command) in the macro. When you press CTRL-F10 in Macro mode, "Functions" displays next to the mode indicator on the status line. With Functions on, every command key you press is inserted into the macro instead of being executed. The following is the alternative to the preceding steps for the example in steps 1 through 4:

5. Press CTRL-F10 to turn on Functions.

6. Press SHIFT-F10, and Editor inserts {Retrieve} into the macro.

7. Press CTRL-F10 again to turn off Functions. The Functions operation is especially useful for entering several keystroke commands sequentially.

Once you have inserted the Retrieve command using either the Valve or Functions command,

8. Type **C:\AUTOEXEC.BAT** to retrieve the AUTOEXEC.BAT file from your hard disk. If the AUTOEXEC.BAT file is stored somewhere other than the C: drive, enter the correct drive.

9. Since Editor needs a return at the end of the filename, you must insert one in the macro. Again, you can use Value (CTRL-V) and press ENTER or use Functions (CTRL-F10) and press ENTER to insert the keystroke. {Enter} is then inserted into the macro as shown here:

```
{:}Retrieves·c:\autoexec.bat~{Retrieve}c:\autoexec.bat{Enter}
```

To have Editor beep after the file has been retrieved, you must use the BELL command from the Macro Commands window. To enter the BELL command,

10. Press CTRL-PGUP to display the Macro Commands window.

11. Type **B** to have Editor move to commands beginning with "B." Since BELL is the first one, just press ENTER, and {BELL} is added to the macro. The editing screen should look similar to the one shown here:

```
{:}Retrieves·c:\autoexec.bat~{Retrieve}c:\autoexec.bat{Enter}{BELL}
```

12. Press F10 to save the macro.

13. Enter a name for the macro. The name must meet the DOS file-naming requirement of eight characters or fewer. The macro will be saved to the current default directory. If you are running Editor under Shell, the default directory is the directory specified on Editor's Program Information screen. If you are running Editor from DOS, the default directory is the directory you were in when you entered Editor.

Now try the macro to make sure it works. First, clear the editing screen by pressing F7 and then typing **N** and **N** to answer No to both prompts. To run the macro you just defined:

1. Press ALT-F10 to execute a macro.

2. When the "Macro:" prompt appears at the bottom of the screen, enter the name you assigned to the macro in step 13 above.

Editor should retrieve the AUTOEXEC.BAT file and then sound a beep. If this does not happen, retrieve the macro and make sure that all of the correct commands and text are in the proper order. Also, check to see if there is a tilde (~) marking the end of the comment field. Misplacing a tilde or forgetting to put one in are the most common sources of problems when creating a macro in Editor.

Editing a Macro

In Editor you can retrieve and edit macro files in any format as long as Editor has the correct .MRS file. For example, you can retrieve and edit the Editor macro described in the previous section so that it pauses and waits for you to input a filename before retrieving the file and beeping.

To retrieve and edit the macro just defined, do the following from an empty editing screen:

1. Press SHIFT-F10 to retrieve the file.

2. At the prompt, enter the filename that you assigned to the macro. If you have changed Editor's default directory since saving the file, you will also need to include the path to the file. Also be sure and include the correct extension. For Editor macros it is .EDM.

3. Delete C:\AUTOEXEC.BAT from the macro to allow you to input any name.

Editor needs a PAUSE macro command following the retrieve. The PAUSE command stops the macro and allows user input until you press the ENTER key. After pressing the ENTER key, the macro continues execution.

4. Move the cursor beneath {Enter} following {Retrieve} as shown here:

```
{;}Retrieves·any·file·into·Editor·then·beeps~{Retrieve}{Enter}{BELL}
```

5. To insert the PAUSE command, press CTRL-PGUP to display the Macro Commands window.

6. Type **P** to have Editor move to the commands beginning with "P." PAUSE is the first command it finds for Editor macros.

7. Press ENTER and Editor inserts {PAUSE} in the macro. The editing screen should look similar to the one shown here:

`{:}Retrieves·any·file·into·Editor·then·beeps~{Retrieve}{PAUSE}{Enter}{BELL}`

8. Save the macro by pressing F10 and entering a name for the macro.

Test the macro to make sure it works from an empty editing screen. To clear the editing screen press F7 and type **N** and **N** to answer No to both prompts. To run the macro you edited:

1. Press ALT-F10 to execute a macro.

2. When the "Macro:" prompt appears at the bottom of the screen, enter the name you assigned to the macro. The macro pauses with the "File to be Retrieved:" prompt displayed at the bottom of the screen.

3. Type in the name of the edited macro file and press ENTER. Be sure to include the full path to the file if it is not in Editor's default directory.

Editor should retrieve the file you specified and sound a beep once the file is retrieved. If the file did not retrieve check to make sure the file is in the default directory, or that the path you entered is correct. If the file retrieved but no beep sounded, retrieve the macro and make sure {BELL} is in the correct position in the macro.

Using Macro Variables

The advanced macros used in Editor allow you to store numbers, text, or keystrokes in temporary variables that you can specify. While a macro is being executed, the contents of variables can be used for comparisons, to print strings of text to the screen, or to execute keystrokes. The contents of variables are temporary and will be lost when you turn off your computer. One variable can hold up to 120 bytes of information.

One of the advantages of using advanced macro commands is that you can name the variables used in a macro. In Office 2.0, macros were limited to using the numbers 0 to 9 as designators. With advanced macros in Office 3.0, you can also define variables using names up to 39 characters for Editor macros and 20 characters for Shell macros.

Assigning contents to a named variable is done using the same commands as with numbered variables. You can assign a number value or text string inside the macro to a variable using the ASSIGN command. An example of this is to put the text string "Spaniel" into the variable "Dogs" using the following command:

```
{ASSIGN}Dogs~Spaniel~
```

Until another value is assigned to the variable "Dogs" it will contain "Spaniel."

The CHAR and TEXT commands both take keyboard input and assign it to a variable. The difference is that CHAR only accepts a single character, and TEXT accepts an entire string. To assign a single character to a variable using the CHAR command, first enter the name of the variable followed by a prompt to display on the screen separated by a tilde ($\sim$), as shown here:

```
{CHAR}Answer~Is this the correct way? (Y/N):~
```

Be sure to mark the end of the prompt with a tilde. This command will assign the first keystroke entered into the *Answer* variable.

The TEXT command also displays a prompt and waits for keyboard input, but Editor waits until ENTER is pressed before assigning the string to the variable you specify. In the following example all keystrokes (up to 120) typed before pressing ENTER are assigned to the *Name* variable:

```
{TEXT}Name~Input the name you wish to use:~
```

Using Control Characters

When using macro commands that display a message or prompt on the screen, you can use *control characters* to change the display format.

There are two types of control characters for advanced macros: *position* and *attribute*.

Position Characters

The position control characters control the placement of the text display. Table 5-1 outlines the available characters, the keystrokes to insert them, how they display in a macro, and how they position the cursor.

A special position control character is CTRL-P or {^P}. It can be used to position the cursor anywhere on the screen. Editor reads the two characters following {^P} and converts them into x and y coordinates for screen column and row and then positions the cursor accordingly. The two values for x and y coordinates are input as follows:

1. Press CTRL-V for Value.

2. Press ALT-*x* where *x* is the number of the column where the cursor will be positioned.

3. Press ALT-*y* where *y* is the number of the row where the cursor will be positioned.

When you execute a macro using this command, any text following this definition is displayed at the position you specify.

Character	Keystroke	Display	Cursor Position
^H	CTRL-V, CTRL-H	{HOME}	Upper-left corner
^J	CTRL-V, CTRL-J	{ENTER}	Start of next line
^K	CTRL-V, CTRL-K	{Del to EOL}	Same position; delete to end of line
^L	CTRL-V, CTRL-L	{Del to EOP}	Upper-left corner; delete to end of page
^M	CTRL-M	{^M}S	Start of same line
^W	CTRL-V, CTRL-W	{Up}	Up one line, same column position
^X	CTRL-V, CTRL-X	{Right}	Right one column
^Y	CTRL-V, CTRL-Y	{Left}	Left one column
^Z	CTRL-V, CTRL-Z	{Down}	Down one line, same column

Table 5-1.   Position Control Characters

Attribute Characters

Attribute control characters affect the text display with the attributes bold, underline, reverse video, and blink. The attribute control characters are shown in Table 5-2.

Both the position and attribute control characters can be used with the CHAR, TEXT and PROMPT advanced macro commands. For example, the following lines in an advanced macro would use the bold and blink attributes:

```
{PROMPT}{^]}This is bold{^\}{^N}{^P}This is blinking{^O}{^P}~
```

Position control characters could also be added to place the text in a certain position.

Editing Multiple Documents

With Editor, you can have up to nine files open for editing at one time. Two of these files are considered active files because they are currently in Editor's two editing screens. When you use SHIFT-F3 or F8 to switch between editing screens, you are switching between the two active files.

Character	Keystroke	Display	Action
^Q	CTRL-Q	{^Q}	Turns off all attributes
^R	CTRL-R	{^R}	Turns on reverse video
^S	CTRL-S	{^S}	Turns off reverse video
^T	CTRL-T	{^T}	Turns on underline
^U	CTRL-U	{^U}	Turns off underline
^N,^P	CTRL-N, CTRL-P	{^N}{^P}	Turns on blink
^O,^P	CTRL-O, CTRL-P	{^O}{^P}	Turns off blink
^]	CTRL-]	{^]}	Turns on bold
^\	CTRL-\	{^\}	Turns off bold

Table 5-2.   Attribute Control Characters

Any other open file can be activated from either editing screen, and it replaces one of the files in the editing screen as an active file.

Opening Multiple Files

Editor keeps track of all open files by numbering them from 1 to 9. These numbers are assigned when you first open the file. To open multiple files from the editing screen, press HOME and type a number from 1 to 9 to assign to that file. Editor clears the editing screen and opens a file with the number you assigned displaying as the file number on the status line. You can then use all of Editor's features to create or edit a file. If you should need to access any other open files, you simply press HOME and the number of the file to retrieve into the editing screen.

Listing Open Files

With nine editing screens it may be difficult to remember which files you have open. For this reason Editor has a listing feature that allows you to see which files are open. To see the list press HOME-0. Editor displays a list of all open files according to the number you assigned as shown in Figure 5-4. The list displays the file number, whether the file has been modified since you retrieved it, and the path and name of the file. If the file has not been saved it is given an [unnamed file] status. If a file is opened but does not contain any text it is given an [empty file] status.

Moving Between Files

You can move between open files by pressing HOME and the number you assigned to the file. The file moves to the current editing screen and replaces any file that may have already existed there. If you press HOME-x, where x is the file number, to try and access a file that is already open in the other editing screen, Editor switches you to the other screen rather than opening multiple copies of the same file.

```
File Modified Filename
1           C:\AUTOEXEC.BAT
2           C:\OFF30\ED_FILES\MACRO1.EDM
3           C:\OFF30\ED_FILES\MACRO2.EDM
4           C:\OFF30\MACRO.WPM
5           C:\OFF30\ALTSHFTA.SHM




Selection: 5
```

Figure 5-4.   Open Files menu

Another way to move between files is to use the listing feature, HOME-0. While the listing of open files is displayed, press the number of the file you want to access. The file you select replaces the file that was in the editing screen when you pressed HOME-0. If the file you select is already active in the second editing screen, Editor switches to that screen instead of placing the same file in both screens.

Closing Multiple Files and Exiting

With multiple files you have the choice of closing each file one at a time or using the Save All command (HOME-F7). Saving each file singly is done the same as if only one file was open. To save multiple files one by one:

1. Press F7 to exit the file.

2. Type **Y** when Editor asks if you want to save the file. If the file is an existing file, the original name displays on the status line.

3. Press ENTER to save the file to its original name or enter a new filename and, if necessary, the path you want the file to be saved to. If you want to save the file to its original name, or if you enter a filename that already exists, Editor displays the "Replace *filename*? (Y/N)N" prompt to have you confirm the replacement.

4. Type **Y** to replace the file or type **N** and Editor asks you again for a name for the file and you can enter a different name.

To save all of the open files and exit from Editor you can do the following:

1. Press HOME-F7 for Save All. Editor displays the "Save All Modified Files? 1 Yes; 2 No; 3 Prompt:" prompt.

2. Type **Y** to continue with the save. Editor displays all of the open files and asks for a filename if the file has not yet been named and saved. If the file has already been saved, Editor prompts you to save the file under its original name and asks if it should replace the original file, just as with a single file.

3. After all the files have been closed, Editor displays the prompt "Exit Editor? (Y/N)N". Type **Y** to exit Editor or type **N** to clear the editing screen and stay in Editor.

Editing in Binary Mode

You can use Editor to retrieve and edit files while they display in a binary format. In Binary mode, each character displays as its ASCII equivalent. To change Editor to Binary mode, do the following from an empty editing screen:

1. Press CTRL-F5 to display the Text In/Out menu.

2. Press **2** for Binary.

3. Press F7 or ENTER to return to the editing window.

In the lower-left corner of the screen the mode indicator should now display BIN as shown here:

BIN   **File 1**   **Ln 1**   **Pos 1**

To retrieve and edit a file in Binary mode:

1. Change to Binary mode as just described.

2. Retrieve the file you want to edit (see "Retrieving a File," earlier in this chapter).

If you want to replace existing characters in the file, press the INS key to change to Typeover mode. The status line on the lower-left corner of the screen displays Typeover instead of the filename when in Typeover mode. This means any character you enter will replace the character at the cursor. To add additional characters to the file, leave Editor in Insert mode so the filename is displayed on the status line in the lower-left corner of the screen. Enter the characters to add to the file.

When you save a file edited in Binary mode it remains in its original file format. Binary mode is especially useful, for example, if you do not want to strip codes from a WordPerfect document that you need to edit within Editor.

Editing with Reveal Codes

It is often helpful, especially in Binary mode, to edit the file while Reveal Codes is active. In Reveal Codes, the screen is split into two windows. The upper window is the editing screen containing the file being edited. The lower window contains a hexadecimal display of the file on the left side of the window and a normal display of the file on the right side. As you move the cursor in the editing window, the highlighted characters in the bottom window also change to reflect the movement. While in Reveal Codes you can use any of Editor's functions to edit the file in the editing

Append

Using the Append command you can attach a block of Editor text to information already in the temporary block buffer or to an existing file.

Keystrokes

1. Press ALT-F4 or F9 to turn on Block.

2. Using the cursor keys, highlight a block of text.

3. Press SHIFT-F4 to append the defined block.

4. Press ENTER to append to the block buffer or enter the path of the existing file to which you want to append the block of text.

Note: The Append command displays an error if you try and append to an empty block buffer or to a nonexistent file.

ASCII Codes

To help edit files in DOS Text or Binary mode, Editor provides an on-screen reference table of ASCII (American Standard Code for Information Interchange) characters as shown in Appendix B.

Keystrokes

1. Press F3 to display the main help screen.

2. Press **A** for ASCII Character Codes to display the table.

3. Press ENTER to exit help.

Backup

To help protect against loss of information, Editor provides you with two different methods to back up your work. One is Timed Backup and the other is Original Backup.

Keystrokes

To perform a timed backup:

1. Press SHIFT-F1 for Setup.

2. Press **2** or **E** to set the Environment options.

3. Press **1** or **B** for Backup.

4. Press **1** or **T** for Timed Backup.

5. Type **Y** to turn on Timed Backup.

6. Enter the number of minutes between backups.

7. Press F7 until you return to the editing screen.

To perform an original backup:

1. Press SHIFT-F1 for Setup.

2. Press **2** or **E** for Environment.

3. Press **1** or **B** for Backup.

4. Press **2** or **O** for Original Backup.

5. Type **Y** to turn on Original Backup.

6. Press F7 until you return to the editing screen.

For more information on using the Backup features see "Backing Up Editor Files," earlier in this chapter.

Binary Mode

You can use Editor to retrieve and edit text files while they are displayed in a binary format. In Binary mode any printer or message control characters display as their ASCII equivalents.

Keystrokes

1. Press CTRL-F5 to display the Text In/Out menu.

2. Press 2 for Binary.

3. Press F7 or ENTER to return to the editing window.

For information on editing in Binary mode see "Editing in Binary Mode," earlier in this chapter.

Block

You can use Block to define a section of text to use with specific functions.

Keystrokes

1. Move the cursor to the position where the block should begin.

2. Press ALT-F4 or F9 for Block. A "Block on" prompt will blink in the lower-left corner on the status line indicating that Block is on.

3. Using the cursor movement keys, set the cursor at the position where the block should end.

4. From the choices listed in the following section, select the function or attribute to be applied to the block.

5. If the command you selected leaves Block on, turn off Block by pressing ALT-F4 or F1 to cancel.

Applications

Each of the following applications can be applied to a defined block to give the block an attribute or to perform a function on the block.

Append to an Existing Block or File   The Append command (SHIFT-F4) attaches a defined block to the end of an existing file or block buffer.

Append to the Clipboard   You can append a defined block to the contents of the Clipboard (CTRL-F1, 3). This will not replace any existing text in the Clipboard, but will add the block to the end.

Assign   Using advanced macros you can assign a block of text to a macro variable. With a block of text defined, press CTRL-PGUP. Editor displays the "Variable:" prompt, and you can enter the name or number of the variable to which you want to assign the block of text.

Backspace   If you press BACKSPACE with Block on, you can delete the contents of the block.

Copy   To copy the contents of the block, press Copy (F4). This copies the block into the temporary block buffer. To retrieve the block, move the cursor to the position where the block should be copied and press SHIFT-F10 to retrieve and then press ENTER.

Delete   Press DEL with Block on to delete the contents of a block.

Move   To move a block and delete it from its original position, press CTRL-F4. This places a copy of the block into the temporary block buffer and removes the contents from the display. To retrieve the block, move the cursor to the position where the block should be placed and press SHIFT-F10 to retrieve and then press ENTER.

Print   To print a defined block press SHIFT-F7. Editor will print the block of text to the device you defined and return to the editing screen.

Search or Search and Replace   You can use Search or Search and Replace by pressing F2 or ALT-F2 with Block on. This specifies the area to search through. The Search and Replace function searches through the block for the text you specify and replaces it with new text that you enter.

Save   You can save a defined block of text by pressing F10 to save. To save the block to the temporary block buffer and replace the present contents press ENTER. You can also save the block to a file by entering a filename and path, if necessary.

Save to the Clipboard   Editor also gives you the option of saving a defined block to Shell's Clipboard. You can save the contents of a block to the Clipboard by pressing CTRL-F1 for Shell and **2** or **S** to save the block. This replaces the contents of the Clipboard.

Switch Letter Cases   Using the Switch function with a block defined allows you to convert all characters in the block to either uppercase or lowercase characters. To do this, define a block of text and press SHIFT-F3 or F8 to switch cases. To convert to uppercase, press **1** or **U**. To switch all characters to lowercase press **2** or **L**.

Cancel

With the Cancel command you can cancel or exit from any feature in Editor that modifies the screen or you can restore deleted text.

Keystrokes

Canceling a Command

To cancel out of a feature in Editor press F1. This exits the feature and returns you to normal operating mode. This also turns off features such as Block and restores the editing screen.

Restoring Deleted Text

Using Cancel's Restore feature you can restore up to the last three deletions. Editor restores the deleted text to the current cursor position.

For information on restoring deleted text see "Restoring Deleted Text or Commands," earlier in this chapter.

Codes

See "Reveal Codes," later in this chapter.

Colors

If you use a color monitor with Editor, you can set your display colors in Setup.

Keystrokes

To set the colors used on your display:

1. Press SHIFT-F1 for Setup.

2. Press **1** or **D** for Display.

3. Press **1** or **C** for Colors.

4. From the color menu, select the color you want displayed for each attribute. As you change the color setup, the sample display on the right side of the screen shows you how the display will appear.

5. Press F7 until you return to the editing screen.

Compose

The Compose feature allows you to create digraphs, symbols, and diacriticals from the WordPerfect character sets.

Keystrokes

To use the Compose feature, you must know the character set number and character number from the character chart in Appendix C. To insert the character you want:

1. Press CTRL-2 to turn on Compose. Editor does not display a prompt.

2. Type the character set number for the character you want to insert.

3. Type a comma (,) or press ENTER as a separator between the values.

4. Enter the character number from the character chart in Appendix C.

Note: Your monitor may not be able to display all of the available characters. If your monitor cannot display a character it appears as a box. To find which characters your monitor can display, retrieve the CHARMAP.TST file from the Office directory. You can also see which characters your printer supports by printing out this file. For a listing of the available characters, see Appendix C, "WordPerfect Characters Chart."

Copy

The Copy command copies a block of text to the temporary buffer or if there is no block defined, then Copy acts like Copy Line (ALT-F6).

Keystrokes

1. Move the cursor to the position where you want the block to begin.

2. Press ALT-F4 for Block. A "Block on" prompt blinks in the lower-left corner on the status line.

3. Using the cursor movement keys, move the cursor to the position where you want the block to end. The text or commands inside the block will be highlighted.

4. Press F4 for Copy.

5. Position the cursor where you want to retrieve the block.

6. Press SHIFT-F10 to retrieve the block. Editor displays the "File to be Retrieved: (Block)" prompt.

7. Press ENTER and Editor retrieves the contents of the block you defined.

Copy Line

Using Copy Line you can have Editor copy any line you specify by giving the line number. Before you use the Copy Line command you must know the number of the line you want Editor to copy.

Keystrokes

1. Position the cursor where you want the copied line to be placed.

2. Press ALT-F6 for Copy Line. At the bottom of the screen, Editor asks for the line number by displaying a "Ln" prompt.

3. Enter the number of the line to copy.

Editor copies the line you specify to the current position of the cursor.

CTRL-HOME

See "Go To" later in this chapter.

Cursor Movement Keys

You can use the keys listed in Table 5-3 for positioning the cursor in Editor. These keystrokes are available from all screens in Editor.

Date

Editor's Date command inserts your computer's current date into the file in the editing screen.

Keystrokes

1. Press SHIFT-F5 for Date.

2. Press **1** or **T** to select Date Text.

Keystroke	Action
LEFT ARROW	Moves left one column
RIGHT ARROW	Moves right one column
UP ARROW	Moves up one line
DOWN ARROW	Moves down one line
CTRL-LEFT ARROW	Moves left one word
CTRL-RIGHT ARROW	Moves right one word
HOME, LEFT ARROW	Moves to the beginning of line
HOME, RIGHT ARROW	Moves to the end of line
HOME, UP ARROW	Moves to the top of screen
HOME, DOWN ARROW	Moves to the bottom of screen
PGUP	Moves up one page
PGDN	Moves down one page
HOME, HOME, UP ARROW	Moves to the top of file
HOME, HOME, DOWN ARROW	Moves to the bottom of file
CTRL-HOME, #	Goes to line number
HOME, #	Edits file number

Table 5-3.   Cursor Keys in Editor

A text string for the date is inserted in the editing screen at the current position of the cursor. The Date function can insert a string in the editing screen up to 58 characters long.

Date Format

You can change the Date Format used in the Date Text.

Keystrokes

1. Press SHIFT-F5 for Date.

2. Press **2** or **F** to select Date Format.

3. Using the options on the menu, set the display format.

4. Press F7 until you return to the main editing screen.

DOS Text Mode

The default editing mode for Editor is DOS Text mode. After using other editing modes, however, you may need to reselect it.

Keystrokes

1. Press CTRL-F5 for Text In/Out.

2. Press **1** to select DOS Text mode.

3. Press ENTER or F7 to exit and return to the editing screen.

For more information on Editor's modes see "Changing Editing Modes" earlier in this chapter.

Duplicate Word

The Dup Word command copies the word in the line directly above the cursor to the line where the cursor is located. Editor duplicates all characters until it finds a space, tab, or return.

Keystrokes

1. Using the cursor keys, position the cursor one line below the beginning of the word you want to duplicate.

2. Press F6 to duplicate the word.

For more information on the Dup Word command, see "Duplicating a Word" earlier in this chapter.

Duplicate Line

The Dup Line command copies the line directly above the line the cursor is on until it finds a return.

Keystrokes

To use the Dup Line command from the editing screen:

1. Using the cursor keys, position the cursor one line below the line to be duplicated.

2. Press SHIFT-F6 to duplicate the line.

For more information on Dup Line see "Duplicating the Previous Line" earlier in this chapter.

Keystroke	Action
DEL	Deletes the character at the cursor
BACKSPACE	Deletes the character to the left of the cursor
CTRL-BACKSPACE	Deletes the word at the cursor
HOME, BACKSPACE	Deletes from current position left to start of the word
HOME, DEL	Deletes from current position right to end of the word
CTRL-END	Deletes to the end of the current line
CTRL-PGDN	Deletes to the end of the current page
INS	Switches between Insert and Typeover modes

Table 5-4.   Editing Keys in Editor

Editing Keys

You can use the keys listed in Table 5-4 for editing text and macro commands in Editor. These editing keystrokes are available from all text editing screens in Editor. Since there are no page breaks in Macro mode, you must be careful when using the Delete to End of Page command (CTRL-PGDN). Make sure that Editor is deleting only what you want to be deleted.

Escape

See "Repeat Value" later in this chapter.

Exit

Use the Exit (F7) command to exit from Editor and return either to Shell or DOS. You can also save the file in the editing screen as part of an exit. See "Saving a File and Exiting Editor," earlier in this chapter.

Exit All

Exit All is used to close multiple open files for editing in Editor and to exit from Editor.

Keystrokes

To use the Exit All command, do the following from any editing screen in Editor:

1. Press HOME, F7 to use Exit All.

2. To save all files that have been edited, press **1** or **Y**. Editor will then close each file individually and ask you for a filename.

    To exit without saving any files press **2** or **N**. Editor will warn you that no files will be saved, and you have the choice of continuing or canceling the exit.

    To have Editor prompt you for a name for each file, press **3** or **P**.

3. To exit from Editor, type **N** when Editor asks if you want to exit.

Expressions

Expressions are logical operations that can be substituted for the value argument in the ASSIGN, CASE, CASE CALL, and IF advanced macro commands. Table 5-5 lists available expressions. Text strings can also be used in the expressions $n1=n2$ and $n1!=n2$. Using text in expressions requires that the text strings be surrounded by quotes.

Function

Using Functions while in Macro mode records every function key you press and inserts them into the macro editing screen instead of executing the function. This is useful when creating a macro that executes several functions sequentially.

Expression	Value Returned
−n1	Opposite of n1
n1 + n2	Sum of n1 and n2
n1 − n2	Difference of n1 and n2
n1*n2	Product of n1 and n2
n1/n2	Quotient of n1 divided by n2
n1%n2	Remainder of n1 divided by n2
!n1	Logical NOT of n1
n1&n2	Logical AND of n1 and n2
n1¦n2	Logical OR of n1 and n2
n1 = n2	If true returns −1
	If false returns 0
n1! = n	n1 not equal to n2
	returns −1
	n1 equal to n2 returns 0
n1 > n2	n1 greater than n2
	returns −1
	n1 less than n2 returns 0
n1 < n2	n1 less than n2 returns −1
	n1 greater than n2 return 0

Table 5-5. Expressions

Keystrokes

1. Press CTRL-F10 from an editing screen in Macro mode.

When you press CTRL-F10 in Macro mode, "Functions" displays next to the mode indicator on the status line.

Go To

The Go To command moves the cursor to the line number you specify. It can be used in both relative and absolute page numbering. Pressing Go To followed by the UP ARROW or DOWN ARROW key moves the cursor to the top or bottom of the current page.

Keystrokes

For relative page numbering:

1. Press CTRL-HOME for Go To.

2. Type the number of the line on the same page followed by a comma (,) to indicate relative page numbering. If Editor is already using relative numbering, you can end the command by pressing ENTER instead of entering a comma.

For absolute page numbering:

1. Press CTRL-HOME for Go To.

2. Type the number of the line on the same page followed by a period (.). If Editor is already using absolute numbering, you can end the command by pressing ENTER.

Help

Editor provides you with extensive on-screen help about its features and options. You can also define your own help screens, with information about operations or commands that you commonly use.

Keystrokes

1. Press F3 for Help from the main Editor screen.

2. Choose one of the following options:

   • Type one of the menu item letters to see information about the specific topic.

   • Press a function key to see information about the feature associated with that key.

- Press F3 for Help again to see the Editor keyboard template.
  This is especially useful since WordPerfect Office does not come with a keyboard template for Editor.

3. Press ENTER or the spacebar to exit a help screen or press ESC to return to the main help screen.

Hints

The help screens are a valuable tool for accessing information about the Editor program. You do not have to press Help (F3) from the main Editor screen. Pressing Help from any Editor menu displays information about the features associated with that screen. For information on creating user-defined help screens see "Creating User-Defined Help Screens," earlier in this chapter.

Line Format

Using the Line Format selection under Options you can set up the TAB key value and turn the Auto Indent feature on or off.

Keystrokes

Vary Tabs

1. Press SHIFT-F8 for Options.

2. Press 1 or L for Line Format menu.

3. Press 1 or V for Vary Tabs.

4. Enter the value for the first TAB, type a comma (,) separator, and enter the number of columns the TAB key moves after the first TAB.

For example, if you want to have the TAB key move to column 4 the first time it is pressed on a line, and then move 5 columns after that, enter **4,5.**

Tab Every

1. Press SHIFT-F8 for Options.

2. Press **1** or **L** for Line Format menu.

3. Press **2** or **T** to set a constant value for the TAB key. Enter the number of columns you want the TAB key to move every time it is pressed.

Hints

You can have the TAB key insert spaces instead of the TAB character by pressing SHIFT-F8, 1, 3. You can also have Editor indent each line automatically to match the line above it. This is useful when using Editor to write program source code. To turn on the Auto Indent feature, press SHIFT-F8, 1. Type **Y** to turn on Auto Indent or **N** to turn it off.

Line Number

In Editor you can choose to have the status line display the current line's number as an absolute number (the line's number in the file) or as a relative number (the line's number on the current page).

Keystrokes

1. Press SHIFT-F1 for Setup.

2. Press **1** or **D** for Display.

3. Press **3** or **A** to set the Line Numbering option.

4. Type **N** to have the status line display relative line numbers or type **Y** to have the status line display absolute line numbers.

5. Press F7 twice to return to the editing screen.

With the status line displaying absolute line numbers, the page number still reflects the current page number, but the line number is the current line's number in the file.

List Files

Using List Files in Editor you can perform many common file-management commands without exiting to DOS. List Files displays the files and subdirectories contained in a given directory, and you can select a function from the menu at the bottom of the screen. For information on the functions available in List Files see "Using List Files," earlier in this chapter.

Macro

The Macro function is for executing a previously defined Editor macro.

Keystrokes

1. Press ALT-F10 for Macro.

2. Enter the filename of the macro to execute. You do not need to type the .EDM filename extension.

If the macro is not located in the default directory, enter the path with the filename.

Macro Commands

From the editing screen there are two possible functions for the Macro Commands feature. The first one is to display a listing of advanced macro commands to use when creating or editing a macro. The other function is to assign contents to a variable.

Keystrokes

To insert macro commands:

1. Press CTRL-PGUP to display the Macro Commands window.

2. Use the cursor keys to highlight the command you want to retrieve to the editing screen or type in the name of the command. Editor searches the list to match the name pattern you enter.

3. With the command you want to retrieve highlighted, press ENTER. Editor retrieves the command into the editing screen at the current position of the cursor.

To assign variables with macro commands:

1. Press CTRL-PGUP twice to assign a variable.

2. Enter the number or name of the variable.

3. Enter the value or text you want to assign to the variable.

Macro Define

To create a macro that executes within Editor, you can use the Macro Define command.

Keystrokes

1. Press CTRL-F6 to turn on Macro Define. You can also press CTRL-F10 in DOS Text mode. Editor displays a prompt asking for a name.

2. Enter a filename or press ALT-*x* where *x* is a letter from A to Z.

3. Enter an optional description about the purpose of the macro. This is useful if you ever need to retrieve and edit the macro. A "Macro Def" prompt blinks at the bottom of the screen while you are in Macro Definition mode.

4. Insert the keystrokes you want to record in the macro.

5. When you finish defining the macro, press CTRL-F6 again to turn off Macro Define.

Editor saves the macro with a .EDM extension appended to the filename you enter.

To execute the macro, press ALT-F10 and enter the name of the macro. If the macro is not located in Editor's default directory, enter the path with the filename.

Macro Variables

See "Using Macro Variables," earlier in this chapter.

Move

The Move command is used to move a defined block of text or commands from one position to another. The block is removed from its original position and copied to the current location of the cursor when SHIFT-F10 is pressed.

2. Press ENTER to save the file to its original name or enter the name and path you want the file to be saved under.

If you want to save the file to its original name or enter a name that already exists, Editor displays the "Replace *filename*? (Y/N)N" prompt to have you confirm the replacement. Type **Y** to continue and replace the file. If you type **N**, Editor again asks you for a name for the file, and you can enter a different name. After completing the save, you will return to the editing screen with the cursor in its original position.

Screen

You can use the Screen command in Editor to rewrite the screen, divide the screen into two editing windows, adjust the scroll regions for the top and bottom of the display, and make size adjustments for nonstandard screens.

Keystrokes

1. Press CTRL-F3 to display the Screen options.

2. Select one of the options listed here:

```
Screen 0 Rewrite; 1 Window; 2 Scroll; 3 Size; 0
```

Options

The following options are available from the Screen menu:

Rewrite   When you rewrite the screen, it automatically updates the screen to reflect any changes in the displayed file.

Window   You can divide the editing screen into two editing windows with this option. First select the option, then enter the number of lines you want in the top window (the bottom window takes the remainder). The screen is divided into two windows separated by a tab indicator. If any files were displayed in the editing screens, they are now displayed with file 1 in the top window and file 2 in the bottom window. Use SHIFT-F3 to switch between the windows.

To return to normal screen display, do the following:

1. Press CTRL-F3 to display the Screen options.

2. Press **1** or **W** to select the Window option.

3. Enter **24** as the number of lines that the top window should use. For a standard display this occupies the entire screen.

Scroll   With this option you can set the minimum number of lines between the top or bottom of the screen and the scroll bar when scrolling through a file. First enter the minimum number of lines Editor should keep between the cursor and the top of the screen. Then enter the minimum number of lines Editor should keep between the cursor and the bottom of the screen. For either one of the scroll regions you can enter **0** if you do not want any buffer between the screen borders and the cursor.

Size   Using the Size option you can set the number of display lines used for monitors that can display more or less than the standard 25 lines of text.

Scroll

Using the Scroll features, ALT-F9, SHIFT-F9, and CTRL-F9, you can reposition the cursor and the current line it is on to the bottom, middle, or top of the display.

Keystrokes

1. To scroll the editing screen so the cursor and the current line it is on are at the bottom of the screen, press ALT-F9; to scroll to the

center of the screen, press SHIFT-F9; or to scroll the editing screen so the cursor and the current line it is on are at the top of the screen, press CTRL-F9.

Search

Editor's Forward Search and Reverse Search commands search from the current cursor position forward to the end of the file or from the cursor backward to the beginning of the file, respectively.

Keystrokes

1. Press F2 for Forward Search or SHIFT-F2 for Reverse Search.

2. Type the word pattern you want Editor to search for.

3. Press F2 to accept the string of text.

Editor searches the file until it finds the next occurrence of the character string you entered. A "*Not Found*" prompt displays if no occurrences of the character string are found.

Setup

The Setup menu allows you to configure Editor settings to meet your needs.

Keystrokes

1. Press SHIFT-F1 for Setup.

2. Make the desired changes to the following options:

```
Setup
    1 - Display
    2 - Environment
    3 - Initial Settings
    4 - Location of Files
```

Options

The following options are available from the Setup menu:

Display From the Display menu you can change the Color Setup menu, the display characteristics for control characters, the print format for control characters, and the line numbering method (absolute or relative).

Environment From the Environment menu you can set Backup options, Beep options, and Wrap options. From the Environment menu you can disable Macro mode so that all macros are displayed in DOS Text format. Editor also gives you the option of having Search distinguish between uppercase and lowercase. The last two items listed let you choose to have PGUP and PGDN act like SCREEN UP and SCREEN DOWN (the + and − keys on the numeric keypad), and the input format for the Value function.

Initial Settings From the Initial Settings menu you can set the display format for the Date command. You can also set Print options for both DOS text files and macro files.

Location of Files Location of Files lets you tell Editor where to create backup files and where to look for macro resource (.MRS) files.

Shell

Using Editor under Shell provides you with several advantages over starting Editor from DOS. You can switch between programs without exiting Editor. You can also create and use Shell macros to help increase productivity. With the Shell Clipboard you can also transfer information between programs.

Keystrokes

Program Switch

To leave Editor resident and go to Shell, press CTRL-ALT-SPACEBAR. You can also access Shell from almost any screen in Editor:

1. Press CTRL-F1.

2. Type **1** or **G** to select Go to Shell.

When you return to Editor the cursor is in the same position and the same information is displayed.

You can also switch to other programs listed on the Shell menu by pressing CTRL-ALT-x where x is the Shell menu letter or number of the Shell option you want to change to.

Clipboard

To define a block and save or append the contents to the Clipboard:

1. Move the cursor to the position where the block should begin.

2. Press ALT-F4 to turn on Block.

3. Use the cursor movement keys to set the cursor at the position where you want the block to end.

4. Press CTRL-F1 to display the Shell Options menu.

5. Press **2** or **S** to save the block to the Clipboard and replace its contents or press **3** or **A** to append the block to the end of the current contents of the Clipboard.

Startup Options

Whether you are starting editor from Shell or from DOS, you can specify several startup switches to modify the way Editor works. If you are running Editor from Shell, the switches must be entered on the Startup Options line in the Program Information screen for Editor. If you are starting Editor from DOS, you can enter the switches on the command line. The following is a listing of the Editor startup options.

filename	Retrieves specified file on startup
/1	For using Editor on a computer with a single floppy drive
/A	Disables Macro mode
/B	Disables Macro mode and starts Editor in Binary mode
/CP	Overrides DOS Code Page command
/D-*directory*	Redirects overflow and temporary files to a specified directory
/D-%*x*	Lets you run multiple copies from the same directory
/F2	Corrects graphic display problems
/H-*directory*	Specifies directory containing user-defined help screens
/L	If run during one session, restores file in next session
/M-*macroname*	Specifies a startup macro
/NF	Corrects display problems with some compatibles and window programs
/NS	Speeds up color monitors
/NT-*x*	Specifies network type where *x* represents the network
/PS-*directory*	Redirects path to setup file
/W-*kilobytes*	Allocates less workspace in memory
/X	Ignores setup file

Switch

The Switch command in Editor normally switches you between the different editing screens. If a block of text is defined, it also gives you the option of converting all text in the block to uppercase or lowercase.

Keystrokes

To use Switch to change editing screens, press SHIFT-F3 from either editing screen. To use Switch in case conversion, do the following:

1. Move the cursor to the position where the block should begin.

2. Press ALT-F4 to turn on Block.

3. Use the cursor movement keys to set the cursor at the position where you want the block to end.

4. Press SHIFT-F3 to convert cases. Editor prompts to convert the entire block to uppercase or lowercase characters.

5. To convert to uppercase press **1** or **U**. To convert to lowercase, press **2** or **L**.

Editor converts the characters in the block and turns off the Block.

Text In/Out

The Text In/Out command sets the mode for the editing screens. The menu displayed when you select Text In/Out depends on the number of .MRS files Editor can locate.

Keystrokes

1. Press CTRL-F5 for the Text In/Out menu.

2. From the menu entries select the default mode for the editing screens.

3. Press ENTER or F7 to accept the selection and return to the editing window.

Value

The Value command has two functions in Editor. One is to enter any ASCII character and the second is to insert a keystroke command in Macro mode without executing the command.

Keystrokes

To use Value to insert an ASCII character, do the following from the editing window:

1. Press CTRL-V.

2. Press ALT-x where x is the value of the ASCII character. This can be decimal or hexadecimal depending on the setup option. See "Setup" earlier in this chapter.

To use Value to insert a macro keystroke command without executing the command, do the following from an editing window in Macro mode:

1. Press CTRL-V.

2. Press the keystroke associated with the command you want to insert.

Editor inserts the command without executing it.

Wrap

The Wrap command searches forward through the file on the editing screen for lines longer than the current default setting. If it encounters a line, you can have it automatically wrap the line to the next line or have Editor ask you for confirmation before wrapping the line.

Keystrokes

1. Using the arrow keys position the cursor where you would like the search to begin.

2. Press CTRL-F2 to begin the search.

3. Type **Y** if you want to confirm each wrap or type **N** to have Editor wrap automatically.

Using File Manager

File Manager is a powerful file and directory organizer. File Manager is similar to the List Files feature found in other WordPerfect Office programs and in WordPerfect. File Manager can do everything that List Files can do and more. For example, in File Manager, you can rename a directory, display two directories at the same time, and sort files alphabetically as well as by date, size, or extension. These are just a few of the advantages File Manager has over the List Files feature. Within individual programs, List Files is a useful feature that can perform many everyday file-organization tasks. However, when you need to do several file-organization tasks or reach the limits of List Files or simply want an easier method to accomplish many of your file and directory organization needs, File Manager is the answer.

Many DOS functions can be performed within File Manager including copying, deleting, moving, and renaming files. For those who are unfamiliar with DOS commands, File Manager is an excellent and easy-to-use tool. For those familiar with DOS, File Manager adds versatility and power to directory and file organization.

The main File Manager screen displays helpful information at the top, such as the current date and time, the name of the directory, and specific information about the directory displayed. Below this information is the name of all the subdirectories and files in the currently displayed directory. At the bottom of the screen are 11 options that perform various functions within File Manager. Each of these options will be discussed at length throughout this chapter.

File Manager allows you to select which files in a directory are displayed and how they are displayed. Using a *filename pattern*, you can list only those files that fit a given pattern. For example, you can tell File Manager to display only play the files in a given directory with .EXE and .BAT extensions. You can also specify how you want the files displayed: alphabetically, by date and time last saved, by size, or by filename extension.

Along with changing the file display, you can also change the way the screen appears in File Manager. File Manager has two separate screens for displaying files. You can list files in Full Screen mode as shown in Figure 6-1, where the files are listed on the full screen, or in Half Screen mode as shown in Figure 6-2, where the current file list only displays on half the screen. With Full Screen mode you can see more files at a time, but you must switch to another screen to see files in a different directory. With Half Screen mode you can display two separate directories simultaneously on the same screen. This feature is useful when comparing directory contents.

File Manager also has the capability of displaying the *tree structure* of a drive. The tree structure only displays the directories on the drive. Displaying the tree structure of a drive helps you see exactly how the drive is organized by showing the different levels of directories on that drive.

With the Look feature you can see the contents of a file in any directory without having to retrieve the file into a program. This is useful if you have forgotten what is in a file or just want to see what is

```
02-24-92  12:58p            Directory C:\OFFICE30\*.*
Free Mem: 206,304    Disk Free: 21,522,432   Used: 2,688,645      Files:   259

. <CURRENT>   <DIR> °         .. <PARENT>     <DIR>
LEARN    .     <DIR>  05-14-90  9:56a  ADD_CONT.SHM    2,403  06-01-90 12:56p
ADD_LST .SHM   2,317  06-01-90 12:56p  ADD_MSG .SHM    1,129  06-01-90 12:56p
ALTC    .EDM   1,692  06-01-90 12:56p  ALTD    .EDM      678  06-01-90 12:56p
ALTE    .EDM   2,920  06-01-90 12:56p  ALTF    .EDM    4,568  06-01-90 12:56p
ALTG    .EDM   1,216  06-01-90 12:56p  ALTI    .EDM    1,351  06-01-90 12:56p
ALTL    .EDM   4,664  06-01-90 12:56p  ALTM    .EDM    4,358  06-01-90 12:56p
ALTN    .EDM   1,290  06-01-90 12:56p  ALTO    .EDM      322  06-01-90 12:56p
ALTP    .EDM     652  06-01-90 12:56p  ALTR    .EDM    5,100  06-01-90 12:56p
ALTS    .EDM   6,864  06-01-90 12:56p  ALTSHFDM.SHM    2,469  06-01-90 12:56p
ALTSHFM2.SHM   1,946  06-01-90 12:56p  ALTSHFM3.SHM    2,218  06-01-90 12:56p
ALTSHFTA.SHM   3,388  06-01-90 12:56p  ALTSHFTD.SHM    1,799  06-01-90 12:56p
ALTSHFTD.WPM  10,533  06-01-90 12:56p  ALTSHFTE.SHM    2,259  06-01-90 12:56p
ALTSHFTM.SHM   1,654  06-01-90 12:56p  ALTSHFTX.SHM    1,986  06-01-90 12:56p
ALTT    .EDM     474  06-01-90 12:56p  ALTU    .EDM      632  06-01-90 12:56p
ALTV    .EDM  39,934  06-01-90 12:56p  ALTW    .EDM    1,078  06-01-90 12:56p
ALTX    .EDM   4,152  06-01-90 12:56p  ALTX    .WPM      902  06-01-90 12:56p
AUTOSC  .SHM   3,818  06-01-90 12:56p  CALC    .EXE   31,232  06-01-90 12:56p
CALC    .HLP  26,258  06-01-90 12:56p ▼ CALC    .SHM    1,464  06-01-90 12:56p

1 *Mark; 2 Delete; 3 Move/Rename; 4 Select Files; 5 Lock; 6 Look; (F7 to Exit,
7 Other Dir; 8 Copy; 9 Word Srch; N Name Srch; F5 Find Files: 6    F3 for Help)
```

Figure 6-1.   File Manager in Full Screen mode

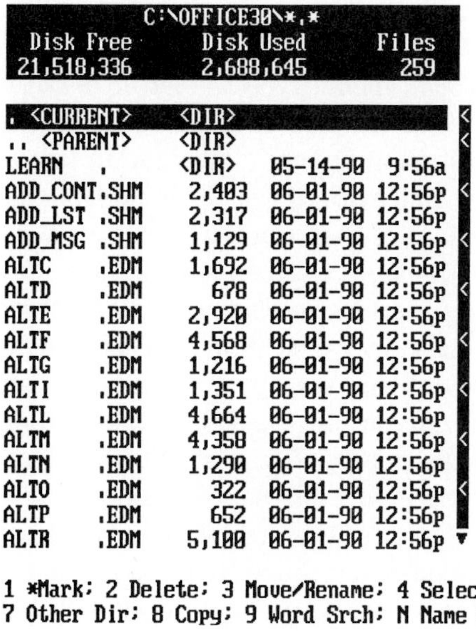

```
                    C:\OFFICE30\*.*
        Disk Free        Disk Used        Files
        21,518,336       2,688,645          259

    .  <CURRENT>    <DIR>                               <
    .. <PARENT>     <DIR>                               <
    LEARN      .    <DIR>      05-14-90   9:56a
    ADD_CONT.SHM       2,403   06-01-90  12:56p  <
    ADD_LST .SHM       2,317   06-01-90  12:56p
    ADD_MSG .SHM       1,129   06-01-90  12:56p  <
    ALTC    .EDM       1,692   06-01-90  12:56p
    ALTD    .EDM         678   06-01-90  12:56p  <
    ALTE    .EDM       2,920   06-01-90  12:56p
    ALTF    .EDM       4,568   06-01-90  12:56p  <
    ALTG    .EDM       1,216   06-01-90  12:56p
    ALTI    .EDM       1,351   06-01-90  12:56p  <
    ALTL    .EDM       4,664   06-01-90  12:56p
    ALTM    .EDM       4,358   06-01-90  12:56p  <
    ALTN    .EDM       1,290   06-01-90  12:56p
    ALTO    .EDM         322   06-01-90  12:56p  <
    ALTP    .EDM         652   06-01-90  12:56p
    ALTR    .EDM       5,100   06-01-90  12:56p  ▼

    1 *Mark; 2 Delete; 3 Move/Rename; 4 Select Files; 5 Lock; 6 Look; (F7 to Exit;
    7 Other Dir; 8 Copy; 9 Word Srch; N Name Srch; F5 Find Files; 6    F3 for Help)
```

Figure 6-2.   File Manager in Half Screen mode

in a file without retrieving it. In the Look mode you can search for specific words and copy and save selected text to the Shell Clipboard.

The Find File and Word Search features are helpful in locating files that you have forgotten the name of. With Find File you can enter any part of a filename, such as an extension, and File Manager helps you find the correct file by listing all the files with that extension. With Word Search you enter a specific word or words that you know are in the file, and File Manager then lists all the files containing the word or words you entered.

A powerful feature in File Manager is Program Launch. Program Launch does as its name denotes: It launches programs or commands from within File Manager. For example, from within File Manager you can highlight the name of an executable file such as WordPerfect, press F9 or **E** for Execute, and the program is started. Several other options available with Program Launch will be discussed in "Using Program Launch" later in this chapter.

File Manager's uses can be as simple as copying a file or as complex as launching a program. But whatever your file and directory organization needs, File Manger can fill them.

Starting File Manager

To start File Manager from the Shell menu, type the letter next to the File Manager entry; the default letter is **F**. To start File Manager from DOS type **fm**. There are several startup options that you can use when starting File Manager. For more information, see "Startup Options" in the "Functions and Features" section of this chapter.

The first time you start File Manager a screen similar to the one in Figure 6-1 appears. The display of the files in Figure 6-1 is referred to as a *file list*. A file list displays directories and individual files found in the specified directory. At the top of this screen, the heading information displays in reverse video. The current date and time, taken from the computer's date and time, are in the upper-left corner. The name of the directory being listed appears at the top middle. The amount of free memory (RAM), the available disk space, the used disk space, and the number of files in the directory appears on the second line. If you have marked files in the directory, the Files entry now displays "Marks:" with the number of files designated, and the "Used" entry now displays "Marked:" and only displays the amount of memory used by the marked files, as shown in Figure 6-3. Knowing the amount of free memory is especially useful when you want to copy files to a floppy disk. You can list the files on the disk in the floppy drive and compare the amount of free memory to the size of the files you want to copy. This way you won't get the frustrating "Disk Full" error message that displays when there is not enough room to copy files.

Below the heading information are the .<CURRENT> <DIR> and ..<PARENT> <DIR> listings. The current directory represents the directory that is currently listed on screen. For example, in Figure 6-3 the current directory is C:\DOCUMENT. The parent directory represents the directory one level above the current directory. In Figure 6-3 the parent directory is C:\. For more on using the current and parent listings see "Changing Directories," later in this chapter.

Directly below the current and parent listings are the names of any subdirectories. Subdirectories help you better organize your files. Directories and subdirectories are often compared to a filing cabinet where the entire cabinet is the root directory (C:\, for example) and the individual drawers of the filing cabinet are the subdirectories. The main dividers within the drawers are also subdirectories and the actual items in the folders are the files. Just as you would never throw all your

```
02-24-92   1:04p          Directory C:\DOCUMENT\*.*
Free Mem: 286,304      Disk Free: 21,331,968  Marked: 28,586        Marks: 12/41

. <CURRENT>    <DIR>                  .. <PARENT>    <DIR>
ADD_CONT.SHM      2,403* 06-01-90 12:56p   ADD_LST .SHM     2,317* 06-01-90 12:56p
ADD_MSG .SHM      1,129* 06-01-90 12:56p   ALTC    .EDM     1,692* 06-01-90 12:56p
ALTD    .EDM        678* 06-01-90 12:56p   ALTE    .EDM     2,920* 06-01-90 12:56p
ALTF    .EDM      4,568* 06-01-90 12:56p   ALTG    .EDM     1,216* 06-01-90 12:56p
ALTI    .EDM      1,351* 06-01-90 12:56p   ALTL    .EDM     4,664* 06-01-90 12:56p
ALTM    .EDM      4,358* 06-01-90 12:56p   ALTN    .EDM     1,290* 06-01-90 12:56p
ALTO    .EDM        322  06-01-90 12:56p   ALTP    .EDM       652  06-01-90 12:56p
ALTR    .EDM      5,100  06-01-90 12:56p   ALTS    .EDM     6,864  06-01-90 12:56p
ALTSHFDM.SHM      2,469  06-01-90 12:56p   ALTSHFM2.SHM     1,946  06-01-90 12:56p
ALTSHFM3.SHM      2,218  06-01-90 12:56p   ALTSHFTA.SHM     3,388  06-01-90 12:56p
ALTSHFTD.SHM      1,799  06-01-90 12:56p   ALTSHFTE.SHM     2,259  06-01-90 12:56p
ALTSHFTM.SHM      1,654  06-01-90 12:56p   ALTSHFTX.SHM     1,986  06-01-90 12:56p
ALTT    .EDM        474  06-01-90 12:56p   ALTU    .EDM       632  06-01-90 12:56p
ALTU    .EDM     39,934  06-01-90 12:56p   ALTW    .EDM     1,078  06-01-90 12:56p
ALTX    .EDM      4,152  06-01-90 12:56p   AUTOSC  .SHM     3,818  06-01-90 12:56p
CALC    .SHM      1,464  06-01-90 12:56p   CALC1   .SHM     4,876  06-01-90 12:56p
CALC_VAL.SHM      1,918  06-01-90 12:56p   CL_PD   .SHM     1,503  06-01-90 12:56p
CL_PD1  .SHM      2,247  06-01-90 12:56p ▼ CL_PM   .SHM     1,949  06-01-90 12:56p

1 *Mark; 2 Delete; 3 Move/Rename; 4 Select Files; 5 Lock; 6 Look; (F7 to Exit,
7 Other Dir; 8 Copy; 9 Word Srch; N Name Srch; F5 Find Files; 6    F3 for Help)
```

Figure 6-3.   Default File Manager screen with marked files

information into one big drawer, you do not want to put all your computer files in one directory.

The main part of the File Manager screen contains the actual file listings. Along with the name of the file, File Manager displays the file's size and the date and time the file was last saved. If there are more files in the directory than can be listed on screen, an arrow displays in the middle of the screen as shown here:

```
ALTSHFTD.WPM     10,533  06-01-90 12:56p   ALTSHFTE.SHM     2,259  06-01-90 12:56p
ALTSHFTM.SHM      1,654  06-01-90 12:56p   ALTSHFTX.SHM     1,986  06-01-90 12:56p
ALTT    .EDM        474  06-01-90 12:56p   ALTU    .EDM       632  06-01-90 12:56p
ALTU    .EDM     39,934  06-01-90 12:56p   ALTW    .EDM     1,078  06-01-90 12:56p
ALTX    .EDM      4,152  06-01-90 12:56p   ALTX    .WPM       982  06-01-90 12:56p
AUTOSC  .SHM      3,818  06-01-90 12:56p ▼ CALC    .EXE    31,232  06-01-90 12:56p

1 *Mark; 2 Delete; 3 Move/Rename; 4 Select Files; 5 Lock; 6 Look; (F7 to Exit,
7 Other Dir; 8 Copy; 9 Word Srch; N Name Srch; F5 Find Files; 6    F3 for Help)
```

Along with displaying useful information, File Manager also gives you many powerful options to manipulate and organize your files. These 11 options are listed on the bottom of the main screen; they will be covered individually in subsequent sections of this chapter.

Moving Around the File List

When you first enter a file list the cursor rests on the current directory listing. The cursor is a reverse video bar that highlights the entire file or directory. While in the file list the following cursor keys help you quickly move through the directory and file listings:

UP ARROW/DOWN ARROW	Moves up/down one file at a time
LEFT ARROW/RIGHT ARROW	Moves up/down the list in Half Screen mode and left/right in Full Screen mode one file at a time
PGUP/PGDN	Moves up/down one screen at a time
HOME, HOME, UP ARROW	Moves to the current directory listing
HOME, HOME, DOWN ARROW	Moves to the last file in the file list

Displaying a Directory Tree

A directory tree displays the directories and subdirectories of a given drive. Directory trees are useful for viewing the organization of a drive, especially with network drives that contain hundreds of directories and subdirectories. If you are not familiar with the organization of a network drive, you can display the tree list for that drive. To display a tree list in the current File Manager screen:

1. Press CTRL-F3, and the following menu appears at the bottom of the screen:

    0 Rewrite; 1 Half Screen; 2 Full Screen; 3 Tree; 4 File List: 0

2. Press 3 or **T** for Tree.

3. Enter the drive at the filename pattern prompt.

By default the filename pattern lists the current directory or file the cursor is highlighting. If you press ENTER to accept the default, the tree displays the drive where the file or directory is found.

After entering the drive letter, File Manager displays a "Scanning Directory Tree" message along with a "Number Directories Found= x" message, where x is the current number of directories found. The "Number of Directories Found= x" message is updated until File Manager reads the entire drive and displays the directory tree. The process of reading the directories is called *scanning*. Scanning a drive can take anywhere from a few seconds to several minutes depending on the size of the drive and the processing speed of the computer. A "Please Wait" message displays while the drive is being scanned. Once File Manager has scanned the drive, a listing similar to the one in Figure 6-4 appears. A directory tree only displays on one side of the screen so it can show the true structure of a drive.

The information displayed in a tree list is similar to that displayed in a file list, except that the information displayed for used disk space and the number of files is for the directory that is currently highlighted. In Figure 6-4, "Used: 2,688,645" refers to the amount of disk space used by the files in the OFFICE30 directory and "Files: 259" indicates that there are 259 files in the OFFICE30 directory. Using the directory tree

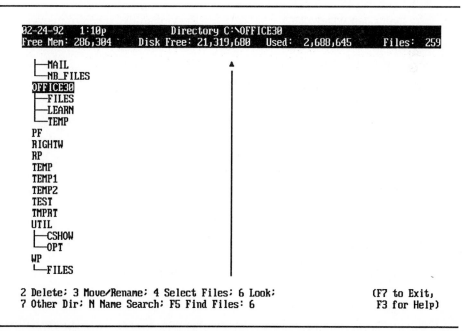

Figure 6-4.   A directory tree

you do not have to list each directory separately to find out how much disk space it uses and how many files it contains.

The options listed at the bottom of the screen are the same as those listed for a file list, with the exception of those options that only work for individual files, such as Mark, Lock, Copy, Word Search, and Find File.

Moving Around the Directory Tree

Within a directory tree, directories are organized in a family structure. Directories one level above another directory are parent directories and directories at the same level are sibling directories. In Figure 6-4 OFFICE30 is the parent directory of FILES, LEARN, and TEMP, which are all sibling directories. This structure exists at all levels of a tree list. While in the tree list the following cursor keys help you quickly move through the directory listings:

UP ARROW/DOWN ARROW	Previous/next directory
LEFT ARROW/RIGHT ARROW	Previous/next directory level
CTRL-LEFT ARROW/RIGHT ARROW	Previous/next sibling directory
PGUP/PGDN	Screen up/down
HOME, HOME, UP ARROW/DOWN ARROW	First/last directory

Moving to a previous or next directory level is especially powerful when you have multiple directory levels. In Figure 6-5, using the LEFT ARROW successively would take you from FM first to TEMP, then to OFFICE30, and finally to the root. After moving up the directory structure with the LEFT ARROW, pressing the RIGHT ARROW would take you back down the exact path to FM.

Marking Files

The first option on the File List screen is Mark. This option is not available on a tree list. Marking files lets you perform a function on

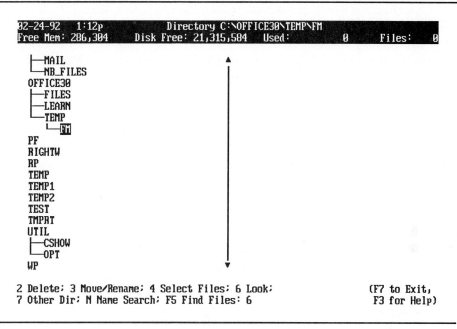

```
02-24-92  1:12p         Directory C:\OFFICE30\TEMP\FM
Free Mem: 206,304   Disk Free: 21,315,584   Used:        0    Files:     0

  ┌─MAIL
  └─NB_FILES
OFFICE30
  ┌─FILES
  ├─LEARN
  └─TEMP
      └─FM
PF
RIGHTW
RP
TEMP
TEMP1
TEMP2
TEST
TMPRT
UTIL
  ┌─CSHOW
  └─OPT
WP

2 Delete; 3 Move/Rename; 4 Select Files; 6 Look;        (F7 to Exit,
7 Other Dir; N Name Search; F5 Find Files: 6            F3 for Help)
```

Figure 6-5.   Directory illustrating moving directory levels

several files at one time. For example, if you wanted to copy three files from a directory on your hard drive to a floppy disk, you could mark the three files and then copy all of them at the same time. Marking files helps you save time and avoids repeating functions over and over again. To mark individual files from a file list:

1. Highlight the file and press **1** or the spacebar, or *****. Once the file is marked, a bolded asterisk appears to the right of the file size.

2. Repeat step 1 for each file you want to mark.

As you can see there are several ways to mark files. Each method of marking a file does exactly the same thing. It is up to you to decide which way is easiest and most convenient. If you need to unmark a file repeat step 1, and the asterisk is removed.

After you have marked files you can use the Delete, Move, Lock, Copy, or Word Search options.

To mark all the files in a directory:

Press ALT-F5 or press HOME, * for Mark/Unmark All.

All the files in the directory are marked. Note that Mark/Unmark All is a toggle; if there were files marked before pressing Mark All, File Manager unmarks the marked files.

Deleting Files and Directories

You can use the Delete feature to delete unwanted files and directories. To delete a file or directory:

1. Highlight the file or directory you want to delete or mark all files you want to delete by pressing 1 or the spacebar or *.

2. Press 2 or **D** for Delete.

3. Type **Y** to delete the file(s) or directory.

As File Manager deletes the file(s) a message displays at the bottom of the screen telling you what files are being deleted. When all files are deleted, a message at the bottom of the screen displays the total number of files deleted.

Deleting Multiple Files

If you are deleting multiple files and answer No to the "Delete marked files? (Y/N)N" prompt, File Manager displays the name of the currently highlighted file and asks if you want to delete that file. This is especially useful if you previously marked files for a different purpose and then decide to delete a single file. Once the file is deleted you can continue with the other tasks you were performing with the marked files.

When deleting several files, you can press Cancel (F1) to stop the deleting process. The number of files deleted displays at the bottom of the screen. File Manager deletes the marked files in the order they appear on the screen, starting from the top and moving from left to right.

Deleting Directories

In order to delete a directory it must be empty (contain no files or subdirectories). If you try to delete a directory that is not empty, File Manager displays the "ERROR: Directory not empty, or is in use" message. If the directory is empty and you are on a network, someone else may be using the directory. If you are using Office PC and think that the directory is empty, it is possible that hidden files exist in the directory. You need to use a utility program to unhide the files and then delete them.

Note: You can only delete one directory at a time because File Manager does not allow you to mark multiple directories.

To delete a directory from the directory tree:

1. Highlight the directory you want to delete.

2. Press **2** or **D** for Delete.

3. Type **Y** to delete the directory.

Once File Manager deletes the directory it is automatically removed from the tree list.

Using the Move/Rename Feature

The Move/Rename feature helps you rearrange files and directories. With the Move/Rename feature you can change the name of a file or directory, move a file or marked files to a different directory, and simultaneously move a file to a different directory and change the name of the file. To rename a file or directory:

1. Highlight the file or directory.

2. Press **3** or **M** for Move/Rename.

3. Type the new filename without a path and press ENTER.

The file or directory you highlighted is then renamed. Renaming a file is useful if you need to give a more descriptive name to certain files. For example if you named all your reports, REPORT.1, REPORT.2, REPORT.3, and so on, after a few days you may forget what is contained in each report. You can use the Rename feature to change the names to COST.RPT, SALES.RPT, and PROFIT.RPT. All this can be done within File Manager with a few easy keystrokes. You can only rename one file at a time.

Sometimes you will need to move a file or files to another directory. You can copy an existing file and then delete it, but with the Move/Rename feature this is done automatically. This is especially useful if you need to move files to make room on your hard drive but still want a copy of the files. To move a file or marked files to another directory:

1. Highlight the file you want to move or mark all files you want to move by pressing **1** or the spacebar or **∗**.

2. Press **3** or **M** for Move/Rename. If you marked files, type **Y** for Yes to move the marked files.

3. Enter the name of the directory to which you want the files moved.

File Manager copies the files to the new directory and deletes them from the original directory.

You can also create a new directory when you move files. Building on the previous example of the report files, let's say you needed to create a special directory for all your report files, to be called RE-PORTS. You would mark all the report files and then type **REPORTS** (the directory name) at the prompt and press ENTER. File Manager would then display the "Create REPORTS? (Y/N)N" prompt. Type **Y** to create the directory. File Manager moves all the marked files to the newly created REPORTS directory.

Along with moving files you can also move and rename a file at the same time. To do so:

1. Highlight the file you want to move and rename.

2. Press **3** or **M** for Move/Rename.

3. Enter the name of the directory you want to move the file to along with the new filename.

File Manager moves the file to the new directory and gives it the new name. You can only move and rename one file at a time. If you mark files and try to move and rename them, File Manager proceeds as if you are trying to create a new directory.

Locking Files

Within File Manager you can lock a file or lock marked files with a password. Locking files encrypts the file, so the only way you can look at it or retrieve it is to know the password. File Locking adds security to confidential files. If you are on a network and save files in a shared network directory, locking files ensures that other network users will not be able to retrieve and modify files if they do not know the password. To lock a file:

1. Highlight the file you want to lock.

2. Press **5** or **k** for Lock.

3. Press **1** or **L** for Lock.

4. Enter a password. The password can be up to 80 characters long.

5. Reenter the password. File Manager asks you to reenter the password to ensure you entered it correctly the first time.

You can lock multiple files with the same password by first marking the files and then following the preceding steps. Once you have locked a file it cannot be locked again. If you try to lock a file that has been locked, File Manager appears to lock it, but it retains the original password. This feature adds extra security to locking files.

File Manager only lets you unlock a file if you know the password. To unlock a file:

1. Highlight the file you want to unlock.

2. Press **5** or **k** for Lock.

3. Press **2** or **U** for Unlock.

4. Enter the password.

File Manager displays a brief message that it is unlocking the file. You can unlock multiple files with the same password by marking the files and following the preceding steps.

Looking at Files and Directories

One powerful feature within File Manager is the Look feature. With Look you can view the contents of a directory or a file without having to retrieve the file into a program. To look at a file:

1. Highlight the file.

2. Press **6** or **L** for Look or press ENTER.

File Manager displays the name of the file along with the size of the file at the top of the screen. If the file is a text file, the text along with some of the codes (bold, underline, indent, tab) are displayed as shown here:

```
Filename: C:\OFF30\TEXT.DOC                          File Size:    1,875
This is how a document displays when viewing it with the Look feature in File
Manager.  Many of the text attributes will be displayed.
This is Bold.
This is Underline.
        This is indented text.
            This is text with tabs.
```

If the file is a macro, File Manager displays the macro summary as shown here:

```
Advanced Macro Summary

    Interpretation:    Shell

    Macro Filename:    ADD_LST

    Macro Description: Add Phone Message info to ADDRESS.NB
```

There may be occasions when you forget exactly what a macro does; the macro summary displayed in the Look screen can help you determine the macro's function if you entered a description when you defined the macro. For this reason it is a good idea to enter descriptions when defining macros.

File Manager displays the contents of any other type of file (.EXE, .COM, and so on) in hexadecimal form as shown here, where FM.EXE is displayed:

```
Filename: C:\OFFICE30\FM.EXE                          File Size:   75,776

00000000: 4D 5A CD 00 94 00 00 00   20 00 9B 04 FF FF E0 16  ╥Z=.ö... .¢. α.
00000010: 00 00 00 00 12 00 25 12   1C 00 00 00 00 00 00 00  ╓.....%. ........
00000020: 00 00 00 00 00 00 00 00   00 00 00 00 00 00 00 00  ........ ........
00000030: 00 00 00 00 00 00 00 00   00 00 00 00 00 00 00 00  ........ ........
00000040: 00 00 00 00 00 00 00 00   00 00 00 00 00 00 00 00  ........ ........
```

File Manager displays the addresses on the left, the hexadecimal codes in the middle of the screen, and the ASCII equivalents on the right.

Moving Around the Look Screen

When you first enter the Look screen the cursor is in the upper-left corner. The following keys move the cursor within the Look screen:

UP ARROW/DOWN ARROW	Moves up/down one line at a time
SCREEN UP/SCREEN DOWN (+/− on the numeric keypad)	Moves up/down one screen at a time
S	Scrolls the file until you press S again
HOME, HOME, UP ARROW/DOWN ARROW	Moves to the beginning or end of the file

Searching in the Look Screen

If you are not sure the file you are looking at contains the information you need, you can search for specific words or word patterns with the Search feature. To use the Search feature while looking at a file:

1. Press F2 for Forward Search or SHIFT-F2 for Reverse Search. Forward Search searches from the cursor forward, and Reverse Search searches from the cursor backward.

2. Enter the word or word pattern you want to find.

If the word or word pattern is found, the cursor moves to the first occurrence of the word and displays it in reverse video. You can repeat the search by pressing Forward Search (F2) or Reverse Search (SHIFT-F2) twice. If the word or word pattern exists on the line more than once, File Manager only finds the first occurrence. For example if you are searching for the word "red" in the following line:

The little red fox and the little red hen

File Manager only finds the first "red" during the search.

Using the Clipboard in the Look Screen

While in the Look screen you can block text and save the information to the Shell Clipboard. Once you save information to the Clipboard you can retrieve it into another Shell-compatible program, such as Notebook, WordPerfect, or Calendar. To save information to the Clipboard:

1. Highlight the file containing the information you want to save to the Clipboard.

2. Press **6** or **L** for Look or press ENTER to display the contents of the file.

3. Use the arrow keys to move the cursor to the portion of the text you want to save.

4. Press ALT-F4 for Block and move the cursor to the end of the text you want to save. The text appears highlighted on the screen. Block is only active in the Look screen.

5. Press CTRL-F1 for Shell.

6. Press **2** or **S** to save the information to the Clipboard or press **3** or **A** to append the information to any existing information in the Clipboard.

File Manager saves all codes within the text to the Clipboard. File Manager does not save any formatting codes that come before the text—such as styles, margin settings, or tab settings—to the Clipboard. Codes within the text, such as bold, underline, and center, are saved to the Clipboard.

You can use the following cursor keys to block text while in Look:

UP ARROW/DOWN ARROW	Blocks entire line of text above or below the cursor
HOME, HOME, UP ARROW/DOWN ARROW	Blocks from the cursor to the beginning or end of the text

The LEFT ARROW/RIGHT ARROW keys do not block, they only move you to the beginning or end of a line.

Changing Directories with Look

You can use Look to change directories and view the files in another directory. This is a fast and easy way to move to different directories. To change to a different directory:

1. Highlight the directory in the file list.

2. Press **6** or **L** for Look or press ENTER.

By default the new directory is automatically displayed. If you want File Manager to prompt you for the filename pattern you can change the Directory Look Method in the Setup menu to Prompt (SHIFT-F1, 5, 2).

Changing Directories

There are several ways to change directories within File Manager. When you change a directory the contents of the new directory replace what was previously displayed on the screen. To change directories using the Other Directory option:

1. Press **7** or **O** for Other Directory, and the "New directory:" prompt appears.

2. Type the path and name of the new directory and press ENTER. The "Filename Pattern:" prompt appears.

3. Press ENTER.

When you use the Other Directory option the new directory becomes the default directory. The default directory is displayed each time you select the Copy, Move/Rename, or Other Directory option.

If you change directories while displaying a directory tree, the contents of the list only change if you enter a new drive letter. If you enter the name of a directory that exists on the drive that is currently displayed, File Manager displays the same list with the directory you just entered highlighted.

You can also use the Look feature to change directories; for information on this feature see "Looking at Files and Directories," earlier in this chapter.

Copying Files

With File Manager you can copy a single file or all marked files to a specified drive or directory. When you copy a file, a duplicate file is created in the specified drive or directory. Copying files is useful when you need to copy files to a floppy disk and you do not want to delete the files from the hard drive. To copy a single file:

1. Highlight the file you want to copy.

2. Press **8** or **C** for Copy. The "Copy file To:" prompt appears.

3. Type in the drive or directory where you want the file copied.

If you need to copy several files in the same directory:

1. Mark all files you want to copy by pressing **1** or SPACEBAR, or typing *****.

2. Press **8** or **C** for Copy. The "Copy marked files? (Y/N)N" prompt appears.

3. Type **Y** for Yes.

4. Type in the drive or directory where you want the files copied.

As File Manager copies the file(s), a message displays at the bottom of the screen telling you what files are being copied and to where they are being copied. After all the files are copied, a message displays the total number of files copied.

If a file by the same name already exists in the destination drive or directory, the "Replace *filename*? (Y/N)N" prompt appears. Type **Y** to replace the file with the file you are copying or type **N** to keep the original file. If you do not want File Manager to prompt you when a file by the same name exists in the destination directory, you can set the Confirm Replace option to No (SHIFT-F1, 2 for a permanent setting or SHIFT-F8, 9 for a temporary setting). If this option is set to No, File Manager overwrites any files with the same name during the copying, moving, and renaming process without a prompt.

Copying Files to a Floppy Disk

You can use File Manager to copy all the files in one directory to a floppy disk to give to a client, boss, or secretary:

1. Press **7** or **O** for Other Directory.

2. Type the name of the directory where the files are located and press ENTER.

3. Press ALT-F5 to mark all files in the directory.

4. Press **8** or **C** for Copy.

5. Type **Y** to copy all marked files.

6. Type in the drive letter where your floppy disk is located and press ENTER.

File Manager copies all marked files to the disk.

Copying Multiple Files

If you are copying multiple files and answer No to the "Copy marked files?" prompt, File Manager displays the name of the currently highlighted file and asks you to enter the destination drive or directory. This is especially useful if you previously marked files for a different purpose and then decide to copy a single file. Once the file is copied you can continue with the other tasks you were performing with the marked files.

When copying several files you can press Cancel (F1) to stop the copying process. The number of files copied displays at the bottom of the screen. File Manager copies the files in the order they appear on the screen, starting from the top and moving from left to right.

Creating a New Directory with Copy

If you want to copy marked files to a new directory, you can create a new directory during the copying process. When prompted for the destination directory, enter the name of the new directory. The "Create *directory name*? (Y/N)N" prompt appears. Type **Y** to have File Manager create the new directory and copy the files into it.

Changing the Default Copy Destination

When copying files, File Manager displays the default directory as the destination directory. You can change the default copy directory with the following keystrokes.

1. Press **7** or **O** for Other Directory.

2. Type the name of the new directory.

3. Press ENTER.

4. Press F1 for Cancel.

The next time you press **8** or **C** for Copy the directory you entered in step 2 appears. This only changes the default directory for copying, which is very useful if you need to copy several files from different directories to one location and do not want to change the default directory.

Using Word Search

If you want a listing of all the files containing a certain word or *word pattern* you can use the Word Search feature. A word pattern is a special way of limiting exactly what words are found during a search. For more information on word patterns see the following section. When you use Word Search, File Manager lists only those files in the current directory that contain the word or word pattern you entered. Word Search is particularly useful if you have forgotten the name of a file, but you do remember a key word or phrase contained in the file. For example, if you wanted to find all the files that contained the name of your client, Tom, you would

1. Press **9** or **W** for Word Search.
2. Type **Tom** and press ENTER.

File Manager displays a "Searching *filename*" message and then displays the number of files in which the word or word pattern is found. File Manager then redisplays the directory list with only those files containing the word "Tom."

Note: If you mark files before performing a word search, File Manager only searches the marked files and then unmarks the files that do not contain the word or word pattern.

If you want to see exactly where the word or word pattern occurs in a file you can use the Look feature and view the contents of the file. File Manager highlights the word or word pattern in the Look screen.

Using Word Patterns

A word pattern is a way of limiting what files File Manager displays. Word patterns can be used when you start File Manager, change directories, enter a filename pattern, or perform a word search.

Using Wildcard Characters in Word Patterns

File Manager uses two wildcard characters: the question mark (?) and the asterisk (*). The ? represents one character and the * represents zero or more characters. A zero character simply means there is no character. The following example illustrates the use of the ? wildcard. Let's say you wanted to list all your sales report files and had given them names such as SALES.RP1, SALES.RP2, SALES.RP3. You could quickly do so with the following steps:

1. Press **7** or **O** for Other Directory.

2. Enter the name of the directory where the reports are located.

3. When prompted for the filename pattern, enter **SALES.RP?** You do not have to enter the directory again.

After entering the filename pattern a screen similar to the one in Figure 6-6 displays.

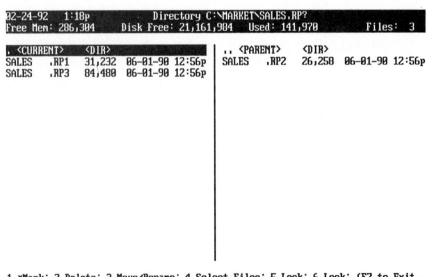

```
02-24-92   1:18p             Directory C:\MARKET\SALES.RP?
Free Mem: 286,304      Disk Free: 21,161,984   Used: 141,970         Files:  3

. <CURRENT>   <DIR>                    .. <PARENT>   <DIR>
SALES   .RP1   31,232  06-01-90 12:56p  SALES   .RP2   26,258  06-01-90 12:56p
SALES   .RP3   84,480  06-01-90 12:56p

    1 *Mark; 2 Delete; 3 Move/Rename; 4 Select Files; 5 Lock; 6 Look; (F7 to Exit,
    7 Other Dir; 8 Copy; 9 Word Srch; N Name Srch; F5 Find Files; 6     F3 for Help)
```

Figure 6-6.   Result of wildcard search for SALES.RP?

The * wildcard is a more global character in that it represents zero or more characters. For example, if you entered **REPORT.***, File Manager would list all files that have a REPORT prefix and any combination of extensions, including no extension. The following example illustrates when you might want to use the * wildcard. Let's say this time you need to list all your reports. Because each report file has a different filename prefix you need to use both the * and the ? wildcards. To list all of your reports:

1. Press **7** or **O** for Other Directory.

2. Enter the name of the directory where the reports are located.

3. When prompted for the filename pattern, enter ***.RP?**

After entering the filename pattern a screen similar to the one in Figure 6-7 displays. The directory name at the top of the screen lists the directory along with the filename pattern.

```
02-24-92   1:23p            Directory C:\MARKET\*.RP?
Free Mem: 286,304      Disk Free: 20,987,904   Used: 304,559           Files:  7

. <CURRENT>    <DIR>               .. <PARENT>    <DIR>
PROGREE .RP2  111,104  06-01-90 12:56p   PROGRESS.RP1   10,509  06-01-90 12:56p
RESEARCH.RP1   10,533  06-01-90 12:56p   RESEARCH.RP2   30,443  06-01-90 12:56p
SALES   .RP1   31,232  06-01-90 12:56p   SALES   .RP2   26,258  06-01-90 12:56p
SALES   .RP3   84,480  06-01-90 12:56p



1 *Mark; 2 Delete; 3 Move/Rename; 4 Select Files; 5 Lock; 6 Look; (F7 to Exit,
7 Other Dir; 8 Copy; 9 Word Srch; N Name Srch; F5 Find Files: 6    F3 for Help)
```

Figure 6-7.   Result of wildcard search for *.RP?

You can also use wildcard characters when performing a word search. The following examples illustrate how wildcard characters work with a word search.

User Input	Result
t?p	This lists all files with a word containing one character between the t and p such as, top, tip, and tap.
work*	This lists all files with the word "work" followed by zero or more characters such as, work, works, working, worker, worked, and worklog.

Wildcard characters are very powerful and can help you save time when listing directories and when doing word searches.

Using Logical Operators in a Word Search

Sometimes the word or word pattern you are looking for is not clear cut. For example, you may want to find files with two words that do not always display together, or you may want to find files that do not contain a certain word. These and other situations are handled by File Manager's logical operators. Logical operators are text strings that tell File Manager that certain conditions exist. The following logical operators are available when performing a word search.

Operator	Text String	Function
AND	; or a space	This finds files that contain the word pattern that is on each side of the ; or space. For example, enter **Defendant; Charles Manson** to find all files with both defendant and Charles Manson.
OR		This finds files that contain the word pattern that is on each side of the , or files that contain either word pattern. For example, enter **Profits,Deficits** to find files with both profits and deficits or files with either word.

| NOT | ~ | This finds files that do not contain the word following the tilde. For example, enter ~**April** to find all files that do not contain the word April. |
| BUT NOT | - | This finds files that contain the word pattern before the hyphen, but not the word pattern after the hyphen. For example, enter **April-memo** to find all files that contain the word April, but not the word memo. |

Logical operators can be combined to limit the search even further.

Using Name Search

The Name Search feature provides a quick and easy way to move to a file. When a directory listing is quite large, using the cursor keys to move to a file would be tedious. With the Name Search feature you can move directly to a file as long as you know the first few letters of the filename. To use Name Search in a file list:

1. Press **N** or F2 for Name Search from a file list.

2. Type the first letter of the filename.

3. Continue typing the remaining letters of the filename, until the file is highlighted.

4. Press SPACEBAR or the LEFT ARROW/RIGHT ARROW keys to end the name search.

When performing a Name Search in a file list, directories are searched only if you enter **/** before typing a letter. You can use the Name Search feature while in a tree list. Follow the preceding steps, replacing the filename with the name of the directory. File Manager

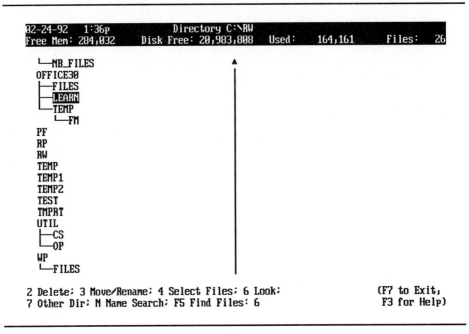

Figure 6-8.   Name Search in a directory tree

only searches the directories that are below the same parent directory. For example, in Figure 6-8 where the cursor is highlighting LEARN, only the FILES, LEARN, TEMP, and FM subdirectories would be searched.

Using Find Files

Find Files is another File Manager feature that helps you quickly locate files. Find Files searches the current drive for all files matching the specified filename pattern. Find Files is useful if you know a filename or part of a filename but do not remember in which directory it is stored. To use Find Files:

1. Press F5 or **F** for Find Files.

2. Enter a filename or filename pattern. You are asked if you want to send the list of files found to the printer.

3. Type **Y** if you want to print the list or type **N** if you only want to view the list on screen.

After Find Files, all the files (including the entire path) containing the filename pattern are displayed on the screen along with the size of the file and date and time the file was last saved, as shown in Figure 6-9. At the bottom of the list, File Manager briefly displays the total number of files found. If there are more files than can display on the screen, the first files found scroll past and only those at the end of the list remain on screen. If this happens, you may want to narrow your filename pattern. To return to the previous file list, press any key.

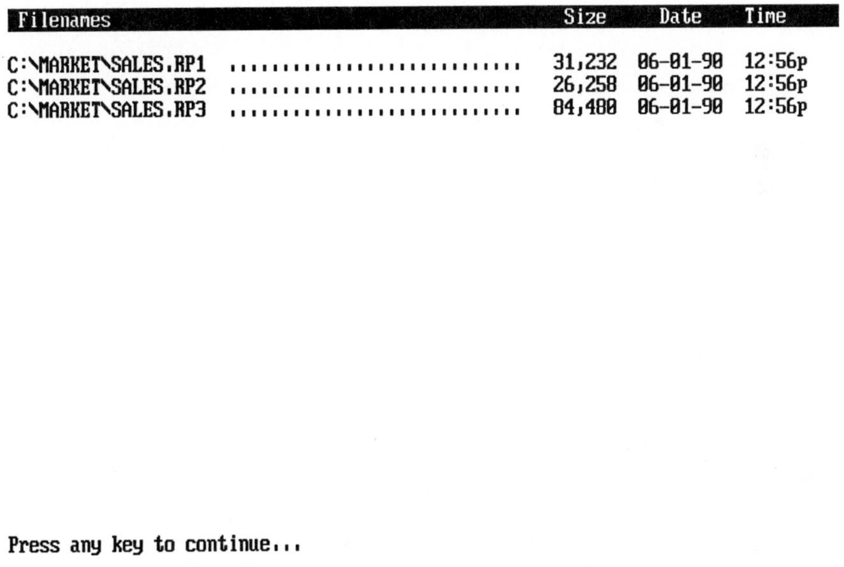

```
Filenames                                      Size    Date    Time
C:\MARKET\SALES.RP1  ...........................  31,232  06-01-90  12:56p
C:\MARKET\SALES.RP2  ...........................  26,258  06-01-90  12:56p
C:\MARKET\SALES.RP3  ...........................  84,480  06-01-90  12:56p




Press any key to continue...
```

Figure 6-9.   Result of Find Files

Using the Date Feature

The Date feature lets you list files saved during a specified time period. This may be useful if you forgot the name of a file but remember approximately when you last modified it, or if you want to check for old files that are cluttering up your directories. To change the date:

1. From a file list press **4, S,** or SHIFT-F8 for Select Files.

2. Press **2** or **D** for Date.

3. Type **Y** for Yes.

4. Enter the earliest date for which you want files listed.

5. Enter the last date for which you want files listed.

6. Press F7 for Exit to return to the file list.

When you return to the file list only those files saved between the specified dates appear. The date on all files is the date the file was last saved. The files are not sorted by date. The only function File Manager performs with this option is not displaying the files that do not match the date specifications entered on the Select Files screen.

You can enter a date on the From line and leave the To line set to All as shown in Figure 6-10 to list all files from that date forward. The example in Figure 6-10 would list all files dated from 2-1-90 to the present. If you enter an ending date only, File Manager lists all files up to the date entered on the To line.

Displaying Directories in Half Screen Mode

File Manager can display two directories on the same screen side by side. Displaying directories side by side is useful when comparing the contents of one directory to another. For example, if you wanted to see if the dates of the files on a floppy disk were the same as the dates of the files on the hard drive, you could display these directories in Half

```
Select Files - List 1

     1 - Filename Pattern:        C:\OFFICE30\*.*

     2 - Date                     YES
         From   (MM-DD-YY):       2-1-90
         To     (MM-DD-YY):       (All)

     Sort files by:               Filename
         3 - Filename
         4 - Extension
         5 - Date & Time
         6 - Size

     7 - Display Mode:            File List

     8 - Directory Look Method:   Prompt

     9 - Confirm Replace:         YES



Selection: 0
```

Figure 6-10.   Date feature selecting all files from 2-1-90

Screen mode. Instead of having to switch screens, you can see both directories at the same time. To change to Half Screen mode:

1. Press CTRL-F3 for Screen.

2. Press **1** or **H** for Half Screen.

Note: You can also switch between Full and Half Screen mode by pressing F8.

If you had two directories listed (one in both screens), they would both appear as shown in Figure 6-11. If you only had one directory listed, a screen similar to the one in Figure 6-12 would appear. To list another directory on the other side of the screen:

1. Press SHIFT-F3 or TAB.

2. Enter the filename pattern.

```
┌─────────────────────────────────────┐┌─────────────────────────────────────┐
│           C:\OFFICE30\*.*            ││         C:\OFFICE30\LEARN\*.*        │
│ Disk Free      Disk Used      Files  ││ Disk Free      Disk Used      Files  │
│ 20,977,664     2,690,181        259  ││ 20,977,664       164,161         26  │
├─────────────────────────────────────┤├─────────────────────────────────────┤
│. <CURRENT>    <DIR>                  ◄│◄ . <CURRENT>    <DIR>                 │
│.. <PARENT>    <DIR>                  │◄ .. <PARENT>    <DIR>                 │
│FILES    .     <DIR>    02-24-92  1:10p│ ADDRESS .NB    3,658  05-03-90 12:21p│
│LEARN    .     <DIR>    05-14-90  9:56a◄ ADVSALES.LRN   1,970  05-03-90 12:21p│
│TEMP     .     <DIR>    02-24-92  1:10p│ ART     .CAL   1,508  05-03-90 12:21p│
│ADD_CONT.SHM   2,403    06-01-90 12:56p◄ ART     .NB    9,814  05-03-90 12:21p│
│ADD_LST .SHM   2,317    06-01-90 12:56p│ ASHSALES.PLN   2,641  05-03-90 12:21p│
│ADD_MSG .SHM   1,129    06-01-90 12:56p◄ CHARMAP .NB   44,206  05-03-90 12:21p│
│ALTC    .EDM   1,692    06-01-90 12:56p│ CHECKOUT.NB    3,147  05-03-90 12:21p│
│ALTD    .EDM     678    06-01-90 12:56p◄ CLIENT  .NB    3,615  05-03-90 12:21p│
│ALTE    .EDM   2,920    06-01-90 12:56p│ CONTACT .NB    6,239  05-03-90 12:21p│
│ALTF    .EDM   4,568    06-01-90 12:56p◄ COUNCIL .ASG   1,024  05-03-90 12:21p│
│ALTG    .EDM   1,216    06-01-90 12:56p│ COUNCIL .DAT   3,584  05-03-90 12:21p│
│ALTI    .EDM   1,351    06-01-90 12:56p◄ COUNCIL .IND   4,096  05-03-90 12:21p│
│ALTL    .EDM   4,664    06-01-90 12:56p│ COUNCIL .STR   4,096  05-03-90 12:21p│
│ALTM    .EDM   4,358    06-01-90 12:56p◄ COUNCIL .TOD     512  05-03-90 12:21p│
│ALTN    .EDM   1,290    06-01-90 12:56p│ COUNCIL .TXX   5,120  05-03-90 12:21p│
│ALTO    .EDM     322    06-01-90 12:56p▼ EMPLOYEE.NB    2,943  05-03-90 12:21p│
└─────────────────────────────────────┘└─────────────────────────────────────┘
```

1 *Mark; 2 Delete; 3 Move/Rename; 4 Select Files; 5 Lock; 6 Look; (F7 to Exit,
7 Other Dir; 8 Copy; 9 Word Srch; N Name Srch; F5 Find Files; 6   F3 for Help)

Figure 6-11.   Half Screen mode with two directories

Note: You can permanently change the screen display defaults with
the Display option on the Setup menu (SHIFT-F1, 3).

In Half Screen mode, arrows divide the screen and point to the directory that is currently active as shown in Figure 6-11. To switch between
the two screens press TAB or SHIFT-F3.

Using Half Screen Mode with a File List and a Directory Tree

You can display both a file list and a directory tree while in Half Screen
mode as shown in Figure 6-13. When displaying both list types you can
move down the tree list and display the contents of the highlighted
directory on the other side of the screen. If Directory Tree Look
Method is set to Automatic (SHIFT-F1, 4) the directory automatically displays on the opposite screen. If it is set to Manual, you must press ENTER
to display the highlighted directory on the opposite screen.

```
                 C:\OFFICE30\*.*
     Disk Free        Disk Used          Files
    20,973,568        2,690,181            259

   .  <CURRENT>     <DIR>                            <
   ..  <PARENT>     <DIR>                            <
   FILES    .       <DIR>      02-24-92   1:10p
   LEARN    .       <DIR>      05-14-90   9:56a      <
   TEMP     .       <DIR>      02-24-92   1:10p
   ADD_CONT.SHM     2,403      06-01-90  12:56p      <
   ADD_LST .SHM     2,317      06-01-90  12:56p
   ADD_MSG .SHM     1,129      06-01-90  12:56p      <
   ALTC    .EDM     1,692      06-01-90  12:56p
   ALTD    .EDM       678      06-01-90  12:56p      <
   ALTE    .EDM     2,920      06-01-90  12:56p
   ALTF    .EDM     4,568      06-01-90  12:56p      <
   ALTG    .EDM     1,216      06-01-90  12:56p
   ALTI    .EDM     1,351      06-01-90  12:56p      <
   ALTL    .EDM     4,664      06-01-90  12:56p
   ALTM    .EDM     4,358      06-01-90  12:56p      <
   ALTN    .EDM     1,290      06-01-90  12:56p
   ALTO    .EDM       322      06-01-90  12:56p ▼
```

1 *Mark; 2 Delete; 3 Move/Rename; 4 Select Files; 5 Lock; 6 Look; (F7 to Exit,
7 Other Dir; 8 Copy; 9 Word Srch; N Name Srch; F5 Find Files: 6   F3 for Help)

Figure 6-12.   Half Screen mode with only one directory

```
        C:\OFFICE30                          C:\OFFICE30\*.*
  Disk Free     Disk Used     Files     Disk Free     Disk Used     Files
 20,971,520     2,690,181      259     20,971,520     2,690,181      259

    └─NB_FILES                      ▲   .  <CURRENT>     <DIR>
 OFFICE30                          <   ..  <PARENT>     <DIR>                      <
    ├─FILES                            FILES    .       <DIR>      02-24-92   1:10p
    ├─LEARN                        <   LEARN    .       <DIR>      05-14-90   9:56a
    └─TEMP                             TEMP     .       <DIR>      02-24-92   1:10p
       └─FM                        <   ADD_CONT.SHM     2,403      06-01-90  12:56p
 PF                                    ADD_LST .SHM     2,317      06-01-90  12:56p
 RP                                <   ADD_MSG .SHM     1,129      06-01-90  12:56p
 RW                                    ALTC    .EDM     1,692      06-01-90  12:56p
 TEMP                              <   ALTD    .EDM       678      06-01-90  12:56p
 TEMP1                                 ALTE    .EDM     2,920      06-01-90  12:56p
 TEMP2                             <   ALTF    .EDM     4,568      06-01-90  12:56p
 TEST                                  ALTG    .EDM     1,216      06-01-90  12:56p
 TMPRT                             <   ALTI    .EDM     1,351      06-01-90  12:56p
 UTIL                                  ALTL    .EDM     4,664      06-01-90  12:56p
    ├─CS                           <   ALTM    .EDM     4,358      06-01-90  12:56p
    └─OP                               ALTN    .EDM     1,290      06-01-90  12:56p
 WP                                ▼   ALTO    .EDM       322      06-01-90  12:56p
```

2 Delete; 3 Move/Rename; 4 Select Files; 6 Look;   (F7 to Exit,
7 Other Dir; N Name Search; F5 Find Files: 6   F3 for Help)

Figure 6-13.   A file list and a directory tree in Half Screen mode

You can copy and move files using a file list and a tree list. To copy or move a file to the directory displayed in a file list to a directory displayed in a tree list:

1. Highlight the file you want to move or copy.

2. Press 8 or **C** for Copy or press **3** or **M** for Move/Rename.

3. When the "Copy file To:" or "Move/Rename To:" prompt displays, press TAB or SHIFT-F3 to move to the tree list. The file in the file list is highlighted.

4. Move the cursor to the directory where you want to copy or move the files to and press ENTER twice.

File Manager copies or moves the file to the specified directory and returns the cursor to the file list. You can use this method with marked files as well. Using this method of manipulating files is fast and efficient since you do not have to remember or type in directory names.

Changing the Directory Look Method

The Directory Look Method determines what happens when you press Look on a directory name while in a file list or a directory tree.

File List

The default Directory Look Method for a file list is No Prompt. With No Prompt, File Manager displays the contents of a directory as soon as you highlight it and press ENTER. If the Directory Look Method for a file list is set to Prompt, you must enter a filename pattern after pressing ENTER on the directory name. If you usually list all the files in a directory, you would want to set the Directory Look Method for a file list to No Prompt; if you use filename patterns frequently to list files, you should set the Directory Look Method to Prompt. To set the default Directory Look Method for a file list:

1. Press SHIFT-F1 for Setup

2. Press **5** or **F** for File List.

3. Press **1** or **N** for No Prompt, or press **2** or **P** for Prompt.

To set the Directory Look Method temporarily until you exit File Manager from the file list:

1. Press **4** or **S** or SHIFT-F8 for Select Files.

2. Press **8** or **L** for Directory Look Method.

3. Press **1** or **N** for No Prompt, or press **2** or **P** for Prompt.

Directory Tree

The default Directory Look Method for a directory tree is Automatic. With the Automatic setting, File Manager displays the contents of a directory as soon as you highlight it while in a directory tree. File Manager displays the directory on the other screen. If the Directory Look Method is set to Manual, you must press ENTER to display the contents of the directory. This option is most useful when you are using Half Screen mode and can see the contents without switching screens. Be aware that if you use the Automatic setting it may slow down your cursor movement within a directory tree due to the time it takes to display each directory. This is most noticeable if you have extremely large directories. To set the default Directory Look Method:

1. Press SHIFT-F1 for Setup

2. Press **4** or **T** for Directory Tree.

3. Press **1** or **M** for Manual or press **2** or **A** for Automatic.

To set the Directory Look Method temporarily until you exit File Manager from the file list:

1. Press **4** or **S** or SHIFT-F8 for Select Files.

2. Press **8** or **L** for Directory Look Method.

3. Press **1** or **M** for Manual, or press **2** or **A** for Automatic.

Printing in File Manager

You may want a printed copy of the contents of a directory or the structure of a drive. With the File Manager Print feature you can print a file list or a tree list. To use the Print feature:

1. Press SHIFT-F7 for Print.

2. Press **2** or **S** for Select Print Device. The following prompt appears:

Print Device (1 LPT1; 2 LPT2; 3 LPT3; 4 Device or Filename): 4

3. Type **1**, **2**, or **3** to select the correct printer port or type **4** to select the device or filename. You only have to select the printer port the first time you print; File Manager will then use that setting until you change it.

4. Press **1** or **P** for Print.

File Manager prints the list on which the cursor is resting. If you have two directories displayed on the screen, File Manager only prints the directory on which the cursor is resting. File Manager prints all the heading information and file information as shown in Figure 6-14, but does not print the options at the bottom of the File Manager screen.

When printing a tree list the connecting lines are not printed. However, the directories are indented to show their different levels. If

```
            02-24-92  15:14p            Directory C:\MARKET\*.*
Free Mem:   277568   Disk Free: 20918272   Used:    304559 Files:        7

. <CURRENT>    <DIR>                  .. <PARENT>    <DIR>
PROGREE .RP2   111104  06-01-90 12:56   PROGRESS.RP1    10509  06-01-90 12:56
RESEARCH.RP1    10533  06-01-90 12:56   RESEARCH.RP2    30443  06-01-90 12:56
SALES   .RP1    31232  06-01-90 12:56   SALES   .RP2    26258  06-01-90 12:56
SALES   .RP3    84480  06-01-90 12:56
```

Figure 6-14.   Printed file list

you want to have the lines printed you can use the Shell Screen Copy feature and retrieve the tree list into WordPerfect to print.

1. Press ALT-SHIFT-MINUS.

2. Press **1** or **R** for Rectangle.

3. Position the cursor at the very top of the tree list, and then press ENTER to anchor the cursor.

4. Use the DOWN ARROW key to move the cursor to the last directory displayed on the current screen as shown here:

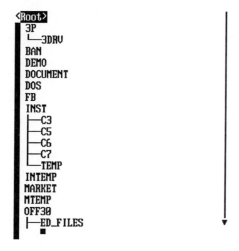

Make sure you do not highlight the options at the bottom of the screen.

5. Use the RIGHT ARROW key to move the cursor to the center line that divides the screen.

6. Press ENTER.

7. Press **1** or **S** for Save. If your tree takes up more than one screen, continue with steps 8 to 11.

8. Use the DOWN ARROW key to display the remaining files.

9. Repeat steps 1 through 6.

10. Press **2** or **A** for Append.

11. Repeat steps 8 to 10 until all the directories in the tree list have been saved to the Clipboard.

Once the information is saved to the Clipboard, enter WordPerfect and press CTRL-F1 for Clipboard and press **2** or **R** for Retrieve Clipboard. You can then send the information to the printer with SHIFT-F7, 1.

Using Program Launch

Program Launch allows you to assign specific actions to a keystroke and perform them on designated files while running File Manager under Shell. Program Launch does not work if File Manager is not running under Shell. With the Program Launch functions you can automate many of your daily file-management tasks.

Using Default Program Launch Functions

File Manager comes with default Program Launch functions for Edit, Execute, and Print. The following list outlines the functions and the keys for the Default Program Launch functions.

Function	Key
Edits a file	F6 or E
Executes a file	F9 or X
Prints a file	SHIFT-F7 or P

Default Edit Function

You can highlight a file and use the Edit function to start the *source program* from the Shell menu for the highlighted file. A source program is the program in which the file was created . The Edit function works with the following files: Calendar, Editor macro files, Notebook (5.0 or later format), PlanPerfect worksheets, WordPerfect, DrawPerfect or PlanPerfect graphics files, and WordPerfect documents (5.0 or later). The Edit function reads the header information in the highlighted file in order to know what source program it should use to edit the file. To use the Edit function:

1. Highlight the file you want to edit.

2. Press F6 or **E**.

The source program starts, and the file you were highlighting is retrieved. After you exit the source program you are returned to File Manager with the same file highlighted. An example of when you might want to use the Edit function is to retrieve a document into Word-Perfect. You can use File Manager to help find the file and then press F6 or **E** to bring the file into WordPerfect. This avoids having to exit File Manager and start WordPerfect, thus saving you keystrokes and time.

Using the Edit Function with Resident Programs   If you try to edit a file whose source program is already resident, File Manager performs a series of checks before retrieving the file.

If the program has two or more editing windows (as in Word-Perfect, DrawPerfect, PlanPerfect, and Editor), File Manager checks the other window and if it is empty retrieves the file into that window. If the second window has a file, File Manager checks to see if the file in the first window has been modified since you retrieved it. If it has not been modified, File Manager retrieves the file selected in File Manager. If the file has been modified, you are asked if you want to save the file. After saving or exiting the file, the screen is cleared and the new file is retrieved.

When using the Edit function on a Calendar file, File Manager asks if you want to replace the old file with the new file or merge the two files.

In order to perform the above checking methods, File Manager uses several Shell macros. The path to these macros should be entered in the Macro Directory option for the Shell Setup options. The following list outlines the names of these macros and the program for which they are used.

Macro Name	Program Name
ED{CL}.SHM	Calendar
ED{DR}.SHM	DrawPerfect
ED{ED}.SHM	Editor
ED{NB}.SHM	Notebook
ED{PL}.SHM	PlanPerfect
ED{WP}.SHM	WordPerfect

Execute Function

The default Execute function executes any .COM, .EXE, or .BAT files. It also executes macro files created in any WordPerfect product. To use the Execute function:

1. Highlight the desired .EXE, .COM, or .BAT file.

2. Press F9 or **X**.

After you exit the program you are returned to File Manager. The Execute function is especially useful with batch files. If you see a *.BAT file while in File Manager and don't remember what it does, you can press F9 or **X** to run the batch file and be returned to File Manager.

When using the Execute function with a Shell macro, you can only execute Shell macros that were defined from the Shell menu. After executing a macro the program is not left resident, and you are not returned to File Manager. Once you press Execute, complete control is given to the macro.

Print Function

The default Print function executes a Shell macro that starts the source program of the highlighted file, retrieves the file into the program, prints the file, and returns you to File Manager. The default Print function works with the same types of files as the Edit function. To use the Print function:

1. Highlight the file you want to print.

2. Press SHIFT-F7 or **P**.

The highlighted file is retrieved into the correct program and printed.

Creating Custom Program Launch Functions

If the default Program Launch functions do not meet all your needs, you can define your own Program Launch functions. For example if you use Lotus 1-2-3 and want to be able to retrieve your spreadsheets into the program using the Program Launch Edit function, you could define your own Program Launch for those specific files. See the example later in this section for specific instructions.

Program Launch functions are assigned to filename extensions you select in the Setup Program Launch screen. You can define Program Launch functions for up to 20 separate filename extensions. Program Launch functions can be assigned to the following Program Launch keys listed here:

Function	**Key**
Edit	F6 or E
Execute	F9 or X
Look	ENTER or 6
Print	SHIFT-F7 or P

Although the function is given a descriptive name, you can also use any key to perform any function. For example, if you want to use ENTER or 6 to edit a file, you can assign the keys and functions accordingly using the Setup menu.

File Manager gives you three different functions to choose from when defining custom Program Launch functions:

• Start a program from the Shell menu and retrieve the highlighted file into the program

• Execute a DOS command and pass the highlighted file to the command line

• Execute a Shell macro and pass the highlighted file as a parameter

To define your own Program Launch Function:

1. Press SHIFT-F1 for Setup.

2. Press 1 or L for Program Launch. The screen shown in Figure 6-15 appears.

3. Use the arrow keys to move to a space that does not have an extension listed. The dots on the top of the screen indicate the periods in the extension of a filename.

Figure 6-15. Main Program Launch screen

4. Press **1** for Name.

5. Enter the extension on which you want the action performed. You can use wildcard characters to define global actions.

6. Select one of the functions listed here:

```
2 - Edit:
3 - Execute:
4 - Look:
5 - Print:
```

7. After selecting a function, a screen similar to the following one appears:

```
Z                                    Q
Z - WP Office Programs -             Z - Applications -
A Appointment Calendar               D DataPerfect
C Connection Station                 P PlanPerfect
E Editor                             R DrawPerfect
F File Manager                       W WordPerfect
M Mail                               Z - Utilities -
N NoteBook                           G Go to Dos For One Command
S Scheduler                          O Other Menu

1 DOS Command; 2 Shell Macro; 3 Clear (use FM default): 0
```

All the options on your current Shell menu are displayed.

8. Select the type of action you want performed from the menu at the bottom of the screen.

9. Enter the command line parameters if necessary. These parameters override any default parameters.

Defining a Shell Program Launch

An option that is available when selecting your own Program Launch functions is to edit the file in one of the programs listed on your Shell menu. After selecting the key to which you want the Launch defined, a copy of your Shell menu appears. Select the letter next to the program for which you want the file retrieved. This option is especially useful with non-WordPerfect products.

After selecting the menu letter, you are prompted for command line parameters. The commands you enter here override anything entered on the Program Information screen of the Shell menu.

Defining a DOS Command Function

When you define a DOS command function, the filename you highlight in File Manager is used in the DOS command. After choosing DOS Command from the menu at the bottom of the Program Launch screen, enter the command you want performed. The filename is passed as the last option unless otherwise specified. To insert the command in another location, enter % % at the location you want the filename inserted. You can also enter & & within the command to have it pause after the command is executed and wait for you to press a key.

If the command you want to execute is an internal DOS command (see your DOS manual) you must specify the path to COMMAND.COM followed by a /C before entering the command.

Defining a Shell Macro Function

When you select Shell Macro as the function type, the Shell macro you are highlighting is executed. If you want the Shell macro to be performed on files with certain extensions, you would enter the path to the Shell macro as the command line parameters. The file you highlight in the file list is passed to the Shell macro as Macro Variable 0.

Program Launch Macro Names

When defining Program Launch macros the macros are assigned specific names. The following list outlines the names of the macros, where *EXT* indicates the extension to which the macro is assigned.

Macro Name	Action Key
ED*EXT*.SHM	Edit
EX*EXT*.SHM	Execute
LK*EXT*.SHM	Look
PR*EXT*.SHM	Print

You can use the action macros to specify what you want done when the target program is already resident. When the macro is executed the selected filename is stored in Macro Variable 0.

File Manager searches for the macros in the Macro Directory option specified in the Shell Setup options menu.

Block

You can use Block to highlight certain information while in the Look screen and save the information to the Shell Clipboard. Block is only active from the Look screen.

Keystrokes

1. Highlight the file containing the information you want to save to the Clipboard.

2. Press **6** or **L** for Look or press ENTER to display the contents of the file.

3. Use the arrow keys to move the cursor to the portion of the text you want to save.

4. Press ALT-F4 for Block; use the UP/DOWN ARROW keys to move to the end of the text you want to save. The text appears highlighted on the screen.

Note: The LEFT ARROW/RIGHT ARROW keys do not block; they only move the cursor to the beginning or end of a line.

5. Press CTRL-F1 for Shell.

6. Press **2** or **S** to save the information to the Clipboard or press **3** or **A** to append the information to any existing information in the Clipboard.

Clipboard

The Clipboard is a temporary storage buffer that aids in transferring information between programs and within programs. File Manager can save entire files or selected information from a file to the Shell Clipboard. You can then retrieve this information into any Shell-compatible program.

273

Keystrokes

Saving an Entire File to the Clipboard

1. Highlight the file you want to save and press CTRL-F1 for Shell.

2. Press **2** or **S** to save the file to the Clipboard or press **3** or **A** to append the file to any existing information in the Clipboard.

Saving Selected Information to the Clipboard

See "Block" in the previous section for steps on saving selected information to the Clipboard.

Copy

With File Manager you can copy a file or all marked files to a specified drive or directory.

Keystrokes

To copy a single file:

1. Highlight the file you want to copy.

2. Press **8**, **C** , or F4 for Copy. The "Copy file to:" prompt appears.

3. Type in the drive or directory where you want the file copied.

To copy multiple files:

1. Press **1**, **M**, or SPACEBAR to mark all the files you want to copy.

2. Press **8**, **C**, or F4 for Copy. The "Copy marked files? (Y/N)N" prompt appears.

3. Type **Y** for Yes.

4. Type in the drive or directory where you want the files copied.

Creating a Directory

You can create directories while in File Manager without exiting to DOS. Directories can be created in three different ways:

- Changing to a new directory
- Copying marked files to a new directory
- Moving marked files to a new directory

Keystrokes

1. Press **7** or **O** for Other Directory, **8** or **C** for Copy, or **3** or **M** for Move/Rename.

2. Enter the name of the new directory. The "Create *directory name*? (Y/N)N" prompt appears at the bottom of the screen.

3. Type **Y** for Yes to create the directory or type **N** for No to cancel the function.

Once File Manager creates the directory it appears in the file list or the directory tree (if created in the directory tree) in the proper location.

Current Directory

The .<CURRENT> <DIR> listing, which appears at the top of a file list, can help you narrow down the file listing of the current directory.

Keystrokes

1. Highlight the .<CURRENT> <DIR> listing.

2. Press ENTER.

3. Type in a filename pattern.

4. Press ENTER.

After using this option to narrow down a file listing you can high-light the .<CURRENT> <DIR> listing again and press ENTER to restore the original file list with the entire directory listed.

Date

The Date option lets you list files saved during a specified time period. This may be useful if you forgot the name of a file but remember approximately when you last modified it, or if you want to check for old files cluttering up your directories.

Keystrokes

1. From a file list press **4**, **S**, or SHIFT-F8 for Select Files.

2. Press **2** or **D** for Date.

3. Type **Y** for Yes.

4. Enter the earliest date for which you want files listed.

5. Enter the last date for which you want files listed.

6. Press F7 for Exit to return to the file list.

For more information on using the Date feature, see "Using the Date Feature," earlier in this chapter.

Delete

With Delete you can delete a file, all marked files, or an empty directory.

Keystrokes

1. Highlight the file or directory you want to delete or press **1**, *, or SPACEBAR to mark the files you want to delete.

2. Press **2** or **D** for Delete.

3. Type **Y** to delete the file(s) or directory.

Directory Tree

A directory tree lists all the directories in a specified drive or volume. A directory tree helps you visualize the organization of the directories.

Keystrokes

1. Press CTRL-F3.

2. Press **3** or **T** for Tree.

3. Enter a drive or volume letter followed by a colon at the "File-name Pattern:" prompt.

For more information on directory trees see "Displaying a Directory Tree," earlier in this chapter.

Directory Look Method

The Directory Look Method determines what happens when you press Look on a directory name while in a file list or a directory tree. For information on changing the Directory Look options see "Changing the Directory Look Method," earlier in this chapter.

Display

The Display option lets you set up permanent display options for File Manager.

Keystrokes

1. Press SHIFT-F1 for Setup.

2. Press **3** or **D** for Display.

3. Make the desired changes to options 1 through 4 (described in the next section).

4. Press F7 twice to return to the main File Manager screen.

Options

The following options are available from the Display menu.

Windows   The Windows options let you specify if File Manager displays in Full Screen mode or in Half Screen mode.

List 1 and List 2   List 1 is the left side and List 2 is the right side if you are in Half Screen mode. The List options determine if the screens display a file list or a directory tree.

Colors   With the Colors options you can determine how the monitor displays different colors and attributes.

If you have a color monitor, the Colors option lets you set colors for normal, bold, underline, and reverse video text. You can also choose how you want underline displayed on a single-color monitor. For monitors with Hercules cards and compatibles you can select the appropriate mode.

Double Directory

File Manager can display two directories side by side using Half Screen mode.

Keystrokes

To temporarily display Half Screen mode:

1. Press CTRL-F3 for Screen.

2. Press **1** or **H** for Half Screen.

To change the default display mode to Half Screen:

1. Press SHIFT-F1 for Setup.

2. Press **3** or **D** for Display.

3. Press **1** or **W** for Windows.

4. Press **1** or **H** for Half Screen mode.

For more information on using Half Screen mode see "Displaying Directories in Half Screen Mode," earlier in this chapter.

File List

A file list contains the names, sizes, and the date and time last modified for all the subdirectories and files in a directory. While displaying a file list you can choose any of the options at the bottom of the menu.

Filename Patterns

Filename patterns help to constrict a file list. File Manager prompts for a filename pattern when you press **7** or **O** for Other Directory or when you look at a directory in a file list (if the Directory Look Method is set to Prompt). You can also enter a filename pattern in the Select Files menu for a file list. When you enter a filename pattern, File Manager only displays those files that match the pattern. You can use two wildcard characters to create filename patterns: an asterisk (*) and a question mark (?). The * stands for zero or more characters and the ? stands for one character. You can enter multiple filename patterns on the same line. For example,

```
Filename Pattern: *.exe,*.com,*.bat
```

would list all the files with an .EXE extension, all files with a .COM extension, and all files with a .BAT extension.

Find Files

Find Files helps you quickly locate files by entering a filename pattern. This is useful if you only remember part of the filename or if you want to know which and how many files meet the specified filename pattern.

Keystrokes

1. Press F5 or **F** for Find Files.

2. Enter a filename or filename pattern. You are asked if you want to send the list of files found to the printer.

3. Type **Y** if you want to print the list or type **N** if you only want to view the list on the screen.

Help

The Help feature displays on-screen information about File Manager features.

Keystrokes

1. Press F3 for Help from the main File Manager screen.

2. To get information, you can type one of the menu item letters to see information about the specific topic; press a function key to see information about the feature associated with that key; or press F3 for Help again to see the File Manager template. This is especially useful since File Manager does not come with a keyboard template.

3. Press ENTER or the spacebar to exit a help screen or press ESC to return to the main Help screen.

Hints

The help screens are a valuable tool for accessing information about the File Manager program. You do not have to press Help (F3) from the main File Manager screen. Pressing Help from any File Manager menu displays information about the features associated with that screen. File Manager displays the keystrokes (if any) for the feature in the upper-right corner of the help screen.

HEX Dump

A HEX dump displays the hexadecimal codes for any file, with the addresses on the left, the HEX codes in the center, and the ASCII values on the right.

Keystrokes

1. Highlight the file you want to display.

2. Press ALT-F3 or **H** for HEX Dump.

HOME, X

Pressing HOME, x, where x is a drive or volume letter, while in a directory tree quickly displays the specified drive. This is a fast way to move between disks or volumes if you are on a network.

Lock

Locking files protects them from being retrieved and modified by users who do not know the password. When a file is locked, you must enter the password to retrieve it into a program. If you look at a locked file within File Manager, the contents are encrypted as shown in Figure 6-16.

Keystrokes

1. Highlight the file you want to lock.

2. Press **5** or **k** for Lock.

3. Press **1** or **L** for Lock.

4. Enter a password. The password can be up to 80 characters long.

5. Reenter the password. File Manager asks you to reenter the password to ensure you entered it correctly the first time.

You can lock multiple files with the same password by first marking the files and then following the preceding steps.
To unlock a previously locked file:

1. Highlight the file you want to unlock.

2. Press **5** or **k** for Lock.

3. Press **2** or **U** for Unlock.

4. Enter the password.

```
Filename: C:\TEST\CHECK.51                          File Size:   61,860

1?87>6:^C

^A+
================================================================================
^G^N
================================================================================

^O^E
================================================================================
^[^RIBXLTXX^Z^Q^X^T^X^O^T

_
1?87>6:^C

^A+
================================================================================
^G^N
================================================================================



Look: 1 Next File; 2 Prev File: 0
```

Figure 6-16.   Locked file displayed in Look

Look

With the Look feature you can view the contents of a directory or file.

Keystrokes

1. Highlight the file or directory you want to display.

Note: If you are in a directory tree and the Directory Look Method is set to Automatic, the contents of the directory displays as soon as you highlight the directory.

2. Press **6**, **L**, or ENTER for Look.

If you are highlighting a file, the contents of the file displays in the Look screen. If you are highlighting a directory, the contents of the directory displays, unless the Directory Look Method for File List is set to Prompt. If it is set to prompt, you are prompted for a filename pattern. For more information on using Look and various applications see "Looking at Files and Directories," earlier in this chapter.

Mark

Marking files lets you perform a function on more than one file at a time. You can copy, move, delete, lock, and search marked files. Marking files avoids repeating functions over and over.

Keystrokes

1. Highlight the file you want to mark.

2. Press **1**, or SPACEBAR, or type * to mark the file.

3. Repeat steps 1 and 2 until all files are marked.

4. Select the desired function you want to perform on the marked files.

Move/Rename

You can change the name of a file or directory, move a file or marked files to a different directory, and simultaneously move a file to a different directory and change the name of the file with the Move/Rename feature.

Keystrokes

1. Highlight the file or directory.

2. Press **3** or **M** for Move/Rename.

3. Enter a new filename without a path, enter a new directory name, or enter a new directory name and a new filename.

Note: You can only move files, not directories, and you can only rename one file at a time.

Name Search

Name Search is a quick and easy way to move to individual files in a file list or directories in a directory tree. With the Name Search feature you can move directly to a file as long as you know the first few letters of the filename.

Keystrokes

1. Press **N** or F2 for Name Search from a file list.

2. Type the first letter of the filename.

3. Continue typing the remaining letters of the filename until the file is highlighted.

4. Press SPACEBAR or the LEFT ARROW/RIGHT ARROW keys to end the name search.

Hints

When performing a name search in a file list, directories are only searched if you type **/** before you type the first letter. When using Name Search in a tree list, File Manager only searches the directories at the current level.

Other Directory

Other Directory allows you to change to another directory listing and display the contents.

Keystrokes

1. Press **7** or **O** for Other Directory.

2. Enter the name of the directory you want to display.

3. Enter a filename pattern.

Hints

With Other Directory you are always prompted for a filename pattern no matter how the Directory Look Method is set. You can also use Other Directory while in a directory tree. Instead of entering a new directory name, enter a new drive or volume.

Parent Directory

The ..<PARENT> <DIR> listing, which appears at the top of a file list, can quickly move you up one directory level. This can be very useful if you are down several levels in a file list.

Keystrokes

1. Highlight the ..<PARENT> <DIR> listing.

2. Press ENTER.

3. If prompted for a filename pattern, type in a filename pattern.

4. Press ENTER.

Program Launch

Program Launch lets you define keys that perform certain actions on designated files. For detailed information on the Program Launch feature, see "Using Program Launch," earlier in this chapter.

Rescan

When you display a directory tree, File Manager creates a scan file. The scan file is created the first time you display the directory tree. Each successive time you display the directory tree it reads the scan file that is already created. File Manager creates the scan file to save time when displaying directory trees over and over again.

If you make changes that affect the directory tree when outside of it, you will need to rescan the directory tree. A rescan updates the tree file for that drive or volume. A tree file for a local drive is named DIR {FM}.TRE and is saved in the root directory. A tree file for a network drive is named *XXX*{FM}*X*.TRE where the first three *X*s are your File ID and the fourth *X* is the drive designation of the network volume; these files are saved in the File Manager default directory.

Keystrokes

1. Display the directory tree that needs to be rescanned.

2. Press **4**, **S**, or SHIFT-F8 for Select Files.

3. Press **9** or **R** for Rescan Directory Tree. File Manager displays the last date the tree file was rescanned.

4. Type **Y** to rescan the directory.

Search

You can search for specific words or hexadecimal codes when displaying files in the Look screen.

Keystrokes

1. Highlight the file you want to display.

2. Press **6**, **L**, or ENTER to display the file in the Look screen.

3. Press F2 for Forward Search or SHIFT-F2 for Reverse Search.

4. Enter the word or word pattern for which you want to search.

Hints

File Manager only finds the occurrence of a word or word pattern once on a single line. You can repeat a search again by pressing F2 twice.

Select Files

Select Files sets the current options for a file list or directory tree display. The changes you make are in effect until you exit File Manager. A separate Select Files screen exists for each file list, and you can switch between the two lists by pressing TAB or SHIFT-F3 while in Select Files. If you want to make permanent changes, use the Setup feature (SHIFT-F1).

Keystrokes

1. Press **4**, **S**, or SHIFT-F8 for Select Files.

2. Make the desired changes to the options shown here:

```
1 - Filename Pattern:          C:\OFFICE30\*.*

2 - Date                       NO
      From  (MM-DD-YY):        (All)
      To    (MM-DD-YY):        (All)

Sort files by:                 Filename
      3 - Filename
      4 - Extension
      5 - Date & Time
      6 - Size

7 - Display Mode:              File List

8 - Directory Look Method:     Prompt

9 - Confirm Replace:           YES
```

3. Press F7 for Exit.

Options

The following options are available from the Select Files menu.

Filename Pattern   Filename Pattern displays as the first option to help you remember what is displayed on screen. You can change the filename pattern in Select Files, but it is usually easier to change it using the <CURRENT> Directory option unless you are making other changes in the Select Files menu.

Date   With the Date option you can determine which files you want to display according to the date and time the file was last modified. By default, File Manager displays all files. For more information on the Date option see "Date" earlier in this chapter.

Sort Files By   With the various sort options you can sort files by filename, extension, date and time last modified, and size. By default, File Manager displays files alphabetically by filename. If you do a name search when files are sorted by extension, File Manager uses the extension to search. If you try to do a name search when files are sorted by date or size, File Manager displays the "Can't do Name Search in this Sort Mode" error message.

Display Mode   With Display Mode you can choose if you want the list displayed as a directory tree or as a file list.

Directory Look Method   You can change the Directory Look Method to Manual or Automatic for a directory tree and to Prompt or No Prompt for a file list. For more information on these options see "Changing the Directory Look Method," earlier in this chapter.

Rescan Directory Tree   This option only displays if you are listing a directory tree. The Rescan option lists the last time the directory was scanned. See "Rescan" earlier in this chapter for more information on when and why you use the Rescan option.

Confirm Replace   If you are displaying a file list you will see the Confirm Replace option. This option determines if File Manager prompts you when you are copying or moving files to a location where a file by the same name already exists. If Confirm Replace is set to Yes (the default), File Manager prompts you to confirm the replacement of an existing file. If it is set to No, File Manager automatically overwrites the existing file without warning.

Setup

From the Setup menu you can set the defaults for Program Launch, Confirm Replace, Display, and Directory Look Method.

Keystrokes

1. Press SHIFT-F1 for Setup.

2. Make the desired changes to the options shown here:

```
1 - Program Launch

2 - Confirm Replace          YES

3 - Display

Directory Look Method
        4 - Directory Tree   Manual
        5 - File List        No Prompt
```

3. Press F7 until you return to the main File Manager screen.

Options

The following options are available from the Setup menu:

Program Launch   Program Launch lets you define keys that perform certain actions on designated files. For detailed information on the Program Launch feature, see "Using Program Launch," earlier in this chapter.

Confirm Replace   The Confirm Replace option determines if File Manager prompts you when you are copying or moving files to a location where that filename already exists. If Confirm Replace is set to Yes (the default), File Manager prompts you to confirm the replacement of an existing file. If it is set to No, File Manager automatically overwrites the existing file without warning.

Display   With the Display option you can permanently set up the way the File Manager screens display. You can specify Full Screen or Half Screen mode, file list or directory tree, and set the colors if you have a color monitor. For more information on the Display option see "Display" earlier in this chapter.

Directory Look Method   You can change the Directory Look Method to Manual or Automatic for a directory tree and to Prompt or No Prompt for a file list. For more information on these options see "Changing the Directory Look Method" in the first section of this chapter.

Shell

The Shell feature lets you exit to Shell without exiting File Manager, save and append text to the Shell Clipboard from the Look screen, and save or append an entire file to the Shell Clipboard.

Keystrokes

1. Press CTRL-F1 for Shell.

2. Choose from the options shown here:

```
1 Go to Shell: 2 Save to Clipboard: 3 Append to Clipboard: 0
```

Options

The following options are available with the Shell feature.

Go to Shell   The Go to Shell option lets you keep File Manager in memory while exiting to Shell. After exiting to Shell you can choose any option on the Shell menu. The File Manager entry on the Shell menu displays an * to remind you that File Manager has been left in memory. Go to Shell is especially useful if you want to go to another program and retrieve the contents of the Clipboard and then return to File Manager.

Save/Append to Clipboard   You can save or append blocked text in the Look screen to the Clipboard or you can highlight a file in a file list and save or append the entire contents to the Clipboard. See "Clipboard" earlier in this chapter for more information.

Sibling Directories

Sibling directories are directories that have the same parent directory. In Figure 6-17, FILES, LEARN, and TEMP are all sibling directories of the parent directory OFFICE30.

Startup Options

Startup options override certain default File Manager conditions on startup. You may put startup options on the command line if you are starting File Manager from DOS or add the options to the Shell Program Information screen for File Manager under Startup Options. The following is a list of all the startup options that you can use with File Manager.

```
02-24-92   1:48p            Directory C:\OFFICE30\*,*
Free Mem: 204,032      Disk Free: 20,967,424    Used: 2,690,181        Files:  259

, <CURRENT>   <DIR>                      | .. <PARENT>      <DIR>
FILES    .    <DIR>    02-24-92  1:10p   | LEARN     .     <DIR>    05-14-90  9:56a
TEMP     .    <DIR>    02-24-92  1:10p   | ADD_CONT .SHM   2,403   06-01-90 12:56p
ADD_LST .SHM  2,317    06-01-90 12:56p   | ADD_MSG  .SHM   1,129   06-01-90 12:56p
ALTC    .EDM  1,692    06-01-90 12:56p   | ALTD     .EDM     678   06-01-90 12:56p
ALTE    .EDM  2,920    06-01-90 12:56p   | ALTF     .EDM   4,568   06-01-90 12:56p
ALTG    .EDM  1,216    06-01-90 12:56p   | ALTI     .EDM   1,351   06-01-90 12:56p
ALTL    .EDM  4,664    06-01-90 12:56p   | ALTM     .EDM   4,358   06-01-90 12:56p
ALTN    .EDM  1,290    06-01-90 12:56p   | ALTO     .EDM     322   06-01-90 12:56p
ALTP    .EDM    652    06-01-90 12:56p   | ALTR     .EDM   5,100   06-01-90 12:56p
ALTS    .EDM  6,864    06-01-90 12:56p   | ALTSHFDM.SHM   2,469   06-01-90 12:56p
ALTSHFM2.SHM  1,946    06-01-90 12:56p   | ALTSHFM3.SHM   2,218   06-01-90 12:56p
ALTSHFTA.SHM  3,388    06-01-90 12:56p   | ALTSHFTD.SHM   1,799   06-01-90 12:56p
ALTSHFTD.WPM 10,533    06-01-90 12:56p   | ALTSHFTE.SHM   2,259   06-01-90 12:56p
ALTSHFTM.SHM  1,654    06-01-90 12:56p   | ALTSHFTX.SHM   1,986   06-01-90 12:56p
ALTT    .EDM    474    06-01-90 12:56p   | ALTU     .EDM     632   06-01-90 12:56p
ALTV    .EDM 39,934    06-01-90 12:56p   | ALTW     .EDM   1,078   06-01-90 12:56p
ALTX    .EDM  4,152    06-01-90 12:56p   | ALTX     .WPM     902   06-01-90 12:56p
AUTOSC  .SHM  3,818    06-01-90 12:56p ▼ | CALC     .EXE  31,232   06-01-90 12:56p

1 *Mark; 2 Delete; 3 Move/Rename; 4 Select Files; 5 Lock; 6 Look; (F7 to Exit,
7 Other Dir; 8 Copy; 9 Word Srch; N Name Srch; F5 Find Files; 6    F3 for Help)
```

Figure 6-17.   Sibling directories

Note: The options marked with an asterisk (*) are available when pressing Other Directory (7) while in File Manager. Place the options after the filename pattern.

/A-*date**	This lists only those files modified after a certain date. Be sure to enter dates as month-day-year (for example, 7-24-92).
/B-*date**	This lists only those files modified before a certain date.
/C	This displays the file list and directory tree of the startup directory side by side.
/CP	This overrides the default code page set by DOS.
/D-*path*	This redirects overflow files to the specified directory.

/FT	This displays a directory tree on startup.
/M-*macroname*	This starts specified macro on startup.
/PS-*directory*	This indicates where setup file should be saved and searched for.
/RN	This replaces files without confirmation when you use Copy or Move.
/RY	This asks before replacing files when you use Copy or Move. This is the default option and is only needed if you change Confirm Replace to No in Setup.
/S*	This lists the files sorted by size.
/T*	This lists the files sorted by date and time.
/X*	This lists the files sorted by extension.

Switch

The Switch feature lets you switch between the two lists in File Manager. Switch also works while in the Select Files screen.

Keystrokes

1. From a directory tree or file list press SHIFT-F3 for Switch.

Note: You can also press TAB to switch between the two lists.

Wildcard Characters

See "Filename Patterns" earlier in this chapter.

Word Search

If you want a listing of all the files that contain a certain word or word pattern, you can use the Word Search feature. Word Search lists only those files in the current directory that contain the word or word pattern you entered.

Keystrokes

1. Press **9** or **W** for Word Search.

2. Type in the word or word pattern and press ENTER.

File Manager displays a "Searching *filename*" message, and then displays the number of files in which the word or word pattern is found. File Manager then redisplays the directory tree with only those files containing the word or word pattern you entered. For more information on using Word Search see "Using Word Search" earlier in this chapter.

Using Mail

The Mail package that comes with Office LAN is a quick and effective way to communicate with other users on your network or even users clear across the country. With Mail you can create and send messages — just as you do on paper with interoffice mail, but in a fraction of the time. You can also use Mail to send existing files and to keep track of phone messages. In addition, Mail lets you send the same message to many users simultaneously.

The main screen in Mail is divided into two windows as shown in Figure 7-1. The window on top is the In Box, and the window on the bottom is the Out Box. This is where you can see all of the messages you send and receive. From the main screen, you can read or delete messages listed in the In and Out Boxes, as well as check the status of any message that you have sent. Along the top of the screen is a heading that displays information about how Mail identifies you, along with the current date and time. The menu at the bottom of the screen outlines the options available from the main screen. These include moving to other screens, reading or deleting messages, and displaying various lists.

From the main screen, you can move to the Send screen, where you specify the recipients for a message and enter the message that you want to send. From the Send screen you can use the List feature to attach existing files to a message or to display a list of known users to select as recipients of a message.

You can move to Mail's Phone Message screen from the main screen. The Phone Message screen resembles a notepad used to keep track of information about missed phone calls. On the Phone Message screen, the person taking the message can list the caller's name and phone number, any message, and how future contact will be made.

As you read a message listed in the In Box you have the opportunity to reply to that message or forward it to another user who might be interested. With the Info Option, you can also view information about a message, such as when it was sent and the other recipients of the message.

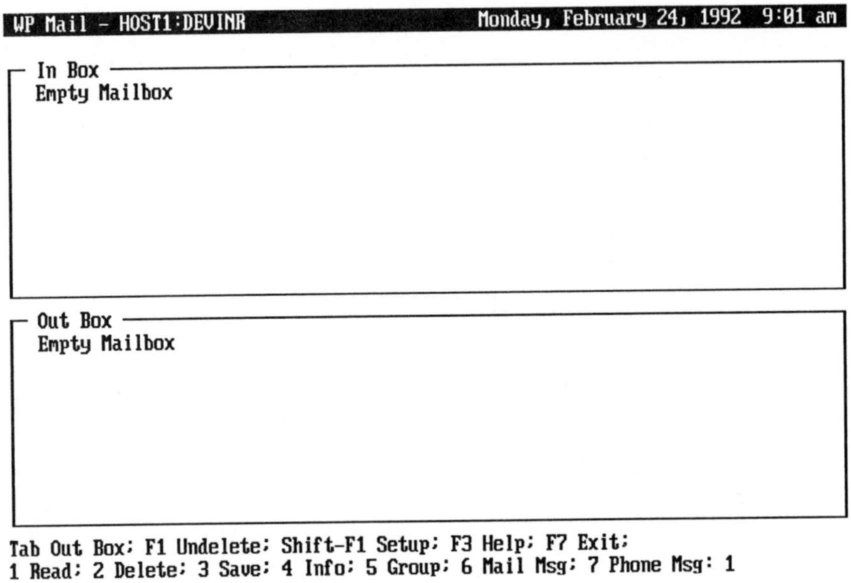

```
┌WP Mail - HOST1:DEVINR                    Monday, February 24, 1992  9:01 am┐
┌─ In Box ──────────────────────────────────────────────────────────────────┐
│ Empty Mailbox                                                               │
│                                                                             │
│                                                                             │
│                                                                             │
│                                                                             │
│                                                                             │
│                                                                             │
└─────────────────────────────────────────────────────────────────────────── 
┌─ Out Box ─────────────────────────────────────────────────────────────────┐
│ Empty Mailbox                                                               │
│                                                                             │
│                                                                             │
│                                                                             │
│                                                                             │
│                                                                             │
│                                                                             │
└───────────────────────────────────────────────────────────────────────────┘
Tab Out Box; F1 Undelete; Shift-F1 Setup; F3 Help; F7 Exit;
1 Read; 2 Delete; 3 Save; 4 Info; 5 Group; 6 Mail Msg; 7 Phone Msg: 1
```

Figure 7-1.   Blank main screen

From Mail you can print the contents of any message or information about the message that you have listed in the In or Out Box. You can also save messages or attached files to disk for future reference.

Mail provides you with a quick and easy way to send letters, memos, or files to a single user or to a group of users. Because of its speed and flexibility, Mail provides an excellent alternative to interoffice memos.

Mail Basics

Before getting started, it is helpful to understand some of the basic terms used in the Mail program. The first term to be familiar with is the basic building block of an Office LAN system, the *host*. A host consists of a set of network directories generated by the system administrator, where Mail stores all of its information. Each host, or group of directories, is then given a name to make identification easier. If a user is assigned to a certain host, or is on a given host, it means the information files for that user are located in the set of Office directories with that particular name.

For example, it is often convenient to group users in the same department on the same host and then give that host the name of the department, such as Marketing or Research. The number of users on a single host is only limited by the number of users that a network allows to use a single file server.

Each user assigned to a given host must have a unique *User ID* and *File ID*. The User ID is the name Mail uses to identify each user, so each User ID must be unique on a single host. The File ID is made up of three letters, usually the user's initials or an abbreviation of his or her name. Mail uses the File ID to name all of the information files associated with that user. For example, if a user has a File ID of AAA, then the In and Out Box files for that user are named AAA. In most situations, only the system administrator will see these files. These initials must also be unique on each host.

Once a host has been defined and users assigned to it, that host can be combined with other hosts to make a larger Mail system. It is important to remember, that each host can be considered an independent Office system that can function on its own.

Starting Mail

To start Mail from the Shell menu, type the letter next to the entry for Mail; the default letter is **M**. To start Mail from DOS, type **ml** and press ENTER. If you are starting Mail for the first time, you will see empty In and Out Boxes as shown in Figure 7-1. The heading along the top of the screen displays the name of the host you are assigned to and your User ID, along with the current date and time. When you are in Mail's main screen, the cursor displays as a reverse video bar in the In or Out Boxes if any messages are listed.

Moving Around in Mail

When you first enter Mail the cursor is resting on the first unread message in the In Box or at the top of the In Box if there are no unread messages. Any unread messages in the In Box appear with a bullet next to the message as in Figure 7-2. (Your screen will also display them in a bold text.) You can use the cursor keys to move up and down in the In and Out Boxes; the TAB key or SHIFT-F3 moves you between the two boxes. You can use the following keystrokes to move the cursor in the main screen:

Keystroke	Movement
UP ARROW/DOWN ARROW	Previous/next message
TAB/SHIFT-F3	Change current box
HOME, UP ARROW/DOWN ARROW	Top/bottom of box display
HOME, HOME, UP ARROW/DOWN ARROW	Top/bottom of box, or first/last message

From either box in the main screen you can read the current highlighted message or look at information about the message. From the main screen, you can also access the Send screen.

Reading Your Mail

Any unread messages in the In Box are bolded and marked on the left with a bullet so you can easily identify them. When entering Mail, the cursor is always placed on the oldest unread message in the In Box. If all messages have been read, the cursor highlights the first message in the In Box.

To read a message in Mail:

1. Use the cursor keys as listed in the preceding section and highlight the message you want to read.

2. Press **1**, **R**, or ENTER.

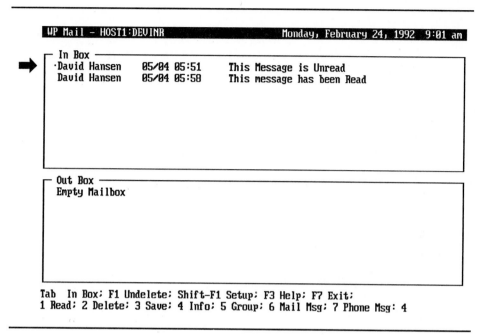

```
 WP Mail - HOST1:DEVINR                    Monday, February 24, 1992  9:01 am
┌ In Box ─────────────────────────────────────────────────────────────────┐
│ ·David Hansen      05/04 05:51      This Message is Unread                 │
│  David Hansen      05/04 05:58      This message has been Read             │
│                                                                           │
│                                                                           │
│                                                                           │
│                                                                           │
│                                                                           │
└───────────────────────────────────────────────────────────────────────┘
┌ Out Box ────────────────────────────────────────────────────────────────┐
│ Empty Mailbox                                                             │
│                                                                           │
│                                                                           │
│                                                                           │
│                                                                           │
│                                                                           │
└───────────────────────────────────────────────────────────────────────┘
Tab  In Box; F1 Undelete; Shift-F1 Setup; F3 Help; F7 Exit;
1 Read; 2 Delete; 3 Save; 4 Info; 5 Group; 6 Mail Msg; 7 Phone Msg: 4
```

Figure 7-2.   Read and unread messages in In Box

Mail displays the sender's full name and User ID, the User IDs of as
many recipients as fit on one line, the date and time the message was
sent, the subject of the message, and the actual message as shown in
Figure 7-3. If there are any files attached to the message, the filename
displays below the actual message. If the message is longer than one
screen, you can use the following keystrokes to move in the Read
screen:

Keystroke	Movement
UP ARROW/DOWN ARROW	Up/down one line
HOME, UP ARROW/DOWN ARROW	Top/bottom of screen
SCREEN UP/SCREEN DOWN ($+/-$ on the numeric keypad)	Top/bottom of screen
HOME, HOME, UP ARROW/DOWN ARROW	Top/bottom of message

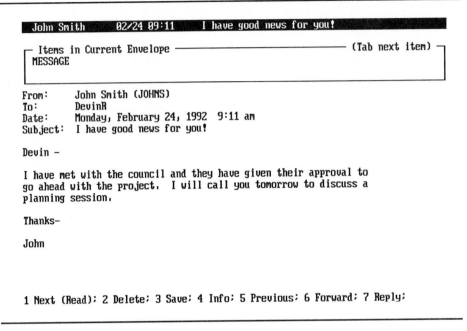

John Smith   02/24 09:11   I have good news for you!
┌ Items in Current Envelope ───────────────────────── (Tab next item) ┐
MESSAGE

From: John Smith (JOHNS)
To: DevinR
Date: Monday, February 24, 1992   9:11 am
Subject: I have good news for you!

Devin -

I have met with the council and they have given their approval to
go ahead with the project. I will call you tomorrow to discuss a
planning session.

Thanks-

John

1 Next (Read); 2 Delete; 3 Save; 4 Info; 5 Previous; 6 Forward; 7 Reply;

Figure 7-3.   Read screen

At the very top of the Read screen is the *items listing,* which contains a listing of all of the files that make up the current Mail message, as shown here:

The items listing includes the message (if a message was sent) and any files attached to the message. You can display the contents of any file in the items listing by pressing TAB to highlight the file. As soon as you highlight a file it is displayed. If you do not want each file you highlight to display, press the ENTER key before pressing TAB. After pressing ENTER, you can move to any file with the TAB key and then press ENTER to display the contents of the file. This saves time if you have several files attached and are only interested in viewing one of the files. If the file is a program file or other non-text file, the display shows the ASCII equivalents of the file contents. For information on saving a file from the Read screen see "Saving a Message or Attached File," later in this chapter.

From the Read screen, you can read the previous message listed in the In Box by pressing **5** or **P**. The next message in the In Box can be read by pressing **1** or **N**. If there is no previous or next message listed in the In Box, Mail exits to the main screen.

Sending a Mail Message

The screen where you create and edit a mail message is the Send screen. The Send screen can be accessed from the main screen by pressing **6, M,** or F9. The Send screen is divided into three sections, as shown in Figure 7-4. You can move between the different fields and

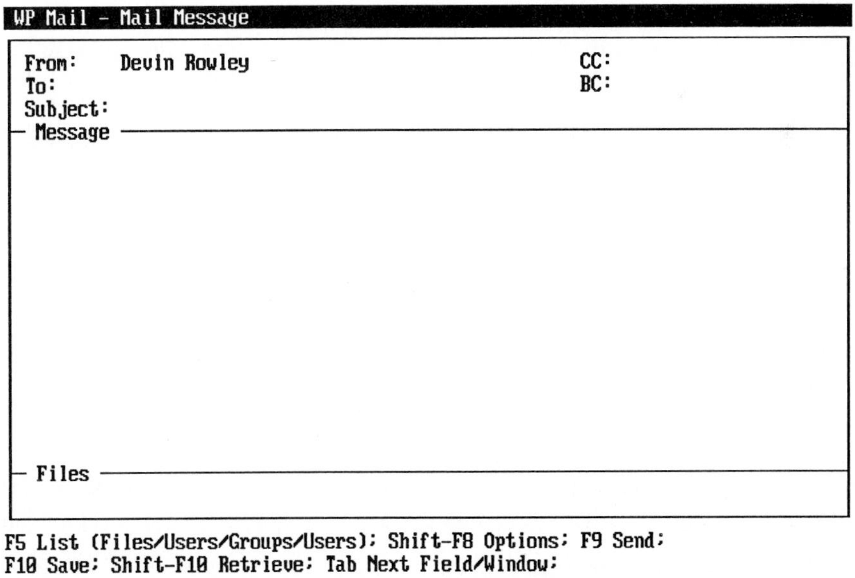

```
 WP Mail - Mail Message
┌──────────────────────────────────────────────────────────────────┐
│  From:     Devin Rowley                         CC:                │
│  To:                                            BC:                │
│  Subject:                                                          │
│ ┌ Message ──────────────────────────────────────────────────────  │
│                                                                    │
│                                                                    │
│                                                                    │
│                                                                    │
│                                                                    │
│                                                                    │
│                                                                    │
│                                                                    │
│                                                                    │
│                                                                    │
│ ┌ Files ──────────────────────────────────────────────────────── │
└──────────────────────────────────────────────────────────────────┘
F5 List (Files/Users/Groups/Users); Shift-F8 Options; F9 Send;
F10 Save; Shift-F10 Retrieve; Tab Next Field/Window;
```

Figure 7-4.   Send screen

sections of the Send screen by pressing TAB. Pressing SHIFT-TAB moves you backwards through the fields. Upon entering the Send screen, the From line automatically lists your User ID. You can change the name on the From line if desired. After you have entered the recipient(s), subject, and message, there are two ways to send a message:

1. Press F9 to send the message. This clears the Send screen but does not exit you out of the screen. This is useful if you want to send several messages at the same time.

2. Press F7 and type **Y** to send the message and exit the Send screen. If you type **N**, the message is not sent, and you return to the main screen. You can later return to the Send screen and the information you entered is still listed.

Entering User IDs

When sending a Mail message you must enter the User IDs for the people to whom you want to send the message. If you already know the User IDs, you can type them in on the To line. Be sure to put a separating comma between each individual User ID as shown here:

```
WP Mail - Mail Message

 From:    Devin Rowley                          CC:
 To:      Johns,Donr,Greg,Cecily                BC:
 Subject:
 Message
```

If you do not enter a comma, Mail sees all IDs as User IDs. If you don't know a person's User ID, you can have Mail display a listing of all known users and their User IDs, using the List feature. To use the List feature:

1. If necessary, press TAB or SHIFT-TAB to move the cursor to the To line.

2. Press F5 to display the List options.

3. Press **2** or **U** to display the user list.

4. Use the arrow keys to move the cursor to the name of the person you want to include on the To line, or press F2 or **N** to activate Name Search and then type in the name of the person. Mail moves through the user list to find and match the characters you type.

5. With the cursor on the person's name, press ENTER to retrieve the User ID to the To line.

You can also use the List feature to retrieve several users from the user list. To do this, use the Mark option to mark all users you want retrieved onto the To line, as follows:

1. If necessary, press TAB or SHIFT-TAB to move the cursor to the To line.

2. Press F5 to display the List options.

3. Press **2** or **U** to display the user list.

4. Use the arrow keys to move the cursor to the name of the person you want to include on the To line, or press F2 or **N** to activate Name Search and then type in the name of the person. Mail moves through the user list to find and match the characters you type.

5. Type an asterisk (*) to mark each user's name on the list.

6. Repeat steps 4 and 5 until you have marked all the names you need.

7. Press F7 to exit the user list and retrieve the User IDs for the marked users to the To line.

You can specify different types of recipients for a message using the To, CC, and BC fields. For more information on the use of these fields, see "Using Carbon and Blind Copy Types," later in this chapter.

Entering a Subject

In the top section of the Send screen you can enter the subject of the message. The information on the Subject line is what Mail displays in the recipient's In Box. To enter a subject for the message:

1. From the To line, press ENTER to move directly to the Subject line. If you press TAB or SHIFT-TAB you will move through the CC and BC fields before moving to the Subject line.

2. Type in a subject for the message.

The subject can contain up to 40 characters. If you try to enter more characters, Mail ignores them. You can use the Bold key (F6) to bold the subject.

Entering the Sender's Name

The From line at the top of the Send screen identifies the person sending the message. When you enter the Send screen, your full name is automatically inserted here. If you are sending a message for another person you can change the name in the From line. The name you enter displays in the recipient's In Box, but your own User ID is displayed when the message is read or the information about the message is viewed. Your User ID is also used if the recipient sends a reply to the message.

Entering a Message

The center section of the Send screen is the Message window, where you enter the message you want to send. With the cursor in the Message window, you can type the text of your message. You can also retrieve the contents of an existing file as your message. Retrieved files can be in DOS Text or WordPerfect format. Only very basic formatting from a WordPerfect document, such as bold and underline, convert when retrieving a file in the Message window. The Message window can hold over 6000 characters. If you try and enter more characters or retrieve a file larger than 6000 characters, Mail displays an error message and ignores the command. Files too large to fit in the Message window can be attached to the message and sent along with it. For more information, see "Attaching Files to a Mail Message," later in this chapter.

To retrieve an existing file into the Message window:

1. Press TAB or SHIFT-TAB to move the cursor to the Message window.

2. Press SHIFT-F10 to retrieve the file.

3. Enter the name of the file to retrieve. If the file is not in Mail's default directory, enter the path to the file.

When you type characters in the Message window, Mail automatically wraps text to the next line. The keystrokes listed in Table 7-1 are available to create and edit your message in the message window.

You can save your message as a file from the Send screen. This is useful, for example, if you want to use it in a memo you are creating in WordPerfect to send to people not on your Mail system. To save a message in the Message window as a file:

1. Press F10 to save the message.

2. Enter the path, if necessary, and filename where you want the message saved.

3. If the filename you enter already exists, Mail asks if it should replace the file. If you type **Y**, the original file is replaced with the current contents of the Message window. Pressing F1 cancels the save and returns you to the Send screen.

Listing Attached Files

The bottom section of the Send screen is for listing any files you want to send with the message. You should use this feature if the information you need to send is larger than 6000 characters or if it contains formatting codes that need to be preserved, as found in tables, graphics, figures, and so on.

When a file is attached to a message, it becomes a part of the Mail message. When the user receives the message, he can save a copy of the file to disk. When a message is deleted, any attached files are also deleted. For more information on file attachments, see "Attaching Files to a Mail Message," later in this chapter.

Replying to a Message

Once you have read a message that has been sent to you, you can use the Reply option to send a message back to the original sender. After

Keystroke	Result
RIGHT ARROW/LEFT ARROW	Moves right/left one character
UP ARROW/DOWN ARROW	Moves up/down one line
END	Moves to end of current line
HOME, UP ARROW/DOWN ARROW	Moves to top/bottom of window
SCREEN UP/SCREEN DOWN (+/− on the numeric keypad)	Moves to top/bottom of window
HOME, HOME, UP ARROW/DOWN ARROW	Moves to top/bottom of message
BACKSPACE	Deletes previous character
DEL	Deletes character at cursor
CTRL-BACKSPACE	Deletes word at cursor
CTRL-END	Deletes to end of line
CTRL-PGDN	Deletes to end of message
HOME, TAB	Inserts tab in message
F6	Turns bold on/off
F8	Turns underline on/off

Table 7-1.   Available Keystrokes in the Message Window

selecting Reply (7 from the Read screen), Mail takes you directly to the Send screen. Mail automatically inserts the name of the user who sent you the message on the To line. The subject is filled in with the same subject as the original message, and "Reply" is added to the end of the Subject line as shown here:

```
From: Devin Rowley                          CC:
To:   JOHNS                                 BC:
Subject: I have good news for you! -Reply
- Message
```

This lets the person who sent the original message know that this is a reply. Mail enters the above information by default, but you can edit it or add to it. For example, you can add more users to the To line or change the Subject line, if you wish.

Once you have completed your reply, you send it the same way you send a normal Mail message:

1. Press F9 to send the message. This clears the Send screen and keeps you in it. Or press F7 and type **Y** to send the message and exit the Send screen. If you type **N**, the message is not sent and you return to the Read screen with the original message displayed.

Forwarding a Message

Another useful feature available from the Read screen is Forward (6). With the Forward option you can forward a copy of the message on the Read screen to other users. The Forward option takes you to the Send screen, fills in the Subject line with the same subject as the original message, and adds "Forwarded" to the end of the Subject line as shown here:

```
 From:    Devin Rowley                            CC:
 To:                                              BC:
 Subject: I have good news for you! -Forwarded
 - Message ──────────────────────────────────────────────
       Forwarded mail received from: JOHNS
```

Mail enters the original subject as a default, but it can be edited. Mail also enters a note at the top of the Message window indicating this is a forwarded message. Enter User IDs for the people you want to receive the forwarded message the same way you do with a normal message. For help on inputting User IDs see "Entering User IDs" under "Sending a Mail Message," earlier in this chapter.

After entering the User IDs, you can enter a message to send with the forwarded message. You might enter a message that says, "Received this information about the committee meeting; thought it might be useful for your next meeting." When you forward a message, the original message is sent as an attached file along with the new message you create. Once you complete the new message, you can send it in the same way you send a normal Mail message:

1. Press F9 to send the message. This clears the Send screen and keeps you in it. Or press F7 and type **Y** to send the message and exit the Send screen. If you type **N**, the message is not sent and you return to the Read screen with the original message displayed.

When the recipient reads the forwarded message, the new message is displayed first. Since the original message is sent as an attached file, it is displayed when TAB is pressed and the second MESSAGE listing is highlighted, as shown here:

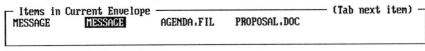

```
┌─ Items in Current Envelope ──────────────────── (Tab next item) ─┐
│ MESSAGE        MESSAGE       AGENDA.FIL    PROPOSAL.DOC           │
│                                                                  │
└──────────────────────────────────────────────────────────────────┘
From:     Devin Rowley (DEVINR)
To:       JACKC
Date:     Monday, February 24, 1992  9:15 am
Subject:  I have good news for you! -Forwarded
```

To display any other files that are attached to the message, you can press TAB to highlight the file to display.

Saving a Message or Attached File

You can save a message or attached file from either the main screen or the Read screen. From either screen, Mail prompts you before saving the message and each file. From the Read screen, the message and any attached files can be saved individually by highlighting the file you want to save and pressing Save (F10). From the Read screen, you can also mark the files you want to save. All files are saved in Mail's default directory, unless you specify a path to another directory. If you specify a new directory during a save, Mail saves all of the files attached to that message in that directory unless you change the path again.

To save a message and attached files from the main screen:

1. Use the cursor keys to highlight the message you want to save.

2. Press 3, S, or F10 to save the message and attached files. At the bottom of the screen, Mail displays the path to the current default directory with the filename MESSAGE. This is the default filename when saving a message.

3. Press ENTER to use the default filename or change the path or filename and then press ENTER. If you specify a new directory, Mail defaults to that directory when saving any other files attached to that message.

4. Mail then prompts you before it saves any files attached to the message. You can save the file listed on the prompt by pressing ENTER.

From the Read screen, the message file and any attached files are displayed in the items listing at the top of the Read screen. From the listing, you can press TAB to highlight the file you want to save. If you want to save multiple files, you can mark them with an asterisk (*). When moving through the items listing, Mail displays the files as they are highlighted. You can speed up the save process by disabling the display. To do this, simply press ENTER from the Read screen, and then press TAB to highlight the files in the listing. You can turn the display on again by pressing ENTER. To save files from the Read screen with the display on or off:

1. Press TAB to highlight the file you want to save, or press TAB to move through the file listing and type an asterisk (*) next to each file you wish to save.

2. Press **3**, **S**, or F10 to save from the Read screen. If you have marked files on the Read screen, type **Y** to save all marked files, or type **N** to save only the file at the cursor.

3. Press ENTER to save the files to Mail's current default directory or type in a new path and filename for the first file. Mail then uses the directory you enter as the default directory for all files in this message.

4. If there's a file with the same name in the directory where you try and save the files, Mail asks if you want to replace the original file or append the new file to the original. To replace, press **1**, **R**, or **Y**. To append, press **2** or **A**.

If you have marked multiple files in the items listing, Mail continues to the next marked file; repeat steps 3 and 4 until all the files are saved.

Saving a Message from the Send Screen

After entering a message on the Send screen, you can save the message as a file before sending it. To save a message from the Send screen:

1. If necessary, press TAB or SHIFT-TAB to move the cursor to the Message window on the Send screen.

2. Press F10 to save the message as a file.

3. Type in the filename for the message. To save the file to a directory other than the current default directory, enter the path with the filename.

Using Carbon and Blind Copy Types

You can assign one of three *copy types* to message recipients. A copy type classifies each recipient according to the way the message is displayed—without changing the contents of the message itself.

The first and most common copy type is *primary*. A primary-type recipient receives the primary copy of a message.

A *carbon copy*-type recipient is listed in the Information screen for that message with CC next to their User ID. A carbon copy-type recipient doesn't have to act on a message; they receive it to be kept informed and as a courtesy. For example, you might send the minutes of a meeting to an employee not directly involved with the issues discussed in the meeting.

The third copy type is *blind copy*. Information about a blind copy recipient is not displayed in the other users' Information screen. Only the sender and the blind copy recipient know that the blind copy recipient has received the message. For example, if someone is transferring to your department, but the transfer is still confidential, you could send that employee a blind copy of all messages pertaining to your department, and none of the other employees in your department will know that the new person is receiving the messages.

If you want to send a message using copy types and know the User IDs, enter the User IDs in the correct field on the Send screen. Use TAB or SHIFT-TAB to move between the copy-type fields and type in the User

IDs. If you don't know the recipients' User IDs, you can use the List feature to have Mail display all known users. You can then mark the users and retrieve them to the appropriate copy-type fields. To use the List feature to send a message using the different copy types from the Send screen:

1. Press TAB or SHIFT-TAB to move the cursor to the To line.

2. Press F5 to display the List options.

3. Press **2** or **U** for User List.

4. Use the arrow keys to move the cursor to the name of the person to include as a recipient, or press F2 or **N** to activate Name Search, and then type in the name of the person. Mail moves through the user list to find and match the characters you type.

5. To mark a user as a primary copy type, type an asterisk (*). To mark a user as a carbon copy type, press **C** or type a plus sign (+). To mark a user as a blind copy type, press **B** or type an ampersand (&).

6. Repeat steps 4 and 5 until you have marked all the names you need.

7. Press F7 to exit the user list and retrieve the marked user IDs into the correct copy-type field, or press F1 to cancel and return to the Send screen.

Note: When the cursor is in either the CC or BC field, marking users with an asterisk (*) retrieves the User ID into the field where the cursor is located, not to the To line.

Creating a Group in Mail

If you send messages to the same users on a continual basis, you may want to define a group. Then, when you want to send a message to these people, you only need to type the group name on the To line instead of entering each individual's User ID. For example, if you work in a

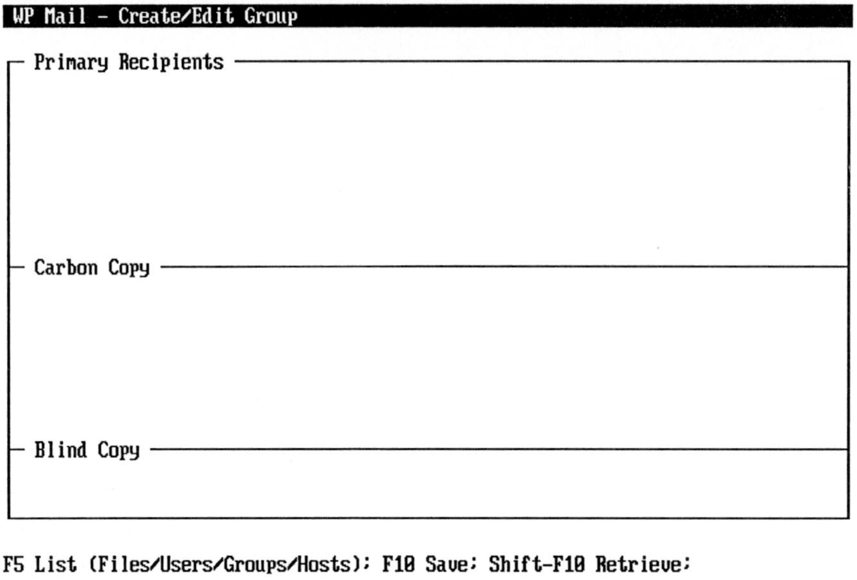

```
WP Mail - Create/Edit Group
┌─ Primary Recipients ──────────────────────────────────────────┐
│                                                                 │
│                                                                 │
│                                                                 │
│                                                                 │
│                                                                 │
│                                                                 │
├─ Carbon Copy ───────────────────────────────────────────────── │
│                                                                 │
│                                                                 │
│                                                                 │
│                                                                 │
├─ Blind Copy ─────────────────────────────────────────────────  │
│                                                                 │
│                                                                 │
│                                                                 │
└─────────────────────────────────────────────────────────────────┘
  F5 List (Files/Users/Groups/Hosts); F10 Save; Shift-F10 Retrieve;
```

Figure 7-5.   Group screen

department and most of the messages you send go to every person in that department, you can make a group containing all the people in your department.

You can define a group of Mail users by using the Group screen. The Group screen is divided into three sections as shown in Figure 7-5. Each of these sections is for listing the different copy-type recipients. The section on top contains primary copy types, the center section is for carbon copy types, and the bottom section is for blind copy types.

Creating a Group from the Main Mail Screen

To enter the Group screen from the main screen and create a group:

1. Press **5** or **G** to enter the Group screen.

2. Press TAB or SHIFT-TAB to move the cursor to the correct copy type.

3. Type in the User ID for the person to include in the group or use the List Users feature (a submenu of the List feature) to mark and retrieve users.

4. Repeat steps 2 and 3 until all users have been added.

Note: Be sure to add separating commas between the User IDs.

5. Press F7 and type **Y** to save the group when exiting the Group screen or press F10 to save the group to the default directory and remain in the Group screen.

6. Enter the filename to use for the group file.

7. If you pressed F7 to save the group, type **Y** to exit the Group screen and return to the main screen. If you pressed F10 to save the group, you remain in the Group screen, and the user names remain on screen. At this point you can add more names to create another group by repeating steps 2 through 7.

Creating Groups from the Send Screen

You can also define a group from the Send screen. To do so:

1. Enter the users you want to include in the group in the correct copy-type fields. You can either type in the User IDs or use the List feature to mark and retrieve the correct User IDs (see "Using Carbon and Blind Copy Types," earlier in this chapter).

2. After entering all of the User IDs for your group, press TAB or SHIFT-TAB to position the cursor in one of the copy-type fields.

3. Press F10 to save the group.

4. Type in a name for the group file. If the filename already exists, Mail asks you to confirm the save. Type **Y** to replace the file, or type **N** to stop the save and enter a new filename. Pressing F1 cancels the save.

Nesting Groups

Mail also allows you to *nest* groups, that is, place the name of one group inside another. Nesting lets you build larger groups by combining existing ones. When combining existing groups to create a new one, it is important to remember two important rules:

- Do not nest groups more than five levels deep. This means that the first group can be listed inside a second group, and that second group can be listed inside a third group, and so on until there are five levels of subgroups below the first group. If you exceed five levels of grouping, Mail displays the "Error: Group nesting too deep" message.

- Never create a group that contains its own name.

To combine (nest) groups into a larger group using the Group screen, you can use List Groups or simply enter the names of the groups to combine on the Group screen and save the new group to a new name. For example, imagine you have already created three groups named GRP1, GRP2, and GRP3, and you want to combine them into one group named BIGGRP1. To do this, you would do the following from the Group screen:

1. Use TAB or SHIFT-TAB to move the cursor to the correct copy-type field for the first group.

2. Type **GRP1**, the name of the first group, in the Group screen.

3. Repeat steps 1 and 2 until all the group names are listed in the correct copy-type section of the Group screen.

4. Press F10 to save the group, and then enter the name for the group. You must enter a name that meets the DOS file-naming criteria. If the group already exists, Mail asks you to confirm the save. Type **Y** to save the group or **N** to cancel the save using the current name.

You can also use the List feature to list system groups created by the system administrator or personal groups that you have already defined. To use List to combine groups, do the following from the Group screen:

1. Use TAB or SHIFT-TAB to move the cursor to the correct copy-type field for the first group.

2. Press F5 to display the List menu.

3. Press **4** or **G** to display the system groups, or press **5** or **P** for Personal Groups. If you select Personal Groups, Mail displays the path to the default directory where the personal groups are saved unless you specify another directory. Press ENTER to have Mail display all files in the default directory with a GRP extension, or enter the path to the directory where you store personal groups.

4. Use the cursor keys to highlight the group you want to retrieve.

5. Enter **+**, **&**, or ***** to mark the file. You can use the same copy-type marking conventions used to mark users.

6. Repeat steps 4 and 5 until all group names are marked with the correct copy type.

7. Press F7 to retrieve the names of the marked groups into the Group screen.

8. Press F10 to save the group, and then enter the name for the group. You must enter a name that meets the DOS file-naming criteria. If the group already exists, Mail asks you to confirm the save. Type **Y** to save the group or **N** to cancel the save using the current name.

Using Groups to Send Messages

You can use existing groups to send mail messages the same way you use individual User IDs. Mail retrieves the User IDs contained in the group file to the To line and sends those users mail as if they had been listed on the To line one by one. You can also have users assigned to copy types inside of group files. When you use a group to send a message, Mail allows you to either list the name of the group file on the To line with the path, if necessary, or retrieve the contents of a group file into the To line to let you edit the user listing.

Entering the name of the group file on the Send screen is the quickest and easiest way to send a message to several users at one time. To enter a group filename when sending mail:

1. Use TAB or SHIFT-TAB to position the cursor on the To line.

2. Type in the group filename and path.

3. Type in the subject and message you want to send.

4. Press F9 to send the message.

If you would like to retrieve a group and edit it before sending a message, do the following from the Send screen:

1. Use TAB or SHIFT-TAB to position the cursor on the To line.

2. Press SHIFT-F10 to retrieve the contents of a group file.

3. Enter the group filename and path.

4. Edit the user listing for the message.

5. Type in the subject and message you want to send.

6. Press F9 to send the message.

Retrieving the contents of the group is useful if you want to delete some of the users in the group or add new users just for this message.

Using List Groups

When a Mail system is created, the system administrator can create groups available to all users on the network. These group files are located in a global group directory. To access these global groups, you can use the Groups option in the List feature. If you want to send a message to users in a global group created by the system administrator:

1. Use TAB or SHIFT-TAB to position the cursor on the To line.

2. Press F5 for the List feature.

3. Press **4** or **G** to list the groups in the global group directory.

4. Use the cursor keys to highlight the group you want to retrieve.

5. Press **1** or **R** to retrieve the contents of the highlighted group file.

After retrieving the contents of the group, you can then add or delete users from the list.

Note: If a group listing is too large to fit on the To line, Mail displays an error message, indicating that there is too much information to fit in the buffer. If this happens you will need to retrieve the group by marking it with an asterisk (*) and then pressing Exit (F7 from the List Groups screen). This retrieves the name of the group but not the entire contents. The message will still be sent to all the users in the group.

With the Groups option, you can also retrieve multiple group names to the To line on the Send screen. To use the List feature to send a message to more than one group:

1. Use TAB or SHIFT-TAB to position the cursor on the To line.

2. Press F5 for List.

3. Press **4** or **G** to list the groups in the global group directory.

4. Use the cursor keys to highlight the group you want to retrieve.

5. Type an asterisk (*) to mark the group filename.

6. Repeat steps 4 and 5 until all the groups are marked.

7. Press F7 to retrieve the groups.

When you send the message with the group names listed on the Send screen, Mail extracts the User IDs from the groups and sends the message to all the users included in the groups.

Copy Types Inside Groups

You can assign copy types to users when a group is created. Mail assigns a copy type depending on the user's copy type inside the group and the field where the group is listed on the Send screen. Blind copy has the highest priority, carbon copy the next priority, and primary the lowest priority. Mail then makes copy-type assignments based on which priority is higher: the copy-type designation inside the group or the copy type of the field where the group is listed on the Send screen.

For example, if you have a group made up of all primary copy-type users, but you type the group name in the CC field on the Send screen, Mail considers all of the primary recipients as carbon copy recipients—the reason being that the carbon copy field has a higher priority than the primary copy type inside the group. However, if there were also blind copy recipients in the same group you retrieved to the CC field, they would remain as blind copy types. The reason they remain blind copy recipients is because their copy type inside the group has a higher priority than the field where they are listed.

The only other situation to be aware of when using copy types is when you list User IDs individually and within a group. In this case, the User ID takes precedence over the copy type inside the group. If user DonR inside a group is listed as a blind copy recipient, and you type his User ID on the To line as a primary type, he is assigned a primary copy type since the individual User ID overrides the copy type in the group.

Attaching Files to a Mail Message

When you send a mail message it is often necessary to send additional files along with the message. These files could be text files, data files, or program files. You can list any files that you want to send as part of the message in the Files window at the bottom of the Send screen. These files actually become part of the message, and when you delete a Mail message from the In Box, you also delete those files. Mail can attach up to 100 files to a single message, but the more files you attach, the longer the message takes to deliver.

If you know the path and filenames for any files you want to attach to a mail message, do the following from the Send screen:

1. Press TAB or SHIFT-TAB to move the cursor to the Files section at the bottom of the screen.

2. Type in the full path and filename for the file you want to attach. Be sure to use commas to separate the filenames if you enter more than one file.

3. Press F9 to send the message.

You can also use the List Files feature to retrieve one or more filenames into the Files window. To attach files using List Files:

1. Press TAB or SHIFT-TAB to move the cursor to the Files section at the bottom of the screen.

2. Press F5 for the List feature. The following menu appears at the bottom of the screen.

`List 1 Files; 2 Users; 3 User IDs; 4 Groups; 5 Personal Groups; 6 Hosts: 1`

3. Press **1** or **F** for Files.

4. Mail displays the path to the current default directory at the bottom of the screen. The path also uses the default filename pattern of *.* to display all files in the directory. You can enter another path, change the filename pattern that is displayed, or press ENTER to display all of the files in the default directory.

5. After selecting the directory containing the files you want to attach, use the cursor keys to highlight the first file to attach and mark it by typing an asterisk (*), or press F2 or **N** to perform a name search in the directory listing, and type the name of the file to attach. Mail moves the cursor as you type the characters to match the filename pattern displayed. When the correct file is highlighted, type an asterisk (*) to mark the file.

6. Repeat step 4 until all the files you want to attach have been marked.

7. Press F7 to retrieve the names of the marked files into the Files section of the Send screen. Mail inserts any separating commas needed.

Note: Do not use the Retrieve option when attaching files using List Files. If you press **1** or **R** for Retrieve, Mail tries to retrieve the entire contents of the file to the Files window and not the name of the file. This normally causes a buffer full error.

Sending a Quick Message

Sometimes all you need to send is a one-line message. For times like this, you can use the Subject line on the Send screen. The Subject line can hold up to 40 characters. When you send a quick message the entire message is displayed in the recipient's In Box. To send a quick message:

1. Enter the recipients' User IDs.

2. Press TAB to move the cursor to the Subject line.

3. Type the message you want to send. It must not be more than 40 characters.

4. Press F9 to send the message.

Sending a Phone Message in Mail

The Phone Message feature automates the message-taking process for phone messages. Using the Phone Message feature avoids having to use paper phone-message pads, which tend to get lost or misplaced. When a phone message is sent, all the information about the phone call is stored on your computer. You can refer back to this information as often as you like.

The Phone Message screen, shown in Figure 7-6, gives information about the caller, his or her phone number, any message that was left, and the next course of action.

To use the Phone Message feature from the main screen:

1. Press 7 or **P** to enter the Phone Message screen.

2. Enter the User ID of the person who received the call or use the List Users option to display a list of all known users and retrieve the User ID from the list.

```
WP Mail - Temporary Send Options

   1 - Message
       Auto-Delete
       Expire After (Days)
       Insert in Out Box
       Notify Recipients
       Priority
       Reply Requested
       Return Notification

   2 - Protection
       Concealed Subject
       Encryption
       Security

   3 - Transport
       Conversion of Enclosures
       Deliver After (Days)
       Routing (Automatic or Explicit)
       Status Information (Remote)


Selection: 0
```

Figure 7-8.   Temporary Send Options menu

Message Options

The Message options apply specifically to the priority of the message and how the message is displayed to both the sender and the recipient. To access the Message options press **1** or **M**.

Auto-Delete   The Auto-Delete option automatically deletes the message from your Out Box after all of the recipients have deleted it from their In Boxes. To change the Auto-Delete option, press **1** or **D**. Type **Y** to turn Auto-Delete on or **N** to turn it off.

Expire After   The Expire After feature expires, or deletes, the message if it is unread from any recipient's In Box after the set number of days has passed. Select Expire After by pressing **2** or **E**. Type the number of days between 1 and 250 for Mail to wait before expiring the message. To turn off Expire After, press **N** for None. It is helpful to set an expire date so the network does not get cluttered with old Mail messages.

Insert In Out Box   If you do not want a message you send to be listed in your Out Box, you can set the Insert in Out Box option to No. To set the option, press **3** or **I** to select Insert in Out Box. Type **Y** to have the message inserted in your Out Box or **N** to not list the message.

Notify Recipients   One of the options you can set for a message is to turn the on-screen notification on or off. To set the notification, press **4** or **N** to select Notify recipients. Type **Y** to turn notification on or **N** to turn notification off. If it is set to Yes, and the recipient is running the Notify program, they receive on-screen notification of all incoming messages. For more information on the Notify program see Chapter 11, "Using Notify, Repeat Performance, and TSR Manager."

Priority   You can set the priority of messages with the Priority option. To set the priority, press **5** or **P** to select Priority. From the menu at the bottom of the screen, press **1** or **L** for Low, **2** or **N** for Normal, or **3** or **H** for High. This affects the way the unread message displays in the recipients' In Boxes.

Reply Requested   You can mark a message to request a reply from the recipient by using the Reply Requested option. When you request a reply, an exclamation mark (!) displays next to the message in the recipient's In Box after it is read to remind him or her to reply. The mark is removed after a reply is sent. To set Reply Requested, press **6** or **Q**. Type **Y** to ask for a reply when convenient, or enter the number of days to use as a deadline for the reply. You can turn off the option by pressing **N**. Reply Requested is useful if you must have an answer to a message because it helps the recipient know which messages need to be responded to.

Return Notification   Return Notification uses on-screen notification to tell you when a message you sent was opened by the recipient. If you set it to Yes and are running the Notify program, you receive notification when the message is opened. To set Return Notification, press **7** or **R**. Type **Y** to turn Return Notification on, or **N** to turn it off. For more information on the Notify program, see Chapter 11, "Using Notify, Repeat Performance, and TSR Manager."

Protection Options

To protect your messages from being read by anyone other than the listed recipients, Mail supplies file encryption and an option to conceal the subject of confidential messages. To access the Protection options, press **2** or **P**.

Concealed Subject   For messages that may have a subject that you don't want to display in your Out Box, in the recipient's In Box, or in the notification window, you can use the Concealed Subject option to block the subject from displaying. Press **1** or **C** to select Concealed Subject, and then type **Y** to block the subject display or **N** to turn off the block. With the option set to Yes, "**CONCEALED SUBJECT**" displays in place of the subject.

Encryption   By default, Mail encrypts all of the messages that it uses. If you would like to change the setting, press **2** or **E** from the Protection Options menu. Press **1** or **N** to have no encryption on the message file, or **2** or **W** to reset the encryption to WordPerfect format.

Security   You can change a message's security stamp using the Security option. Press **3** or **S** to set the option and then select the security stamp you want to display with the message from options 1 to 6 on the menu displayed at the bottom of the screen. The Security option does not actually protect the message in any way, it only displays a message's security level. This may help the user know the sensitivity of the issues discussed in a message.

Transport Options

The Transport options affect the way a message is delivered and the amount of information that displays in the sender's Information screen. (The Transport options are only useful if you are using a Mail system with more than one host.) To access the Transport options, press **3** or **T**.

Conversion of Enclosures   Conversion of Enclosures is only needed if you are sending to a mail system that requires translation through a *gateway,* or portal, to another delivery system or operating system. This allows for the conversion of messages and/or attached files to another format when passing through a gateway. To set the file conversions allowed, press **1** or **C** and select the conversions from the menu displayed. Press **1** to allow no files to change, press **2** to allow the message file to convert, or press **3** to allow the message and any attached files to be converted. The conversions allowed may differ from gateway to gateway.

Deliver After   You can defer the delivery date of a message by using the Deliver After option. To set the number of days to wait, press **2** or **D**. Type the number of days to wait, or press **I** for Immediate Delivery. This is useful if you are going to be out of the office, but must have a message delivered on a certain day. Mail will take care of business while you are away.

Routing   *Routing* is the path that the message takes to get to its destination. *Automatic routing* uses the paths defined by your system administrator; *explicit routing* follows a path that you specify on the Send or Phone Message screen. To use explicit routing you must be familiar with the structure of the global mail system and know which paths are valid. To set the routing, press **3** or **R**, and then press **1** or **A** for Automatic or **2** or **E** for Explicit.

Status Information (Remote)   Remote Status Information refers to the level of information that is returned to the sender about any messages sent to another host. This can range from no information to information about when the file is deleted from the recipient's In Box. To set the level of information, press **4** or **S** for Status Information (Remote). Then press **1** for no status, **2** for information on when the message was delivered, **3** to return the time and date the message was read, or **4** to tell you when the message was deleted from the recipient's In Box. Each option you select includes the options below it, so 2 includes 1, 3 includes 2 and 1, and so on.

Printing in Mail

While in the Mail program, you can print a message with all of its attached files, or mark only the files you want to print from the Read screen. If the attached files contain formatting codes you may want to print them in the program that supports the formatting codes. Mail only supports WordPerfect 4.2 formatting codes.

To print the message and all attached files:

1. Use the cursor keys to highlight the message to print.

2. Press SHIFT-F7 to print the message.

Mail then prints the message and any attached files to the device you specify.

To selectively mark and print files, do the following from the main screen:

1. Use the cursor keys to highlight the message to print.

2. Press **1** or **R** to go to the Read screen.

3. Use the TAB key to move the cursor through the file listing at the top of the Read screen. Mark all files you want to print by typing an asterisk (*).

4. Press SHIFT-F7 to print all marked files to the device specified.

Selecting a Print Device

Mail supports printing either to a local printer via a parallel port or to a network printer. To select a local print device:

1. Press SHIFT-F7 to display the Print menu.

2. Press **4** or **V** to define a printing device.

3. Press **1** through **3** to select a local port as the print device.

To define a network printer or print queue for Mail:

1. Press SHIFT-F7 to display the Print menu.

2. Press **4** or **V** to define a printing device.

3. Press **4** or **D** to define a print device.

4. At the prompt, enter the name of the print queue for the network printer.

Selecting a Printer Definition

Before you can print properly in Mail, you must select the correct printer definition. To select a printer definition:

1. Press SHIFT-F7.

2. Press **3** or **D** for Printer Definition

3. Enter the number of your printer or the number of a printer that your printer emulates.

4. Press F7 until you return to the main Mail screen.

Page Format

On the Print menu you can select **2** or **F** to set up the page format for printing in Mail. From the Page Format menu you can set page length, left and right margins, and the margin at the top of the page as shown in Figure 7-9.

To display the Page Format menu, do the following:

1. Press SHIFT-F7 to display the Print menu.

2. Press **2** or **F** to display the Page Format menu.

3. Set the options on the menu.

4. Press F7 twice to return to the original screen.

Print Options

With the 6/14/90 version of Office the Print Options menu is accessed via the Setup screen or the Print menu. The Print Options menu lists features available for printing and page formatting in Mail. From the Print Options menu you can specify the size of a printed page in terms of lines and columns, as well as margins. You can also select a printer device file (.PRD) and a print device or port.

```
WP Mail - Page Format
    1 - Form length in lines: 66
    2 - Number of text lines: 54

    3 - Top margin (in lines): 6

    4 - Left margin (column #):  10
    5 - Right margin (column #): 74




Selection: 0
```

Figure 7-9.   Page Format menu

To display the Print Options menu under the Setup screen, do the following from the main screen:

1. Press SHIFT-F1 to display the Setup menu.

2. Press 2 or **P** to display the Print options.

After you finish setting the Print options, press F7 until you return to the main screen. Changes to these options remian in effect until you choose them again, no matter which menu you use to change them.

Changing the Date and Time Formats

The Date/Time option on Mail's Setup menu changes how the date and time are displayed in the main screen heading, the In Box, and the Information screen. To change this information:

1. Press SHIFT-F1 for Setup from the main Mail screen.

2. Press 4 or **E** for Environment.

3. Press **1** or **F** for Date/Time Formats. The following menu appears along the bottom of the screen:

1 Heading Date; 2 Heading Time; 3 In Box; 4 File Info; 5 Recipient Info: 0

Note: You can also press SHIFT-F5 to select the Date/Time Formats menu from the main Mail screen.

4. Select an option from the menu.

Options

The following options are available from the Date/Time Format screen.

Heading Date Heading Date changes how the date is displayed on the main screen in Mail. To set the display format for the date you can use any of the characters displayed in Figure 7-10. Along with the special characters, you can enter text, punctuation, or spaces to format the display.

```
WP Mail - Setup: Date/Time Format

Character   Meaning
   1        Day of the Month
   2        Month (number)
   3        Month (word)
   4        Year (all four digits)
   5        Year (last two digits)
   6        Day of the Week (word)
   7        Hour (24-hour clock)
   8        Hour (12-hour clock)
   9        Minute
   0        am / pm
   %        Used before a number, will:
              Pad numbers less than 10 with a leading zero
              Abbreviate the month or day of the week

Examples:  3 1, 4      = January 1, 1991
           %6 %3 1, 4  = Tue Jan 1, 1991
           %2/%1/5 (6) = 01/01/91 (Tuesday)
           8:90        = 10:55am


1 Heading Date; 2 Heading Time; 3 In Box; 4 File Info; 5 Recipient Info: 0
```

Figure 7-10.   Date/Time format screen

Heading Time   You can change how the current time is displayed in the main screen heading with Heading Time. You can set the time to display with a leading 0 or remove any leading characters. A leading 0 is inserted by entering a percent sign (%) in front of the time format string.

In Box   With In Box you can set the display format for the time and date that is shown in the In Box next to each message. This time and date reflect when the message was originally received. Since the space to display the date and time string is limited to 15 characters, it is important to keep the string short.

File Info   File Info affects the display of the creation date and time for all messages displayed in the Information screen.

Recipient Info   Recipient Info formats the date and time information displayed on the Information screen. This affects the date and time display for when the message was delivered, opened, and deleted.

Using the Clipboard with Mail

The Shell Clipboard is one of the main tools that all the WordPerfect Office programs use to integrate and share information. You can use the Clipboard to transfer information from Mail to another program and vice versa. While in Mail, the Shell Clipboard lets you block and save information from the Read screen and the Information screen. This information can be retrieved into another Shell-compatible program. You can also save information from another program to the Clipboard and retrieve it into Mail.

Saving and Appending Information to the Clipboard

To define a block from the Read or Information screen or from a file display and save or append the contents to the Clipboard:

1. Move the cursor to the beginning of the text.

2. Press ALT-F4 for Block.

3. Use the cursor-movement keys to move the cursor to where the block should end. The text or commands inside the block should be highlighted.

4. Press CTRL-F1 to display the Shell Options menu.

5. Press **2** or **S** to save the block to the Clipboard, or press **3** or **A** to append the block of text.

Saving information to the Clipboard overwrites any information already in the Clipboard. Appending information to the Clipboard adds it to the end of any existing information.

Retrieving Text from the Clipboard

To retrieve the contents of the Clipboard into Mail, do the following from the Group or Send screen:

1. Use the arrow keys to position the cursor where you want to retrieve the contents of the Clipboard.

2. Press CTRL-F1 to display the Shell Options menu.

3. Press **4** or **R** to retrieve the contents of the Clipboard.

Retrieving Another User's Mail

In Mail you can retrieve another user's mail and read his or her messages. This requires a password to be set either by your system administrator or the other users themselves. By default Mail maintains maximum security, which denies access to another's mail.

To retrieve another user's mail, you can do the following:

1. Have the other user set a password in Mail under Setup by pressing SHIFT-F1, 4, 3.

Environment Options

The Environment options let you change the default settings for Date/ Time Formats, the function of the PGUP and PGDN keys, and passwords. These settings remain in effect until you change them again.

Keystrokes

1. Press SHIFT-F1 for Setup.

2. Press **4** or **E** for Environment. The following options appear:

```
 WP Mail - Setup: Environment

   1 - Date/Time Formats

   2 - Page Up/Down Same as Next/Previous        No

   3 - Password
```

3. Select and modify the desired option.

4. Press F7 until you return to the main screen.

Options

The following options are available from the Environment menu.

Date/Time Formats   Several of the screens in Mail use the current DOS date and time in their displays. You can set the format of these displays using this option. For more information on changing these options, see "Changing the Date and Time Formats," earlier in this chapter.

Page Up/Down Same as Next/Previous   By default the PGUP and PGDN keys take you to the next screen of a message or, when using the

Look option in the List function, to the next page of the file. You can change the PGUP and PGDN keys to take you to the next message or file with this option.

Password   With the Password option you can set and remove a password for Mail. For more information on passwords see "Password," later in this chapter.

Forward

The Forward option allows you to forward a mail message you have received to another user on your Mail system.

Keystrokes

1. From the main Mail screen, highlight the message in your In Box you want to forward.

2. Press **1**, **R**, or ENTER for Read.

3. Press **6** or **F** for Forward.

4. Enter the User ID of the person(s) to whom you want to forward the message.

5. Enter any additional information in the Message window.

6. Press F9 to forward the message. For more information on forwarding messages see "Forwarding a Message," earlier in this chapter.

Help

The Help feature displays on-screen information about the Mail features.

Keystrokes

1. Press F3 for Help from the main Mail screen. Mail displays the screen shown in Figure 7-11.

2. To access help you can type one of the menu item letters to see information about the specific topic; press a function key to see information about the feature associated with that key; or press F3 again to see the Mail template, which is especially useful, since Mail does not come with a keyboard template.

3. Press ENTER or the spacebar to exit a help screen, or press ESC to return to the main help screen.

Hints

The help screens are a valuable tool for accessing information about the Mail program. You do not have to press Help (F3) from the main Mail

---

```
Press any function key to get information about the use of the key.
Press Help (F3) again to see a template for the function keys.
Type one of the following letters for information about specific topics:

        A - Starting Mail            N - Updating In Box
        B - Sending a Message        O - Setup Options
        C - Sending a Phone Message  P - Entering Text
        D - Reading Mail             Q - Printing Mail
        E - Saving Mail              R - Send Options
        F - Envelope Information     S - Copy Types
        G - Deleting Mail
        H - Selecting Recipients
        I - Defining a Group
        J - Selecting Groups
        K - Sending Files
        L - Moving the Cursor        Y - Customer Support
        M - Exiting Mail             Z - Extended Character Set


A-Z Topic: 0           (ESC Topics; Space Exit; Function Key Help for Key)
```

Figure 7-11.   Main Mail help screen

screen. Pressing Help from any Mail menu displays information about the features associated with that screen. Mail displays the keystrokes (if any) for the feature in the upper-right corner of the help screen.

Information Screen

The Information screen displays helpful information for all messages in your In Box or Out Box. The information in this screen includes who the message is from; the date of the message; the subject; the message recipients; the size, date, and time the message and any attached files were sent; the time the message was sent and delivered; and specific options. The information displayed depends on whether you look at the screen from the In Box or the Out Box.

Keystrokes

To view the Information screen for a message, do the following from the main screen:

1. Use the cursor keys to highlight the message for which you want to display the Information screen.

2. Press 4 or **I** to display the Information screen.

3. To return to the main screen, press F7 or ENTER.

In the Information screen you can also move to the Read screen, delete the message, save the message, and move to the next or previous message displayed on the main screen.

List

The List feature in Mail can be used to display lists of files, users, hosts, and groups.

Keystrokes

1. Press F5 for List. The following menu displays:

List 1 Files; 2 Users; 3 User IDs; 4 Groups; 5 Personal Groups; 6 Hosts: 1

List Files

Using List Files in Mail, you can perform many common file-management commands without exiting to DOS. List Files displays the files and subdirectories contained in a given directory. From the List Files screen, you can retrieve, delete, move, rename, or look at a file. Unless you mark several files on which to perform the function, the function is only performed on the file that is currently highlighted in the file listing. You can also perform a name search while in List Files. If you want to change to another directory, you can use the Other Directory option. List Files is especially useful for retrieving files into the Message window in the Send screen and attaching files to send with a message.

Keystrokes

1. Press F5 for List.

2. Press **1** or **F** for Files.

3. Mail displays the current default directory. Press ENTER to select the directory, or enter a path to another directory.

Changing directories in List Files changes the current default directory for Mail.

List Groups

Using the List Groups option you can look at a listing of all of the global groups created by your system administrator or the groups you have created.

Keystrokes

1. Press F5 for List.

2. Press **4** or **G** for Groups to list the global groups, or press **5** or **P** for Personal Groups to look at a listing of the group you have created. After selecting Personal Groups, Mail displays the current default directory. Press ENTER to have Mail list all of the group files in the default directory, or enter the directory where your personal group files are stored.

If you are using a group to send a message, you can mark and retrieve a group from the List Groups screen. You can also look at the contents of the group by pressing ENTER.

List Hosts

The List Hosts option under the List feature is used to display all of the known hosts in your Mail system. From the List Hosts screen you can also look at host-specific user lists.

Keystrokes

1. Press F5 for List.

2. Press **6** or **H** for Hosts.

From the List Hosts screen, you can view the users on a specific host by highlighting the host and pressing **1, U,** or ENTER.

List Users

The List Users option displays all of the known users on your Mail system.

Keystrokes

    1. Press F5 for List.

    2. Press **2** or **U** for Users.

From the List Users screen, you can see information about each user, such as his or her department, phone number, and User ID.

Mark

You can use the Mark option when using the List Users, List User IDs, List Groups, or List Personal Groups options to retrieve several users or groups to the To line at one time. The Mark option lets you mark users or groups as primary, carbon, or blind copy types.

Keystrokes

    1. Press F5 to display the List options.

    2. Press **2** or **U** for Users, **3** or **I** for User IDs, **4** or **G** for Groups, or **5** or **P** for Personal Groups.

    3. Use the arrow keys to move the cursor to the name of the person or group you want to include on the To line, or press F2 or **N** to activate Name Search, and begin typing the name of the person or group. Mail moves through the list to find and match the characters you type.

4. Type *, &, or + to mark the user name or group name.

5. Repeat steps 3 and 4 until you have marked all the names or groups.

6. After marking all names or groups, press F7 to exit and retrieve the IDs or group names to the To line.

Message Options

See "Message Options" under "Setting Send Options in Mail," earlier in this chapter.

Options

The Options menu is used specifically for setting temporary Send options for the current message. The choices listed under Options are the same as those displayed on the Send menu under Setup.

Keystrokes

1. Press SHIFT-F8 from the Send screen.

2. Press **1** or **M** to display the Message menu, press **2** or **P** to display the Protection menu, or press **3** or **T** to display the Transport menu.

3. Change the desired options.

4. Press F7 twice to return to the Send screen.

For information on the individual options see "Setting Send Options in Mail," earlier in this chapter.

Password

If you would like another user to retrieve your mail but passwords for all users have been disabled by the system administrator, you can set a personal password. With a password set, any user that knows your password can retrieve your mail with full access rights.

Keystrokes

To set a password:

1. Press SHIFT-F1 for Setup.

2. Press 4 or **E** for Environment.

3. Press 3 or **W** for Password.

4. Press 1 or **S** and enter a password.

5. Reenter the password when prompted. This confirms and activates the password.

With a password set, every time you start Mail you are prompted to enter your password.

To remove a password, press 3 or **W** followed by 2 or **R**.

Note: If you press ENTER for your password, a Null password is defined. With the Null password set, *any* user can access your mail.

Phone Message

The Mail program lets you send phone messages to any user on your Mail system.

Keystrokes

1. From the main Mail screen, press 7 or **P** for the Phone Message screen.

2. Enter the User ID of the person to whom you are sending the phone message, or use the List Users option to display a list of all known users and retrieve the User ID from the list.

3. Enter the name of person who left the message in the Caller field.

4. Enter the name of the company or organization the caller represents at the Of line.

5. Enter the caller's phone number in the Phone field.

6. If necessary enter a message in the Message window.

7. Use TAB to move through comments that apply and type an asterisk (*) or press the spacebar to mark them.

8. When you are done entering the message, press F9 to send the message.

For more information on the Phone Message feature, see "Sending a Phone Message in Mail," earlier in this chapter.

Print

In Mail you can print a message with all of its attached files, or mark only the files you want to print from the Read screen.

Keystrokes

To print the message and all attached files:

1. Use the cursor keys to highlight the message to print.

2. Press SHIFT-F7 to print the message.

Mail then prints the message and any attached files to the device you have previously specified.

To selectively mark and print files, do the following from the main screen:

1. Use the cursor keys to highlight the message to print.

2. Press **1** or **R** to go to the Read screen.

3. Use the TAB key to move the cursor through the file listing at the top of the Read screen. Mark all files you want to print by typing an asterisk (*).

4. Press SHIFT-F7 to print all marked files to the device specified.

For more information on printing in Mail see "Printing in Mail," earlier in this chapter.

Print Options

With the 6/14/90 release of Office the Print Options menu is accessed via the Setup screen. The Print Options menu lists features available for printing and page formatting in Mail. From the Print Options menu you can specify the size of a printed page in terms of lines and columns, as well as margins. You can also select a printer device file (.PRD) and a print device or port.

Keystrokes

1. Press SHIFT-F1 for Setup.

2. Press **2** or **P** to display the Print options.

After you finish setting the Print options, press F7 until you return to the main screen.

Protection Options

See "Protection Options" under "Setting Send Options in Mail," earlier in this chapter.

Reply

With the Reply option you can have Mail automatically send a reply to the sender of a message without having to enter all of the usual information on the Send screen.

Keystrokes

1. From the Read screen of the message to which you want to reply, press **7** or **R** for Reply.

2. Enter the reply.

3. Press F9 to Send the reply.

See "Replying to a Message," earlier in this chapter.

Resend

From the main screen you can resend any message listed in the Out Box. You can resend the message as it is, edit the information in the original message, or change the users you want to receive the message. This avoids having to reenter an entire message when you only want to change part of the information.

Keystrokes

1. From the Out Box use the arrow keys to highlight the message to resend.

2. Press **1**, **R** or ENTER for Read.

3. Press **7** or **R** for Resend. This displays the Send screen with the original message and recipients listed.

4. If necessary, edit the message or user list.

5. Press F9 to send the message.

Note: Any Send options you set for the first message must be reset.

Retrieve

You can use the Retrieve feature in Mail to retrieve the contents of a text file into the Message window or to retrieve a group of users to the To field.

Keystrokes

To retrieve the contents of an existing file into the Message window:

1. Press TAB or SHIFT-TAB to move the cursor into the Message window.

2. Press SHIFT-F10 to retrieve a file.

3. Enter the name of the file to retrieve. If the file is not in Mail's default directory, enter the path to the file.

To retrieve the users from inside a Group file to the To line:

1. Press TAB or SHIFT-TAB to move the cursor to the To line.

2. Press SHIFT-F10 to retrieve a file.

3. Enter the name of the group file to retrieve. If the file is not in Mail's default directory, enter the path to the file.

Note: You can also use Retrieve to retrieve another user's mail.

Save

Mail lets you save the contents of a message and/or any attached files. For more information on using the Save feature, see "Saving a Message or Attached File," earlier in this chapter.

Screen Update

It is very common to receive a message while you are in Mail. Mail checks for any incoming files and updates the status of your screen every five seconds. If you should need to update or rewrite the screen at any time, you can also do it manually using the Screen Update feature.

Keystrokes

1. Press CTRL-F3 from the main screen. If there are no changes to make, Mail leaves the screen intact. If there are new messages to display, Mail inserts them in your In Box.

Search

When you are reading a message, looking at the Information screen for a message, or looking at the contents of a file in List Files you can use the Search feature in Mail to find a word or string of words.

Keystrokes

1. Press F2 for Forward Search or SHIFT-F2 for Reverse Search.

2. Type the word pattern for which to search.

3. Press F2 or ENTER to begin the search.

Mail searches forward or backward until it finds the next occurrence of the character string you entered and highlights the string. If no match is found, Mail beeps to signal the search failed.

Note: The Search begins at the line below the cursor for a Forward Search and at the line above the cursor for a Reverse Search.

Send

With the Send option (F9), you can send a message to a user or users. See "Sending a Mail Message," earlier in this chapter.

Send Options

The Send options let you set default or temporary settings for Mail messages. These options affect the Message options, the Protection options, and the Transport options.

Keystrokes

To permanently set the Send options:

1. Press SHIFT-F1 for Setup.

2. Press **1** or **S** for Send options.

3. Choose the desired option and make the necessary changes.

To change the Send options for the current message only:

1. Press SHIFT-F8 from the Send screen.

2. Choose the desired option and make the necessary changes.

For more information on the individual Send options, see "Setting Send Options in Mail," earlier in this chapter.

Setup

Using the Setup menu you can permanently configure the options in Mail to meet your needs. The changes you make in the Setup menu remain in effect until you change them again. Mail saves the settings in your personal Setup file in the MSETPC directory.

Keystrokes

1. Press SHIFT-F1 to display the Setup menu. The following menu appears:

```
WP Mail - Setup

   1 - Send

   2 - Print

   3 - Display

   4 - Environment
```

2. Press **1** or **S** to set the Send options, **2** or **P** to display the Print options, **3** or **D** to configure your display, and **4** or **E** to make changes to Mail's environment options.

For more information on the individual Setup options, see "Send Options," "Print Options," "Display Options," and "Environment Options," in the "Functions and Features" section of this chapter.

Shell

The Shell feature lets you exit to Shell without exiting Mail, save and append text to the Shell Clipboard, and retrieve text from the Clipboard.

Keystrokes

1. Press CTRL-F1 for Shell.

2. Choose from the options shown here:

`1 Go to Shell; Clipboard 2 Save; 3 Append: 0`

For more information on the Shell options see "Using the Clipboard with Mail," earlier in this chapter.

Startup Options

Startup options override certain default Mail conditions on startup. You may put startup options on the command line if you are starting Notebook from DOS or add the options to the Shell Program Information screen for Mail. The following is a list of all the startup options that you can use with Mail.

/@U-User ID   This option specifies the Office User ID of the person whose In and Out Boxes Mail should access. By default, this is the user who has logged onto the network and started Mail. This can only be accomplished if a personal password has been set by that user or a system password has been set by the system administrator. For information on setting a personal password, see "Password," earlier in this chapter. For information on system passwords, contact your system administrator.

/C   This option checks for any unread messages in your In Box. To use this option under Shell, Mail must be set to start resident. If any unread messages are found, Mail starts before the Shell menu is displayed. If no unread messages are found, Mail remains resident, but the program is not entered before Shell. If this option is run from DOS, Mail starts if unread messages are found; if no new messages are found, you return to the DOS command line. This is commonly used in the AUTO-EXEC.BAT file before starting Shell.

/CM   This option is similar to /C, but only checks for unread messages and notifies you if any are found. Mail is not automatically started.

/CN   This option is similar to /C, but if used under Shell, Mail is not left resident in memory if no unread messages exist. If used on from DOS, /CN works the same as /C.

/CP-*x*   This option sets the code page for correct character display. This gives Mail the code page to use regardless of the current DOS code page.

/D-*path* This option specifies the default directory for Mail to use. This is where Mail opens its temporary files and should normally point to a local directory or to your personal work directory.

/M-*macro* This option specifies a macro to execute each time Mail is started when using Mail under Shell. If the macro is not located in the current default directory for Mail, or in the global macro directory specified in Shell, be sure to list the full path to the macro.

/NF   This option sets Mail's screen display to No Flash. This can be used to try and correct common display problems for Mail when used under window or program management products other than Shell.

/NS   This option speeds up display on some color monitors by eliminating the synchronization process. This may cause snow on some monitors.

/NT-*x*   This option specifies the network type you are using where *x* represents the number of the network.

/NU   This option eliminates occasional pauses in Mail's operations by turning off the Auto-Update feature. However, any new messages received after using this option are not displayed in your In Box.

/PH-*path*   This option specifies the location of the Host directory. This is also where Mail looks for your personal information files.

/SS-*row, column*   This option customizes the screen display by specifying the rows and columns on the display.

Transport Options

See "Transport Options" under "Setting Send Options in Mail," in the first section of this chapter.

Undelete

When you delete a message from your In or Out Box, Mail stores that message in a temporary buffer to allow you to undelete or restore it if you desire. You can restore the last three messages deleted from your In and Out Boxes, for a total of six messages.

Keystrokes

1. Use TAB or SHIFT-TAB to position the cursor in the correct window on the main screen.

2. Press F1 to restore the message.

3. Press **1**, **R**, or **Y** to restore the message displayed at the bottom of the screen, or press **2** or **P** to view the previous message in the deletion buffer. Press **1**, **R**, or **Y** to restore the correct message when displayed at the bottom of the screen.

Underline

In the Message or subject window on the Send screen, you can use underline when creating or editing a message.

Keystrokes

To add underline:

1. Use the cursor keys or editing keys to position the cursor where the underline text should start.

2. Press F6 for Underline and type the word or words you want underlined.

3. Press F6 again to turn off Underline.

To delete underline codes:

1. Use the cursor keys or editing keys to position the cursor where the text to be underlined begins.

2. Press CTRL-RIGHT ARROW for Word Right or CTRL-LEFT ARROW for Word Left until the cursor is on the first letter of the underlined word.

3. Press DEL. The "Delete Underline (Y/N)?N" prompt appears.

4. Type **Y** to delete the underline codes.

Using Notebook

The Notebook program is an information organizer. With Notebook you can keep track of similar information in one file. You might use a Notebook file to keep track of employee information, frequently called phone numbers, research notes, and so on. There is no limit to the type of information you can store in a Notebook file. Notebook is similar to a database in that it allows you to creatively organize information, but is much easier to use. With the Notebook program you can determine exactly what information is contained in a Notebook file and how the information should appear on screen, thus giving you great flexibility.

Notebook files can be retrieved into WordPerfect (4.2 and above) and used as secondary merge files. Secondary merge files contain information that is merged with a primary merge file. For example, if you are sending a form letter to 100 clients you can enter the names and addresses of the clients in a secondary merge file. You can then create one letter as the primary file and merge all 100 client names and addresses into the primary file. Secondary merge files automate many daily office tasks. Secondary merge files can also be retrieved into Notebook and used as Notebook files. Managing and editing secondary merge files in Notebook is much easier than managing and editing them in WordPerfect.

Learning Notebook Terminology

In order to better understand the Notebook program, it is helpful to be familiar with a few basic terms that will be used throughout this chapter.

Fields and Records

A Notebook file consists of *fields* and *records*. The fields and records contain the actual information in the Notebook file. A field contains the specific information within a record. For example, if you have a Notebook file containing the name, phone number, and position of each of your employees, the name, phone number, and position would be the fields in that Notebook file. The actual name, phone number, and position of each employee is the field data. You can have up to 100 fields in a Notebook file, but a more realistic limit is between 25 and 30. Unlike most database programs, Notebook's fields are variable in length. Having variable-length fields means, for example, that you do not have to decide in advance how many characters a last name or phone number will need. After creating a field in Notebook, you can enter up to 4000 characters for the field data, even if the screen is set to only display 10 characters for the field. If you enter more information than can be seen on screen, use the arrow keys to scroll to the remaining information. Variable-length fields are not limited by the display size.

A record contains all the fields or all the information for one item. In the previous example, each employee would have his or her own record. If you entered information for 50 employees you would have 50 records in your Notebook file.

List Display and Record Display

Notebook has two main screens: one for viewing information and the other for viewing and entering information. The first screen is the List Display screen. The List Display screen appears when you first retrieve a Notebook file. The List Display screen lists selected fields and the data from the selected fields from each record in your Notebook file. In Figure 8-1, the first and last name, extension, division, and job title of the employee appear on the List Display screen. When you create or edit your own Notebook files, you can choose which information you want to display on the List Display screen. From the List Display you can view information, but you cannot edit or enter new information. The purpose of the List Display is to help you quickly locate information for all the records in the Notebook file.

```
 First Name     Last Name      Extension  Division     Job Title
 Erin           Dobrinski      7860       Accounting   Auditor
 Jackson        Wentworth      7059       Marketing    Sales Representative
 Pamela         Goldberg       7624       Development  Researcher
```

1 Create; 2 Delete; 3 Edit; 4 Options; 5 Name Search: 3   Record 1

Figure 8-1.   Sample List Display

```
┌─────────────────────────────────────────────────────────────┐
│                    COMPANY PHONE DIRECTORY                    │
├─────────────────────────────────────────────────────────────┤
│  First Name: Erin                   Last Name: Dobrinski      │
│   Extension: 7860                  Home Phone: 555-2639       │
│     Address: 1212 S. Main                                     │
│              Snowville, AZ  55512                             │
├─────────────────────────────────────────────────────────────┤
│   Hire Date: 12/04/90              Birth Date: 01/30/61       │
│                                                               │
│    Division: Accounting             Job Title: Auditor        │
│                                                               │
│       Notes: Master's degree in accounting.                  │
│              Graduated in top third of her class.            │
│                                                               │
└─────────────────────────────────────────────────────────────┘
```

Tab Next Field; F2 Search; F7 Exit; F9 Create;   Record 1

Figure 8-2.   Sample Record Display

The second main Notebook screen is the Record Display screen. The Record Display lists all the fields for one record. In Figure 8-2 all the data in the fields for Erin Dobrinski display. From the Record Display you can enter new records or edit existing records.

Field Labels and Field Names

All fields within a Notebook file have a *field label* and a *field name*. The field labels are the descriptions you see when you enter the Record Display screen. A field label helps you know what information you should enter for each field. In Figure 8-2 the field labels are First Name, Last Name, Extension, Home Phone, Address, Hire Date, Birth Date, Division, Job Title, and Notes. You can enter any text for the field label. The more descriptive the label, the easier it is for you and other users to know what information is wanted for each field. The field labels only display in the Record Display screen.

The field names are the names given to the field when the Notebook file is created. The field names display at the top of the List Display as shown here:

First Name	Last Name	Extension	Division	Job Title
Erin	Dobrinski	7860	Accounting	Auditor
Jackson	Wentworth	7859	Marketing	Sales Representative
Pamela	Goldberg	7624	Development	Researcher

The field names can be the same as the field labels, but they do not have to be. A field name can be 39 characters long, while a field label can be any length. Field names are important for merging Notebook files and for creating primary files in WordPerfect for use with Notebook files. These issues will be discussed later in this chapter.

Starting Notebook

To start Notebook from the Shell menu, type the letter next to the Notebook entry; the default letter is N. To start Notebook from DOS type **nb**. There are several startup options that you can use when starting Notebook. For more information, see "Startup Options," in the "Functions and Features" section of this chapter.

The first time you start Notebook an empty List Display screen appears. The words "Empty Notebook" appear at the top of the screen indicating that you do not have any information in the Notebook file.

Exiting and Saving Notebook Files

To exit Notebook and save the current file:

1. Press F7 from the List Display screen.

2. Type **Y** for Yes at the "Save file" prompt.

3. Press ENTER to accept the default filename or enter a new filename.

4. Type **Y** for Yes to exit Notebook.

The first time you save and exit a Notebook file, Notebook displays a default filename. If you are using Office PC the default filename is NOTEBOOK.NB. If you are using Office LAN the default filename is *XXX*_FILE.NB, where *XXX* represents your File ID. Once you have saved a file with the default filename, Notebook automatically retrieves that file each time you start the program. For this reason, you should save the Notebook file that you use most often with the default filename. If you do not save any of your Notebook files with the default filename, Notebook will go to the empty List Display on startup.

Creating a Notebook File

Before you can enter information in Notebook, you must create a Notebook file. Included with your WordPerfect Office 3.0 package are several model Notebook files. You can use these files as they are or you can modify them to fit your needs. If the information you need to enter into a Notebook file does not fit into any of these model files, you will need to create a Notebook file.

Organizing the Information

Before creating a Notebook file, you need to decide what information you want to have in it. For example, a birthday Notebook file for your company might include the full name of each employee, the date of birth, and the employee's address.

Once you decide what information needs to be in the Notebook file, you need to determine how you want it to appear in the record display, where you enter the information. Think of the record display as the form you fill in when entering the information. You can organize the record display any way you want. It is usually best to first sketch out a design for the record display. For the example above, the sketch might look something like this:

```
Employee Birth Date Record
Name:
Birth Date:
Address:
```

Creating the Record Display

Once you determine what information you want in the Notebook file and get an idea of how you want it to appear, you are ready to create the Record Display.

Adding the Fields

The first thing you need to add to the Record Display is the name of each of the fields you want to have in the Notebook file. A field contains the individual information within the record. In this example, the fields are name, birth date, and address. You can have up to 100 fields in one Notebook file, but a more practical limit is between 25 and 30. If you have too many fields, it becomes difficult to view the information in the Record Display, which is limited to one screen. To add the fields to the Record Display from a blank Notebook screen:

1. Press 4 or **O** for Options.

2. Press **1** or **R** for Record Display Format. When you enter the record display, the cursor rests on the "D" in "Default field" as

shown in Figure 8-3. This default field is used as the first field in the record display.

3. Press CTRL-END to delete the Default field label.

4. Press SHIFT-F8 for Edit Fields.

5. Press **3** or **N** for Name.

6. Type **Name** for the first field name. As soon as you begin typing, Notebook deletes the old field name.

7. Press ENTER.

8. Press **4** or **C** for Create to add the second field. As soon as you press Create, an "Enter field name" prompt displays at the bottom of the screen.

9. Type **Birth Date** at the cursor and press ENTER. This overwrites the F02 field name.

Default field:
F01

Ctrl-F3 Line Draw;   Shift-F8 Edit Fields;   F7 Exit;   Insert

---

Figure 8-3.   Blank record display

10. Press **4** or **C** for Create to add the third and final field.

11. Type **Address** at the cursor and press ENTER. This overwrites the F03 field name.

All the fields are now added to the Record Display and your screen should look like this:

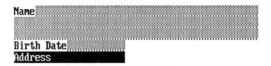

Sizing and Positioning the Fields

Once you have entered all the field names, you need to size the fields and position them in an organized and logical format. At this point you need to look at the sketch you created to determine how the fields should display on screen. For this example, each field requires only one line. To edit the size of the fields:

1. Press TAB once to move the cursor to the Name field.

2. Press **1** or **S** for Size. Once you press Size, any arrow keys you press adjust the size of the field.

3. Press the UP ARROW key twice to change the size of the Name field to one line. A status line in the lower-right corner of the screen displays the field's exact size. In this example, the status line should read "Field display size 1x46."

Note: The size of a field only relates to its display size; it has nothing to do with the amount of information you can enter in the field. You can enter up to 4000 characters in one field. It is helpful to make the fields large enough so that the screen displays as much information as is necessary to quickly see what the field contains. The information that displays is also the information that prints when you print the Record Display.

4. Press the RIGHT ARROW key four times to lengthen the width of the field. The status line should now read "Field display size 1x50." The Name field is now the appropriate size.

5. Press TAB to move to the Birth Date field.

6. Press **1** or **S** for Size. Since this field is already one line, you need only change the length of the field.

7. Press the RIGHT ARROW key until the status line at the bottom of the screen reads "Field display size displays 1x50."

8. Press TAB to move to the Address field and repeat steps 6 and 7.

9. Press F7.

Your screen should look like the one shown here:

```
Name
```

```
Birth Date
Address
```

Once the fields are the correct size, you can move and organize them in any way you wish. At this point, you are allowed a lot of freedom and creativity. There is no right or wrong way to organize the information; it is strictly a matter of personal preference. The only thing you need to keep in mind is that if other users are going to use this Notebook file you want it to be as simple and organized as possible. To position the fields in the employee birthday file:

1. Press the UP ARROW until the cursor moves to the line above the Name field.

2. Press the ENTER key seven times to move the fields to the middle of the screen.

3. Press SHIFT-F8 for Edit Fields. The cursor should be on the Name field.

4. Press the RIGHT ARROW key eight times to move the field to the middle of the screen.

When you first enter the Edit Fields screen, Notebook defaults to the Position option, displaying it in underline. Notebook always underlines the current option in the Edit Fields menu, so if you are not sure what option you have selected, you can check the options line at the bottom of the screen and see which one is highlighted.

5. Press TAB to move to the Birth Date field.

6. Press the RIGHT ARROW key eight times to move the field to the middle of the screen.

7. Press the UP ARROW key once to move the field up one line.

8. Press TAB to move to the Address field.

9. Repeat steps 6 and 7.

10. Press F7 to exit the Edit Fields screen.

Your screen should look like the one shown here:

Adding the Field Labels

Field labels are the descriptions that display when you are entering the actual information into the record. The field labels can be the same as the field names, but they do not have to match. In the employee birthday file, the field names and field labels will match. An example of when you might not want your field names and field labels to match is if you have a Notebook file that needs descriptive field labels. For example, if you have a Notebook file that keeps track of when checks are mailed, your field name could be Date, but your field label might be Date Mailed. The more descriptive the field label, the easier it is to know exactly what information should be entered.

Your cursor should be on the Address field in the employee birthday Notebook file. To add the field labels:

1. If INS displays in the bottom-right corner of your screen, press the INS key to toggle to Typeover mode. This prevents you from adding unnecessary spaces and codes to the record display.

2. Press HOME, LEFT ARROW to move the cursor to the edge of the screen.

3. Press the RIGHT ARROW key four times to move the cursor.

4. Press F6 to turn on Bold, and type **ADDRESS:**.

5. Press the UP ARROW key until the cursor is on the same line as the Birth Date field.

6. Press HOME, LEFT ARROW to move the cursor to the edge of the screen.

7. Press the RIGHT ARROW key once to move the cursor.

8. Press F6 to turn on Bold, and type **BIRTH DATE:**.

9. Press the UP ARROW key until the cursor is on the same line as the Name field.

10. Press HOME, LEFT ARROW to move the cursor to the edge of the screen.

11. Press the RIGHT ARROW key seven times to move the cursor.

12. Press F6 to turn on Bold, and type **NAME:**.

Your screen should look like this:

```
      NAME: Name
BIRTH DATE: Birth Date
   ADDRESS: Address
```

Along with the field labels you can also add other comments or titles to help you further organize your record display. For this example it would be helpful to have a title at the top of the screen indicating the purpose of the record. To add a descriptive title to the Record Display:

1. Press the UP ARROW key four times.

2. Press the SPACEBAR 20 times so the title will be centered on the screen.

3. Press F6 to turn on Bold.

4. Type **EMPLOYEE BIRTH DATE RECORD.**

Your screen should look like this:

EMPLOYEE BIRTH DATE RECORD

```
      NAME: Name
BIRTH DATE: Birth Date
   ADDRESS: Address
```

Adding Line Draw to the Record Display

After you have added the field labels, you don't necessarily have to do anything else to the Record Display. But by adding line-draw characters, you can better organize and divide the Record Display. To add line draw to the employee birthday Notebook file:

1. Press HOME, HOME, UP ARROW to move the cursor to the top-left corner of the screen.

2. Press the DOWN ARROW twice.

3. Press CTRL-F3 for Line Draw.

4. Press 2 to choose the double line-draw character.

5. Press HOME, RIGHT ARROW to draw a line from the cursor position to the other edge of the screen.

6. Press the DOWN ARROW key 13 times to draw the right edge of the box.

7. Press HOME, LEFT ARROW to draw the bottom of the box.

8. Press HOME, UP ARROW to draw the left edge of the box.

9. Press 6 or **M** for Move. When you press Move, you can move the cursor without drawing any lines.

10. Press the DOWN ARROW key three times.

11. Press 2 to choose the double line-draw character.

12. Press HOME, RIGHT ARROW to draw a double line under the EMPLOYEE BIRTH DATE RECORD title.

13. Press **6** or **M** for Move.

14. Press the DOWN ARROW key four times.

15. Press **1** to choose the single line-draw character.

16. Press HOME, LEFT ARROW to draw a single line under the Name field.

17. Press **6** or **M** for Move.

18. Press the DOWN ARROW key two times.

19. Press **1** to choose the single line-draw character.

20. Press HOME, RIGHT ARROW to draw a single line under the Birth Date field.

21. Press F7 three times to exit Line Draw mode and return to the List Display.

After drawing all the lines, your completed record display should look like the one shown in Figure 8-4. To see the Record Display screen, press ENTER from the List Display. Although the process of creating a record display is lengthy, with a little practice it becomes quite easy.

Creating the List Display

Once you create the Record Display, you are ready to create the List Display. The List Display appears when you first retrieve your Notebook file. The List Display displays selected information from each record in the Notebook file. How the information displays and how it is ordered is up to you. When organizing the List Display you need to keep in mind that the purpose of this screen is to help you quickly locate the most important information in the Notebook file. To move to the List Display Format screen:

1. From the main Notebook screen, press **4** or **O** for Options.

2. Press **2** or **L** for List Display Format.

3. Press **1** or **L** for List Display. The screen shown in Figure 8-5 displays.

```
┌──────────────────────────────────────────────────────────┐
│┌────────────────────────────────────────────────────────┐│
││                EMPLOYEE BIRTH DATE RECORD                ││
│├────────────────────────────────────────────────────────┤│
││      NAME:                                               ││
│├────────────────────────────────────────────────────────┤│
││BIRTH DATE:                                               ││
│├────────────────────────────────────────────────────────┤│
││   ADDRESS:                                               ││
││                                                          ││
││                                                          ││
│└────────────────────────────────────────────────────────┘│
└──────────────────────────────────────────────────────────┘
```

Tab Next Field; F2 Search; F7 Exit; F9 Create;   RECORD 1

Figure 8-4.   Final Employee Birth Date Record Display screen

Options: List Display Format

```
Name
Name
```

Order	Field Name		Sort Type	Direction
1	Name		Alpha/Numeric	Ascending

                                              Field display size 79
Tab Next Field; ↔ Size; ↕ Name; Ins Insert; Del Delete; 0

Figure 8-5.   List Display screen

When you first enter the List Display Format screen the first field, in this example the Name field, is the only field that displays. At this point you need to decide which fields you want to display. Because there are only three fields in the employee birthday file, there is enough room for all of them to display on the List Display screen. To add the other fields to the List Display:

   1. Press the LEFT ARROW key until the field display-size message at the bottom-right corner of the screen indicates 25.

   2. Press TAB to move to the next field. Since there is not another field listed, the cursor moves to the end of the Name field.

   3. Press INS to insert a new field. By default the first field name, in this case Name, appears.

   4. To change to the next field press the UP ARROW or DOWN ARROW key until the Birth Date field appears.

   5. Press the RIGHT ARROW key until the field display-size message at the bottom-right corner of the screen indicates 20.

   6. Press TAB to move to the next field.

   7. Press INS to insert a new field.

   8. Press the UP ARROW or DOWN ARROW key until the Address field appears.

   9. Press the RIGHT ARROW key until the Address field extends to the right edge of the screen. The List Display Format screen should look like this:

```
Options: List Display Format

Name
Name                              Birth Date        Address

Order   Field Name                         Sort Type       Direction
1       Name                               Alpha/Numeric   Ascending
```

10. Press F7 to exit.

11. Press **N** when prompted to update the sort list.

Defining a Sort List

After creating the List Display, the final step in creating a Notebook file is defining a sort list. The sort list determines in what order the various records in the Notebook file are sorted. In the employee birthday file the Name field is displayed first, but it would be easier to see which birthdays are coming up if the list was sorted by birth date first. With Birth Date as the first sorting field, all the names will be in order according to the birth date, but the Name field will still display first on the list display. To define the sort list from the List Display Format menu:

1. Type **2** or **S** for Sort List. By default the Name field, the first field in the list display, is listed.

2. Press INS to insert a new field in the first line of the sort list. The first field displays again.

3. Type **B** to change to the field that begins with B, in this case the Birth Date field. You can also press the spacebar to display a different field. The sort list should look like this:

```
Options: List Display Format

Name                    Birth Date           Address


  Order   Field Name                  Sort Type      Direction
  1       Birth Date                  Alpha/Numeric  Ascending
  2       Name                        Alpha/Numeric  Ascending
```

4. Press F7 three times to return to the List Display screen.

For this example you do not need to change any of the other options. For information on the Sort List options see "Editing a Sort List" later in this chapter. In this example there is no need to sort the address. When you begin to enter information in the employee birthday file, the Notebook will be sorted first by birth date and then by name. So all the birthdays in January will be listed first. In order for the Notebook to sort correctly you need to enter the dates in numerical format, such as 2/22, 12/11, and so on. If there are any birthdays on the same day, they will be sorted by name.

Now that you have defined the sort list, you can save the employee birthday file and begin using it to enter information.

Summary of Steps

Creating an entire Notebook file from start to finish is a lengthy process, especially if it is your first time. In order to help you remember exactly what to do when creating a Notebook file, the following lists the basic steps.

1. Organize the information
2. Create the Record Display
    a. Add the fields
    b. Size and position the fields
    c. Add the field labels
    d. Add line draw to the Record Display
3. Create the List Display
4. Define a sort list

Editing a Record

If the information in one of your Notebook files changes or needs to be updated, you can edit a single record or several records. For example, if you have an employee Notebook file and one of your employees receives a new phone number, you would need to edit the file to reflect this change. Table 8-1 lists the editing keys available while in the record display.

Keystroke	Action
BACKSPACE	Deletes the character to the left of the cursor
DEL	Deletes the character at the cursor
HOME, DEL	Deletes entire record
CTRL-BACKSPACE	Deletes the word at the cursor
CTRL-END	Deletes to the end of the current line starting at the cursor
CTRL-PGDN	Deletes all text in the field starting at the cursor
INS	Switches between Insert and Typeover mode

Table 8-1.   Editing Keys in Record Display

Keystroke	Action
UP ARROW/DOWN ARROW	Moves up/down one line
LEFT ARROW/RIGHT ARROW	Moves left/right one character
CTRL-LEFT ARROW/RIGHT ARROW	Moves left/right one word
HOME, LEFT ARROW/RIGHT ARROW	Moves to the beginning or end of a line
END	Moves to end of a line
PGUP	Moves up one record
PGDN	Moves down one record
HOME, PGUP	Moves to previous marked record
HOME, PGDN	Moves to next marked record
TAB	Moves to next field in record
SHIFT-TAB	Moves to previous field in record

Table 8-2.   Cursor Keys in Record Display

Table 8-2 lists the cursor keys available in the record display. To edit a record in your Notebook file from an empty Notebook screen:

1. Press SHIFT-F10 to retrieve the Notebook file.

2. Enter the name of the Notebook file you want to edit.

3. Use the DOWN ARROW key to highlight the record you want to edit.

4. Press ENTER to see the Record Display.

5. Press the TAB key until you are at the field that needs to be modified.

6. Use the editing keys to delete any unwanted information.

7. Type in the new information.

8. Press F7 to exit the Record Display and return to the List Display.

9. Repeat steps 3 through 8 until you have edited all the records that need to be changed.

10. Press F7 to exit Notebook.

11. Press ENTER at the "Save file? (Y/N) Yes" prompt.

12. Press ENTER again to save the file with the same name or enter a new filename.

13. If you save the file with the same name, type **Y** to replace the existing file.

14. Type **Y** to exit Notebook.

Editing the Record Display Format

If the information needed in a Notebook file changes or if you need to rearrange the format of the record display, you can do so from the Record Display Format screen. For example, if you are using the model Notebook files shipped with WordPerfect Office 3.0 and need to delete one of the fields it contains and modify the size of another field, you can do so from the Record Display Format screen. After retrieving the Notebook file you want to edit:

1. Press 4 or **O** for options from the List Display or press SHIFT-F8.
2. Press 1 or **R** for Record Display Format.

From this screen you can change or add line draw to the Record Display screen. You can also edit the field labels that are displayed.

Note: If you are going to make any changes to the actual fields, it is a good idea to make changes to the line-draw characters and field labels after making the other changes.

Using Line Draw

You do not have to use line draw in the Record Display. However, line draw helps the Record Display look more organized and professional. To access the line draw options:

1. Press CTRL-F3. The following options appear:

1 |; 2 ‖; 3 *; 4 Change; 5 Erase; 6 Move: 1

Line Draw Options

The first three options on the Line Draw menu allow you to draw lines with the specified characters. When using line draw you can use the following cursor keys:

Cursor Keys	Action
Arrow key	Draws one character at a time
HOME, arrow key	Draws a line until another line-draw character or edge of screen is encountered
HOME, HOME, arrow key	Draws a line to the edge of the screen

You can change the character displayed for the third option with Change. After selecting Change, choose the number corresponding to one of the characters listed or enter a new character by pressing Other. If you want to use a character not listed on the keyboard, you can enter its decimal equivalent. See Appendix B for the decimal values of ASCII characters.

If you make a mistake when using the line-draw characters, use the Erase option. Once you press Erase, all cursor keys erase existing lines and field label characters. Always use the Erase option and not the DEL key.

When you are drawing lines you may also need to move the cursor without drawing a line or erasing existing lines. The Move option allows you to do this without exiting Line Draw mode. After you press Move, the cursor keys move without performing any other line-draw functions.

Editing Field Labels

The field labels help identify what information should be entered in the Record Display. If you need to change or add field labels you can do so from the Record Display Format screen. When you are entering the field labels you can use boldfacing and underlining to make the labels more noticeable.

Editing Fields

If you need to edit, delete, or add to the field information for a Notebook file, you can do so with the Edit Fields options. To access the Edit Fields screen:

1. Press SHIFT-F8 from the Record Display Format screen.

A screen similar to the one in Figure 8-6 appears with the information for your Notebook file. The Edit Fields options are listed at the bottom of the screen. The currently selected option is underlined. The default option when you enter this screen is Position. While in the Edit Fields screen, the TAB key moves you through the fields.

Size   The Size option lets you increase or decrease the size of the field. The upper-left corner of the field is fixed, and any changes you make to the size will use that corner as the reference point. The status line at the bottom-right corner of the screen lists the display size of the currently highlighted field. This is useful if you are trying to make two fields the same size or if you want to compare the size of two fields.

Position   The Position option lets you move the field to a different location in the Record Display. This is the default option when you enter the Edit Fields screen.

Name   The Name option lets you change or edit the name of a field that is already created. As soon as you begin typing, the old name

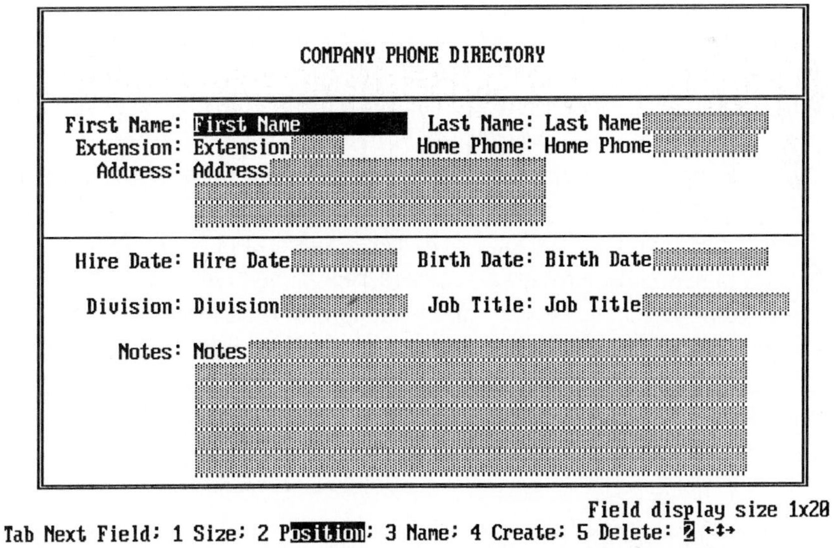

```
                      COMPANY PHONE DIRECTORY


   First Name: First Name            Last Name: Last Name
   Extension: Extension              Home Phone: Home Phone
     Address: Address



    Hire Date: Hire Date             Birth Date: Birth Date

     Division: Division               Job Title: Job Title

        Notes: Notes




                                            Field display size 1x20
   Tab Next Field: 1 Size: 2 Position: 3 Name: 4 Create: 5 Delete: 2 ←↕→
```

Figure 8-6.   Edit Fields screen with sample Notebook file

is deleted. This option is especially useful if you are trying to standard-ize the field names of all your Notebook files.

Create   The Create option adds a new field to the Record Display. As soon as you press Create, Notebook prompts you for the field name. When you create a new field, it is inserted below the last field in the record display. The field may initially display on top of another label or line-draw character. This will be corrected after entering a name and positioning the field. When you first create a field its size is 1 by 21. After creating the field, you can move and size it according to your needs.

Delete   With the Delete option you can delete unwanted fields from the Record Display. The Delete option deletes the field from the Record Display as well as from all previously created records. Before Notebook deletes a field, the "Delete the field from EVERY RECORD? (Y/N)N" message displays, warning you that the field along with all information previously entered will be deleted. Notebook does not allow you to delete a field from a record if it is the only field in the record.

Using the List Display

As previously mentioned, the List Display is the first screen that ap-pears when you start Notebook. It displays selected information from each record in the Notebook file. From the List Display screen you can only view information; you cannot edit information. The fields in the List Display are listed at the top of the screen and appear bolded. Below the field names are the entries from each record as shown in Figure 8-7. At the bottom of the screen are the various options available from the List Display along with number of the currently highlighted record. The cursor is a reverse video bar that highlights the entire line of informa-tion. Table 8-3 lists the cursor keys available in the list display, along with their actions.

Using List Display Options

The following options are available from the List Display screen:

```
1 Create; 2 Delete; 3 Edit; 4 Options; 5 Name Search: 3
```

Create   The Create option displays a blank Record Display screen so you can enter information for a new record. You can also press INS or F9 to create a new record.

Delete   The Delete option deletes the entire record from the Notebook file. Before the record is deleted, Notebook displays the "Delete record? (Y/N)Y" prompt. Type **Y** if you want to delete the record or type **N** if you do not want to delete the record. You can delete multiple files by marking them with an asterisk and then selecting Delete. For more information on marking records see "Marking Notebook Records" later in this chapter.

Edit   The Edit option accesses the Record Display for the highlighted record. You can also press ENTER or Switch (SHIFT-F3) to edit the record. After pressing Edit you can change or add information to the record.

```
First Name    Last Name      Extension  Division     Job Title
Erin          Dobrinski      7860       Accounting   Auditor
Jackson       Wentworth      7059       Marketing    Sales Representative
Pamela        Goldberg       7624       Development  Researcher
```

```
1 Create; 2 Delete; 3 Edit; 4 Options; 5 Name Search: 3        Record 1
```

Figure 8-7.   Sample list display

Keystroke	Action
UP ARROW or PGUP	Moves up one record
DOWN ARROW or PGDN	Moves down one record
SCREEN UP (+ on the numeric keypad)	Moves up one screen
SCREEN DOWN (− on the numeric keypad)	Moves down one screen
HOME, HOME, UP ARROW	Moves to first record
HOME, HOME, DOWN ARROW	Moves to last record
CTRL-HOME, x	Moves to record number specified by x
HOME, PGUP	Moves to previous marked record
HOME, PGDN	Moves to next marked record
ENTER	Moves to Record Display of highlighted record

Table 8-3.   Cursor Keys in List Display

Options   The Options selection displays the screen used for setting or changing temporary Notebook options. From this screen you can change the format of the record and list display, turn Auto-Sort on or off, change the language, text, and date format, and define dialing instructions. Any changes you make in this screen are saved with the current Notebook file only. To change these settings for all future Notebook files, use Setup Options (SHIFT-F1).

Name Search   The final option on the List Display menu is Name Search. Name Search allows you to quickly move to a record by typing in the first few letters of the first field. As soon as you press Name Search, Notebook highlights the first field in the sorting order. This helps you to know what field Name Search is actually searching since the first sorting field may not be the first displayed field. For more information on Name Search see "Using Name Search" later in this chapter.

Editing the List Display Format

You can edit or add to the list display from the List Display Format screen. For example, if you are using a Notebook file that displays employees' names, addresses, and phone numbers and you find the addresses are not useful, you could delete the address field from the list display. You could then replace it with another field from the record display or change the size of the other two fields in the list display. To edit a list display:

1. Press **4** or **O** for Options or press SHIFT-F8.

2. Press **2** or **L** for List Display Format.

3. Press **1** or **L** for List Display.

A screen similar to Figure 8-8 appears, listing the information for your Notebook file. At the top of the screen are the current fields in the list display. To change these options:

4. Press TAB to move to the field you want to edit.

5. Use the options at the bottom of the menu to make the desired changes.

Options: List Display Format

First Name	Last Name		Extension	Division		Job Title	
First Name	Last Name		Extension	Division		Job Title	

Order	Field Name	Sort Type	Direction
1	First Name	Alphabetic	Ascending
2	Last Name	Alphabetic	Ascending

Field display size 13

Tab Next Field: ↔ Size: ↕ Name: Ins Insert: Del Delete: 0

Figure 8-8.   List Display Format screen

List Display Format Options

From the List Display Format menu you can change the size of a field, replace a field with another field, delete a field, or add a field to the List Display. If you make a mistake when editing the list display format you can press Cancel (F1) to exit the screen without saving your changes.

Changing the Size of a Field

The LEFT ARROW and RIGHT ARROW keys change the size of the highlighted field. Press the RIGHT ARROW key to increase the display size and the LEFT ARROW key to decrease the size. The status line at the bottom-right corner of the screen lists the current display size of the highlighted field. You can also change the size of the space between the fields.

Changing the Name of a Field

If you want to replace a field that is currently displayed in the List Display with another field:

1. Press TAB to move to the field you want to change.

2. Press the UP ARROW or DOWN ARROW key until the field you want to display appears.

Instead of using the arrow keys, you can type the first letter of the field you want to display. For example, if you want the Address field to display, type **a** and Address automatically appears as the field. If there is more than one field with the same first letter, continue typing the letters in the field until the correct field appears.

Inserting a New Field

To add a field to the List Display:

1. Press TAB to move to where you want to insert the new field.

2. Press INS.

3. Press the UP ARROW or DOWN ARROW key until the correct field name appears.

If you insert a field before existing fields, Notebook automatically shifts the existing fields to the right.

Deleting a Field

To delete a field from the List Display:

1. Press TAB to move to the field you want to delete.

2. Press DEL or BACKSPACE to delete the field. Notebook displays the "Remove field from list display? (Y/N)N" message.

3. Type **Y** to delete the field.

When you delete a field in the list display it does not remove any data from the Notebook file, it only removes the field from the list display.

Sorting a Notebook File

By default Notebook automatically sorts your Notebook file according to the sort list. For more information on setting up and editing a sort list see the next section in this chapter. If you do not want Notebook to automatically sort your file each time a change is made, you can turn off Auto-Sort. If you have a large Notebook file it's a good idea to turn off Auto-Sort. This way Notebook is not sorting the file every time you make a change, which slows down the performance of the program. To turn off Auto-Sort for the current Notebook file:

1. Press 4 or **O** for Options or press SHIFT-F8.

2. Press 3 or **A** for Auto-Sort.

3. Type **N** for No.

If you want to turn Auto-Sort off for all newly created Notebook files:

1. Press SHIFT-F1 for Setup.

2. Press **2** or **I** for Initial Settings.

3. Press **1** or **A** for Auto-Sort.

4. Type **N** for No.

If you turn Auto-Sort off, you can still sort your file manually. From the List Display:

1. Press CTRL-F9.

2. Type **Y** to sort the file.

If you do not want to sort the entire Notebook file, you can mark records with an asterisk and then sort them manually. This increases the sorting speed tremendously.

Editing a Sort List

The sort list determines what fields Notebook uses when sorting a notebook file and how the fields are sorted. If you do not set up a sort list, Notebook automatically sorts the file by the first field in the list display. The sort list is useful if you want to display the fields one way, but sort them another. For example, if you have a Notebook file that keeps track of equipment that has been loaned out, you can display the name of the person who has checked out the equipment in the first column, but sort it by the date the equipment is due.

Notebook allows you to have up to 14 different fields in the sort list. It is best to only list fields that are especially useful because the more fields you sort by, the longer it takes to sort the list. If you find you need to sort by a field that is not listed, you can always add the field to the sort list.

To edit a sort list:

1. Press **4** or **O** for Options or press SHIFT-F8.

2. Press **2** or **L** for List Display Format.

3. Press **2** or **S** for Sort List. A screen similar to Figure 8-9 displays the current sort list information.

4. Press TAB to move to the desired column and make the necessary changes to the sort list.

Sort List Options

The Sort List screen lists the order in which Notebook sorts the fields. Notebook does not allow you to change this option. The next items listed are the name of the field, followed by the sort type, and the direction for sorting.

```
Options: List Display Format

First Name    Last Name         Extension  Division       Job Title

Order    Field Name                          Sort Type    Direction
  1      First Name                          Alphabetic   Ascending
  2      Last Name                           Alphabetic   Ascending
```

```
Ins Insert; Del Delete; Space/Letter Select Field: 0
```

Figure 8-9.   Sort List screen

Adding or Changing a Field Name

If you want to add a field to the sort list, press INS. Notebook adds the new field at the current cursor position and moves any other fields down one level. When you first add a field, Notebook always displays the name of the first field in the list display. To change the name press the spacebar or type the first letter of the field name you want to display. You can change the names of existing fields in the same manner. If you want to delete a field from the sort list, highlight the field name and press DEL or BACKSPACE.

Changing the Sort Type

Notebook can sort fields in alphabetic/numeric order or in alphabetic order. With an alphabetic/numeric sort each character in the field is ranked by the first number (moving to the second and so on, when needed). This is especially significant with numbers. The following example illustrates how a list of numbers is sorted using an alphabetic/numeric sort:

```
100
5
56
7
```

In an alphabetic sort, Notebook looks at the entire sequence of numbers to determine the sort order. The above example would be sorted as follows:

```
5
7
56
100
```

Use an alphabetic sort for zip codes, phone numbers, and monetary values.

Changing the Sort Direction

You can sort a field in ascending or descending order.

Using Name Search

You can use Name Search to quickly move to a record in the List Display. To use Name Search:

1. Press **N** or **5** for Name Search.

2. Type the first letter of the field you want to find.

The cursor highlights the field that matches the letter or letters you type. If there are several fields with the same information, you can press TAB to extend the search to the next field. After pressing TAB, Notebook displays the entire information in the first field followed by an arrow, indicating you have extended the search. For example, let's say you have a Notebook file containing a field for first and last names and you want to search for the name Chris Howard. After searching for Chris you find there were several fields with the name Chris. To extend the search to the next field, press TAB. Notebook would display the "Chris → " prompt. At this point you would type **Howard** to have Notebook continue the search.

When you press Name Search, Notebook searches the first field in the sorting order. The fields, and the order in which Notebook searches the fields, are entirely dependent on how the sort order is set up in the sort list. For more information on the sort list see "Sorting a Notebook File," earlier in this chapter.

Using Search

Along with searching for names in the List Display, you can also search for words or word patterns in all or selected records in a Notebook file. A word pattern may contain wildcard characters. The asterisk (*) as a wildcard character stands for zero or more characters. The question mark (?) represents one character. Search is especially useful if you want to find a certain word or word pattern that is not displayed on the List Display screen. You can use the Search feature from the List Display or from the Record Display.

Searching Records

You can perform a forward search, which searches from the current cursor position to the end of the file, or you can perform a reverse search, which searches from the current cursor position to the beginning of the file. Search does not search the record the cursor is highlighting. To use Search:

1. From the List Display or Record Display press F2 for Forward Search or press SHIFT-F2 for Reverse Search. The following prompt displays:

```
-> Search:
1 Records: All   2 Field: All   0
```

2. If you want to perform a global search on all fields in all records, type in the word or word pattern you want to search for and press ENTER. Or if you only want to search a selected field, press **2** for Field and type in the first letter of the field name you want to search. You can also press the UP ARROW or DOWN ARROW key to display the field names. After selecting the field name press ENTER and type in the word or word pattern for which you want to search.

If the word or word pattern is found, Notebook highlights the record if you are in the List Display. You can press ENTER to display the entire record if the List Display does not show enough information. If you are in the Record Display, Notebook displays the next record in the Notebook file containing the word or word pattern. Notebook positions the cursor on the field that contains the word or word pattern. If Notebook does not find the word or word pattern, the "* Not found *" message displays at the bottom of the screen.

If you only want to Search selected records, you can mark the records with an asterisk and search only the marked records. To mark and search selected records:

1. Mark the record. If you are in the List Display, highlight the record and type an asterisk (*). If you are in the Record Display press HOME, and type an asterisk (*) or press ALT-F5 to mark the record that is currently displayed.

2. Press F2 for Forward Search or press SHIFT-F2 for Reverse Search.

3. Press **1** for Records and press the UP ARROW key to display "Marked" and press ENTER.

4. If you want to search all fields in the marked records, type in the word or word pattern you want to search for and press ENTER. Or if you only want to search a selected field, press **2** for Field and type in the first letter of the field name you want to search. After selecting the field name press ENTER and type in the word or word pattern for which you want to search.

If the word or word pattern is found, Notebook highlights the record if you are in the List Display. You can press ENTER to display the entire record if the List Display does not show enough information. If you are in the Record Display, Notebook displays the next record in the Notebook file containing the word or word pattern. Notebook positions the cursor on the field that contains the word or word pattern. If Notebook does not find the word or word pattern, the "* Not found *" message displays at the bottom of the screen.

Searching and Marking Records

Along with searching records, Notebook can search and mark records if the word or word pattern is found. This is useful if you want Notebook to automatically search all the records in a Notebook file and not stop each time it finds an occurrence of the word or word pattern. With Search and Mark, Notebook marks the records that contain the word or word pattern. You can perform a forward Search and Mark or a reverse Search and Mark. Search and Mark works exactly like Search except Notebook displays the "Mark with confirm? (Y/N)N" prompt before beginning the search. If you type **Y** for Yes, Notebook stops and asks you to confirm the marking of each record. If you type **N** for No, Notebook automatically marks all records containing the word or word pattern. If you mark records before using Search and Mark and change option 1 from ALL to MARKED, Notebook only searches the marked records and unmarks those that do not contain the word or word pattern.

Printing in Notebook

Notebook lets you print a single record or the information displayed on List Display. To print a single record or the List Display:

1. Press SHIFT-F7 for Print from the desired screen.

2. Press **1** or **P** for Print.

When you print from the List Display, Notebook only prints the information that displays on screen.

You can print selected records from the List Display by marking the records with an asterisk (*) and then printing the list. Printing marked records is useful if you have a Notebook file that lists employee birthdays, for example. From the List Display you could mark and then print a list of all the birthdays for the current month.

Setting Up the Printer

Before printing you must select the proper settings for your printer. To set up your printer:

1. Press SHIFT-F7 for Print. The following menu appears:

```
Print

     1 - Print

     2 - Options

     3 - Device or File

     4 - Select Printer              GENERIC
```

2. Press **3** or **D** for Device or File and enter the correct port or press **4** and enter a device or filename. After selecting a device or filename type **Y** if the device you entered is a network printer. If you are printing to a network printer you can also use your own

network redirection command to direct printer output and select the appropriate port.

3. Press **4** or **S** for Select Printer.

4. Enter the number corresponding to your printer. If your printer is not listed, select one that your printer emulates.

5. If you want to change the print options press **2** or **O** for Options and make the desired changes (for more on print options, see the next section).

Changing Notebook's Print Options

With Notebook's print options you can indicate how printed information should appear on the page. To change any of the print options:

1. Press SHIFT-F7 for Print.

2. Press **2** or **O** for Options. The following menu appears:

```
Print: Options
       1 - Page Length (in lines)      66
       2 - Number of Lines             54
       3 - Top Margin (in lines)       6
       4 - Left Margin (column #)      0
       5 - Right Margin (column #)     79
```

3. Select an option and make the desired changes. The options are described in the following section.

Options

Notebook stores the changes you make to the print options in the Notebook setup file, and they remain in effect for all Notebook files until you change them again.

Page Length   Enter the length of the current page. The default for an 11-inch page in a 10 point font is 66 lines. If you wanted to print on legal-size paper you would change this to 72 lines.

Number of Lines   Enter the number of text lines you want printed on each page. The default is 54, which gives you 9 inches of text if you are using a 10 point font.

Top Margin   Enter the number of lines from the top that the text should begin to print. Six lines equal 1 inch in a 10 point font.

Left/Right Margin   Enter the column position from the left and right edges. The default settings are 10 for the right margin and 79 for the left margin.

Marking Notebook Records

Just as you can mark files while in File Manager or List Files, Notebook lets you mark records and perform various functions on the marked records. If you are in the List Display, type an asterisk (*) to mark the highlighted record. You can mark or unmark all records in the List Display by pressing ALT-F5. In the List Display the status line in the lower-right corner of the screen indicates how many records are marked as shown here:

```
1 Create; 2 Delete; 3 Edit; 4 Options; 5 Name Search; 3    Marks 2    Record 3
```

If you are in the Record Display screen press ALT-F5 to mark the currently displayed record. An asterisk appears in the lower-right corner, along with the number of marked records and the total number of records in the file.

After you have marked records, you can use the Delete, Print, Save, Save to the Clipboard, Append to the Clipboard, Search, and Search and Mark functions.

Using a Modem with Notebook

One of the advantages of using Notebook to organize names and phone numbers is its modem capabilities. With a modem attached to your computer and phone, you can dial phone numbers directly from your Notebook files. Once you find the name of the person you want to call, one keystroke (F4) dials the number. You can also manually dial any number while in Notebook. For example, if you are in Notebook and you remember you need to make a call and the number is not in your Notebook file, you can manually type in the number and Notebook dials it for you. To manually dial a number press SHIFT-F4.

Setting Up the Dial Feature

Before you can use Notebook to dial phone numbers, you must set up the modem within Notebook and define the dialing instructions.

Setting Up the Modem

In order for Notebook to communicate with your modem, you must select the proper settings. To set up your modem with Notebook:

1. Press SHIFT-F1 for Setup.

2. Press 4 or **M** for Modem. The following screen appears:

```
Setup: Modem

     1 - COM Device (1-4)           1

     2 - Initialization String      Default Touch-Tone Dialing

     3 - Termination String         Default Termination
```

3. Press **1** or **C** for COM Device.

4. Type the number from 1 to 4 that corresponds to the serial port to which your modem is attached.

5. Press **2** or **I** for Initialization String. The information in the initialization string accesses the dial tone on the telephone line.

6. Select one of the options shown here:

```
Sample AT Commands for Initialization

ATD        Get the attention of the modem and dial.
ATDT           - Touch-Tone dialing.
ATDT9W         - Dial 9 and wait for an outside line.
ATDP           - Pulse dialing.
```

Notebook has predefined initialization strings for the AT command set for touch-tone dialing and pulse dialing. If your modem needs other commands, select **3** or **E** for Edit and enter the appropriate commands from your modem manual. In the middle of the screen is a sample list of AT initialization commands to help you modify the string.

7. Press **3** or **T** for Termination String. The information in the termination string disconnects the modem and turns control over to the telephone.

8. Select **1** or **D** for Default Termination if your modem uses the standard AT command set termination string or press **2** or **E** for Edit and enter the appropriate termination string commands for your modem. A sample list of AT termination commands displays in the middle of the screen.

9. Press **F7** twice to return to the List Display.

You only have to set up the modem commands once. The changes you make remain in effect until you change them again. These settings are saved to your Notebook setup file. If you are using Office PC the filename is NOTEBOOK.SYS. If you are using Office LAN the filename is *XXX*_NB.SYS, where *XXX* is your File ID.

Setting Up the Dialing Instructions

After setting up the modem commands, you need to define the specific dialing commands for each Notebook file you want to use with the Dial feature. The dialing instructions tell Notebook what to do when you use the Dial feature. You must define a separate dialing instruction for each field in each Notebook file that contains a phone number. To define a dialing instruction:

1. Press SHIFT-F10 and enter the name of the Notebook file you want to retrieve and define dialing instructions for.

2. Press **4** or **O** for Options or press SHIFT-F8.

3. Press **7** or **D** for Dialing Instructions. A screen similar to Figure 8-10 appears. Notebook lists the first field under Field Name.

4. If the correct field is not displayed, use the UP ARROW or DOWN ARROW key to display the field containing a phone number.

5. Press TAB to move to Dialing Instruction.

6. Enter any of the special dialing characters listed on screen. A dialing instruction may contain up to 29 characters.

7. Repeat steps 4 through 6 for each field containing a phone number you want to dial.

8. Press F7 until you are prompted to save the file. These changes affect the current Notebook file only.

Options: Dialing Instructions

Field Name	Dialing Instruction
▲ Extension	@
Home Phone	9@
Address	[None]
Hire Date	[None]
▼ Birth Date	[None]

Special Dialing Characters

@ = Dial using the field contents   ? = Prompt the user for instructions
A-Z = Replace with a dialing sequence   0-9 = Dial the selected digit
                                         , = Pause two seconds

Dialing Sequences

A - ?	J -	S -
B -	K -	T -
C -	L - 1	U -
D -	M -	V -
E -	N -	W -
F -	O - 9	X -
G -	P -	Y -
H -	Q -	Z -
I -	R -	

↕ Prev/Next Field; Tab Edit Dialing Instruction; A-Z Edit Sequence; @ (F3 Help)

Figure 8-10.   Dialing Instructions options

Dialing Characters   If you simply want to dial the number as it displays in the field, type @ for the dialing instructions. If you want to be prompted for input, type ?. For example, if your Notebook lists a long distance phone number without an area code you could type ?@ for the dialing instructions. Notebook would prompt you for input and then dial the number in the field. You can also enter numbers 0 to 9 in the dialing instruction. This is especially helpful if you need to dial a certain number to get an outside line. For example, if you have to dial 9 before placing an outside call, you would type **9**@ as the dialing instruction. Notebook also has the ability to insert a pause in the dialing instruction. A comma (,) pauses dialing for 2 seconds. A pause is useful if you are calling a number that connects you to a main switchboard and then asks you to enter the extension. For example, if you enter **299-4646,,,,,,,,,,5436** Notebook dials the number 299-4646, pauses for 20 seconds, and then dials the extension 5436.

Dialing Sequences   Dialing sequences can also be added to the dialing instructions. A dialing sequence is a string (up to 20 characters) of numbers and/or special dialing characters. This string is assigned to a letter from A to Z. Dialing sequences make it possible for you to dial numbers longer than 29 characters. To define a dialing sequence:

1. Press 4 or **O** for Options or press SHIFT-F8.

2. Press 7 or **D** for Dialing Instructions.

3. Type the letter to which you want to define the sequence.

4. Enter numbers or special characters you want in the sequence.

5. Press F7 twice to exit.

Unlike the dialing instructions, a dialing sequence is available for all Notebook files. A dialing sequence is useful if you are calling international numbers. You could enter the international country codes in a dialing sequence instead of entering them for each field that dials an international number.

Using the Clipboard with Notebook

The Shell Clipboard is one of the main tools that all the WordPerfect Office programs use to integrate and share information. While in Notebook, the Shell Clipboard lets you save information from a field and retrieve it to a different location in Notebook or to a different Shell-compatible program. The Clipboard also lets you retrieve information you have saved to the Clipboard from another program into a field in Notebook.

Saving and Appending Fields to the Clipboard

To save or append information:

1. While in the Record Display, move the cursor to the field you want to save.

2. Press CTRL-F1 for Shell.

3. Press **2** or **S** for Save Field or press **3** or **A** for Append Field.

Saving information to the Clipboard overwrites any information already in the Clipboard. Appending to the Clipboard adds the information to the end of any existing information.

Saving and Appending an Entire Record to the Clipboard

If you want to save all the information in one record to the Clipboard:

1. Highlight the record in the List Display.

2. Press CTRL-F1 for Shell.

3. Press **2** or **S** for Save Record or press **3** or **A** for Append Record.

You can also mark selected records and save or append the marked records to the Clipboard. The entire contents of the records are saved to the Clipboard. When this information is retrieved into WordPerfect, the header information and the contents of the records are retrieved. The records are in secondary merge format and can be added to an existing secondary merge file or merged into a primary merge file. For information on Notebook headers and secondary merge files, see "Using a Notebook File in WordPerfect" later in this chapter.

Retrieving Text from the Clipboard

To retrieve information saved to the Clipboard into Notebook:

1. In the Record Display, move the cursor to the field in which you want to retrieve the information.

2. Press CTRL-F1 for Shell.

3. Press **4** or **R** for Retrieve from Clipboard.

You can retrieve any text into a field in Notebook. For example, if you were typing a letter to someone while in WordPerfect and needed to use some of the information in a Notes field in their Notebook record, you could easily do so with the previous steps.

You can also retrieve an entire record from a WordPerfect secondary merge file that has been saved to the Clipboard. To retrieve the record into Notebook:

1. From the List Display, press CTRL-F1 for Shell.

2. Press **4** or **R** for Retrieve Records.

If the information in the Clipboard is not in secondary merge format, Notebook displays an error message. If the information is not in the text format that is currently selected in Notebook, an error message also displays. You can change the text format to match the format of the information (SHIFT-F8, 5). When you retrieve records from a secondary merge file, Notebook inserts the fields in position order, not according to field name.

Note: Since Notebook does not have a cut and copy feature, you can use the Clipboard to save a record from one Notebook file and then retrieve it into another Notebook file.

Merging Notebook Files

If you need to combine two existing Notebook files into one file, you can use the Notebook Merge feature. You might want to combine Notebook files if you and your partner both have a client Notebook file and share a secretary. You could merge your two Notebook files so the secretary would have a master Notebook file containing both lists of clients. The Merge feature allows you to combine multiple Notebook files and control exactly how they are combined.

To merge two files:

1. Retrieve the file you want to use as the master file. All fields in the master file and field positions of the master file are maintained after the merge.

2. Retrieve the second file. If you use List Files, Notebook asks you to verify that you want to retrieve the file into the existing document. Type **Y** for Yes.

At this point a screen similar to Figure 8-11 appears, unless all the fields in the two files match exactly (if they do match, they are automatically merged). You can only access this screen when you are performing a merge. At the top of the screen, Notebook lists the current and the retrieved files. Notebook lists three options in the middle of the screen: Merge Files, Merge Type, and Extra Fields. Below the options are the results of the merge, both by name and by position. On the left side of the screen is the Name Merge Result and on the right is the Position Merge Result. Once you decide which type of merge you are going to perform, you only need to be concerned with the result information for that type. Below the result information are the definitions of the markers that indicate the status of the fields.

Selecting a Merge Type

After the Merge Records screen appears, the first thing you need to do is decide what type of merge you want to perform. As mentioned previously, the results of both types are listed in the middle of the screen. If all of the fields do not display, press the UP ARROW or DOWN ARROW key to see the additional fields.

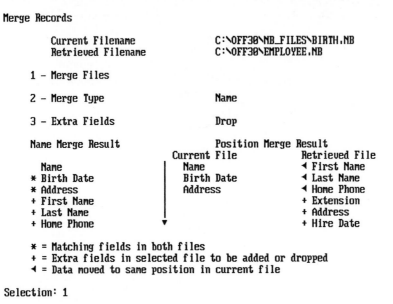

```
Merge Records

        Current Filename              C:\OFF30\NB_FILES\BIRTH.NB
        Retrieved Filename            C:\OFF30\EMPLOYEE.NB

    1 - Merge Files

    2 - Merge Type                    Name

    3 - Extra Fields                  Drop

    Name Merge Result                 Position Merge Result
                               Current File        Retrieved File
       Name                    Name               ◄ First Name
     * Birth Date              Birth Date         ◄ Last Name
     * Address                 Address            ◄ Home Phone
     + First Name                                 + Extension
     + Last Name                                  + Address
     + Home Phone      ▼                           + Hire Date

     * = Matching fields in both files
     + = Extra fields in selected file to be added or dropped
     ◄ = Data moved to same position in current file

Selection: 1
```

Figure 8-11.   Merge Records screen

Name Merge

Name merge is the default merge type, and for most cases is the type of merge you should use. Because name merge uses field names to determine which fields match, it is a good idea to standardize your field names across Notebook files.

A name merge merges all fields with matching field names. If there are field names in the retrieved file that do not match any of the field names in the current file, you can choose to add or drop the fields. If you add the fields, they are added to the bottom of the record display in all fields but information is only added to the records where they originally existed. The following shows the results of a name merge:

```
Name Merge Result

       Name
     * Birth Date
     * Address
     + First Name
     + Last Name
     + Home Phone
```

In this example, the Birth Date and Address fields are in both files so the information in those fields remains in the merged file. When the field names match, an asterisk (*) appears next to the field name. The First Name, Last Name, and Home Phone field names only exist in the retrieved file. You can choose to add or drop these fields by selecting Extra Fields. If you add the fields they are added to the bottom of the record display.

Position Merge

A position merge merges the fields according to their position (creation order). You would use a position merge if you have Notebook files with the same information in the same order but with different field names. With a position merge, you can also merge two WordPerfect secondary merge files that do not have Notebook headers. Because secondary merge files do not have field names, a name merge will not work.

With a position merge you may have dissimilar information in the same field. For example if field 1 contains names of employees in the current file and addresses in the retrieved file, the merged file would contain both names and addresses in the first field. A position merge always keeps the field name from the current file.

The following example shows the results of a position merge:

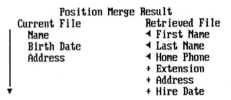

```
                Position Merge Result
        Current File           Retrieved File
          Name                 ◄ First Name
          Birth Date           ◄ Last Name
          Address              ◄ Home Phone
                               + Extension
                               + Address
                               + Hire Date
```

In this example, the contents of the First Name field from the retrieved file are retrieved into the Name field, the contents of the Last Name field from the retrieved file are retrieved into the Birth Date field, and the contents of the Home Phone field are retrieved into the Address field. Fields that are merged into the same position in the current file are marked with a ◄ . The Extension, Address, and Hire Date fields can be added or dropped from the merged file. Fields that can be dropped or added are marked with a plus sign (+).

Merging the File

After selecting the type of merge you want to perform and choosing to add or drop extra fields, you are ready to perform the actual merge. To merge the file:

1. Press **1** for Merge Files. You can also press F7 to begin the merge.

Note: If you decide you do not want to perform the merge press Cancel (F1) to exit the merge screen.

The merged file appears on the List Display screen. You can edit the file at this point or save it. If you are saving the file be sure to change the filename if you do not want to overwrite one of your existing Notebook files.

Using a Notebook File in WordPerfect

You can retrieve a Notebook file into WordPerfect and use it as a secondary merge file. With this capability, you can create, edit, and add to Notebook files from within WordPerfect.

When you retrieve a Notebook file into WordPerfect 5.0 or 5.1, a header displays at the top of the file. Figure 8-12 displays a sample header. Most of the header information is not used when merging the file, but it helps you to know what information is contained in the Notebook file.

You can set up a primary merge file using fields from a Notebook file as the secondary merge file. When you set up the primary file you can indicate the field numbers displayed in the header to the left of the field names or the actual field names used in the Notebook file.

Avoiding and Fixing Corrupted Notebook Files

Once in a while a Notebook file may become corrupted. A corrupted Notebook file may display strange characters in the List Display or

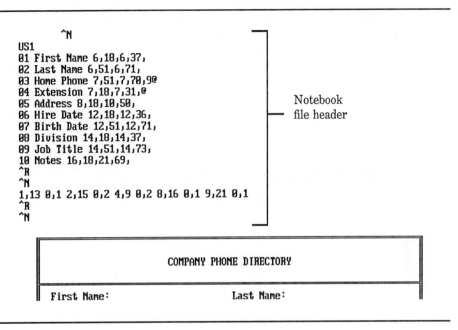

```
      ^N
US1
01 First Name 6,18,6,37,
02 Last Name 6,51,6,71,
03 Home Phone 7,51,7,70,9@
04 Extension 7,18,7,31,@
05 Address 8,18,10,50,
06 Hire Date 12,18,12,36,
07 Birth Date 12,51,12,71,
08 Division 14,18,14,37,
09 Job Title 14,51,14,73,
10 Notes 16,18,21,69,
^R
^N
1,13 0,1 2,15 0,2 4,9 0,2 8,16 0,1 9,21 0,1
^R
^N
```

Notebook
file header

```
┌──────────────────────────────────────────────┐
║                                                ║
║             COMPANY PHONE DIRECTORY            ║
║                                                ║
╟────────────────────────────────────────────────╢
║  First Name:                  Last Name:       ║
```

Figure 8-12.   Sample Notebook file header

Record Display. With corrupted Notebook files, the Record Display screen becomes scrambled and does not function properly. Here are a few suggestions to help you avoid corrupting your Notebook files:

• When creating the Record Display, exit and then reenter if the cursor keys begin to perform strangely or the screen looks odd.

• Do not add formatting codes to a Notebook file while in Word-Perfect.

If a file becomes corrupted here are some possible ways to correct the problem:

• Always make a backup copy.

• Change the text format to another format (4.2, 5.0, 5.1) and then change the format back. This strips out codes that may be causing problems.

- Retrieve the file into WordPerfect and use Reveal Codes to search for any unwanted codes.

- If the problem is in the Record Display Format screen, move to the top-right corner of the screen. With the cursor to the right of any text or line-draw characters, press CTRL-END to clear any unwanted and nondisplayable characters. Repeat this for each line of text on screen.

Auto-Sort

Auto-Sort automatically sorts the List Display anytime changes are made to the contents. Auto-Sort helps keep the List Display up-to-date and organized. See "Sorting a Notebook File," earlier in this chapter for more information.

Keystrokes

To change the Auto-Sort option for the current Notebook:

1. Press **4** or **O** for Options or press SHIFT-F8.

2. Press **3** or **A** for Auto-Sort.

3. Type **Y** for Yes to turn on Auto-Sort or type **N** for No to turn off Auto-Sort.

To change the Auto-Sort option for all newly created Notebook files:

1. Press SHIFT-F1 for Setup.

2. Press **2** or **I** for Initial Settings.

3. Press **1** or **A** for Auto-Sort.

4. Type **Y** for Yes to turn on Auto-Sort or type **N** for No to turn off Auto-Sort.

Backup

To avoid accidental loss of your Notebook files due to computer or power failure, the Timed Backup feature automatically backs up your Notebook files at regular intervals. If you are using Office PC, the backup file is {NB}NB.BK!. If you are using Office LAN, the backup file is *XXX*}NB.BK!, where *XXX* is your File ID. As soon as you exit Notebook properly, these files are deleted. For this reason, as soon as you experience a computer or power failure, enter Notebook and retrieve this file and then save it with a new name. If you do not rename the file, Notebook displays the "Old Backup file exists: (1) Rename, (2) Delete" prompt the next time it tries to back up your existing file.

Keystrokes

1. Press SHIFT-F1 for Setup.

2. Press **1** or **B** for Backup.

3. Press **1** or **T** for Timed Backup.

4. Type **Y** to turn on Timed Backup or type **N** to turn off Timed Backup.

If you turn on Timed Backup:

5. Enter the number of minutes between each backup.

6. Press **3** or **B** for Backup Directory and enter the directory where you want the backup file stored.

Bold

You can boldface text or field labels in the Record Display. Any information you boldface in the Record Display also appears boldfaced in the List Display.

Keystrokes

1. Press F6 for Bold.

2. Enter the text you want boldfaced.

3. Press F6 to turn off Bold.

Cancel

Cancel (F1) backs you out of a Notebook menu or prompt. Cancel also restores deleted information in some parts of the program. You can undelete a record or the contents of a field.

Keystrokes

To back out of a menu or prompt and return to the previous menu or screen:

1. Press F1 for Cancel.

To undelete the last deleted record:

1. Press F1 for Cancel from the List Display. Notebook displays the "Restore last deleted record? (Y/N)N" prompt.

2. Type **Y** to restore the record.

You can also undelete the text of a field or an entire record from the Record Display.

1. Press F1 for Cancel from the Record Display. If you have deleted text from one of the fields, Notebook displays the "Restore original field contents? (Y/N)N" prompt. If you have not deleted text from a field but have deleted a record, the "Restore last deleted record? (Y/N)N" prompt displays.

2. Type **Y** or **N** to either prompt.

With the "Restore original field contents?" prompt displayed, you can also press F1 again to restore the last deleted record.

Note: If you delete a record larger than 4K, Notebook cannot restore it because it is too big to fit in the buffer that holds all deletions.

Date

From the Record Display, Notebook's Date feature inserts your current system's date into any field in the Record Display. You can also choose to replace the current contents of a field with the date. From the List Display, the Date feature changes the format of the dates inserted with the Date feature.

Keystrokes

To insert the date in a field or replace the contents of a field with the date:

1. From the Record Display, press SHIFT-F5 for Date.

2. Press **1** or **T** for Date Text to insert the current date in the field or press **2** or **R** for Replace Date to replace the current contents of the field with the date.

A text string for the date is inserted in the field at the current position of the cursor. The Date feature can insert a date string up to 58 characters.

To change the date format:

1. From the List Display, press SHIFT-F5 for Date.

2. Using the menu options, set the display format.

3. Press F7 to return to the list display.

Delete

You can delete an entire record, a field, or selected text from a field while in Notebook. From the List Display highlight the record you want to delete and press BACKSPACE or DEL. To delete a record from the Record

Display, display the record you want to delete and press HOME, DEL. For information on deleting selected text in the record display see Table 8-2 earlier in this chapter.

Dial

The Dial feature lets you dial phone numbers in the Record or List Display if your computer is attached to a modem. Before dialing a number you must set up the modem in Notebook and define the dialing instructions. For information on these processes see "Using a Modem with Notebook," earlier in this chapter.

Keystrokes

To dial a phone number from the List Display:

1. Highlight the record containing the number you want to dial.

2. Press F4 for Dial. If more than one field contains dialing instructions, Notebook displays the "TAB Next Field" message.

3. If necessary, press TAB until the correct field is highlighted, and then press ENTER. Notebook displays a "Dialing" message followed by the number it is dialing.

4. Pick up the phone.

5. After the "Press any key after picking up phone" message appears, press any key to disconnect the modem.

Note: Make sure you do not press a key before this message displays. If you do, the call will not be completed.

To dial a number from the Record Display:

1. Use the TAB key to highlight the field containing the number you want to dial. If you do not move the cursor to the field you want to dial, Notebook searches through the record and dials the first field with dialing instructions.

2. Press F4 for Dial. Notebook displays a "Dialing" message followed by the number it is dialing.

3. Pick up the phone.

4. After the "Press any key after picking up phone" message appears, press any key to disconnect the modem.

Note: Make sure you do not press a key before this message displays. If you do, the call will not be completed.

Dialing Instructions

Dialing instructions tell Notebook what to do when you press Dial (F4). Before you can dial a phone number in a record, you must define the dialing instructions. You must define the dialing instructions for each phone field in every Notebook file with which you want to use the Dial feature. Dialing instructions are saved with each Notebook file.

Keystrokes

1. Press SHIFT-F10 and enter the name of the Notebook file for which you want to retrieve and define dialing instructions.

2. Press 4 or O for Options or press SHIFT-F8.

3. Press 7 or D for Dialing Instructions. Notebook lists the first field in the record under the Field Name title.

4. If the correct field is not displayed, use the UP ARROW or DOWN ARROW key to display the field containing a phone number.

5. Press TAB to move to the Dialing Instruction field.

6. Enter any of the special dialing characters listed on screen. A dialing instruction may contain up to 29 characters.

7. Repeat steps 4 through 6 for each field containing a phone number you want to dial.

8. Press F7 twice to save the changes for the current Notebook.

For more information on dialing instructions and the special dialing characters, see "Using a Modem with Notebook," earlier in this chapter.

Display

If you have a color monitor, the Display option lets you set colors for normal, bold, underline, and reverse video text. You can also choose how you want underline displayed on a single-color monitor. For monitors with a Hercules card you can select the mode.

Keystrokes

1. Press SHIFT-F1 for Setup.

2. Press 3 or **D** for Display. The following menu appears:

```
Color Setup

Monitor Characteristics: 0
    1 Color monitor
    2 Single color monitor (eg. Black & White or Compaq)
    3 Hercules RamFont Card (InColor or Graphics Plus)
```

3. Choose the option that corresponds to your monitor and make the desired selections.

Help

Notebook provides you with extensive on-screen help about features and options.

Keystrokes

1. From the main Notebook screen press F3 to display the main Notebook help screen.

2. To access help you can then type one of the menu-item letters to see information about the specific topic; press a function key to see information about the feature associated with that key; or press F3 for Help again to see the Notebook keyboard template. This is especially useful since WordPerfect Office does not come with a keyboard template for Notebook.

3. Press ENTER or the spacebar to exit help or press ESC to return to the main help screen.

Hints

The help screens are a valuable tool for accessing information about the Notebook program. You do not have to press Help (F3) from the main Notebook screen. Pressing Help from any Notebook menu displays information about the features associated with that screen.

Initial Settings

The Initial Settings menu lets you change the default settings for the Auto-Sort, Language, Text Format, and Date Format options. When you change these settings, the changes only affect newly created Notebook files. If you have a Notebook file retrieved or saved on disk, the changes will not affect that file. Any changes made via the Initial Settings menu are saved in the Notebook setup file. If you are using Office PC the filename is NOTEBOOK.SYS. If you are using Office LAN the filename is *XXX*_NB.SYS, where *XXX* is your File ID.

Keystrokes

1. Press SHIFT-F1 for Setup.

2. Press **2** or **I** for Initial Settings.

3. Select the desired option and make the necessary changes.

For more information on the individual options, see the option name in the "Functions and Features" section of this chapter.

Language

Notebook supports several language codes. When you change the language code the format in which the date displays is altered. Notebook supports the following language codes:

Language	Code	Language	Code
Catalan	CA	German–Switzerland	SD
Czechoslovakian	CZ	Greek	GR
* Danish	DK	* Icelandic	IS
Dutch	NL	Italian	IT
English–Australia	OZ	* Norwegian	NO
English–U.K.	UK	Portuguese–Brazil	BR
English–U.S.	US	Portuguese–Portugal	PO
* Finnish	SU	Russian	RU
French–Canada	CF	Spanish	ES
French–France	FR	* Swedish	SV
German–Germany	DE		

* Has a unique sorting sequence.

Keystrokes

To change the language code for the current Notebook only:

1. Press **4** or **O** for Options or press SHIFT-F8.

2. Press **4** or **G** for Language.

3. Enter the two-character language code.

To change the language code for all newly created Notebook files:

1. Press SHIFT-F1 for Setup.

2. Press **2** or **I** for Initial Settings.

3. Press **2** or **G** for Language.

4. Enter the two-character language code.

The language information is taken from the WP.LRS file. You can add language codes to this file or modify the existing information by retrieving the file into Notebook and making the necessary changes.

Line Draw

When creating a Record Display, you can use line-draw characters to organize and divide the fields in the record. If you use too many line-draw characters you may fill up the Record Display buffer. If your printer supports line-draw characters, they will print as part of the Record Display. If they do not print correctly but your printer does support the characters, you can use the WPOPTR program to enter the correct decimal values for those characters. For information on adding line draw to the Record Display see "Creating a Notebook File," earlier in this chapter.

List Files

Using List Files in Notebook, you can perform many common file-management commands without exiting to DOS. List Files displays the files and subdirectories contained in a given directory. From the List Files screen, you can retrieve, delete, move, rename, or look at a file. You can also perform a word search or name search. If you want to change the default directory you can use the Other Directory option. List Files is especially useful for listing the directory of a Notebook file you want to retrieve but whose filename you cannot remember.

List Display Format

The List Display Format screen lets you change the format of the List Display. From this screen you can change which fields display and in what order they appear. You can also define the sort list from the List Display Format screen. For more information on editing the List Display see "Editing the List Display Format," earlier in this chapter.

Manual Dial

With the Manual Dial feature you can dial any phone number from within the Notebook program. If you are using Notebook and need to make a call and the phone number is not in your Notebook file, you can use Manual Dial. If you have defined any special dialing sequences, you can use them when entering a number for Manual Dial.

Keystrokes

1. From the List Display or Record Display, press SHIFT-F4 for Manual Dial. Notebook displays the "Enter Phone Number" prompt at the bottom of the screen.

2. Enter the phone number you wish to dial.

3. Pick up the phone.

4. After the "Press any key after picking up phone" message appears, press any key to disconnect the modem.

Note: Make sure you do not press a key before this message displays. If you do, the call will not be completed.

Mark

For information on marking records see "Marking Notebook Records," earlier in this chapter.

Merge Format

You can merge two Notebook files into one file with the Merge feature. When merging Notebook files, you can use a Name merge or a Position merge. A Name merge compares the names of the fields in both files. If there are matching field names, the fields are merged. If there are fields that do not match, you can choose to add the fields to the merge file or drop the fields.

A Position merge merges the information according to the position (creation order) of the field. If there are more fields in the second file you are merging, you can choose to add the fields to the merge field or drop the fields. For more information on using the merge format see "Merging Notebook Files," earlier in this chapter.

Middle

The Middle feature lets you move the highlighted record to the middle of the screen when the cursor is in the lower half of the screen. You must have more than one screen of records in the List Display to use the Middle feature. If Scroll Lock is on, the cursor remains in the middle of the screen.

Keystrokes

1. Press SHIFT-F9 for Middle.

Modem

You can use a modem to dial phone numbers while in Notebook. Before you can use a modem you must set up the modem information. Once you set up the modem information it remains in effect for all Notebook files.

Keystrokes

1. Press SHIFT-F1 for Setup.

2. Press **4** or **M** for Modem.

3. Select **1** or **C** for COM Device.

4. Type the number from 1 to 4 that corresponds to the serial port to which your modem is attached.

Note: If you use the COM3 or COM4 port and Notebook will not communicate with your modem, you may need to change the I/O address to 3E8-3EF hex for COM3 or 2E8-2EF hex for COM4.

5. Press **2** or **I** for Initialization String.

6. Select the correct initialization string or press **3** or **E** to insert the codes needed for your modem.

7. Press **3** or **T** for Termination String.

8. Select **1** or **D** for Default Termination if your modem uses the standard AT command set termination string or press **2** or **E** for Edit and enter the appropriate termination string commands for your modem.

9. Press F7 twice to return to the List Display.

For more information on setting up a modem see "Using a Modem with Notebook," earlier in this chapter.

Name Search

You can use the Name Search feature to quickly move to a field in the list display.

Keystrokes

1. Press **N** or **5** for Name Search.

2. Type in the first letter of the record you want to find.

Notebook Options

For each Notebook file you create you can change several options, including the Record Display Format, List Display Format, Auto-Sort, Language, Text Format, Date Format, and Dialing Instructions options.

Keystrokes

1. Press **4** or **O** for Options or press SHIFT-F8.

2. Select the desired option and make the necessary changes.

The changes made to the Notebook options are not saved until the Notebook file is saved. For more information on the individual options, see the option name in the "Functions and Features" section of this chapter.

Record Display Format

The Record Display Format screen lets you create or edit the Record Display for a Notebook file. Within the Record Display Format screen you can add or delete fields, edit the size and position of fields, add field labels, and add line-draw characters. For information on creating and using the Record Display Format screen to create a record display see "Creating the Record Display," earlier in this chapter. For information on editing an existing record display see "Editing the Record Display Format."

Retrieve

Use the Retrieve feature to retrieve Notebook files. If you retrieve a file into an existing file and all field names do not exactly match, Notebook displays the Merge Records screen.

Keystrokes

1. Press SHIFT-F10 for Retrieve.

2. Enter the name of the Notebook file you want to retrieve. If the file is not in the default directory, enter the full path name.

If the file has an .NB extension, you do not have to enter the extension. Notebook automatically looks for the .NB extension.

Note: You can also use the Retrieve option in List Files to retrieve Notebook files.

Save

The Save feature lets you save Notebook files without exiting Notebook. You cannot save an empty Notebook file. If you mark records and then press Save, only the marked records are saved.

Keystrokes

1. From the List Display press F10 for Save.

2. Type the name you want the file saved under or press ENTER to save the file with the existing name.

Search and Search and Mark

The Search and Search and Mark features find specified words or word patterns in your Notebook records. You can search all records with Search or only marked records with Search and Mark. You can search all fields in a record or specified field. For more information on Notebook's search abilities, see "Using Search," earlier in this chapter.

Setup

From the Setup menu you can permanently change the Backup, Initial Settings, Display, and Modem options. Any changes made from this menu affect all newly created Notebook files. These changes are saved in the Notebook setup file. If you are using Office PC the filename is NOTEBOOK.SYS. If you are using Office LAN the filename is *XXX*_NB.SYS, where *XXX* is your File ID.

Keystrokes

1. Press SHIFT-F1 for Setup. The following menu displays:

```
Setup
    1 - Backup
    2 - Initial Settings
    3 - Display
    4 - Modem
```

2. Select the desired option and make the necessary changes.

For more information on the individual options, see the option name in the "Functions and Features" section of this chapter.

Shell

The Shell feature lets you exit to Shell without exiting Notebook, save and append text to the Shell Clipboard, and retrieve text from the Clipboard.

Keystrokes

1. From the List Display, press CTRL-F1 for Shell.

2. Choose from the options shown here:

```
1 Go to Shell; 2 Save Record; 3 Append Record; 4 Retrieve Records: 0
```

For more information on the Shell options see "Using the Clipboard with Notebook," earlier in this chapter.

Sort

If you turn off the Auto-Sort feature you can manually sort your Notebook file with the Sort feature. If you have only modified a few records you can mark those records and then sort the file. Notebook only sorts the marked records. You can only sort a file from the List Display. It is a good idea to turn off Auto-Sort and use manual sort with large Notebook files.

Keystrokes

1. Press CTRL-F9 for Sort. The "Sort Entire File? (Y/N)Y" prompt appears.

2. Type **Y** for Yes or type **N** to sort only marked records.

Note: If you have a record of over 4000 characters, you will receive the "Error record too big to sort" message when sorting.

Startup Options

Startup options override certain default Notebook conditions on startup. You can put startup options on the command line if you are starting Notebook from DOS or you can add the options to the Shell Program Information screen for Notebook.

The following is a list of all the startup options that you can use with Notebook.

/CP-*xxx*	Overrides the default code page set by DOS.
/D-*path*	Specifies a directory for Notebook temporary files. If this is not specified, the default directory is used. If you are running Notebook from a network drive, you may want to use this option to redirect these files to the local hard drive, RAM drive, or personal network drive.
/D-%*x*	Allows you to run several Notebook files from the same directory. *X* represents the number or letter of the temporary file for this Notebook file.
/M-*macro*	Invokes a Shell macro at startup of Notebook. This option only works if you are running Notebook from the Shell menu.
/NT-*x*	Specifies the network type you are using, where *x* is the number of the network.
/NS	Inhibits synchronization of output to color monitors. This switch will speed up the display, but it may cause snow on some monitors.
/PS-*path*	Indicates where setup files are located. If you are on a network and your system administrator has put all your setup files in one location, use this option.

/SS-RW,CL	Overrides the automatic row and column settings, which allows you to display more or fewer rows and/or columns if your monitor supports such a mode.
/W-*xx*	Allocates less memory for Notebook work space.

Switch

The Switch feature lets you switch between the List Display and the Record Display.

Keystrokes

1. From the List Display or Record Display press SHIFT-F3.

Text Format

Notebook files can be saved in WordPerfect 4.2, 5.0, or 5.1 format. The Text Format option determines in which format the Notebook file will be saved. Lower text formats are compatible with higher formats, but higher formats are not downward compatible. For example, if you save a Notebook file in 4.2 format, you can retrieve that file into 5.0 or 5.1. But if you saved a Notebook file in 5.0, you cannot retrieve it into 4.2. You can convert Notebook files to other formats by changing the text format and then saving the file. Many times you can salvage corrupted Notebook files by changing the text format. If you have a file that is not displaying correctly, try saving it in a different format and then retrieving the file.

Keystrokes

To change the text format for the current Notebook file only:

1. Press 4 or **O** for Options or press SHIFT-F8.

2. Press 5 or **T** for Text Format.

3. Enter the desired option.

To change the text format for all newly created Notebook files:

1. Press SHIFT-F1 for Setup.

2. Press 2 or **I** for Initial Settings.

3. Press 3 or **T** for Text Format.

4. Enter the desired option.

Underline

You can underline the text or field labels you enter in a Record Display. Any information you underline in the Record Display also appears underlined in the List Display.

Keystrokes

1. Press F8 for Underline.

2. Enter the text you want underlined.

3. Press F8 to turn off Underline.

Using Scheduler

Scheduler is a personal time management utility that allows you to interact with the other users on the Office system. With Scheduler, you can organize meetings with one person or with every user on the system. You can also specify resources to use. A *resource* is defined by the system administrator, and can be anything from rooms to cars to equipment. Since Scheduler is interactive, it allows users included in events either to accept or delete the event. Each resource is assigned an owner, who must be a valid user. The owner of a resource is responsible for accepting or deleting events for that resource. If you delete an event, you can also send a reply explaining why you did so.

Scheduler also interacts with your personal Appointment Calendar to give you a more complete personal schedule using either program. Unlike Scheduler, however, Appointment Calendar cannot interact with other people's calendars and, consequently, cannot be used to organize events including others on the Office system.

Scheduler can search through other users' schedules when looking for available times to schedule an event. Any user on the system can access this information, but the program does not give specific information about what items it found, only when the event is taking place. It also provides a screen to display the results of a search in a more graphical format so you can quickly select the time you want to use.

Scheduler Basics

Before getting started, you need to know some of the basic terms and functions of the Scheduler program. The basic building block of an Office system is called the host. A *host* consists of a set of network directories in which Scheduler stores all of its information. Each host, or group of directories, is created and named by your system administrator. If a user is assigned to a certain host, or is on a given host, it means the information files for that user are located in the set of Office directories with that particular name.

For example, it is often convenient to group users that are in the same company department on the same Office host, and then give that host the name of the department, such as Marketing or Research. The number of users on a single host is only limited by the number of users that a network allows to use a single file server.

Each user that is assigned to a given host must have a unique Office User ID and File ID. The *User ID* is the name by which Office knows each user, so each User ID must be unique on each individual host. The *File ID* is made up of three letters, usually the user's initials or an abbreviation of her or his name. Scheduler uses the File ID to name all of the information files associated with that user. For example, if your File ID is AAA, your information files are named AAA. These initials must also be unique on each host.

Once a host has been defined and users assigned to it, that host can be combined with other hosts to enlarge the delivery area and increase the number of users you can access using Office. Keep in mind, however, that each host can function independently of any other hosts.

Starting Scheduler

To start Scheduler from the Shell menu, type the letter next to the entry for Scheduler—the default letter is **S**. If you are starting Scheduler from DOS, enter **sc**. The first screen you see when starting Scheduler is the Event screen, which consists of a title bar, Request box, Organized box, and a menu, listing options for the Event screen. The Request box displays any scheduled events in which you are included, and allows you to accept or delete an event (see "Accepting or Deleting an Event"). The Organized box displays a list of all events that you have organized and allows you to check the status of any user included in events that you have organized. The menu at the bottom of the Event screen lists the options available from the Event screen, as well as the keys used to access other screens in Scheduler. When you enter Scheduler for the first time, an empty Event screen appears, as shown in Figure 9-1. In the Event screen, the cursor displays as a reverse video bar in the Request or Organized box.

Screens in Scheduler

Scheduler has six screens that you use regularly when organizing events or updating your schedule.

Event Screen

Upon entering Scheduler, you see the Event screen, Scheduler's main screen. A heading at the top of the screen lists the host you are

```
 Events for - HOST1:DEVINR            Monday, February 24, 1992   9:05 am 
┌ Requests for Devin Rowley ─────────────────────────────────────────────┐
│ No requests                                                             │
│                                                                         │
│                                                                         │
│                                                                         │
│                                                                         │
│                                                                         │
│                                                                         │
└─────────────────────────────────────────────────────────────────────────┘
┌ Organized by Devin Rowley ─────────────────────────────────────────────┐
│ No organized events                                                     │
│                                                                         │
│                                                                         │
│                                                                         │
│                                                                         │
│                                                                         │
└─────────────────────────────────────────────────────────────────────────┘
 TAB Organized box; SHIFT-F1 Setup; F2 Search; F3 Help; F7 Exit;
 1 Month/Week; 2 Delete; 3 Accept; 4 Info; 5 Groups; 6 Sched: 4
```

Figure 9-1.   Blank Event screen

assigned to, along with your Office User ID. The right side of the heading displays the current date and time. You can configure the way the date and time are displayed using the Date and Time Format options under Setup (see "Date/Time Formats").

When you first enter Scheduler, the cursor highlights the first unopened event in your Request box. If there are no unopened events, the cursor highlights the first event in your Request box. Any events in your Request box that you haven't looked at appear boldfaced with a bullet to the left of the item (as well as boldfaced on your screen), as shown here:

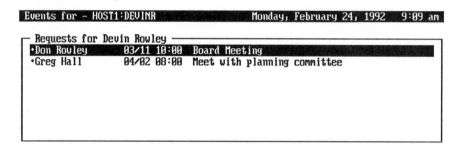

Any events that you have looked at but have not yet responded to display a bullet to the left but are not bolded. Once you accept an event, the bullet is removed. You can use the arrow keys to move the cursor up and down in the Request and Organized boxes. Pressing TAB or SHIFT-F3 moves you between the two boxes.

Month Screen

From the Event screen, you can move to the Month screen by pressing **M**. Pressing **1** displays either the Month or Week screen, depending on which screen you viewed last. Even after you exit and reenter Scheduler, when you press **1** for Month/Week Scheduler displays the last screen you viewed. The Month screen, shown in Figure 9-2, displays a calendar on the left of the screen and a single day on the right. The Day window displays the schedule for the date that is currently highlighted in the Calendar window, and changes as you move from day to day on the calendar. You can move between the two windows by pressing TAB or SHIFT-F3.

```
┌─────────────────────────────────────────────────────────────────────┐
│ Month for - HOST1:DEVINR              Monday, February 24, 1992  9:09 am │
│                                                                       │
│  Sun Mon Tue Wed Thu Fri Sat          Wednesday, March 11, 1992        │
│  ┌──────────────────────────┐    ┌──────────────────────────────────┐ │
│  │       March 1992         │    │ 8:00 am                          │ │
│  │                          │    │ 8:30 am                          │ │
│  │  1│ 2│ 3│ 4│ 5│ 6│ 7     │    │ 9:00 am                          │ │
│  │                          │    │ 9:30 am                          │ │
│  │  8│ 9│10│·11│12│13│14    │    │10:00 am  ┌Board Meeting          │ │
│  │                          │    │10:30 am  │                        │ │
│  │ 15│16│17│18│19│20│21     │    │11:00 am  │                        │ │
│  │                          │    │11:30 am  │                        │ │
│  │ 22│23│24│25│26│27│28     │    │12:00 pm  └                        │ │
│  │                          │    │12:30 pm                          │ │
│  │ 29│30│31│                │    │ 1:00 pm                          │ │
│  │        April 1992        │    │ 1:30 pm                          │ │
│  │                          │    │ 2:00 pm                          │ │
│  │      │  │ 1│·2│ 3│ 4     │    │ 2:30 pm                          │ │
│  │                          │    │ 3:00 pm                          │ │
│  │  5│ 6│ 7│ 8│ 9│10│11     │    │ 3:30 pm                          │ │
│  │                          │    │ 4:00 pm                          │ │
│  │ 12│13│14│15│16│17│18     │    │ 4:30 pm                          │ │
│  │                          │    │ 5:00 pm                          │ │
│  └──────────────────────────┘    └──────────────────────────────────┘ │
│ 1 Date; 2 Sched:               (Shift-F1 Setup; Shift-F3 Week; F3 Help; F7 Event) │
└─────────────────────────────────────────────────────────────────────┘
```

Figure 9-2.   Month screen

The date that is highlighted in the Calendar window depends on how you entered the Month screen. If you highlight an event in the Request window on the Event screen and press **1** or **M** to enter the Month screen, the highlighted date in the Calendar window is the starting date for that event. If there are no events in the Request window on the Event screen, the highlighted date is the current date. With the cursor in the Day window, you can view the information for a listed event by moving the cursor to highlight the event and pressing ENTER. You can use the keystrokes listed in Table 9-1 to move the cursor on the Month screen.

Week Screen

You can access the Week screen from the Event screen by pressing **W**. Pressing **1** displays either the Week or Month screen, depending on

Keystroke	Action
LEFT/RIGHT ARROW	Moves back/forward one day
UP/DOWN ARROW (Calendar)	Moves back/forward one week
UP/DOWN ARROW (Day)	Moves up/down one interval
PGUP/PGDN	Moves back/forward one day
HOME, RIGHT/LEFT ARROW	Moves to the first/last day of week
SCREEN UP/SCREEN DOWN	Moves forward/back one month
(+/− on the numeric keypad)	
HOME, UP/DOWN ARROW	Moves to the first/last day of month
HOME, PGUP/PGDN	Moves forward/back one year
HOME, HOME, UP/DOWN ARROW	Moves to the first/last day of year

Table 9-1.   Cursor Keystrokes in the Month screen

which screen you viewed last. The Week screen, shown in Figure 9-3, displays your schedule in a window format. Each window on the screen represents a single day, and any events for a given day are listed in the

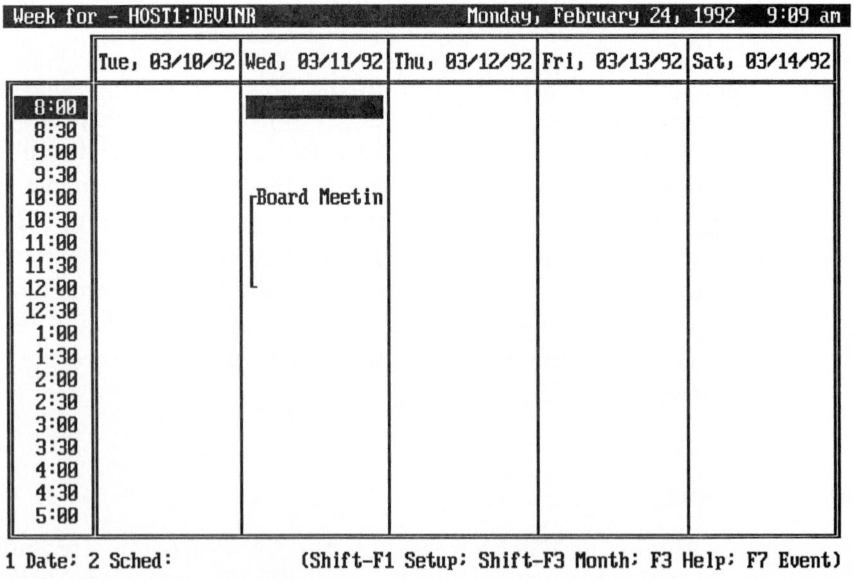

```
Week for - HOST1:DEUINR                    Monday, February 24, 1992   9:09 am

        │Tue, 03/10/92│Wed, 03/11/92│Thu, 03/12/92│Fri, 03/13/92│Sat, 03/14/92│
 ┌──────┤             │             │             │             │             │
 │ 8:00 │             │▐▌▌▌▌▌▌▌      │             │             │             │
 │ 8:30 │             │             │             │             │             │
 │ 9:00 │             │             │             │             │             │
 │ 9:30 │             │             │             │             │             │
 │10:00 │             │┌Board Meetin│             │             │             │
 │10:30 │             ││            │             │             │             │
 │11:00 │             ││            │             │             │             │
 │11:30 │             ││            │             │             │             │
 │12:00 │             ││            │             │             │             │
 │12:30 │             │└            │             │             │             │
 │ 1:00 │             │             │             │             │             │
 │ 1:30 │             │             │             │             │             │
 │ 2:00 │             │             │             │             │             │
 │ 2:30 │             │             │             │             │             │
 │ 3:00 │             │             │             │             │             │
 │ 3:30 │             │             │             │             │             │
 │ 4:00 │             │             │             │             │             │
 │ 4:30 │             │             │             │             │             │
 │ 5:00 │             │             │             │             │             │

 1 Date; 2 Sched;        (Shift-F1 Setup; Shift-F3 Month; F3 Help; F7 Event)
```

Figure 9-3.   Week screen

window for that day. The leftmost window on the screen shows time intervals throughout the day. You can set the increments used in the time display using the Setup menu (see "Changing Scheduler Display Options"). The current date on the Week screen depends on how you entered that screen. If you highlight an event in the Request window on the Event screen and press **1** or **W** to enter the Week screen, the current date is the starting date for that event. If there are no events in the Request window on the Event screen, the Week screen displays the current date.

Schedule Screen

Press **6**, **S**, or F9 from the Event screen to move to the Schedule screen shown in Figure 9-4. From the Schedule screen, you enter information

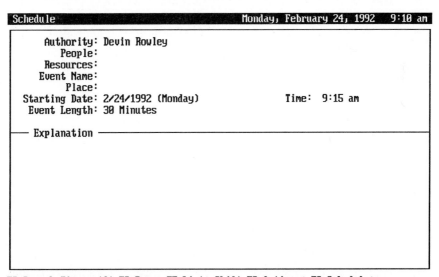

Figure 9-4.   Schedule screen

about an event you are organizing. This information includes who you want to include in the event, any resources, the name or subject of the event, the event location, starting date and time, and event length. An Explanation window is provided for entering detailed information about the event. For help on using the Schedule screen, see the section "Organizing an Event," later in this chapter.

Search Screen

From the Event and Schedule screens, pressing F2 moves you to the Search screen shown in Figure 9-5. From the Search screen, you can check the schedules of users and resources to find a free time to schedule an event. You can perform a search before or after entering information on the Schedule screen. If you perform the search after

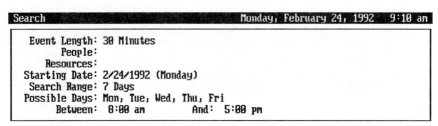

```
Search                              Monday, February 24, 1992   9:10 am
  Event Length: 30 Minutes
        People:
     Resources:
 Starting Date: 2/24/1992 (Monday)
  Search Range: 7 Days
 Possible Days: Mon, Tue, Wed, Thu, Fri
       Between:  8:00 am        And:  5:00 pm

Press F2 to search for free times.




F2 Search; Alt-F3 Busy; F5 List; F9 Sched;   (Tab Next field; F3 Help; F7 Exit)
```

Figure 9-5.   Search screen

entering the information on the Schedule screen, Scheduler duplicates the information you list on the Schedule screen to perform a search. If you move directly to the Search screen without entering information on the Schedule screen, you can enter the necessary information on the Search screen.

Busy Screen

The Busy screen is accessible from the Schedule or Search screens. As shown in Figure 9-6, the Busy screen graphically outlines the schedules of the users and resources that you want to include in an event. You can view the Busy screen from the Search screen by pressing ALT-F3. You can also begin a search and move directly to the Busy screen from the Schedule screen by pressing ALT-F3. Using this method, Scheduler takes the information from the Schedule screen, along with the current Search settings from the Setup options, and searches for available times.

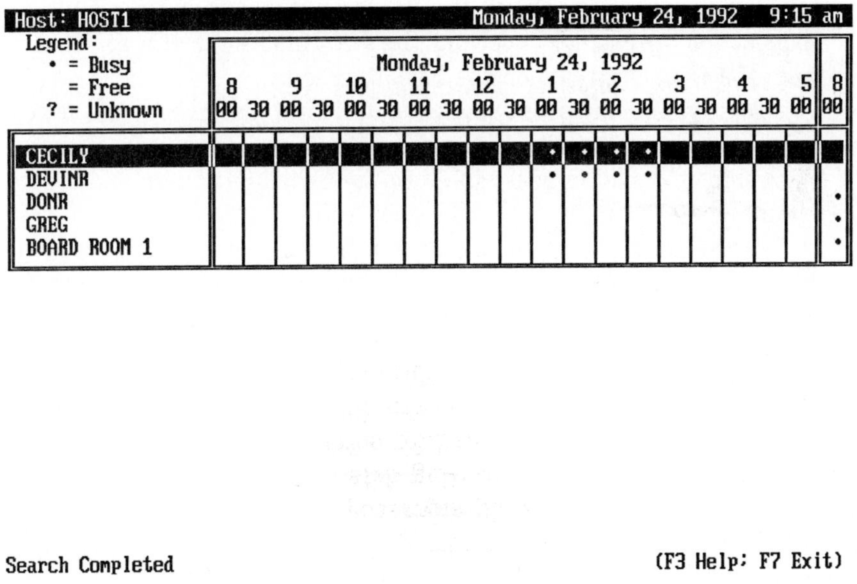

Figure 9-6.   Busy screen showing events

The Busy screen display format is similar to the Week screen. It displays schedule information for the users and resources you specify. The default indicators on the Busy screen are blanks for free times, a bullet for busy times, and ? for unknown schedules. An unknown schedule is common when a search is in progress, and should eventually be replaced by spaces or bullets. For more information on the Busy screen, see "Using the Busy Screen," later in this chapter.

Organizing an Event

Whenever you need to schedule a meeting, conference, or appointment with other users on the Office system, you can use Scheduler. When you organize an event, Scheduler sends information about the event to the users you request, and to the users who "own" any resources that you include in the event. These users can then either accept or delete and reject the event. You can see the status of any user or resource that you request for an event by viewing the Information screen for that event from the Organized box on the Event screen.

To organize an event in Scheduler, first determine the necessary users and resources. Then plan the date, time, and length of the event. With this information, you can go to the Schedule screen and create the event.

For example, you can organize a meeting with several other users on the system, and schedule a conference room and projector that your system administrator has defined as available resources. After determining that you want the meeting to take place on February 24, 1992, beginning at 9:00 A.M. and lasting for three hours, you are ready to schedule the event.

1. Press **6** or **S** from the Event screen, **2** or **S** from the Month or Week screen, or F9 from any of these screens to move to the Schedule screen. A blank Schedule screen displays (see Figure 9-4).

2. The first line on the screen is the Authority line, which lists who has requested the event. Your full name displays here by default. You can enter another name if necessary, but the event displays in

your Organized box since you actually organized it. To enter a different name, press SHIFT-TAB to move the cursor to the Authority line and enter the name.

3. If you know the Office User IDs of the people you want to schedule in the event, type them on the People line with separating commas. You can also display a list of known users by pressing F5 and 2 or **U**. If you only need to retrieve a single user, use Name Search or the cursor keys to highlight the name, type an asterisk (*), and press F7 to retrieve the appropriate User ID onto the Schedule screen. If you want to include several users, highlight their names and mark them by typing an asterisk (*). When you have marked all of the users, press F7 to exit the List and retrieve the User IDs to the Schedule screen.

4. Press ENTER or TAB to move the cursor to the Resources line. You can type in the Office Resource IDs for the resources to include. Alternatively, you can press F5 and 3 or **R** to have the List feature display a list of known resources, and retrieve the resources from the list, as with the users in step 3. Resources are optional to an event, so you can skip this field if you do not need any resources.

5. Press ENTER or TAB to move the cursor to the Event Name field. In this field, enter the name or subject of the event you are organizing. You must assign a name or subject to each event before you can schedule the event.

6. Press ENTER or TAB to move the cursor to the Place field. Enter the location of the event. For this example, you would enter **Conference Room**. This is also an optional field.

7. Press ENTER or TAB to move the cursor to the Starting Date field. This is the day that the event takes place. If it is a multiple-day event, this is the first day of the event. For this example, the date would be 2/24/92.

8. Press ENTER or TAB to move the cursor to the Time field. This is the beginning time for the event. For the example, enter **9:00A** or **9A**.

9. Press ENTER or TAB to move the cursor to the Event Length field. This indicates the length of the event. For this example, type in **3 Hours** or **3h**.

10. If necessary, press ENTER or TAB to move the cursor to the Explanation window. In this window, you can give more detailed information about the event and can discuss any preparations users may need to make before the event.

11. When you have entered all of the information concerning the event, press F9 to schedule it. Scheduler completes the schedule request, clears the display, and leaves you in the Schedule screen. You can also press F7 after completing the information about the event. Schedule then asks "Schedule event? (Y/N)N". Type **Y** to schedule the event and exit the Schedule screen, or **N** to exit the Schedule screen without completing the schedule request. If you exit the Schedule screen without scheduling the event, Scheduler retains the information you have entered on the Schedule screen so you can return and finish the event.

After completing the schedule request, Scheduler distributes the event to the appropriate users and displays the event in their Request box. If you view the information for the event from your Organized box, you can check the status of any users and resources included in the event. The Information screen tells the organizer when an event has been opened or looked at, accepted and deleted. It also displays any reasons a user has given for deleting an event.

Accepting or Deleting an Event

When you are scheduled for an event, you can either accept the event and have it added to your schedule, or delete the event and have it removed from your Request box. You can change the status of an event from any of the screens in Scheduler that display your schedule, including the Event, Month, and Week screens. You can also change the status of an event when you have the Information screen for that event displayed. In addition, you can use Appointment Calendar to accept any events that display in Scheduler. For help on using Scheduler and Calendar together, see "Integrating Appointment Calendar and Scheduler," later in this chapter.

To accept an event in Scheduler, use the cursor keys to highlight the desired event. The cursor keys used to accept an event vary depending on which screen you are in. With the cursor on the event, press 3 or **A** to accept the event and have it inserted into your schedule. When you accept an event, the organizer's information is updated to reflect your acceptance.

In Scheduler, you can delete an event from any of the screens that display a schedule listing. Highlight the event using the cursor keys and press **2, D,** or DEL to delete the event. Scheduler displays the following prompt:

```
1 (Y) Delete; 2 Reply and Delete: 0
```

If you want to delete the event without returning a reason to the organizer, press **1, D,** or **Y.** If you want to delete the event and send a reply to the organizer, press **2** or **R.**

Searching for Available Times

Using Search in Scheduler, you can check the schedules of any users and resources you want to include in an event to find an available free time. Scheduler takes the information you enter on the Search screen, or information from the Schedule screen and the default Search settings, and checks the schedules you indicate. A list of available free time blocks displays chronologically on the Search screen, as shown in Figure 9-7. You can also view the information for individual users by pressing ALT-F3 to view the Busy screen. Using information from the search, you can select a time for the event you wish to schedule.

For example, if you wanted to schedule a two-hour meeting sometime during the week beginning February 24, 1992, you would do the following from the Search screen:

1. Type **2h** in the Event Length line for a two-hour block.

2. Press ENTER or TAB to move to the People line. Type the Office User IDs for the people to search for, or use the List feature to mark and retrieve users from the User List.

3. Press ENTER or TAB to move to the Resources line. To include resources in the search, type the Resource IDs for any resources you need, or use the List feature to mark and retrieve resources from the resource list.

4. Press ENTER or TAB to move to the Starting Date line and type in 2/24/92 for the starting date.

5. Press ENTER or TAB to move to the Search Range field. Since the meeting should take place on a regular workday, seven days covers the entire range of Possible Days listed below.

6. Press ENTER or TAB to move to the Possible Days field. Scheduler only lists free times on the days specified here that fall within the search range. Press ENTER or TAB to skip this field and leave the regular weekdays displayed.

7. Enter the times range that Scheduler should search on the days you specify. If you want to change the daily time interval, enter the new times.

8. Press F2 to initiate the search.

```
 Search                             Monday, February 24, 1992   9:16 am
 ┌──────────────────────────────────────────────────────────────────┐
 │   Event Length: 30 Minutes                                         │
 │         People: DEVINR, GREG, JACKC, JOHNS                         │
 │      Resources:                                                    │
 │  Starting Date: 2/24/1992 (Monday)                                 │
 │   Search Range: 7 Days                                             │
 │  Possible Days: Mon, Tue, Wed, Thu, Fri                            │
 │        Between: 8:00 am          And:  5:00 pm                     │
 └──────────────────────────────────────────────────────────────────┘

 Search Completed

 Between:                            And:
   2/24/1992 (Monday)      9:20 am   2/24/1992 (Monday)      5:00 pm
   2/25/1992 (Tuesday)     8:00 am   2/25/1992 (Tuesday)     5:00 pm
   2/26/1992 (Wednesday)   8:00 am   2/26/1992 (Wednesday)   5:00 pm
   2/27/1992 (Thursday)    8:00 am   2/27/1992 (Thursday)    5:00 pm
   2/28/1992 (Friday)      8:00 am   2/28/1992 (Friday)      5:00 pm
   3/2/1992 (Monday)       8:00 am   3/2/1992 (Monday)       5:00 pm


 Enter Select; Alt-F3 Busy:                  (F1 Cancel; F3 Help; F7 Exit)
```

Figure 9-7.   Search Times screen

Scheduler initially displays information about available times based on the schedules of users and resources on the host you are on. If you included users and resources on another host in your search, Scheduler has to send a request to the other host and process the returned results before it gives you a complete listing of available times. If you try to schedule the event before the search is complete, Scheduler displays the "Search Not Complete!" message. You can finish scheduling the event, but the information you enter may cause scheduling conflicts.

As Scheduler updates the time display, it also indicates how many users and resources it has received information from, as shown here:

```
Information from 4 of 6 users, 0 of 1 resources

Between:                              And:
  2/24/1992 (Monday)      9:15 am     2/24/1992 (Monday)      5:00 pm
  2/25/1992 (Tuesday)     8:00 am     2/25/1992 (Tuesday)     5:00 pm
  2/26/1992 (Wednesday)   8:00 am     2/26/1992 (Wednesday)   5:00 pm
  2/27/1992 (Thursday)    8:00 am     2/27/1992 (Thursday)    5:00 pm
  2/28/1992 (Friday)      8:00 am     2/28/1992 (Friday)      5:00 pm
  3/2/1992 (Monday)       8:00 am     3/2/1992 (Monday)       5:00 pm
```

When all the information has been received and processed, Scheduler displays the message "Search Completed". If no block of time fits all of the search criteria you specified, Scheduler displays the message "No Times Found".

Once you have completed a search on the Search screen, you can use that information to schedule the event by doing the following from the Search screen:

 9. Highlight the block of free time you want to use and press F9 or ENTER to select it.

10. Scheduler prompts you for the starting time of the event, as shown here:

```
Starting Date: 2/24/1992 (Monday)          Starting Time:  9:15 am
```

11. Press ENTER to accept the time or enter a different time. After you enter the starting time, the Schedule screen is displayed with the information from the Search screen and the starting date and time you selected.

12. Press F9 to schedule the event and remain in the Schedule screen, or press F7 and type **Y** to schedule the event and exit the Schedule screen.

If you complete a search and find that another search is necessary, you can edit the information on the Search screen and begin another search by pressing F1 to cancel the current search, editing the information, and pressing F2 to begin a new search.

Using the Busy Screen

When searching for individual free times, it is often useful to view the schedule information for the users and resources in the search. From the Busy screen, you can see when other users and resources have events scheduled. This can help if a search finds no free times for the conditions you specify. In this case, you may have to exclude some users and resources from the event, or schedule them and let them decide how to resolve their scheduling conflict. From the Busy screen, you can see which users and resources may have existing conflicts.

To use the Busy screen, shown earlier in Figure 9-6, you can initiate a search from the Search screen and then watch the Busy screen as the returning information updates the display. You can also input the event information on the Schedule screen and press ALT-F3 to initiate a search. In this case, Scheduler uses the default Search Range, Possible Days, and Time Range settings to complete the search. The Starting Date and Time listed on the Schedule screen are used to mark the start of the search.

When you press ALT-F3, Scheduler moves from the Schedule screen to the Busy screen. From the Busy screen, information about the individual users and resources displays automatically. You can press F7 to return to the Search screen and finish scheduling the event from there, as outlined in "Searching for Available Times," earlier in this chapter.

Using the Information Screen

For each event organized in Scheduler, you can view an Information screen for specifics on the event. You can do this from the Request or Organized box on the Event screen, or from the Month or Week screen.

From the Month and Week screens, you can also look at Information screens for appointments from Appointment Calendar.

The Information screen outlines your current status for the event in the upper-right corner, and lists who organized the event, when the event was organized, its starting date, time and length, and the Office users that are included. In addition, from the Organized box on the Event screen, the Information screen displays the status of each user that you scheduled for the event.

Viewing Information from the Event Screen

To display the Information screen from the Event screen, highlight the event to display and press **4**, **I**, or ENTER. (The screen that appears depends on whether you opened the screen from the Request or Organized box.) From an Information screen opened in the Request box, as shown in Figure 9-8, you can press **3** or **A** to accept the event, or

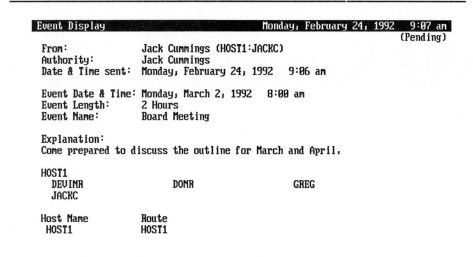

Figure 9-8.   Information screen from Request box

```
┌─────────────────────────────────────────────────────────────────────┐
│ Event Display                          Monday, February 24, 1992  9:01 am │
│                                                                       │
│ From:              Devin Rowley (HOST1:DEVINR)                        │
│ Authority:         Devin Rowley                                       │
│ Date & Time sent:  Monday, February 24, 1992    9:00 am              │
│                                                                       │
│ Event Date & Time: Tuesday, March 3, 1992    9:00 am                 │
│ Event Length:      30 Minutes                                         │
│ Event Name:        Discuss agenda for Board Meeting                   │
│                                                                       │
│ Explanation:                                                          │
│ Discuss the agenda for the 3/10 Board Meeting.                        │
│                                                                       │
│                    Opened        Action                               │
│ HOST1                            02/24 09:00  Delivered               │
│   CECILY           02/24 09:00   02/24 09:00  Accepted                │
│   CONNIE           02/24 09:01                                        │
│   DEVINR                                                              │
│   DONR             02/24 09:00   02/24 09:00  Deleted                 │
│     This is not for my department.                                    │
│   EARNIE                                                              │
│   GREG                           02/24 09:01  Accepted                │
│   JACKC                                                               │
│                                                                       │
│ 1 Month/Week; 2 Delete; 3 Renotify; 4 Next; 5 Previous; 7 Resched: 0  │
└─────────────────────────────────────────────────────────────────────┘
```

Figure 9-9.   Information screen from Organized box

2 or **D** to delete it. If you delete the event, you can simply delete it, or tell the organizer why you deleted the event. In addition, you can press 4 or **N** to display the next event listed in the Request box, or **5** or **P** to display the previous event listed in the Request box. If there is no next or previous event, you are returned to the Event screen.

As with events listed in the Request box, you can display the Information screen from the Organized box by highlighting the event to display and pressing 4, **I**, or ENTER. When you view the information for an event from the Organized box on the Event screen, you see all the information the event recipients see, plus the status of each user scheduled in the event, as shown in Figure 9-9. From the Information screen opened from the Organized box, you can also delete or reschedule the current event, or renotify all users that have not accepted or rejected the event. To delete the current event:

1. Press **2** or **D** for Delete.

2. Press **1, O,** or **Y** to delete the event from your Organized box, but leave it in the recipients' Schedulers, or press **2** or **A** to delete the event from all schedules. This also removes the event from any Appointment Calendars.

To reschedule the current event, do the following from the Information screen:

1. Press **7** or **R** for Reschedule.

2. Press **1** or **D** to delete the event from all Schedulers and Calendars and reschedule it, or press **2** or **R** to leave the original event, but use its information to schedule a new event.

3. Scheduler automatically takes you to the Schedule screen and copies information from the current event into the appropriate fields. Edit the necessary fields and schedule the event by pressing F9, or by pressing F7 and **Y**.

You can also use the Renotify option to have an on-screen notification window display for all recipients that have not yet accepted or deleted the event. To renotify all users with a pending status, press **3** or **T** from the Information screen under the Organized box.

Viewing Information from the Month and Week Screens

An Information screen opened from the Month or Week screen outlines the specifics of an event. To display an Information screen from the Month or Week screen, as shown in Figure 9-10, highlight the correct event and press ENTER. With the information about the event displayed, you can press **3** or **A** to accept an event, or **2** or **D** to display the delete options. Your current status for the event is displayed in the upper-right corner of the Information screen for that event.

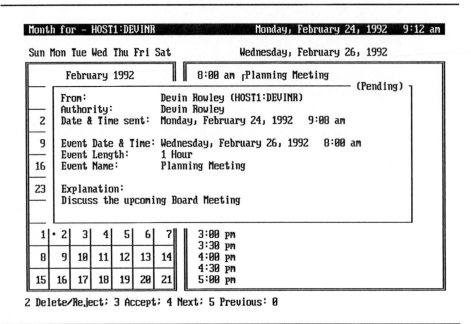

Month for - HOST1:DEVINR   Monday, February 24, 1992   9:12 am

Sun Mon Tue Wed Thu Fri Sat   Wednesday, February 26, 1992

February 1992   8:00 am ⌐Planning Meeting
                                                          (Pending)
          From: Devin Rowley (HOST1:DEVINR)
          Authority: Devin Rowley
    2   Date & Time sent: Monday, February 24, 1992   9:08 am

    9   Event Date & Time: Wednesday, February 26, 1992   8:00 am
          Event Length: 1 Hour
   16   Event Name: Planning Meeting

   23   Explanation:
          Discuss the upcoming Board Meeting

    1 · 2   3   4   5   6   7   3:00 pm
                                  3:30 pm
    8   9 10 11 12 13 14   4:00 pm
                                  4:30 pm
   15 16 17 18 19 20 21   5:00 pm

2 Delete/Reject; 3 Accept; 4 Next; 5 Previous: 0

Figure 9-10.   Information screen from Month screen

If you press ENTER with a conflicting time highlighted, Scheduler displays a listing of the events covering that time. From this listing, you can highlight the correct event and press **4** or **I** to display the Information screen for that event, or **3** or **A** to accept the event, or **2** or **D** to display the delete options for that event.

Creating and Using Groups in Scheduler

If you schedule the same users or resources on a regular basis, you may want to define a group for them. Then, when you want to schedule the group, you just need to type the group name on the People or Resources line instead of entering each user or resource individually. For example, if most of the meetings you schedule are for every person in your

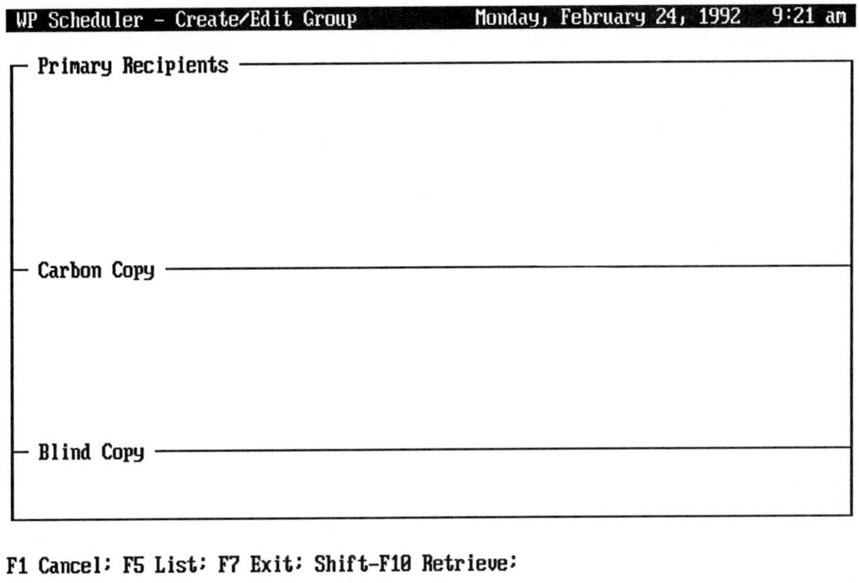

```
WP Scheduler - Create/Edit Group        Monday, February 24, 1992   9:21 am
┌─ Primary Recipients ──────────────────────────────────────────────────┐
│                                                                        │
│                                                                        │
│                                                                        │
│                                                                        │
│                                                                        │
│─ Carbon Copy ──────────────────────────────────────────────────────────│
│                                                                        │
│                                                                        │
│                                                                        │
│─ Blind Copy ───────────────────────────────────────────────────────────│
│                                                                        │
│                                                                        │
└────────────────────────────────────────────────────────────────────────┘

F1 Cancel; F5 List; F7 Exit; Shift-F10 Retrieve;
```

Figure 9-11.   Group screen

department, you can make a group containing all the names of the people in your department.

The Group screen is divided into three sections, as shown in Figure 9-11. In each section, you can list users that will receive the different copy types. If you're just using the group to schedule users, you do not need to use the different copy types. If you're going to use the group with the Mail program and you want to use different copy types, see "Using Carbon and Blind Copy Types" in Chapter 7, "Using Mail." The section on the top of the Group screen is for primary copy types, the center section is for carbon copy types, and the bottom section is for blind copy types. Scheduler allows you to include or exclude users or resources specified as carbon or blind copy types. To set this option permanently, do the following from the Event screen:

1. Press SHIFT-F1 for Setup.

2. Press 3 or S for Schedule.

3. Press **3** or **C** for Schedule CC Recipients in Groups, or **4** or **B** for Schedule BC Recipients in Groups.

4. Type **Y** to include these users when scheduling, or **N** to exclude them when using groups. You can also set this as a temporary option by pressing SHIFT-F8 from the Schedule screen and using steps 3 and 4.

To enter the Group screen from the Event screen and create a group of users or resources:

1. Press **5** or **G** to enter the Group screen.

2. Press TAB or SHIFT-TAB to move the cursor to the desired copy type box.

3. Enter the User ID or Resource ID for the person or resource you want to include in the group, or use List Users or List Resources to mark and retrieve users and resources. The List feature only retrieves names into the primary copy type window.

4. Repeat steps 2 and 3 until you have entered all users or resources into the correct section of the screen. Be sure to add separating commas between the users or resources.

5. After entering all of the names to include in the group, press F10 to save the group and remain in the Group screen, or press F7 and type **Y** to save the group when exiting the Group screen.

6. Enter the filename to use for the group file. Scheduler then asks if you want to add .GRP to the filename, indicating a user group file. Type **Y** if it is a user group. If you type **N**, Scheduler asks if you want to add .RSC, indicating a resource group file. If there is already a file with the same name, Scheduler prompts you to confirm the save. To replace the existing group, type **Y**. To enter a different filename for the group, type **N** and enter another filename. The group file is then saved in the default directory.

7. If you pressed F7 to save the group, type **Y** to exit the Group screen and return to the Event screen. If you pressed F10 to save the group, you remain in the Group screen and the user names or resource remain on the screen. To exit the Group screen, press F7 and **N**.

Creating Groups from the Schedule Screen

You can define a group of users or resources from the Schedule screen as well as from the Group screen. To create a group file from the Schedule screen, enter the users or resources to include in the group on the People or Resources line. Again, you can either type in the User or Resource ID, or use the List feature to mark and retrieve the correct names. After entering all of the User or Resource IDs to include in the group, press F10 with the cursor in the correct field to save the group. Type in the name to use for the group file. If the filename already exists, Scheduler asks you to confirm the save. Type **Y** to replace the file, or **N** to stop the save and enter a new filename.

Nesting Groups

Scheduler also allows you to *nest* groups, or place the name of one group inside another group. This feature lets you build larger user groups by combining existing groups. When combining existing groups, remember two important rules:

- Do not nest groups more than five levels deep. In other words, a group can be listed inside a second group, which can be listed inside a third group, and so on until there are five levels of subgroups below one group. If you exceed five levels of grouping, Scheduler first tells you there is a problem with the group you specified, and then displays the "Error: Groups nested too deep" error message.

- Never create a group that contains its own name. Scheduler considers this an error in group nesting and returns the errors just mentioned.

To combine groups into a larger group using the Group screen, you can use List Groups or simply enter the names of the groups to combine on the Group screen and save the new group to a new name. For example, imagine you have already created three groups named SCGRP1, SCGRP2, and SCGRP3 and you want to combine them into one group named BIGSCGRP. To do this from the main Scheduler screen:

1. Press **5** or **G** for Groups.

2. Type the name of the first group, **SCGRP1**, in the Group screen.

3. Repeat steps 1 and 2 until all the group names are listed with a comma separating each group.

4. Press F10 to save the group.

5. Type in the name to use for the group file. If the filename already exists, Scheduler asks you to confirm the save. Type **Y** to replace the file, or type **N** to stop the save and enter a new filename. Pressing F1 cancels the save.

You can also use the List feature to list system groups created by the system administrator, or personal groups that you have already defined. Since Scheduler considers all users as primary recipients, you can only use List to retrieve group names into the primary window on the Group screen. To use List to combine existing groups into a new group:

1. Press TAB or SHIFT-TAB to move the cursor to the primary copy type field for the first group.

2. Press F5 to display the List menu.

3. Press **5** or **G** for Groups. The following menu appears:

Global: 1 Users; 2 Resources; Personal: 3 Users; 4 Resources: 1

4. Select the desired option. If you select Personal User or Resource Groups, Scheduler displays the path to the default directory in which your personal groups are saved. Press ENTER to have Scheduler display all files in the default directory with a .GRP or .RSC extension or enter a new directory if necessary.

5. Use the cursor keys to highlight the group you want to retrieve.

6. Mark the file with an asterisk (*).

7. Repeat steps 5 and 6 until all group names are marked. You cannot combine User and Resource groups; a group can only contain users or resources.

8. Press F7 to retrieve the names of the marked groups into the Group screen.

9. Press F10 to save the group and then enter a name. You must enter a name that meets the DOS file-naming criteria. If the group already exists, Scheduler asks you to confirm the save. Type **Y** to save the group, or **N** to cancel the save using the current name.

Integrating Appointment Calendar and Scheduler

So that you can integrate your personal Appointment Calendar and your network Scheduler into a complete personal schedule, Appointment Calendar and Scheduler pass information back and forth using special files. Scheduler tells your calendar about any event listed in your Scheduler, and Appointment Calendar tells Scheduler about any appointments that you set up in your Calendar.

From your personal Calendar, you can accept or delete any events that are pending in your Scheduler. When you start Appointment Calendar, it automatically looks for any pending events in your Scheduler and asks you if you want to accept the event, delete or reject the event, or wait and leave the event pending.

To accept the event, press **1** or **A** and the event status is updated in your Scheduler and the event inserted into your Calendar file. To delete the event, press **2** or **D**. Appointment Calendar displays the same prompt as Scheduler when deleting an event. You can delete the event without returning a reason by pressing **1**, **D**, or **Y**. You can send a reply with the deletion by pressing **2** or **R** and then entering the reply.

Each time you create an appointment in your Calendar, it will be sent to your Scheduler, where it displays on the Month and Week screens. The Information screen for such appointments indicates that they are from the Appointment Calendar and lists the information you entered in Appointment Calendar, as shown here:

```
From:               WP Calendar
Event Date & Time: Friday, May 22, 1992   9:00 am
Event Length:       2 Hours
Event Name:         Meet with John to discuss developmen

Explanation:
Meet with John to discuss development
```

An appointment from your Calendar cannot be deleted from within Scheduler. You have to enter your Appointment Calendar to remove the event from your Calendar and Scheduler.

Resetting the Scheduler Path

Sometimes during maintenance and rebuilding of Office systems, the communications files between Scheduler and Appointment Calendar can lose their synchronization. When communication between the two fails, you must reset the Scheduler path in Appointment Calendar. This deletes *all* Scheduler information from your Calendar and requests that Scheduler resend all of its information. After resetting the path, you must enter Scheduler so it can process the resend request and create a new communications file. When you restart Appointment Calendar, it inserts all events that have already been accepted, and asks you to accept or delete any pending events. For more information on resetting your Scheduler path in Appointment Calendar, see Chapter 3, "Using Appointment Calendar."

Printing in Scheduler

In Scheduler, you can print your schedule for a day, week, month, or year. To print your schedule:

1. Press SHIFT-F7 for Print.

2. Press **1** or **P** for Print.

Before printing your schedule, you must first select a printer definition and the print device or port you want Scheduler to print to.

Selecting a Printer Definition

To select the printer definition for your printer:

1. Press SHIFT-F7 to display the Print menu.

2. Press **4** or **S** for Select Printer to display a listing of all available printer drivers.

3. Type the number next to the printer definition for your printer, and press ENTER. If your printer does not appear on the list, select a printer that your printer can emulate.

Selecting a Print Device

Scheduler supports printing either to a local printer via a parallel port, or to a network printer. To select a local print device:

1. Press SHIFT-F7 to display the Print menu.

2. Press **3** or **D** for Device or File.

3. Press **1** through **3** to select a local LPT port as the print device.

To define a network printer or print queue for Scheduler:

1. Press SHIFT-F7 to display the Print menu.

2. Press **3** or **D** for Device or File.

3. Press **4** or **D** to input the print device.

4. At the prompt, enter the name of the file server and network printer or print queue.

5. Type **Y** to indicate that this is a network printer. If you type **N**, Scheduler attempts to print to a file with the name you just entered.

Changing Print Options

With Scheduler's print options, you can indicate how printed information should appear on the page and what information should be printed. You can specify the margins, any indents, the number of days per page, if you want the date printed if there is no information for a particular day, what merge format to use if you are printing to a file, how many days of information to print, and what information to print. To change any of the preceding options:

1. Press SHIFT-F7 for Print.

2. Press 2 or **O** for Options. The following menu appears:

```
Page Size

        1 - Page Length (in lines)      66
        2 - Number of Lines             54

        3 - Top Margin (in lines)       6
        4 - Left Margin (column #)      10
        5 - Right Margin (column #)     74
        6 - Columns to Indent           2

Options

        7 - One Day per Page            No
        8 - Print Empty Days            Yes
        9 - Duration                    Today
```

3. Select an option and make the desired changes. The options are described in the following section.

Options

Scheduler stores the changes you make to the print options in the Scheduler setup file and they remain in effect until you change them again.

Page Length   Enter the length of the current page. The default is 66 lines for an 11-inch page in a 10 point font. If you wanted to print on a legal-size piece of paper, you would change this to 72.

Top Margin   Enter the number of lines from the top that the text should begin. Six lines equals 1 inch in a 10 point font.

Left/Right Margin   Enter the column position from the left and right edges. The default settings are 10 spaces for the right and 74 spaces for the left, which equals 1 inch for each in a 10 pitch font. If you were going to insert the page into a binder of some sort, you might want to increase your left margin.

Number of Columns to Indent   When printing Scheduler information, you can use this option to indent information printed under the date.

One Day Per Page   If you want each day of Scheduler information to print on a separate page, set this option to Yes.

Print Empty Days   By default, Scheduler does not print any text for days that do not contain any scheduled events. If you want to print these days, set this option to Yes. The only information that prints is the date.

Duration   The Duration option lets you decide exactly how many days of information you want printed. All of the options except for Today start printing from the day on which the cursor is resting. You can select Today, Day, Week, Month, or Year.

Exporting Your Schedule as a WordPerfect Merge File

Scheduler's Export feature allows you to create a secondary merge file for WordPerfect using the events in your Scheduler. You can set the way the information is exported and how much information is put in the merge file using the Export menu shown here:

```
Export

     1 - Export to a Merge File

Options

     2 - Content            Individual Events
     3 - Export Empty Days   No
     4 - Export Empty Times  Yes
     5 - Duration            Today
```

To export Scheduler information into a merge file:

1. Press CTRL-F5 to display the Export menu.

2. Press **2** to select the contents of the file.

3. Press **1** or **D** to export the events as they display, with one merge record being one day, or press **2** or **I** to export the events as individual events, with one merge record being one event.

4. Press **3** or **D** for Export Empty Days.

5. Type **Y** to export empty days as blank records, or **N** to skip all empty days.

6. Press **4** or **T** for Export Empty Times.

7. Type **Y** to export all empty times, or **N** to skip any empty time intervals.

8. Press **5** or **U** to select the Duration or time interval to cover in the export. The following options appear:

```
1 Today; 2 Day; 3 Week; 4 Month; 5 Year: 0
```

9. Select the desired option. The day, week, month, and year intervals all begin from the date highlighted on the Month or Week screen.

10. Press **1** to select the option Export to a Merge File. Scheduler displays the default filename *XXX*SCHED.MRG, where *XXX* is your unique Office File ID. You can change the filename, or insert a path where the file should be placed. If you don't specify a path, the file is placed in the default directory. Then you can retrieve this file into WordPerfect as a secondary merge file. You can also retrieve it in Office's Notebook to view the information it contains. When creating a primary merge document in WordPerfect 5.0 or later, use the file header information displayed in Table 9-2 to specify the correct information from the export file.

Individual Event *Merge File Format*		Display *Merge File Format*	
Position	**Field Name**	**Position**	**Field Name**
1	User Name	1	Date
2	Authority	2	Events
3	Organizer	3	User Name
4	Event Name		
5	People		
6	Resources		
7	Place		
8	Starting Date		
9	Time		
10	Event Length		
11	Explanation		

Table 9-2.   Scheduler File Header Information

Changing Scheduler Display Options

From the Setup menu, you can select the Display option to set the screen display attributes for the Scheduler screens. From the Display screen, you can also set the display colors. To change the display options:

1. Press SHIFT-F1 for Setup.

2. Press **1** or **D** for Display. The following options appear:

```
Setup: Display Options                    Monday, February 24, 1992   9:22 am

   1 - Display Hours - Begin          8:00 am
                       End            5:00 pm

   2 - Day Screens Time Interval      30 Minutes

   3 - First Day of the Week          Sunday

   4 - Days on Week Screen            5

   5 - Busy Screen Time Interval      30 Minutes

   6 - Busy Screen Marks - Busy         •
                           Free
                           Unknown      ?

   7 - Colors/Attributes
```

Options

The following options are available from the Setup: Display Options screen.

Display Hours   Press **1** or **H** to set the time range to display on the Month and Week screens. Enter the times to use as the beginning and ending times for the display. The default is 8:00 A.M. to 5:00 P.M. If your standard business day differs from this, you may want to change the times.

Day Screens Time Interval   Press **2** or **D** to set the size of the time blocks displayed on the Month and Week screens.

First Day of the Week   Press **3** or **F** to select which day Scheduler displays as the first day of the week on the Month screen. Press the arrow keys to move through the days of the week, and press ENTER to select the desired day.

Days on Week Screen   Press **4** or **W** to set the number of Day windows to display on the Week screen. You can set a maximum of 17 days. The higher the number, the more days displayed. However, the full date of each window cannot be displayed if the windows are too small.

Busy Screen Time Interval   Press **5** or **B** to set the size of the time blocks displayed on the Busy screen. The smaller the time interval, the more accurate the Busy display becomes.

Busy Screen Marks   Press **6** or **M** to choose what characters display on the Busy screen—indicating busy, free, and unknown times. These can be any two characters from the normal ASCII character set. See Appendix B for an ASCII Character Chart. Characters not found on the keyboard can be entered by holding down the ALT key while entering the ASCII decimal value for the character.

Colors/Attributes   Press **7** or **C** to set the colors and attributes display for Scheduler. If you have a color monitor, or a monochrome monitor that displays different shades, press **1** or **S** to display the Screen Colors menu, or select **2** or **F** to set the display speed. From the color screen, you can set the background and foreground colors for the attributes that Scheduler supports.

Changing Scheduler Environment Options

From Environment Options screen, you can change many of Scheduler's default conditions. To change any of the Environment options:

1. Press SHIFT-F1 for Setup.

2. Press **2** or **E** for Environment. The following menu appears:

```
 Setup: Environment Options              Monday, February 24, 1992   9:22 am

   1 - Beep on Error                No

   2 - Check Resources at Startup   No

   3 - Date / Time Formats

   4 - Password
```

Options

The following options are available from the Setup: Environment Options screen.

Beep on Error   Press **1** or **B** to turn on or off the beep as an error indicator.

Check Resources at Startup   Press **2** or **C** to check any resources you own for pending events each time you start Scheduler. If this option is set to Yes, Scheduler notifies you if there are any pending events for a resource you own. This is helpful because you do not have to retrieve the resource to know if events are pending.

Date/Time Formats   For information on setting Date and Time Formats, see the section "Changing the Date and Time Formats," later in this chapter.

Password   Press **4** or **W** to set or remove a password in Scheduler. To set a password, press **1** or **S** and enter the password. With a password set in Scheduler, anyone, including yourself, must enter a password before your schedule is displayed. Scheduler prompts you to reenter the password before accepting it. To remove a password, press 2 and enter the password.

Changing Schedule Options

The Schedule options change the settings for the Scheduler and Search screens. To change the Schedule options permanently:

1. Press SHIFT-F1 to display the Setup menu.

2. Press 3 or S to select the Schedule option. The Schedule Options screen appears, as shown in Figure 9-12.

```
 Schedule Options                       Monday, February 24, 1992   9:00 am

   1 - Notify                        Yes

   2 - Return Notification - Open    No
                             Accept  No
                             Delete  No

   3 - Schedule CC Recipients in Groups  Yes

   4 - Schedule BC Recipients in Groups  Yes

   5 - Mode of entering Event Length     Event Length

   6 - Possible Days for scheduling      Mon, Tue, Wed, Thu, Fri

   7 - Scheduling Hours - Begin          8:00 am
                          End            5:00 pm

   8 - Event Length                      30 Minutes

   9 - Search Range                      7 Days

 Selection: 0
```

Figure 9-12.   Schedule Options screen

To set the Schedule options on for a single event you are scheduling from the Schedule screen:

1. Press SHIFT-F8 to display the temporary Schedule Options screen and set the desired options.

Options

The following options are available from the Schedule Options screen.

Notify   Press **1** or **N** to turn Notify on or off. With Notify on, any recipients must have Notify loaded to display an on-screen notification window. See Chapter 11 "Using Notify, Repeat Performance, and TSR Manager."

Return Notification   Press **2** or **R** to set the different levels of Return Notification. With these options turned on, you receive on-screen notification indicating when a user opens, accepts, or deletes an event.

Schedule CC Recipients in Groups   Press **3** or **C** to set the option for using carbon copy recipients if they are included in a group you use. If you set this option to No, any carbon copy recipients in the group are not included when the group is used to organize an event. If you set this option to Yes, these users are included as normal recipients.

Schedule BC Recipients in Groups   Press **4** or **B** to set the option for using blind copy recipients if they are included in a group you use. If you set this option to No, any blind copy recipients in the group are not included when the group is used to organize an event. If you set this option to Yes, these users are included as normal recipients.

Mode of Entering Event Length   Press **6** or **P** to indicate the method used to specify an event length. Scheduler lets you specify the actual length of the event, or enter the event's ending date and time.

Possible Days for Scheduling   Pressing **6** or **P** lets you specify which days to include as a default on the Search screen. You can enter the days to include by typing the first letter or two of each day, with a comma separating the days.

Scheduling Hours   Press **7** or **S** to set the default starting and ending times for the Search screen.

Event Length   Press **8** or **E** to enter the default event length for both the Schedule and Search screens. This event length is used as the default even if Ending Date and Time is used as the mode of entering event length.

Search Range   Press **9** or **S** to set the default search range for the Search screen. Scheduler uses this option to set the search length, beginning at the time specified as the starting date and time on the Search screen.

Changing the Date and Time Formats

The Date/Time Formats option on Scheduler's Setup menu changes how the date and time are displayed in the screen headings, the date display in the Month screen, and the time display in the Month and Week screens. To change this information:

1. Press SHIFT-F1 for Setup from the main Scheduler screen.

2. Press **2** or **E** for Environment.

3. Press **3** or **D** for Date/Time Formats. The following menu appears along the bottom of the screen:

1 Combined Date/Time format; 2 Date format; 3 Time format; 0

Note: You can also press SHIFT-F5 to select Date/Time Format from the main Scheduler screen.

4. Select the format you want to change.

Formats

The following format options are available from the Date/Time Format screen.

Combined Date/Time Format   The Combined Date/Time Format changes how the date is displayed on the header of all Scheduler screens. To set the display format for the date, you can use any of the characters displayed in Figure 9-13. Along with the special characters, you can enter text, punctuation, or spaces to format the display.

Date Format   You can use Date Format to change how dates above the day are displayed in the Month screen. This option also determines the order in which you enter dates when using the Go To Date feature.

```
Date and Time Format                    Monday, February 24, 1992   9:00 am

   Character      Meaning
      1           Day of the month
      2           Month (number)
      3           Month (word)
      4           Year (all four digits)
      5           Year (last two digits)
      6           Day of the week (word)
      7           Hour (24 hour clock)
      8           Hour (12 hour clock)
      9           Minute
      0           am / pm
      #           Week  (number)
      %           Used before a number, will:
                      Pad numbers less than 10 with a leading zero
                      Output only 3 letters for the month or day of the week
      $           Include leading space on numbers less than 10
                  (% and $ must directly precede number)

   Examples: 3 1, 4   = January 15, 1991
             2/1/5 (6) = 1/15/91 (Tuesday)
             8:90      = 10:55am

1 Combined Date/Time format; 2 Date format; 3 Time format; 0
```

Figure 9-13.   Date/time format characters

Time Format   The Time Format option changes the way the times are displayed in the Month and Week screens. You can set the time to include a leading space by inserting a dollar sign ($) directly before the time format that makes times align correctly. You can set the time to include a leading 0 (zero) by entering a percent sign (%) in front of the time format string.

Retrieving a Resource Schedule

In Scheduler, each resource has a user designated as its owner. The owner is responsible for maintaining the schedule for that resource by accepting and deleting events in the resource's Scheduler. To retrieve the schedule of a resource that you own, do the following from the Event screen:

1. Press F5 for the List feature.

2. Press **6** or **O** for Owner. Scheduler displays a list of all resources that you own, similar to the one shown here:

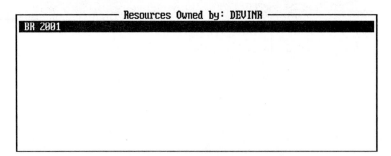

3. Use the cursor keys to highlight the resource you want to re-trieve.

4. Press ENTER to retrieve the resource.

Once you retrieve a resource's schedule, you can accept or delete events as you wish. To retrieve your own schedule, press SHIFT-F10 for Retrieve, and your Office User ID displays as a default. Press ENTER to retrieve your schedule.

Scheduling with Multiple Hosts

When using Office in a multi-host system, you should understand how an event gets from a user on one host to a user on another host. The path a scheduled event takes from the organizer to a recipient on another host is called its *route*. Since routing paths are usually set up by your system administrator, Office users normally do not need to worry about how an event should be delivered.

When you send an event in Scheduler and let the event follow the default system path, the routing of the event is *automatic*. You can also set up *explicit* routes that override any existing system routes.

If you want to use explicit routing for an event, you must know the recipient's User ID on her or his own host, the name of her or his host, and the names of any hosts that handle the event from Scheduler. For example, if you are on host Research and your recipient is on host Sales and has the User ID DonR, you could enter the following when specifying the users to deliver the message to:

Sales:DonR

While this route works with automatic routing if the system administrator has configured the system route correctly, it only works for explicit routing if the event can be sent directly from the local host, Research, to the destination host, Sales, without having to be sent to other hosts to complete the delivery.

The method you use to route your Scheduler events depends mainly on how your administrator has configured your system. For example, if all of the Office User IDs are unique across all known hosts, you do not need to specify the destination host as shown in the previous example. Scheduler can look through the list of users, and if there is only one user with the specified User ID, Scheduler routes the event automatically. However, if it finds duplicate User IDs and no host name is specified, Scheduler proceeds as if the user is on the same host. If this is not the case, Scheduler uses the first user on the user list with that User ID.

For information on how your system is configured and how to route Scheduler events correctly, contact your system administrator.

Bold

In the Event Name and Place fields, and the Explanation box on the Schedule screen, you can use bold to make text more noticeable.

Keystrokes

To add bold:

1. Use the cursor keys or editing keys to position the cursor where the bold text should start.

2. Press F6 for Bold and type the word or words you want in boldface.

3. Press F6 again to turn off Bold.

To delete bold codes:

1. Use the cursor keys or editing keys to position the cursor where the bold text begins.

2. Press CTRL-RIGHT ARROW for Word Right or CTRL-LEFT ARROW for Word Left until the cursor is on the first letter of the boldfaced word.

3. Press DEL. The "Delete Attribute Code (Y/N)?N" prompt appears.

4. Type **Y** to delete the bold codes.

Note: In earlier versions of Office, the code is deleted without a prompt.

Busy Screen

See "Using the Busy Screen" earlier in this chapter.

Cancel

You can use Cancel to quit any current operation and return to the previous screen. This includes searches for available times and scheduling an event.

Keystrokes

1. Press F1 to cancel any Scheduler process. If necessary, Scheduler prompts for you to confirm the cancellation before clearing any screens.

Date/Time Formats

The Date/Time Formats option on Scheduler's Setup menu changes how the date and time are displayed in the main screen headings, the dates in the Month screen, and the times in the Month and Week screens.

Keystrokes

1. Press SHIFT-F1 for Setup from the main screen.

2. Press **2** or **E** for Environment.

3. Press **3** or **D** for Date/Time Formats.

Note: You can also press SHIFT-F5 to select Date/Time Format from the main Scheduler screen.

4. Select an option from the menu to change the desired format.

For information on the individual options, see "Changing the Date and Time Formats" earlier in this chapter.

Display Options

From the Setup menu, you can change various Scheduler Display settings. Any changes made to the Display options remain in effect until you change them again.

Keystrokes

1. Press SHIFT-F1 for Setup.

2. Press **1** or **D** for Display.

3. Select the desired option and make the necessary changes.

For information on the individual Display options, see "Changing Scheduler Display Options" earlier in this chapter.

Environment Options

From the Setup menu, you can change various Environment options. These options include Beep on Error, Check Resources at Startup, Date/Time Formats, and Password. Any changes made to the Environment options remain in effect until you change them again.

Keystrokes

1. Press SHIFT-F1 for Setup.

2. Press **2** or **E** for Environment.

For information on the individual Environment options, see "Changing Scheduler Environment Options" earlier in this chapter.

Export

See "Exporting Your Schedule as a WordPerfect Merge File" earlier in this chapter.

Go To Date

On the Month, Week, and Busy screens, you can use the Go To Date function to move to any date in Scheduler.

Keystrokes

1. Press CTRL-HOME to display the Go To Date prompt shown here:

Enter date (mm/dd/yyyy): 6/14/1990 (Thursday)

2. Enter a new date in the format shown. The default format is mm/dd/yyyy, which is month, day, year. You can enter partial dates if you want to use the current day or month.

3. Press CTRL-HOME to display the current date, and press ENTER to return to the current date.

You can also change the date format to day/month/year or year/month/date using the Date Format option on the Date/Time Format screen (see the section "Changing the Date and Time Formats" earlier in this chapter).

Help

The Help feature displays information about the Scheduler features.

Keystrokes

1. Press F3 for Help from the main Scheduler screen. Scheduler displays the screen shown in Figure 9-14.

2. To access help you can then type one of the menu-item letters to see information about the specific topic; press a function key to see information about the feature associated with that key; or press F3 for Help again to see the Scheduler template. This is especially useful since WordPerfect Office does not come with a keyboard template for Scheduler.

3. Press ENTER or SPACEBAR to exit a help screen, or ESC to return to the main Help screen.

Hints

The Help screens are a valuable tool for accessing information about the Scheduler program. Pressing Help from any Scheduler menu displays information about the features associated with that screen. Scheduler displays the keystrokes (if any) for the feature in the upper-right corner of the Help screen.

Help   Version 3.0   06/14/90
                                                        SC - Other

          Press a Function Key for information about the use of the key.
          Press the Help Key (F3) to see a template for the function keys.
          Type one of the following letters for information about specific topics:

                A - Entering Text   I - Retrieving a User/Resource
                B - Exiting Scheduler   J - Setup Options
                C - Exporting Data   K - Shell Interaction
                D - Go to Date   L - Starting Scheduler
                E - Creating Groups   M - Viewing Events
                F - List
                G - Main Screens   Y - Customer Support
                H - Printing   Z - IBM Character Set

     A-Z Topic: 0   (ESC Topics; Space Exit; Function Key Help for Key)

Figure 9-14.   Scheduler main Help screen

List

You can use the List feature in Scheduler to display lists of files, users, resources, hosts, groups, and owners.

Keystrokes

1. Press F5 for List. The following menu appears:

```
List: 1 Files; 2 Users; 3 Resources; 4 Hosts; 5 Groups; 6 Owner; 2
```

List Files

Using List Files in Scheduler, you can perform many common file-management commands without exiting to DOS. List Files displays the files and subdirectories contained in a given directory. From the List Files screen, you can retrieve, delete, move, rename, or look at a file. The function is only performed on the file that is currently highlighted in the file listing unless you mark several files on which you want the function performed. You can also perform a Name search while in List Files. If you want to change to another directory, you can use the Other Directory option. List Files is useful for retrieving the contents of files into the Explanation window.

Keystrokes

1. Press F5 for List.

2. Press 1 or **F** for Files.

3. Scheduler displays the current default directory. Press ENTER to select the directory, or enter a path to another directory to list. Changing directories in List Files changes the current default directory for Scheduler.

List Groups

Using the List Group option, you can look at a listing of either all of the global groups created by your system administrator, or your personal groups in your default directory.

Keystrokes

1. Press F5 for List.

2. Press **5** or **G** for Groups. The following menu appears:

Global: 1 Users; 2 Resources; Personal: 3 Users; 4 Resources: 1

3. Select the desired option. If you choose Personal, Users, or Resources, Scheduler displays the current default directory. Press ENTER to have Scheduler list all of the group files in the default directory, or a enter a new directory.

Hints

If you are using a group to schedule an event, you can mark and retrieve a group name from the List Group screen using F7, or retrieve the contents of a group using the Retrieve option **1** or **R**. You can also look at the contents of the group or perform a Name search to find a specific group file.

List Hosts

The List Hosts option under the List feature displays a listing of all known hosts, and gives you access to host-specific user and resource listings. You can add users or resources to the People or Resource line with the List Hosts option.

Keystrokes

1. Press F5 for List.

2. Press **4** or **H** for Hosts.

3. Use the UP ARROW or DOWN ARROW key to highlight the desired host.

4. Press **1** or **U** to display a user list for the highlighted host, or **2** or **R** to display a resource list.

List Resources

You can use the List Resources option under the List feature to display all of the known resources on your Office system.

Keystrokes

1. Press F5 for List.

2. Press **3** or **R** for Resources.

From the List Resources screen, you can see information about the resources, such as a description, the owner, and the Resource ID.

List Users

You can use the List Users option under the List feature to display all of the known users on your Office system.

Keystrokes

1. Press F5 for List.

2. Press **2** or **U** Users.

From the List Users screen, you may be able to see information about users, such as their department, phone number, and User ID.

Print

From the Event, Week, or Month screen, you can print a list of all scheduled items for a specified number of days.

Keystrokes

1. Press SHIFT-F7 to display the Print menu.

2. Press **1** or **P** for Print.

For more information on printing in Scheduler, see "Printing in Scheduler" earlier in this chapter.

Print Options

Using the Print Options menu in Scheduler, you can select and format any printed output.

Keystrokes

1. Press SHIFT-F7 to display the Print menu.

2. Press **2** or **O** for Options.

3. Select the desired option and make the necessary changes.

For information on the individual print options, see "Changing Print Options" earlier in this chapter.

Renotify

For any events you have organized, you can renotify any pending users to remind them to respond to the event.

Keystrokes

To renotify any pending users about an event that you have organized, do the following from the Organized box on the Event screen:

1. Use the cursor keys to highlight the correct event.

2. Press **3** or **T** to send a reminder to any users that have not yet responded to your event.

If the users you schedule are using the Notify program, they receive on-screen notification about the event.

Reschedule

If you are the organizer of an event, you can reschedule an event and leave the original in your Organized box, or delete and reschedule the event and replace the original event on the Event screen with the rescheduled event.

Keystrokes

To reschedule an event that you have organized and that is listed in your Organized box, do the following from the Event screen:

1. If necessary, press TAB or SHIFT-TAB to move the cursor to your Organized box.

2. Use the cursor keys to highlight the event to reschedule.

3. Press **7** or **R** to reschedule the event.

4. Press **1** or **D** to delete the original event from your Organized box and all recipients' Requested boxes and reschedule. Or press **2** or **R** to reschedule the event and leave the original event in place.

5. Scheduler takes the information from the event and displays it on the Schedule screen for you to edit. After making any modifications, press F7 and type **Y** to schedule the event and exit the Schedule screen, or press F9 to reschedule the event and remain in the Schedule screen.

If you reschedule an event without deleting the original, both of the events display in the recipients' schedules. Rescheduling does not automatically replace or remove the original event.

Retrieve

When you use Scheduler's Retrieve function from the Event screen, you can retrieve the schedule for another user or resource if they have a password set. When you use Retrieve from the Schedule, Search, and Group screens, it retrieves the contents of a specified file, such as a group or text file, into the field where the cursor is currently located.

Keystrokes

To use Retrieve to view the schedule for another user or resource, do the following from the Event screen:

1. Press SHIFT-F10 to use Retrieve.

2. Enter the Office User ID or Resource ID for the schedule to retrieve.

3. If a password is set in the schedule to retrieve, enter the password to gain full access, or, if no password is set, you have very limited access without any rights to modify that schedule.

4. To retrieve your own schedule again, press SHIFT-F10. Your User ID displays by default. Press ENTER to retrieve your schedule.

To use Retrieve on the Schedule, Search, and Group screens to retrieve a file, do the following:

1. Use TAB, SHIFT-TAB, or the cursor keys to position the cursor where the contents of the file should be placed.

2. Press SHIFT-F10 to use Retrieve.

3. Enter the path, filename, and extension of the file to be retrieved.

Scheduler retrieves the contents of the file you specify to the current cursor location.

Return Notification

To notify you of any changes in the status of users and resources that you schedule for an event, you can use Return Notification. This feature displays on-screen notification to tell you if a user or resource's owner opens, accepts, and/or deletes an event that you have scheduled.

Keystrokes

To set the Return Notification options permanently, do the following:

1. Press SHIFT-F1 for Setup.

2. Press 3 or S for Schedule.

3. Press **2** or **R** from the Schedule Options menu to set Return Notification.

4. Type **Y** to turn on Return Notification, or **N** to disable it for each of the three options listed.

You can also set Return Notification temporarily by doing the following from the Schedule screen:

1. Press SHIFT-F8 to display the Temporary Schedule Options menu.

2. Press **2** or **R** from the Schedule Options menu to set Return Notification.

3. Type **Y** to turn on Return Notification, or **N** to disable it for each of the three options listed.

The temporary setting for Return Notification is only set until the Schedule screen is exited.

Schedule Options

You can set permanent or temporary Schedule options that affect the Schedule, Search, and Busy screens.

Keystrokes

To set the Schedule options permanently, do the following:

1. Press SHIFT-F1 to display the Setup menu.

2. Press **3** or **S** to select the Schedule option.

3. Select the desired option and make the necessary changes.

To set the Schedule options on a temporary basis, do the following from the Schedule screen:

1. Press SHIFT-F8 to display the temporary Schedule Options menu and set the desired options.

For information on the individual Schedule options, see "Changing Schedule Options" earlier in this chapter.

Search

See "Searching for Available Times" earlier in this chapter.

Setup Options

In Scheduler, you can permanently configure the Display, Environment, and Schedule options from the Setup menu. Any changes you make in these options are recorded in your personal Scheduler set file and remain in effect until you change them again.

Keystrokes

1. Press SHIFT-F1 to display the Setup menu.

2. Select options from one of the three submenus and make the desired changes.

See also the sections "Display Options," "Environment Options," and "Schedule Options."

Shell

There are several advantages to using Scheduler under Shell rather than running from the DOS command line. You can move between programs while Scheduler stays resident in memory. Shell also provides the Clipboard, a temporary memory buffer where information can be transferred between programs.

Keystrokes

Program Switch

To leave Scheduler resident and go to Shell, you can press CTRL-ALT-SPACEBAR. You can also use the Shell function from most screens in Scheduler:

1. Press CTRL-F1.

2. Press **G** or **1** to select Go To Shell.

These functions remove Scheduler from base memory, but save it on your hard disk or in expanded memory. When you return to Scheduler, you are in the same position with the same display as when you left.

You can also switch to other programs listed on the same Shell menu as Scheduler by pressing CTRL-ALT-x, where x is the Shell menu letter or Shell option you want to change to.

Startup Options

Scheduler provides several startup options that change some of the default environment settings. If you are running Scheduler under Shell, you can enter these options on the line on the Shell Program Information screen for Scheduler. If you start Scheduler from DOS, enter the startup options on the command line following the sc command to start Scheduler.

The following startup options are available for Scheduler:

/@U-*User ID*	Specifies the Office User ID of the person whose Scheduler you want to retrieve. By default, this is the user who has logged onto the network on the computer starting Scheduler. Retrieving another user's schedule can only be accomplished if a personal password has been set by that user, or a system password by the system administrator. For information on setting a personal password, see the section "Password" under "Changing Scheduler Environment Options." For more information on system passwords, contact your system administrator.
/C	Checks for any unopened events in your Request box. For you to use this option under Shell, Scheduler must be set to start resident. If any unopened events are found, Scheduler starts before the Shell menu is displayed. If no unopened events are found, Scheduler remains resident, but is not entered before Shell. If this option is run from DOS, Scheduler starts if unopened events are found. If no unopened events are found, you return to the DOS command line. This option is commonly used in the AUTOEXEC.BAT file before starting Shell.
/CM	Similar to /C, but only checks for unopened events and notifies you if any are found. Scheduler is not automatically started.
/CN	Similar to /C, but if used under Shell, Scheduler is not left resident in memory if no unopened events exist. If used from DOS, /CN works the same as /C.
/CP-*x*	Changes the default code page used by DOS.
/D-%*x*	If you attempt to start multiple copies of Scheduler using the same default directory, this option allows you to number the temporary files to keep Scheduler from returning an error.

/D-*path*	Specifies the default directory for Scheduler to use. This is where Scheduler opens its temporary files, and should normally point to a local directory, or to your personal work directory.
/M-*macro*	When you are using Scheduler under Shell, this option specifies a macro to execute each time Scheduler is started. If the macro is not located in the current default directory for Scheduler, or in the global macro directory specified in Shell, be sure to list the full path to the macro.
/MONO	Enhances the display capabilities of monitors that can display both color and monochrome, but are currently running in monochrome mode.
/NF	Sets Scheduler's screen display to the Non-flash mode. This option can be used to try to correct common display problems for Scheduler when used under window or program management products other than Shell.
/NK	Disables enhanced keyboard calls to prevent problems with some TSR programs or compatibles.
/NT-*x*	Specifies the Office designation for the software that your network uses, where *x* is the number or letter of the network type.
/NU	Eliminates occasional pauses in Scheduler's operations by turning off the Auto-Update feature. However, any new events you receive after using this option are not displayed in your In Box.
/PH-*path*	Gives Scheduler the location of the user listing file, USERID.FIL. This is also where Scheduler looks for your personal information files.
/RP	If you own a resource, this option checks for any pending events in that resource's Scheduler on startup. If any are found, the resources with pending events are displayed. This is similar to the /CM option, but is for resources.

/SS-*row,column*   Customizes the screen display format by specifying the rows and columns on the display.

/W-*x*   Sets the size of the workspace that Scheduler keeps in memory. *x* is the number of kilobytes Scheduler can use.

Switch

Moves the cursor between windows on the Event screen, and switches between the Month and Week screens.

Keystrokes

1. Press SHIFT-F3 on the Event, Month, or Week screen.

Underline

In the Event Name and Place fields, and the Explanation box on the Schedule screen, you can use underlining to make text more noticeable.

Keystrokes

To add underline:

1. Use the cursor keys or editing keys to position the cursor where the underlined text should start.

2. Press F8 for Underline and type the word or words you want underlined.

3. Press F8 again to turn off Underline.

To delete underline codes:

1. Use the cursor keys or editing keys to position the cursor where the underlined text begins.

2. Press CTRL-RIGHT ARROW for Word Right or CTRL-LEFT ARROW for Word Left until the cursor is on the first letter of the underlined word.

3. Press DEL. The "Delete Attribute Code (Y/N)?N" prompt appears.

4. Type **Y** to delete the underline codes.

Note: In earlier versions of Office the code is deleted without a prompt.

Using Shell

TEN

The Shell program is the integrating force of all Office programs as well as other WordPerfect and non-WordPerfect products. As an information integrator, Shell helps you organize all of your programs on a menu so you can start them by pressing a single letter. You can also add batch files, Shell macros, and submenus to a Shell menu. From the Shell menu you can temporarily exit to DOS without exiting the Shell menu to perform necessary tasks.

With programs listed on the Shell menu, you can switch between programs without exiting the programs. For example, if you are in Mail and need to check an item on your Calendar, you could switch to Calendar, check the information, and then go back to Mail without ever exiting Mail. The Switch feature speeds up many daily tasks that involve the use of several programs.

The Shell Clipboard is the main integrator of information between programs. With the Clipboard you can save or append information from a Shell program to a temporary buffer. You can then retrieve this information into another program. For example, if you are typing a memo in WordPerfect and need to add part of the information to your Calendar, you could save the information to the Clipboard, switch to the Appointment Calendar program, and retrieve the information. The Clipboard is an excellent tool for sharing information between programs.

Along with information integration, Shell also supplies valuable information about your computer memory with the Memory Map. The Memory Map lets you know where your memory is allocated and how much memory you have.

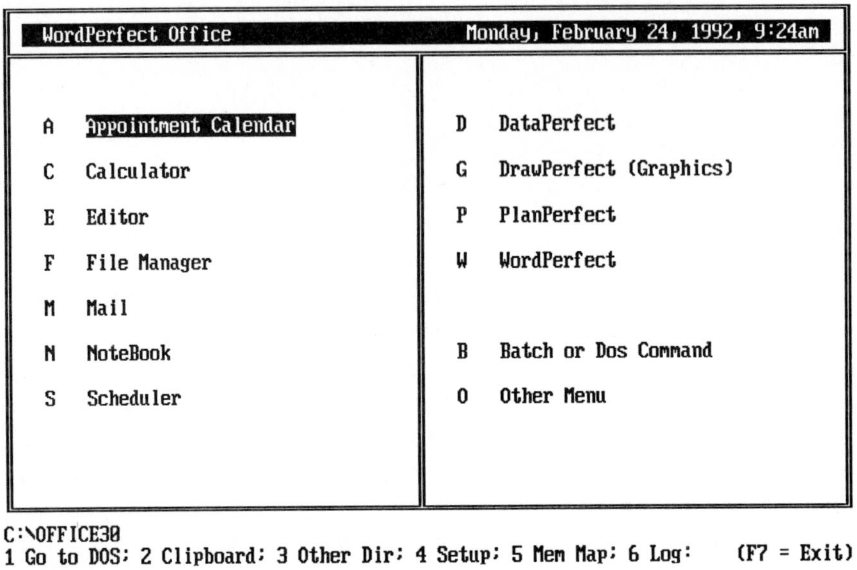

```
┌──────────────────────────────────────────────────────────────────┐
│ WordPerfect Office                    Monday, February 24, 1992, 9:24am │
├────────────────────────────────────┬───────────────────────────────┤
│                                     │                               │
│   A   Appointment Calendar          │   D   DataPerfect             │
│                                     │                               │
│   C   Calculator                    │   G   DrawPerfect (Graphics)  │
│                                     │                               │
│   E   Editor                        │   P   PlanPerfect             │
│                                     │                               │
│   F   File Manager                  │   W   WordPerfect             │
│                                     │                               │
│   M   Mail                          │                               │
│                                     │                               │
│   N   NoteBook                      │   B   Batch or Dos Command    │
│                                     │                               │
│   S   Scheduler                     │   O   Other Menu              │
│                                     │                               │
│                                     │                               │
└────────────────────────────────────┴───────────────────────────────┘
C:\OFFICE30
1 Go to DOS: 2 Clipboard: 3 Other Dir: 4 Setup: 5 Mem Map: 6 Log:    (F7 = Exit)
```

Figure 10-1.   Default Shell menu (LAN version)

Starting Shell

To start Shell, change to the directory where the SHELL.EXE file is located and type **shell**. If the office directory is in your path, you can simply type **shell**. The first time you start Shell, a menu similar to the one shown in Figure 10-1 displays.

If the Shell menu automatically appears when you turn on your computer, the command to start Shell has been added to the AUTO-EXEC.BAT file. If the Shell menu does not automatically appear when you start your computer and you would like it to, you can add the command to your AUTOEXEC.BAT file. For information on editing your AUTOEXEC.BAT file, check your DOS manual and/or consult your system administrator. If you are using Office LAN, you can use the SETMEUP program to have the SHELL command automatically added to your AUTOEXEC.BAT file. For information on using the SETMEUP program, see Appendix A, "LAN User Installation." If you are using Office LAN, your AUTOEXEC.BAT file should look something like this:

```
PATH=f:\office
f:\office\notify
f:\office\cl/i
f:\office\shell
```

You must put the SHELL command after the NOTIFY and CL/I commands.

If you are using Office PC your AUTOEXEC.BAT file should look something like this:

```
PATH=c:\office30
c:\office30\cl/i
c:\office30\shell
```

These sample AUTOEXEC.BAT files only include the necessary commands for Office; your AUTOEXEC.BAT may have more commands.

The default Shell menu shown in Figure 10-1 lists a menu title in the upper-left corner and the current date and time in the right corner. On the left side of the screen are menu entries for all of the Word-Perfect Office programs. On the right side of the screen are other WordPerfect programs. These programs do not come with Office but are listed here for your convenience if you have already purchased them or plan to do so in the future. Below the other WordPerfect programs are the Batch or DOS Command (to go to DOS) and Other Menu options. The Other Menu listing brings up a predefined Shell submenu.

The information on the default Shell menu varies depending on the version of Office you are using. If you are using Office PC, you will not have the options for Mail and Scheduler shown in Figure 10-1. If you are using Office LAN, your system administrator may have changed the Shell menu to meet your network setup.

Below the actual Shell menu in the left-hand corner is the Shell default directory. This is the directory from which Shell was executed. Below the default directory is the main Shell menu.

Default Shell Files

The actual information on the Shell menu is stored in a Shell menu-information file. The first time you start Shell, it uses a default menu-information file called SHELL.NEW. As soon as you make any changes to the Shell menu or setup options, Shell makes a copy of this file and changes the name of the file. If you are using Office PC, the menu-information file is named SHELL.FIL. If you are using Office LAN, the file is named *XXX*SHELL.FIL, where *XXX* represents your File ID. When Shell starts it looks for these default filenames. If the default file is not found, it uses the SHELL.NEW file. If you ever have problems with the wrong Shell menu appearing, make sure the correct menu-information file is being used. You can see what menu-information file is being used by pressing Help (F3). The full path and filename of the menu-information file display in the upper-left corner. Shell lists this file as shown here:

Menu: C:\OFFICE30\SHELL.FIL

Exiting Shell

You can exit the main Shell screen by pressing Exit (F7). If there are no programs resident, you are immediately returned to DOS. If there are programs listed on the Shell menu that are resident, indicated by an asterisk next to the menu entry, the "Save information in all programs? (Y/N)Y" prompt displays. If you type N for No, any and all information in the resident programs is lost and you are exited to DOS. If you type Y for Yes, Shell returns you to the programs resident in memory and lets you save the file and exit the program. If the resident program is a WordPerfect Corporation product, Shell only takes you into those programs where files have been modified and not yet saved. For example, if you had Editor and Notebook resident when you tried to exit, and you had not made any changes to the document in Editor, Shell would only take you into Notebook to save the modified file. For non-WordPerfect programs, Shell enters each resident program and lets you perform the necessary action. After all programs are exited, Shell displays the "Exit shell? (Y/N)N" prompt. Type Y to exit the Shell or N to remain in the Shell menu.

Using the Go to DOS Feature

On the main Shell menu, select option 1 for Go To DOS. When using this option, Shell and any other programs that are in memory are left resident while you go to DOS. A screen similiar to the one shown here displays:

```
Enter the DOS command 'EXIT' (or Press F7) to return to the shell.

(shell) C:\OFFICE30>
```

While in DOS you can perform any DOS command. To return to the Shell menu press F7 or type **exit**.

Note: If you are using Office LAN, your system administrator may have disabled the Go To DOS option.

Switching Programs

The Switch feature allows you to quickly switch between the programs on your Shell menu. To switch to another program press CTRL-ALT-*x*, where *x* is the menu letter of the program to which you want to switch. As soon as you press CTRL-ALT-*x*, you switch to the other program and the first program is left in memory or swapped to disk. If you do not have enough memory or disk space to start another program Shell displays an error message.

You can also use the Switch feature to go to Shell. To switch to the Shell menu press CTRL-ALT-SPACEBAR. An asterisk displays next to the program left in memory as shown in Figure 10-2. When you return to the Shell menu when a program is resident, Shell always highlights the resident program. If there are several programs resident, the program you left most recently is highlighted. The Switch feature can also utilize the Shell menu items at the bottom of the screen. For example, if you want to go to DOS while in a program listed on the Shell menu, press CTRL-ALT-1. The 1 accesses the Go To DOS option from the Shell menu. This allows you quick and easy access to many of the Shell features.

You can use the Switch feature from any screen or menu within a program as long as the Allow Switch Anytime? option is set to Yes on the Program Information screen. The only exception to this is if a program is using a graphics display mode. The Switch feature does not work while in a graphics mode. If the Allow Switch Anytime? option is set to No, Switch only works from screens and menus that normally allow you to exit to DOS.

```
┌──────────────────────────────────────────────────────────────────────┐
│ WordPerfect Office                    Monday, February 24, 1992, 9:01am│
├─────────────────────────────────────┬──────────────────────────────── │
│                                      │                                 │
│   A    Appointment Calendar          │   D    DataPerfect              │
│                                      │                                 │
│   C    Calculator                    │   G    DrawPerfect (Graphics)   │
│                                      │                                 │
│   E    Editor                        │   P    PlanPerfect              │
│                                      │                                 │
│   F    File Manager                  │   W    WordPerfect              │
│                                      │                                 │
│   M    Mail                          │                                 │
│                                      │                                 │
│ * N    NoteBook                      │   B    Batch or Dos Command     │
│                                      │                                 │
│   S    Scheduler                     │   O    Other Menu               │
│                                      │                                 │
│                                      │                                 │
│                                      │                                 │
└─────────────────────────────────────┴─────────────────────────────────┘
C:\OFFICE30
1 Go to DOS; 2 Clipboard; 3 Other Dir; 4 Setup; 5 Mem Map; 6 Log:    (F7 = Exit)
```

Figure 10-2.   Program in resident memory

Using Switch with Non-Shell-Compatible Programs

If the Switch feature does not work properly while using a non-WordPerfect product, you can define a Go To Shell macro that allows you to exit to Shell without exiting the program. A Go To Shell macro only works with programs that have the ability to execute a single DOS command without exiting the program. A Go To Shell macro records the keystrokes that a program uses to go to DOS. These keystrokes are then executed when you use the Switch feature. To define a Go To Shell macro:

1. Enter the program for which you are defining a Go To Shell macro.

2. Press CTRL-SHIFT-F10 to begin defining the Shell macro. The "Define shell macro:" prompt displays.

3. Enter **goshell.*x*,** where *x* represents the Shell menu letter of the program for which you are defining the macro.

4. Enter a macro description.

5. Perform the keystrokes that normally exits you to DOS from that program.

6. As soon as you are at the Shell menu, press CTRL-SHIFT-F10 to end the macro.

Once you define the macro, enter the letter you used for that program in step 3 on the Program Information screen. You must also set the Allow Switch Anytime? option to No. Shell will then look for the Go To Shell macro each time you use the Switch feature.

If you have problems returning to the program that is using a Go To Shell macro, you can create a Return From Shell macro. To create a Return From Shell macro:

1. Go to DOS, using the program's internal commands.

2. Press CTRL-SHIFT-F10 to begin defining the Shell macro. The "Define shell macro:" prompt displays.

3. Enter **rtshell*x***, where *x* represents the Shell menu letter of the program for which you are defining the macro.

4. Enter a macro description.

5. Perform the keystrokes that normally return you to that program from DOS. Usually this is simply pressing the menu letter for the specific program.

6. As soon as you are in the program, press CTRL-SHIFT-F10 to end the macro.

Note: Go To Shell and Return From Shell macros can also be defined for programs that have display problems when using the Switch feature when Allow Switch Anytime? is set to Yes.

Editing the Shell Menu

The default Shell menu that comes with WordPerfect Office lists many of the entries you will use, but it can be customized to meet your

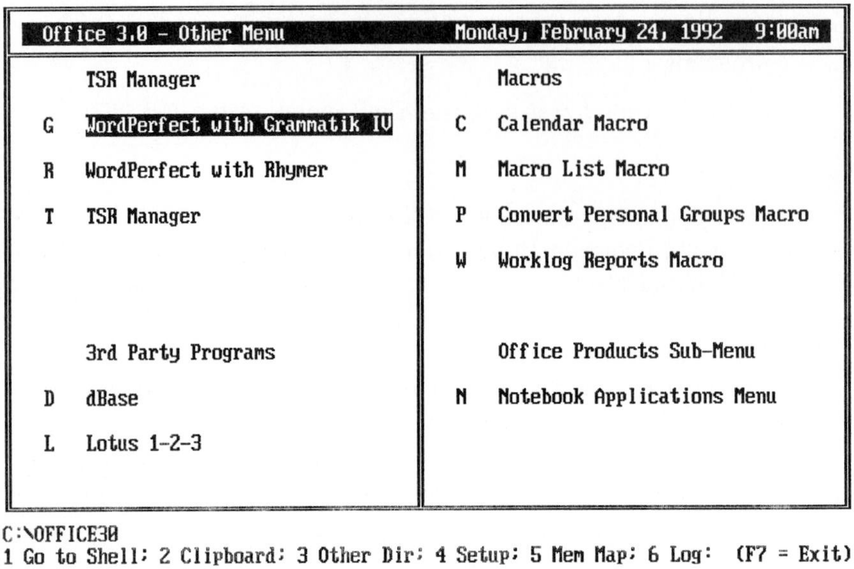

```
╔═══════════════════════════════════════════════════════════════════╗
║ ▓Office 3.0 - Other Menu▓           Monday, February 24, 1992   9:00am║
╟──────────────────────────────────┬──────────────────────────────────╢
║      TSR Manager                 │     Macros                       ║
║                                  │                                  ║
║  G  ▓WordPerfect with Grammatik IV▓ │  C  Calendar Macro               ║
║                                  │                                  ║
║  R  WordPerfect with Rhymer      │  M  Macro List Macro             ║
║                                  │                                  ║
║  T  TSR Manager                  │  P  Convert Personal Groups Macro║
║                                  │                                  ║
║                                  │  W  Worklog Reports Macro        ║
║                                  │                                  ║
║                                  │                                  ║
║      3rd Party Programs          │     Office Products Sub-Menu     ║
║                                  │                                  ║
║  D  dBase                        │  N  Notebook Applications Menu   ║
║                                  │                                  ║
║  L  Lotus 1-2-3                  │                                  ║
║                                  │                                  ║
╚══════════════════════════════════╧══════════════════════════════════╝
C:\OFFICE30
1 Go to Shell; 2 Clipboard; 3 Other Dir; 4 Setup; 5 Mem Map; 6 Log:  (F7 = Exit)
```

Figure 10-3.   Sample customized Shell menu

individual needs and preferences. For example, Figure 10-3 lists several third-party products, macros, and other possible entries. You can add, delete, move, copy, and swap entries on the Shell menu. You can also edit the information contained in the Program Information screen for each Shell entry. You cannot edit a Shell menu item while it is resident in memory. When you enter the Setup menu the menu title at the bottom of the screen changes, and the Shell menu title is replaced with the words "Setup Menu."

Adding and Deleting Shell Entries

You can have a maximum of 20 entries on each Shell menu. The 20 entries include actual menu items, as well as descriptive headings. Each menu item is double-spaced. To add a space for a Shell entry to your Shell menu:

1. Press **4** for Setup.

2. Use the arrow keys to move the cursor to the entry where you want to add a space. You can also type the menu letter to move directly to the item if you are adding a space above a previously existing menu item.

3. Press 3 for Add.

4. Press F7 to return to the main Shell screen.

After pressing Add, all the items at and below the highlighted bar are moved down one space and a space is inserted. After inserting the space you can use the Edit feature to add the necessary information about the item you want to add. The Add option only adds a space to your menu, it does not add the actual entry. For information on adding a Shell entry see "Using the Program Information Screen," later in this chapter.

If there is a menu item you want to delete from your Shell menu you can use the Delete option. The Delete option removes the entry and moves all entries below it up one space. To delete an item from the Shell menu:

1. Press 4 for Setup.

2. Use the arrow keys to move the cursor to the entry you want to delete. You can also type the menu letter to move directly to the item.

3. Press 4 for Delete. Shell displays the "Delete this entry from shell menu? (Y/N)N" prompt.

4. Type **Y** to delete the item from the Shell menu.

5. Press F7 to return to the main Shell screen.

Deleting an entry deletes the menu entry as well as all the information entered on the Program Information screen. At any time before you press Exit (F7) to return to the main Shell screen, you can press Cancel (F1) to cancel the changes you have made to the menu and restore the original contents.

Moving Shell Entries

If you do not like the order in which your Shell menu items display, you can easily move, copy, or swap them to different locations on the menu. Moving, copying, and swapping are all done with the Move option on the Shell Setup menu. To use the Move feature:

1. Press **4** for Setup.

2. Use the arrow keys to move the cursor to the entry you want to move. You can also type the menu letter to move directly to the item.

3. Press **5** for Move. The "Move entry to which letter?" prompt appears at the bottom of the screen.

4. Enter the letter to which you want to move the entry. The following prompt appears:

```
1 Move; 2 Copy; 3 Swap: 1
```

5. Select the desired option.

The Move option moves the item to the new location. If there is already a menu item listed in the new location, Shell displays the "Overwrite this entry? (Y/N)N" prompt. Type **Y** if you want to overwrite the existing entry and replace it with the item you are moving. The Copy option makes a copy of the menu item and moves it to the new location, while still maintaining the original entry. If there is already a menu item listed in the new location, you are asked if you want to overwrite the entry. The Copy option is useful if you want to start the same program but possibly change some of the information, such as the startup options, on the Program Information screen. For example, you could copy the entry for Notebook and, on the second menu entry, list a specific notebook file on the startup options line you want retrieved. The Swap option swaps the item you highlight with the item letter you enter. The only thing that changes when using Swap is the position on the Shell menu. Both entries keep their original menu letters.

Using the Program Information Screen

Once you have positioned the Shell entries in the proper location, you are ready to edit the actual information that Shell uses to start the program. The information you enter on the Program Information screen depends on the type of menu item you are editing. Shell lets you have a normal program entry, which is an executable program such as Word-Perfect. You can also list a DOS command or batch file, a Shell macro, or a submenu.

To access the Program Information screen:

1. Press 4 for Setup.

2. Use the arrow keys to move to the entry you want to edit.

3. Press 1 for Edit.

The following sections explain what information is needed on the Program Information screen for each of the possible entries.

Creating a Menu Item for a Normal Program Entry

Most items on a Shell menu are classified as normal program entries. All of the WordPerfect Office programs are normal Shell entries. Word-Perfect, PlanPerfect, DataPerfect, and DrawPerfect are also normal Shell entries, along with other third-party programs that use an executable file. Figure 10-4 shows a sample Program Information screen for WordPerfect 5.1.

```
                              Program Information

Menu Letter:              W

Menu Description:         WordPerfect 5.1

Menu Item Type:           Normal        Pause: NO

Default Directory:        c:\document

Program Name:             c:\wp51\wp.exe

Clipboard  Filename:

Macros Names - End of Line: EOL .SHM  Go to: GOSHELL .SHM  Return: RTSHELL .SHM

Startup Options:

Prompt for startup options? NO      Swap Shell out?            NO

Start resident?             NO      Allow switch anytime?      YES

     Type the letter (A-Z) used to start the program.

                                             (F7 = Exit, F3 = Help)
```

Figure 10-4.   Sample Program Information screen for WordPerfect 5.1

The first option on the Program Information screen is Menu Letter. This can be any single letter from A to Z. It is helpful to choose a letter that corresponds to the name of the program, and thus make Shell more intuitive. In the example in Figure 10-4, "W" is used for WordPerfect. If you enter a letter that is being used by another entry on the Shell menu, Shell displays the "Duplicate menu letter, clear duplicate entry? (Y/N)N" prompt. If you answer Yes, Shell removes the letter from the other entry and allows you to use it on the current entry. All other program information for the other entry is maintained, only the letter is cleared. If you answer No, you can enter a letter not being used by another Shell entry.

The next option on the Program Information screen is Menu Description. Enter the name of the program on this line. Shell accepts up to 30 characters for this entry. After entering a menu description you need to enter the menu item type. As soon as you move to this entry the following prompt displays at the bottom of the screen:

```
Select DOS/Batch, Macro, Submenu or Normal
by typing the bolded letter of the desired Menu Item Type.
```

Press **N** for Normal. To the right of the Menu Item Type option is the Pause option. Set Pause to Yes if you have a program that displays results or messages after exiting the program. With Pause set to Yes, the program prompts you to press any key to continue. Most normal programs do not require a pause. For the WordPerfect example in Figure 10-4 a pause is not necessary.

The Default Directory option lets you specify the default directory the program will use. If no directory is specified, the program uses the default Shell directory as its default directory. In Figure 10-4, C:\DOCUMENT is the default directory. With this specified, every document is retrieved from or saved to this directory unless you add a path to the filename or change the default directory within WordPerfect. This is especially useful if you have a working directory that is always used while in WordPerfect or any other program. This is also useful if you are using Office LAN and you do not have access rights to the directory where WP.EXE is located and want a personal network directory or local directory to be the default directory. If you enter a directory that does not exist, Shell displays the "Does not exist, Create? (Y/N)Y" message. Type **Y** for Yes, and Shell creates the directory. If you entered the wrong directory, type **N** and enter the correct directory.

Note: If a default document directory is specified in the WP 5.1 Setup menu, it always overrides the setting on the Shell menu. However, temporary files are saved in the directory specified on the Shell menu unless the /D startup option is used to redirect the temporary files.

The Program Name option lets you enter the full pathname and filename of the program. It is strongly recommended that you include the full path to the program. This avoids the problem of not being able to find the program or the correct version of the program. The default Shell menu that comes with Office 3.0 does not include full pathnames. It is a good idea to edit these entries. If you enter an incorrect path or filename, Shell tells you that it does not exist and asks if that is OK. If you type **Y** for Yes the entry remains. If you type **N** for No, Shell clears the information, and you can enter the correct information.

The Clipboard Filename option is for use with programs that are not fully Shell compatible. With this option, you can save text to this filename and as soon as you exit the program the contents of the file are saved to the Shell Clipboard. Once the text is in the Shell Clipboard, you can retrieve it into a program on the Shell menu.

The Macro Names option lets you enter the correct letter for the End of Line macro, Go To macro, and Return macro. The letter you enter here must match the letter you used when defining the macro. The End of Line macro lets you add a character or keystroke to the end of a line of information retrieved into this program from the Clipboard. In order for the macro to work you must retrieve the information from the Clipboard with ALT-SHIFT-+. For example, if you are retrieving information from Editor into WordPerfect and you want to delete the hard return at the end of each line, you can use an End of Line macro. To define this macro:

1. Start Editor from the Shell menu.

2. Press CTRL-SHIFT-F10 and enter **eol*x*.shm**, where x is the letter you indicated on the Shell menu.

3. Enter a description.

4. Press the DEL key.

5. Press CTRL-SHIFT-F10 to end the macro definition.

Now each time you retrieve information into WordPerfect with ALT-SHIFT-+, the last character of the line will be deleted—in the previous example, a hard return character.

The Go To and Return macros are for use with programs that do not recognize the Go To Shell feature. For more information on using and defining these macros, see "Using Switch with Non-Shell Compatible Programs." For the WordPerfect example in Figure 10-4 none of these macros are used.

The Startup Options entry lets you enter any startup options recognized by the program you are defining. For the WordPerfect example, you could enter a filename or any of the valid startup options. You can enter up to 30 characters, and you can also add a prompt on this line as shown here:

```
Startup Options:              ?"Enter Filename"
```

This instructs Shell to pause, display the prompt, and allow input. You must put the prompt in quotes and precede it with a question mark. In this example, you can enter a specific filename each time you start the program. As soon as you press ENTER, the program is executed. You can enter multiple prompts on the Startup Options line. If you do not have enough room or want to enter different startup options each time you start the program, you can set the Prompt For Startup Options? entry to Yes. With this option set to Yes, Shell displays an "Enter options:" prompt before entering the program. If you have startup options on the Startup Options line and Prompt For Startup Options? set to Yes, the options on the Startup Options line are passed to the program first.

With the Swap Shell Out? entry, you can decide if you want to remove Shell from memory when using this program. This is useful for programs that are too big to fit in memory while Shell is running. If this option is set to Yes, all Shell functions are disabled. Shell macros will not work, and you cannot use the Go To Shell feature. For WordPerfect Corporation programs, Go To DOS replaces the Go To Shell feature.

The Start Resident? entry lets you set a program to start as soon as Shell is loaded. If you use this option with non-WordPerfect Corporation products, you may see unexpected results if you try to use the Switch feature or Go To Shell feature immediately after the program has been loaded. If you always start a program immediately after starting Shell, set this option to Yes.

The Allow Switch Anytime? entry lets you use the Switch feature from any menu or screen in a program. If you experience screen display problems with this option set to Yes, set the option to No and define a Go To Shell macro. This option does not work if Swap Shell Out? is set to Yes. For more information on this option see "Switching Programs" earlier in this chapter.

You can also set the menu item type to Normal to create Shell menu headings. Figure 10-5 shows a sample Program Information screen for a Shell heading. To create a heading make sure you leave the Menu Letter and Program Name options blank.

Creating a Menu Item for a DOS Command or Batch File

You can put a DOS command or batch file as a Shell menu item. When using a DOS command, Shell remains in memory and you are returned

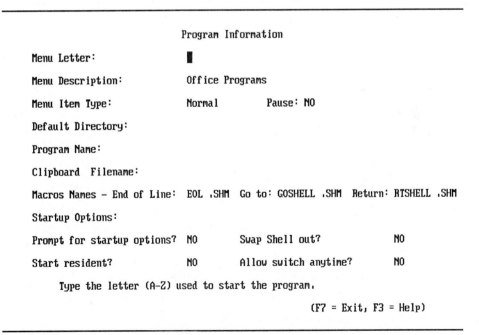

```
                         Program Information

Menu Letter:             █

Menu Description:        Office Programs

Menu Item Type:          Normal        Pause: NO

Default Directory:

Program Name:

Clipboard  Filename:

Macros Names - End of Line:  EOL .SHM  Go to: GOSHELL .SHM  Return: RTSHELL .SHM

Startup Options:

Prompt for startup options?  NO       Swap Shell out?          NO

Start resident?              NO       Allow switch anytime?    NO

       Type the letter (A-Z) used to start the program.

                                          (F7 = Exit, F3 = Help)
```

Figure 10-5.   Sample Program Information screen for a Shell heading

to DOS to execute the specified commands. You can use a DOS command such as DIR, CHKDSK, or FORMAT. Figure 10-6 shows a sample Program Information screen with the necessary information to use the DOS FORMAT command from the Shell menu. You can also create batch files that automate certain tasks and then run them directly from the Shell menu. For example, if you are on a Novell network and have to use a CAPTURE command to attach to various printers, you could put the commands in a batch file and then execute them from the Shell menu.

As previously described, the first entry on the Program Information screen is Menu Letter. This can be any letter from A to Z. It is helpful to choose a letter that corresponds to the command or batch file. In the example in Figure 10-6, "F" is used for Format. If you enter a letter that is being used by another entry on the Shell menu, Shell displays the "Duplicate menu letter, clear duplicate entry? (Y/N)N" prompt. If you answer Yes, Shell removes the letter from the other entry and allows you to use it on the current entry. Only the menu letter is removed. All other information is retained. If you answer No, enter a letter not being used by another Shell entry.

```
                         Program Information

Menu Letter:              F

Menu Description:         Format a Disk in A:

Menu Item Type:           DOS/Batch       Pause: YES

Default Directory:

Program Name:             c:\dos\format.com

Clipboard  Filename:

Macros Names - End of Line:  EOL .SHM  Go to: GOSHELL .SHM  Return: RTSHELL .SHM

Startup Options:          a:

Prompt for startup options?  NO         Swap Shell out?          NO

Start resident?              NO          Allow switch anytime?    NO

      Type the letter (A-Z) used to start the program.

                                         (F7 = Exit, F3 = Help)
```

Figure 10-6.   Sample Program Information screen for a DOS command

The next option on the Program Information screen is Menu Description. Enter a name that describes the command or batch file. In the example in Figure 10-6, "Format a Disk in A:" is the description. Shell accepts up to 30 characters for this entry. After entering the menu description you need to enter the menu item type. Enter **D** for DOS/ Batch.

To the right of the Menu Item Type option is the Pause option. Set Pause to Yes if the command or batch file displays results or messages after executing. With Pause set to Yes, a prompt displays below any message, prompting you to press any key to continue. For example, if you use the CHKDSK command and want to see the results, you would set Pause to Yes.

Specifying a default directory is optional for a DOS command or batch file. If you enter a full path and filename for the command or batch file on the Program Name line, Shell changes to this directory before executing the command or the batch file. In Figure 10-6 C:\DOS\FORMAT.COM is listed for the program name.

The Clipboard Filename and Macro Names options are not used with a DOS command or batch file unless the batch file executes a program.

At the Startup Options entry, enter any parameters you want inserted after the command. In the example in Figure 10-6, "a:" is the startup option. With this specified, the FORMAT command will execute, and "a:" specifies the A: drive as the location of the disk to be formatted. If you do not always want the disks in the A: drive formatted, you could enter **?"What drive"** to prompt for a drive letter before the formatting began. If there is not enough room on the Startup Options line, you can set Prompt For Startup Options? to Yes.

The Swap Shell Out?, Start Resident?, and Allow Switch Anytime? options do not apply to DOS commands or batch files.

Creating a Menu Item for a Shell Macro

If you use certain Shell macros frequently, you can add them to the Shell menu for easy execution. Figure 10-7 shows a sample Program Information screen for a Shell macro.

The first entry on the Program Information screen is Menu Letter, which can be any letter from A to Z. It is helpful to choose a letter that corresponds to the Shell macro. If you enter a letter that is being used

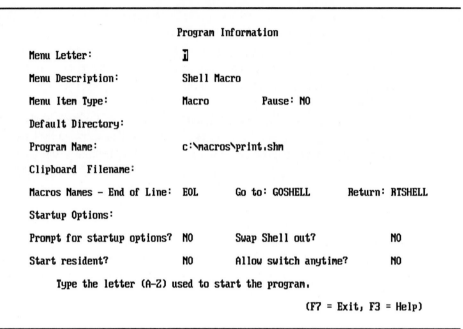

Figure 10-7. Sample Program Information screen for a Shell macro

by another entry on the Shell menu, Shell displays the "Duplicate menu letter, clear duplicate entry? (Y/N)N" prompt. If you answer Yes, Shell removes the letter from the other entry and allows you to use it on the current entry. All other program information for the other entry is maintained, only the letter is cleared. If you answer No, enter a letter not being used by another Shell entry.

The next option on the Program Information screen is Menu Description. Enter a name that describes the Shell macro. After entering the menu description you need to enter the menu item type. Enter **M** for Macro.

The Pause option is not applicable to a macro item type. You can enter a default directory if the macro uses the EXEC DOS command to perform certain functions and you want a certain directory used.

At the Program Name entry, enter the full path and filename of the Shell macro.

The Clipboard Filename and Macro Names options are not used with a Shell macro.

At the Startup Options entry, enter any parameters you want used with the macro. These options are passed to the macro variable 0. You can then have a macro command look to macro variable 0 for certain specifications. If there is not enough room on the Startup Options line or you want to enter different startup options each time you execute the macro, you can set Prompt For Startup Options? to Yes.

You can set a Shell macro to start resident. With this option set to Yes, as soon as Shell is loaded the macro executes. The Swap Shell Out? and Allow Switch Anytime? options do not apply to Shell macros.

Creating a Menu Item for a Submenu

If you cannot fit all the entries on a single Shell menu, you can create a submenu. Submenus must be started from a parent Shell menu. You can create as many submenus as you need, but you can only have up to 20 different menus active at one time. Figure 10-8 shows a sample Program Information screen for a submenu.

```
                         Program Information

Menu Letter:            S

Menu Description:       WordPerfect Submenu

Menu Item Type:         Submenu        Pause: NO

Default Directory:      c:\wp

Program Name:

Clipboard  Filename:

Macros Names - End of Line:  EOL .SHM  Go to: GOSHELL .SHM  Return: RTSHELL .SHM

Startup Options:        c:\wp\wpmenu.fil

Prompt for startup options? NO      Swap Shell out?            NO

Start resident?             NO      Allow switch anytime?      YES

        Type the letter (A-Z) used to start the program.

                                        (F7 = Exit, F3 = Help)
```

Figure 10-8.   Sample Program Information screen for a submenu

The first entry on the Program Information screen is Menu Letter. This can be any letter from A to Z. If you enter a letter that is being used by another entry on the Shell menu, Shell displays the "Duplicate menu letter, clear duplicate entry? (Y/N) N" prompt. If you answer Yes, Shell removes the letter from the other entry and allows you to use it on the current entry. All other program information for the other entry is maintained, only the letter is cleared. If you answer No, enter a letter not being used by another Shell entry.

The next option on the Program Information screen is Menu Description. Enter a name that describes the contents of the submenu. In Figure 10-8 the submenu contains all WordPerfect products so the description is "WordPerfect Submenu." It is a good idea to add the word "submenu" to the description. After entering the menu description you need to enter the menu item type. Enter **S** for Submenu.

The Pause entry must be set to No for a submenu.

The Program Name, Clipboard Filename, and Macro Names entries are not applicable for a submenu item type.

At the Default Directory entry, enter the directory you want to be the default for the submenu. If you do not enter anything here, the default directory of the current Shell is used.

You must enter a filename for the submenu at the Startup Options entry. In Figure 10-8 the filename is C:\WP\WPMENU.FIL. The first time you enter the submenu from the parent menu, "ERROR: file not found" displays at the bottom of the screen. As soon as you make any changes to the Shell menu the file is created. You can also add other Shell startup options on this line. When using a submenu, any options specified for the parent Shell menu are used unless you specify different options on the Startup Options line. If there is not enough room on the Startup Options line or if you want to enter different startup options each time you start the submenu, you can set Prompt For Startup Options? to Yes.

You can set a submenu to start resident. With the Start Resident? option set to Yes, the submenu appears before the parent Shell menu. If you set a program to start resident on a submenu, you must set the submenu to start resident.

The Swap Shell Out? and Allow Switch Anytime? options do not apply to submenus.

Changing Shell Options

From the Shell Setup menu you can change various Shell options. Once you change these options they remain in effect until you change them again. These options must be set for each Shell submenu. Any changes made to the options are stored in the Shell menu-information file. If you are using Office PC, the menu-information file is SHELL.FIL. If you are using Office LAN, the menu-information file is *XXX*SHELL.FIL, where *XXX* represents your File ID. To change the Shell options:

1. Press **4** for Setup.

2. Press **2** for Options. The following menu appears:

```
Options

        1 - Colors

        2 - Date Format:          6, 3 1, 4   8:90

        3 - Menu Title:           WordPerfect Office Lan

        4 - Work Log Setup

        5 - Screen Save (minutes): 0

        6 - Macro Directory:

        7 - Password

        8 - Allow Go to DOS:      YES
```

3. Select the desired option and make the necessary changes.

Options

The following options are listed on the Shell options menu.

Colors   The Colors option sets the default screen colors for your Shell menu. These colors are used by Office programs until you set default colors for the programs individually. Calculator always uses the Shell colors. You can choose the colors that Shell displays if you have a color monitor, how screen attributes will display if you have a single color or monochrome monitor, or the mode for a Hercules card.

Date Format   The Date Format determines how the date displays in the upper-right corner of the Shell menu. After selecting this option choose from any of the special characters listed. You can add spaces, punctuation, or text to the date format.

Menu Title   With the Menu Title option you can change the title that displays in the upper-left corner of the Shell menu. For example, you could change the title to "John's Shell Menu" or any other specialized text. The menu title can contain up to 30 characters.

Work Log Setup   The Work Log Setup option is used to indicate the name of the file where all work logs are output. If you do not enter a filename on this screen you cannot use the Work Log feature. This option also lets you turn on the Program and Project Logging options as well as the Timed Backup option.

Screen Save   The Screen Save feature lets you have Shell blank out your screen after the number of minutes specified for this option. Screen Save helps avoid the screen etching that occurs when the same image is left on a monitor for prolonged periods of time. If this option is set to 0, Screen Save is not active.

Macro Directory   The Macro Directory option tells Shell where to look when executing Shell macros and where to save Shell macros when a directory is not specified. Because Office 3.0 comes with several pre-defined macros, it may be useful to move them to their own directory. If you create a directory for Shell macros, be sure to use this option to specify where the Shell macros are located. For more information on Shell macros see "Using Shell Macros" in this chapter.

Password   The Password option lets you set a password for your Shell menu. With a password set, you can only access options 1 through 6 on the Options menu, and you cannot use any of the other Program Information screen Setup menu items such as Edit, Add, Delete, and Move. A password protects your Shell menu from being changed without your permission.

Allow Go To DOS   This option is primarily used by the system administrator to limit a user's ability to go to DOS from his or her Shell menu. If you want to disable the Go To DOS option on the Shell menu, set this option to No. Along with setting this option to No, you must also put a password on the Shell menu so users cannot change the option back to Yes. When Allow Go To DOS is set to No, the main Shell menu looks like this:

```
2 Clipboard; 3 Other Dir; 4 Setup; 5 Mem Map; 6 Log:
```

Using Shell as a Memory Manager

Shell lets you control the type of memory and the amount of memory that is available for programs run from the Shell menu. When you use the Switch feature to start a program while another is still running, the program that is not currently being used is swapped to memory or to disk. If you do not use any startup options when you start Shell, Shell uses all available expanded memory and disk space when swapping a program. Thus the more expanded memory and disk space you have, the more programs you are able to keep resident at the same time.

Specifying Memory Type and Amount

You can give Shell specific instructions on the type and amount of memory to use. These instructions are given in the form of startup options. The following startup options help manage memory while in Shell.

/O   *[amount of expanded memory];RAM drive path[amount of RAM drive memory to use];hard disk path[amount of hard disk space to use]*

By default Shell uses the maximum memory available in each of these locations.

/V   *RAM drive path[amount of RAM drive memory to use];hard disk path[amount of hard disk space to use]*

With the /V option Shell does not use an expanded memory.

/NE

The /NE option does not let Shell use any expanded memory, and does not allow you to set limits for the other sources of memory like the /V option.

/NO

The /NO option disables Shell from using any expanded memory or disk space. Only normal RAM memory is available for switching programs.

Using the Memory Map

After modifying the amount and type of memory available to the various programs on the Shell menu, you can use the Memory Map to see exactly how much memory each program is using and how much memory and disk space you have left. To view the Memory Map from the main Shell screen:

1. Press 5 for Memory Map. A screen similar to Figure 10-9 appears.

The programs are listed in the order in which they were activated. Next to each program is the amount of memory it is using. If a "D" appears to the right of the program it has been swapped to disk. If an "E" appears it has been swapped to expanded memory.

At the bottom of the screen, Shell lists the amount of available memory, available expanded memory, and free disk space.

When using Memory Map with submenus, only the program memory information for that submenu is listed. The amount of available memory displayed at the bottom of the screen does take into account the memory that is being used by the parent menu. Shell simply does not list the individual program memory information each program on the parent menu is using. This case is also true if you are in a parent menu with a submenu resident.

```
                 ┌─────────────────────────────────────────┐
                 │                Memory Map                 │
                 │                                           │
                 │   Program Description      Memory Used     │
                 │ ┌─────────────────────────────────────┐  │
                 │ │ 1 DOS                         40752   │  │
                 │ │ 2  (Unknown Name)             24912   │  │
                 │ │ 3  (Unknown Name)              3536   │  │
                 │ │ 4 Program                    120704   │  │
                 │ │ 5 Shell                       50128   │  │
                 │ │ 6 NoteBook                   195240 E │  │
                 │ │ 7 Mail                       414064 E │  │
                 │ │ 8 Scheduler                  414064 E │  │
                 │ │ 9 Appointment Calendar        95904 D │  │
                 │ │10 Calculator                  34208 D │  │
                 │ └─────────────────────────────────────┘  │
                 │                                           │
                 │ ┌─────────────────────────────────────┐  │
                 │ │ Available Memory:            414016   │  │
                 │ │ Available Expanded Memory:        0   │  │
                 │ │ Available Disk Space:      24150016   │  │
                 │ └─────────────────────────────────────┘  │
                 └─────────────────────────────────────────┘
```

E = This program has been swapped into Expanded Memory.

D = This program has been swapped to Disk.

(Press any key to return to the shell)

Figure 10-9.   Memory Map

Using Clipboard

The Shell Clipboard is a very powerful tool that enables information to be shared between all Shell-compatible programs. In this instance a fully Shell-compatible program is one that is written to be used with the WordPerfect Office Shell. All WordPerfect products are fully Shell compatible. Once information is saved to the Shell Clipboard it can be retrieved into other programs. From the Shell menu you can view and manage the contents of the Shell Clipboard. To access the Clipboard from the main Shell screen:

1. Press **2** for Clipboard. The following menu appears:

1 Clear; 2 Save as Text File; 3 Retrieve Text File; 0

2. Press **1** or **C** if you want to clear or delete the contents of the Clipboard. Press **2** or **S** if you want to save the contents of the Clipboard to a file. Press **3** or **R** if you want to retrieve the contents of a text file to the Clipboard.

Saving the contents of the Clipboard is useful with programs that are not Shell compatible. If you have information in a program and you want to take it to another program that does not recognize the Clipboard, you could save the information to the Clipboard. After saving the information to the Clipboard, you can use the Clipboard menu to save it to a file. The file is in ASCII format. After saving the file, you can retrieve it directly into the program.

Retrieving the contents of a text file to the Clipboard is useful if you want to use information from a program that is not Shell compatible. This way the information is saved to the Clipboard via a file and can then be transferred to other Shell-compatible programs.

Using Screen Copy

The Screen Copy feature lets you copy text from a program that is not fully Shell compatible or from a screen that does not allow information to be saved to the Clipboard directly. You must be running under Shell to use Screen Copy, and Shell cannot be swapped out. To use the Screen Copy feature:

1. Press ALT-SHIFT-MINUS.

2. Press **1** or **R** for Rectangle or **2** or **B** for Block.
   Rectangle captures rectangularly-shaped text and is usually used when you want to capture the contents of the entire screen. Block captures irregularly shaped text. Block does not capture border characters, such as ASCII line-draw characters.

3. Use the arrow keys to position the cursor where you want to begin the block.

4. Press ENTER to anchor the cursor.

5. Use the arrow keys to highlight the desired text.

6. Press ENTER to store the information. The following menu will appear:

Clipboard: 1 Save; 2 Append; 3 Format; 4 Macro Variable: 1

7. Press **3** or **F** for Format.

8. Select the character you want inserted at the end of each line of text.

9. Press **1** or **S** to Save the information to the Clipboard, or press **2** or **A** to Append the information to any existing text in the Clipboard.

Note: Steps 7 and 8 are optional. The default character is a hard return.

If the information is going to be used in a fully Shell-compatible program, you can retrieve it with the Clipboard Retrieve option in that program. If the information is going to be used in a non-Shell-compatible program:

1. Enter the program and move to the location in which the text is to be inserted.

2. Press ALT-SHIFT-+.

The information is retrieved, inserting the end of line character you selected for the Format option at the end of each text string. Screen Copy is a valuable tool for programs that are not fully Shell compatible.

Using Work Log

Shell has a Work Log feature that allows you to record the time and keystrokes used while in a program. The Work Log feature is useful for keeping track of exactly how much time is spent on a certain project and then using that information for billing purposes. There are four main steps to using the Work Log feature: (1) setting up the original work log file; (2) entering the specific information for the current work log; (3) starting the individual work log; and (4) outputting and using the work log information.

Setting Up the Work Log File

Before you can begin to use Work Log, you must indicate a work log file where the information can be output. Office comes with a predefined Notebook file for outputting the work log information. This file is called WORKLOG.NB and is located in the directory where your main Office 3.0 files are stored. You need to enter the directory and filename for this file in the Shell Options menu.

1. Press **4** for Setup.
2. Press **2** for Options.
3. Press **4** or **L** for Work Log Setup. The following screen appears:

```
                        Work Logging Setup

Work Logging Filename:         ████████████████████████

Project Logging:               NO

Program Logging:               NO

Timed Backup:                  NO

Timed Backup Period (minutes): 0
```

4. Enter the full path and filename to the WORKLOG.NB file. If you are on a network make sure you copy this file to a personal network directory or to your local hard drive. You can change the name of this file, but not the format.

5. If you want the Project Logging or Program Logging option to automatically start when Shell is loaded, type **Y** for Yes for these options.

6. If you want the log file to be automatically backed up, type **Y** at the Timed Backup option and then enter the number of minutes between backups.

```
Work Logging                         Elapsed Time: [None]

    Project/Client Information
        1 - Project:        [None]
        2 - Project ID:     [None]

    User Information
        3 - User:           DRH
        4 - User Job Type: [None]

    Add a Line to Comments
        5 - Project Description:
        6 - Program Comments:

    Work Logging Status
        7 - Project Log:   NO
        8 - Project Timer: NO
        9 - Program Log:   NO

    Forced Record Output (& reset times)
        A - All Records      R - Project Record      S - Program Records

F9: Output All Records; F10: Backup Current Record(s)
Enter Selection: 0
```

Figure 10-10.   Work Logging screen

Entering the Information for the Work Log

After indicating the filename for a work log, you can enter the information for the project or program log. The first information you enter is the descriptive information. From the main Shell screen:

1. Press **6** for Log. The screen shown in Figure 10-10 appears.

2. Press **1** or **P** for Project and enter the name of the project you need to log; for example, type **Smith vs. Jones.**

3. Press **2** or **I** and enter the project ID; for example, type **Continuance Papers.**

4. Press **3** or **U** and enter your user name. If you are using Office LAN this is automatically inserted.

5. Press **4** or **J** and enter your user job type; for example, type **Law Clerk.**

Note: If you change options 1 through 4 while a log is active, Shell asks if you want to output the file after making the changes. If you answer Yes, a new log entry starts with the information you changed. If you answer No, the log continues, but uses the new information.

After the information is entered you need to turn on the Project or Program Log option if they aren't set to start automatically in the Work Logging Setup screen.

1. Press **7** or **L** for Project Log and/or press **9** or **G** for Program Log. You can use them together or singly.

A project log keeps track of the time and keystrokes spent on a project. The program log makes a separate record in the WORKLOG.NB file for each program you use. The record contains the length of time in the program and the number of keystrokes performed while in the program.

If you want to stop a project log without outputting the records and resetting the counters, you can use option 8, Project Timer, to turn off the timer. This allows you to perform tasks that are not related to the project and then resume work on the project without starting a new log.

Outputting the Work Log Information

When you are finished with a project or program log, you need to output the information to the WORKLOG.NB file. Until the information is output to this file there is no way to access the logs. Once the information is in this file, you can use it for billing purposes or for general information. To output a log file:

1. Press **6** for Log.

2. Press F9 or **A** for All Records, **R** for Project Record, or **S** for Program Records.

These records are added to the WORKLOG.NB file listed on the Shell Setup menu. When you output the records all timers are reset. To view the logs:

1. From the main Shell menu enter the Notebook program.

2. Press SHIFT-F10 and enter the correct path and filename of your WORKLOG.NB file, such as **C:\OFFICE30\WORKLOG.NB**.

Once the file is retrieved all the records you have output are listed here. To see more detailed information, highlight the record you want to view and press ENTER. A screen similar to Figure 10-11 appears. You can use this information as is or save specified fields to the Clipboard and retrieve them into WordPerfect to create a billing form. For information on using the Clipboard with Notebook, see Chapter 8, "Using Notebook." There are predefined macros that help to automate the process. For information on these macros, see Appendix E, "WordPerfect Office Predefined Macros."

Using Shell Macros

Shell macros are another very powerful way in which you can combine and integrate information between programs listed on the Shell menu.

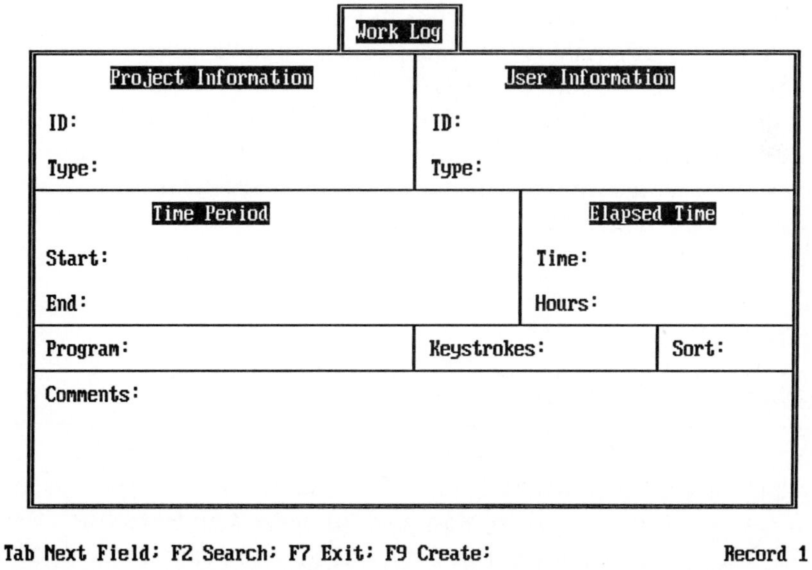

Figure 10-11.   Record Display screen for WORKLOG.NB

Shell macros execute prerecorded keystrokes and commands that aid you in increasing speed and performance. For example you might create a macro that takes you into Notebook, copies selected information from an address notebook to the Clipboard, exits Notebook, starts Word-Perfect, and inserts the information from Notebook into a letter. The possibilities for creating and using Shell macros are virtually limitless. To execute a Shell macro:

1. Press ALT-SHIFT-F10 from the location where the macro was created. Shell displays the "Shell macro" prompt. If the macro was named with an ALT-SHIFT name, you can simply press ALT-SHIFT-x, where x is the letter assigned to the macro.

2. Enter the name of the macro.

As soon as you enter the name the macro begins.

When you execute a Shell macro, Shell looks for the macro in the program default directory specified on the Shell Program Information screen for the current program. If it is not found there it looks in the directory specified in the Shell Options menu for the Shell macro directory. If you are using Office LAN and a path is not specified for the Shell macro directory, Shell looks in the directory where the main Shell menu-information file is found. If you are running Office PC, Shell looks in the directory where SHELL.EXE is found. To make sure the correct macro is executed it is a good idea to specify an entire path and filename when executing the macro. Indicating a directory on the macro default directory in the Options menu also avoids problems with finding the correct macro files.

Creating a Shell Macro

Shell macros can perform very basic as well as very sophisticated functions. This section is designed to help you learn the basics of creating a Shell macro. For information on creating advanced Shell macros and using the advanced Shell macro commands, see Appendix F, "Advanced Macro Commands."

One of the purposes of Shell macros is to automate tasks done on a regular basis. For example, if you make weekly backup copies of certain directories, you can create a Shell macro to automate this task. The following steps create a Shell macro that will start File Manager, change to a specified directory, and make a backup copy of all the files in the directory to a disk in drive A:. To define this macro, from the main Shell screen:

1. Press CTRL-SHIFT-F10 for Define Macro.

2. Enter **Backup** as the name of the macro.

3. Enter **Backup Directory** as the description for the macro.

4. Press **F** or the corresponding letter on your Shell menu that starts File Manager.

5. Press **4** or **S** for Select Files.

6. Press **9** or **R** for Confirm Replace.

7. Type **N** for No.

8. Press F7.

Steps 5 through 8 allow the backup to proceed if duplicate copies exist on the disk in drive A:, without prompting you to replace the existing files.

9. Press **7** or **O** for Other Directory. At this point a pause command needs to be inserted into the macro so you can enter the desired directory each time you run the macro.

10. To insert the pause, press CTRL-SHIFT-PGUP.

11. Press **1** or **P** for Pause.

12. Type in the name of a valid directory. This is not necessarily the directory that will be used in the macro, but must be entered so the macro will continue. This step will not be recorded.

13. Press ENTER three times.

14. Press ALT-F5 to mark all the files in the directory.

15. Press **8** or **C** for Copy.

16. Type **Y** for Yes.

17. Type **a:** or **b:** for the drive to which the files should be copied. File Manager copies the files to the specified drive. Make sure you have a disk in the drive.

18. Press F7 to exit File Manager.

19. Press CTRL-SHIFT-F10 to end the macro.

After defining the macro you could put it as an entry on your Shell menu and then simply press the menu letter any time you need to back up a directory.

When you create Shell macros, they are saved to the directory specified when you name the macro. If you do not specify a full path when naming the macro, the macro is created in the directory specified for the default macro directory in the Shell Setup options. If you are using Office LAN and have not specified a directory in the Shell Setup options, Shell creates the macro where the main Shell menu-information file is found. If you are running Office PC, Shell creates the macro in the directory where SHELL.EXE is found.

Allow Go To DOS

The Allow Go To DOS option enables or disables the ability to choose the Go To DOS option on the main Shell menu. This option is usually set by the system administrator to prevent users from going to DOS from the Shell menu.

Keystrokes

1. From the main Shell screen, press 4 for Setup.

2. Press 2 for Options.

3. Press 8 or **G** for Allow Go To DOS.

4. Type **Y** to enable the feature, or type **N** to disable the feature.

Note: Unless a password is set, users can change this option whenever they want.

Allow Switch Anytime?

When Allow Switch Anytime? is set to Yes, you can go to Shell from any location, except a graphics mode, while in a program. Allow Switch Anytime? makes moving between programs fast and simple. You must be able to swap the program to expanded memory or to disk in order for Allow Switch Anytime? to work. If you experience screen display problems when using this option with a non-WordPerfect product, you need to turn the option off and define a Go To Shell macro. For information on defining a Go To Shell macro see "Using Switch with Non-Shell-Compatible Programs," earlier in this chapter.

Note: Allow Switch Anytime? does not work with any programs that rely on DOS interrupt 21H for keyboard input.

Keystrokes

1. Press 4 for Setup.

2. Use the arrow keys to highlight the program for which you want to set the Allow Switch Anytime? option.

3. Press 1 for Edit.

4. Press SHIFT-TAB once to move to the Allow Switch Anytime? option.

5. Type **Y** for Yes or **N** for No.

6. Press F7 twice to return to the main Shell screen.

Cancel

Cancel backs you out of a Shell menu or prompt. Cancel also lets you exit the Shell Setup menu without saving any changes.

Keystrokes

To back out of a menu or prompt:

1. Press Cancel (F1). Shell returns you to the previous menu or screen.

To exit the Shell Setup menu without saving any of the information you added or edited:

1. Before exiting the Setup menu, press F1 for Cancel. The "Exit WITHOUT saving changes? (Y/N)N" prompt appears.

2. Type **Y** to exit without saving your changes or type **N** to remain in the Setup menu.

Clipboard

The Shell Clipboard is a temporary buffer available for all fully Shell-compatible programs. You can save and append information to and retrieve information from the Clipboard. From the main Shell screen you can manage the contents of the Clipboard.

Keystrokes

1. Press **2** for Clipboard. The following menu appears:

1 Clear; 2 Save as Text File; 3 Retrieve Text File; 0

2. Select the desired option.

For more information on the Shell Clipboard see "Using Clipboard," earlier in this chapter.

Colors

The Colors option sets the default screen colors for your Shell menu. These colors are used by most Office programs until you set default colors for the programs individually. Calculator always uses the Shell colors. You can choose the colors that Shell displays if you have a color monitor, how screen attributes will display if you have a single color or monochrome monitor, or the mode a Hercules card will use.

Keystrokes

1. Press **4** for Setup.

2. Press **2** for Options.

3. Press **1** or **C** for Colors. The following menu displays:

```
                          Color Setup

Monitor Characteristics: 0
      1 - Color Monitor
      2 - Single color Monitor (eg. Black & White or Compaq)
      3 - Hercules RamFont Card (InColor or Graphics Plus)
```

4. If you have a color monitor, press **1** or **C**. If you have a single color or monochrome monitor, press **2** or **S**. If you have a Hercules RamFont Card, press **3** or **H**.

5. Shell asks if it should use a fast screen display, which may cause some snow to display during a screen rewrite. Type **Y** to use fast display, or **N** to disable it.

6. Depending on the type of monitor you selected, you can either set the colors that display for different attributes or how those attributes are represented.

7. After completing the setup, press F7 until you return to the main screen.

Date Format

The Date Format option lets you select how the date displays on the main Shell screen.

Keystrokes

1. Press **4** for Setup.

2. Press **2** for Options.

3. Press **2** or **D** for Date Format.

4. Enter any of the special characters listed on the screen or any text characters you want to display in the date.

5. Press F7 twice to return to the main screen.

Default Directory

The Default Directory option displays on the Program Information screen. This option specifies the default directory a normal program or submenu uses. If no directory is specified, the program uses the default Shell directory as its default directory.

Keystrokes

To change the default directory for an entry on the Shell menu:

1. Press **4** for Setup.

2. Use the arrow keys to highlight the entry you want to edit.

3. Press **1** or ENTER to display the Program Information screen.

4. Press ENTER four times to move to the Default Directory entry.

5. Enter the directory you want to be used as the default directory.

6. Press F7 twice to return to the main Shell screen.

Exit

Exit (F7) lets you exit Shell submenus and prompts. Exit also exits the Shell menu. If you try to exit the Shell menu when programs or submenus are resident, Shell displays the "Save information in all programs? (Y/N)Y" message. If you type **N** all information in the resident programs is lost. If you want to save the information in the programs type **Y**.

Go To DOS

The Go To DOS option lets you exit to DOS without exiting the Shell menu. When you go to DOS a second copy of COMMAND.COM is loaded and you can execute any DOS commands. This is helpful if you want to execute DOS commands but you do not want to exit your Shell menu or any of the programs that are resident on the Shell menu. If you are in a submenu, the Go To DOS option is replaced with Go To Shell as shown here:

```
1 Go to Shell; 2 Clipboard; 3 Other Dir; 4 Setup; 5 Mem Map; 6 Log:   (F7 = Exit)
```

This option exits you to the parent Shell menu. If there are no other submenus loaded you can use the Go To DOS option from this Shell menu.

Keystrokes

1. From the main Shell menu press **1** for Go To DOS.

2. Perform the desired commands.

3. Press F7 or type **exit** to return to the Shell menu.

Help

The Help feature displays on-screen information about Shell features.

Keystrokes

1. Press F3 for Help from the main Shell screen.

2. Type one of the menu item letters to see information about the specific topic.

3. Press ENTER or press the spacebar to exit a help screen or press ESC to return to the main help screen.

Hints

The help screens are a valuable tool for accessing information about the Shell program. You do not have to press Help (F3) from the main Shell screen. Pressing Help from any Shell menu displays information about the features associated with that screen. Shell displays the keystrokes (if any) for the feature in the upper-right corner of the help screen.

Macro Directory

The macro directory tells Shell where to save Shell macros if a full pathname is not included when saving a macro. The default macro directory keeps all of your macros in a single location. If you do not specify a pathname with a macro or indicate a macro directory and you are using Office PC, Shell saves macros in the directory where SHELL.EXE is located. If you are using Office LAN, Shell uses the directory where your Shell menu-information file (*XXX*SHELL.FIL) is located.

When executing a Shell macro, Shell first looks in the program default directory. If the macro is not found in the default directory, Shell looks in the macro directory defined on the Shell Setup screen.

Keystrokes

1. Press **4** for Setup.

2. Press **2** for Options.

3. Press **6** or **M** for Macro Directory.

4. Enter a directory.

5. Press F7 twice to return to the main Shell screen.

Note: If you specify a macro directory and you are using the pre-defined Shell macros that are shipped with Office 3.0, make sure to move these files to the specified macro directory. For specific information on the predefined macros, see Appendix E, "Predefined WordPerfect Office Macros."

Memory Map

The Memory Map displays the current distribution of memory among programs that are in resident memory as well as the amount of free memory and free disk space.

Keystrokes

To access the Memory Map:

1. Press 5 from the main Shell screen.

For more information on the Memory Map see "Using Shell as a Memory Manager," earlier in this chapter.

Menu Title

The menu title displays in the upper-left corner of the screen. You can edit the title to contain any text you want to display. You can enter your name, a description of the Shell menu, or anything else that fits your needs. You can enter a maximum of 30 characters.

Keystrokes

1. Press **4** for Setup.

2. Press **2** for Options.

3. Press **3** or **T** for Menu Title.

4. Enter the text you want to display in the upper-left corner of the Shell menu.

5. Press F7 twice to return to the main Shell screen.

Options

From the Shell Setup menu you can change various Shell options.

Keystrokes

1. Press **4** for Setup.

2. Press **2** for Options.

3. Select the desired options and make the necessary changes.

4. Press F7 twice to return to the main Shell screen.

For information on each option see "Changing Shell Options," earlier in this chapter.

Other Directory

The Other Directory option on the main Shell menu lets you change the default directory for Shell. If a default directory is not specified on the Program Information screen for a menu entry, this directory becomes that entry's default directory.

Keystrokes

1. Press **3** for Other Directory.

2. Enter the new directory.

Password

The Password option adds security to your Shell setup. With a password added to your Shell menu, only those who know the password can change the entries on your Shell menu. Even when a password is set, anyone can enter the Shell Options menu and change the Colors, Date Format, Menu Title, Work Log Setup, Screen Save, and Macro Directory options.

Keystrokes

To add a password:

1. Press **4** for Setup.

2. Press **2** for Options.

3. Press **7** or **P** for Password.

4. Enter your password.

5. Reenter the same password.

6. Press F7 twice to exit to the main Shell screen.

To remove a password:

1. Press **4** for Setup.

2. Enter your password.

3. Press **2** for Options.

4. Press **7** or **P** for Password.

5. Press ENTER twice. This removes the current password.

```
                    Program Information
Menu Letter:

Menu Description:

Menu Item Type:        Normal        Pause: NO

Default Directory:

Program Name:

Clipboard  Filename:

Macros Names - End of Line:  EOL .SHM  Go to: GOSHELL .SHM  Return: RTSHELL .SHM

Startup Options:

Prompt for startup options? NO      Swap Shell out?        NO

Start resident?            NO        Allow switch anytime?  NO

       Type 'Y' for Shell to pause after executing this menu item.  Or Type
       'N' for control to be returned immediately to Shell without pausing.
                                              (F7 = Exit, F3 = Help)
```

Figure 10-12.   Empty Program Information screen

Program Information Screen

The Program Information screen is used to enter and store all information needed to run a program, DOS command or batch file, Shell macro, or submenu from a Shell menu. Figure 10-12 shows an empty Program Information screen.

Keystrokes

1. Press 4 for Setup.

2. Use the arrow keys to move the cursor to the entry that you want to change or to a blank entry if you want to add a new Shell menu item.

3. Press 1 for Edit.

4. Enter the necessary information.

While you are in the Program Information screen you can press PGUP or PGDN to move to the next entry on the Shell menu. The TAB, SHIFT-TAB, ENTER, or UP ARROW and DOWN ARROW keys move you through the entries on the Program Information screen. For information and examples of what information needs to be entered for the various menu types see the corresponding sections under "Using the Program Information Screen," earlier in this chapter.

Screen Copy

The Screen Copy feature lets you copy text to the Clipboard or to a program that is not fully Shell compatible. For information on how to use the Screen Copy feature see "Using Screen Copy," earlier in this chapter.

Screen Save

Shell has an automatic screen saver utility. When Screen Save is on, your Shell menu blanks out after a specified number of minutes. Screen Save only works when the Shell menu is displayed. Screen Save helps prevent menu images that remain on the screen for long periods of time from being permanently etched on your screen.

Keystrokes

1. Press **4** for Setup.

2. Press **2** for Options.

3. Press **5** or **S** for Screen Save.

4. Enter the number of minutes after which you want Screen Save to activate. The Shell menu has to be displayed continuously for the number of minutes specified before Screen Save activates.

Setup

The Setup menu allows you to edit, add, delete, and move Shell menu items. You can also access the Shell Options menu from Setup. Any changes you make to the Shell Setup menu are saved until you change them again.

Keystrokes

1. Press 4 for Setup. The following menu displays at the bottom of the screen:

1 Edit: 2 Options: 3 Add: 4 Delete: 5 Move:

2. Enter the desired selection and make the necessary changes.

Options

The following options are available from the Shell Setup menu.

Edit   The Edit option lets you edit the Program Information screen for an existing menu item or add information for a new menu item. You cannot edit a menu item that is resident in memory.

Options   With Options you can change various Shell options. For more information on these individual options see the corresponding option name in this section of the chapter.

Add   The Add option lets you add a blank space for a menu entry to the Shell menu. You can only add a space if there is at least one empty space in the lower-right corner of the menu. After adding a space, you need to use the Edit option to insert the information for the new entry.

Delete   Delete lets you delete the currently highlighted Shell menu entry. You cannot delete an item that is resident in memory. When you delete an item, the entry on the Shell menu as well as all the information in the Program Information screen is deleted.

Move   The Move option lets you move, copy, or swap Shell menu items. After moving the cursor to the item you want to move press Move. As soon as you press Move, the Shell menu displays all available positions to which you can move the entry. Blank spaces are also given letters as shown in Figure 10-13. Once you press the letter to move to, you can choose to move, copy, or swap the menu entry.

```
┌────────────────────────────────────────────────────────────────────┐
│ Setup Menu                                                           │
├──────────────────────────────────┬───────────────────────────────────┤
│ H                                │ M                                 │
│                                  │                                   │
│ I    Office Programs             │ Q    Applications                 │
│                                  │                                   │
│ A    Appointment Calendar        │ B    DataPerfect (dataBase)       │
│                                  │                                   │
│ C    Calculator                  │ D    DrawPerfect                  │
│                                  │                                   │
│ E    Editor                      │ P    PlanPerfect                  │
│                                  │                                   │
│ F    File Manager                │ W    WordPerfect                  │
│                                  │                                   │
│ N    Notebook                    │ R                                 │
│                                  │                                   │
│ J                                │ G    Go to DOS For One Command     │
│                                  │                                   │
│ K                                │ O    Other Menu                   │
│                                  │                                   │
│ L                                │ S                                 │
└──────────────────────────────────┴───────────────────────────────────┘
C:\OFFICE30
Move entry to which letter?
```

Figure 10-13.   Blank menu items available for move

Startup Options

Startup options override certain default Shell conditions on startup. You may put startup options on the DOS command line if you are starting Shell from DOS or add them to your AUTOEXEC.BAT file if you are starting Shell automatically when you turn on your computer. The following is a list of all the startup options that you can use with Shell.

/C-*x*	Allocates the amount of memory assigned to the Clipboard (*x*). 5K is the default. You cannot indicate less than 3K or certain Shell functions will not work properly.
/CP-*xxx*	Overrides the default code page set by DOS.
/D-*path*	Redirects overflow files to the specified directory. If you are using Office LAN, you may want to redirect these files to a personal network directory or to your local hard drive or RAM drive. If you are using Office PC and have a RAM drive, redirecting these files to the RAM drive may increase the speed of some of the Shell features.
/L	Displays the Work Logging screen on startup. This option is useful if you use the Work Log feature regularly.
/M-*macro name*	Starts specified Shell macro on startup.
/N	Restricts Shell from starting any programs that are set to start resident on the Program Information screen.
/NA	Disables attributes that cause problems on certain monitors when macro prompts display.

/NE	Disables Shell from using expanded memory when swapping programs out of memory.
/NF	Disables fast text display that causes problems on some monitors.
/NG	Keeps Shell from checking for graphics mode.
/NO	Keeps Shell from using disk space when swapping programs out of memory.
/NS	Starts the nonsynchronized version of the program, which may correct screen display problems on some monitors.
/NT-x	Selects a different network type, where x is the network number.
/O-[x];path[y];path[y]	Specifies the expanded memory swapping limits (x) as well as disk location (*path*) and limits (y) to use for program swapping.
/PS-*directory*	Indicates where the Shell menu-information file will be created as well as where Shell should look for the file after it is created. The directory you specify with the /PS option is the only directory Shell looks in for the information file.
/SS-*rows, columns*	Changes the default screen size on non-standard screens.
/V-path[x];path[x]	Lets Shell swap to disk or RAM drive (*path*) and to limit the amount of disk space used (x). With this option expanded memory is not used even if present.
/W-xx	Allocates memory (x) for executing Shell macros. This may need to be increased if your macros are not running properly.

Submenu

You can create submenus from your existing Shell menus. Submenus are useful if you do not have enough room on a Shell menu to enter the necessary menu items or if you want to divide your entries into specific applications. You can create as many submenus as needed, but you can only have up to 20 menus active at one time. The default Shell menu that ships with Office 3.0 has two separate submenus.

When you create a submenu, it is saved in the directory specified with the submenu filename. If a directory is not specified with the filename, it is saved in the default directory specified on the Program Information screen. If a default directory is not specified, the file is saved to the directory specified as the macro directory for the parent Shell. If a macro directory is not specified, the submenu file is saved in the current directory.

For information on creating a submenu see "Creating a Menu Item for a Submenu," earlier in this chapter.

Swap Shell Out

The Swap Shell Out feature lets you load a program from the Shell menu and then swap Shell out of memory. This is helpful for programs that are too big to fit in memory with Shell loaded. If you try entering a program and see the "ERROR: insufficient memory" message, you can change the Swap Shell Out? option on the Program Information screen to Yes. When Swap Shell Out? is set to Yes, you cannot use any Shell features while in the program.

Keystrokes

1. Press 2 for Setup.

2. Use the arrow keys to highlight the program you want to swap Shell out of.

3. Press **1** for Edit.

4. Press SHIFT-TAB three times to move to the Swap Shell Out? option.

5. Type **Y** for Yes.

6. Press F7 twice to return to the main Shell screen.

Work Log

The Work Log feature lets you keep a record of the amount of time and or keystrokes performed for a certain project or for individual programs. For more information on the Work Log feature see "Using Work Log," earlier in this chapter.

Using Notify, Repeat Performance, and TSR Manager

E
L
E
V
E
N

As part of the Office PC package, you receive two utility products: Repeat Performance and TSR Manager. If you are using Office LAN, you also have a third utility product: Notify.

When you are using Mail and Scheduler on an Office LAN system, Notify lets you see on-screen notification when you receive a Mail message or when you are scheduled for an event. You can use Repeat Performance to improve the performance of your computer's keyboard. Among other things, Repeat Performance controls the speed at which you can enter text, the number of keystrokes that are stored while the computer is processing, and the tone of your computer's beep. TSR Manager, or TSRM, helps you manage any TSR (terminate-and-stay-resident) programs you use. It provides a menu screen similar to Shell's from which TSR programs can be loaded and accessed. With TSRM, you can use resident programs while you are using Shell.

Notify

LAN When you receive Mail messages or are scheduling events with Scheduler under Office LAN, you can use Notify to inform you of these items through an on-screen window. The window shown here

```
╔════════ WP Mail from Devin Rowley ════════╗
║ This is a Notification Window              ║
║                                            ║
║                                            ║
╚════════ (Press CTRL-ENTER to clear) ═══════╝
```

tells you the subject of the Mail message or the name of the scheduled event, and which program, Mail or Scheduler, is sending the notification. Notify displays the window for a few seconds and suspends operation of your computer while it is displayed. The window is then erased from the screen and operation of your computer resumes. After a short time, Notify repeats the cycle, briefly displaying the window and then erasing it again. This cycle continues until you clear the notification by pressing CTRL-ENTER or CTRL-ALT-ENTER.

You can also use Notify to display alarms for Appointment Calendar. This saves memory since the Appointment Calendar alarm module (CL/I) does not need to be loaded into memory. Like Mail and Scheduler, when Notify displays an alarm for an appointment, it tells you that the notification came from the Appointment Calendar.

Besides displaying an on-screen window, Notify beeps to attract your attention. You can specify the tones and the duration of the tones that Notify uses. You can specify up to ten tones. Other Notify options set the amount of time the on-screen window displays and the duration of the pause between notification displays of the same window. You can even specify different tone strings, which alter the sound of your computer's beep, to indicate different priority levels on incoming messages and alarms.

When loaded, Notify stores your Office User ID and File ID. This makes the rest of the Office programs have a shorter startup period, since they do not have to search to find this information. When loaded, Notify simply passes this information to any Office program that you start.

Loading Notification Support

You can load Notify into memory either from a DOS command line or from your AUTOEXEC.BAT file when you start your computer. To load Notify from the DOS command line, type **notify**. If the directory in which the Office programs are located is listed in your DOS path statement, Notify loads and displays a message similar to the one shown here:

```
Resident Portion of NOTIFY has been loaded.
Initials - DVN
User ID  - DEVINR
Method   - File Polling
Network  - Novell NetWare
```

You can also have Notify loaded automatically each time you start your computer by adding the command, NOTIFY.EXE, to start Notify from your AUTOEXEC.BAT file. If you ran the SETMEUP program that comes with Office, you were given the option of having the command to load Notify inserted into your AUTOEXEC.BAT file. If you told SETMEUP not to insert the command for Notify, or have not run SETMEUP, you need to run SETMEUP or edit your AUTOEXEC.BAT file using Editor and add the command yourself. The command for loading Notify should be placed in the file after the commands for logging on to your network and before Office Shell is started. For information on using the SETMEUP program, see Appendix A, "LAN User Installation." For more on using Editor to edit your AUTOEXEC-.BAT file, see Chapter 5, "Using Editor."

Clearing Notification

When your system administrator sets up Office LAN on your network, she or he can select one of two ways for notification to take place. The first method gives users notification from Mail and Scheduler only when they are logged on to the network and have Notify loaded. The second method creates a file where Mail and Scheduler store all notifications for incoming messages and events. Then, when you run Notify, it periodically checks this file for any new notification information to give you. That is, even if you are gone for a week, when you return and load Notify, each message received over that week displays on the screen. To allow for both of these situations, Notify provides a way to clear notification messages one at a time or to clear all notification messages at once.

Clearing a Single Notification

When Notify displays on-screen notification for an incoming Mail message or scheduled event, you can clear the single notification by pressing CTRL-ENTER. If your system administrator has set up Office so that you only see notification for messages received when you are logged on to the network, the displayed notification *and* notification for any other messages received at nearly the same time will be cleared. In other words, if you get two messages or events at approximately the same time, you may only see one notification. However, if your Office system stores notifications in a special file, you receive both notification messages. After clearing the first notification by pressing CTRL-ENTER, you have to press CTRL-ENTER again to clear the second notification. Pressing CTRL-ENTER in this case only clears one notification message at a time.

Clearing Multiple Notifications

If your system administrator has set up Office to use a special file in which to store notifications, you may need to clear several notifications at once. This could happen if you have been away from your computer for an extended period of time or if you haven't run Notify for several days. In such a situation, where you will probably be checking your Mail and Scheduler anyway, you may want to clear all of the stored notifications at once. To clear multiple notifications, press CTRL-ALT-ENTER. You can also use CTRL-ALT-ENTER to clear a single notification, but you may clear more on-screen notifications than intended.

Specifying Notification for Different Priority Messages

In Mail, you can assign any one of three priority levels to a message you send. Notify allows you to specify different notification tones to distinguish between different priority messages. With this feature, you will know the priority of all messages you receive without entering Mail. To set up different notification tones for different priority messages, you need to use the /Bx startup option. The /B stands for "beep" and x represents the priority. For example, if you want to set different tone strings for different priorities, you need to include /BH for high priority messages, /B for normal priority Mail messages and Scheduler notifications, and /BL for low priority messages. Notify also allows you to use /BA to set a distinct tone string for Appointment Calendar alarms.

Following any of the /Bx startup options, you need to specify three things:

• The repeat interval at which the tones should sound. This only applies when a notification window for the same message is displayed repeatedly. If you specify a 1, Notify plays the tones you list each time it displays that window. If you specify a 2, the tone only plays every other time the window is displayed, and so on.

• The frequency in hertz for the tones to use. For a listing of the available tones and their corresponding frequencies, consult Table 11-1.

• The duration of each tone based on 1/18th of a second. A 1 means 1/18 of a second, a 9 indicates one half of a second, and so on.

These three pieces of information are listed with the /B*x* startup option as follows:

/Bx-repeat interval,tone,duration,tone,duration, . . .

You can list up to ten tones and their corresponding durations for each priority.

For example, if you wanted "For He's A Jolly Good Fellow" to play for all high priority messages each time the notification window was displayed, and to have each tone last about 1/3 of a second, you would list the following for Notify:

notify /BH-1,523,6,440,6,28,1,440,3,28,1,440,3,415,3,440,3,466,9,440,9

Table 11-2 lists some examples of tone strings used by Notify. As shown previously, you can list separate tone strings for each priority level and Appointment Calendar alarms using the /B*x* startup option. However, since DOS only allows you to enter 127 characters on the command line, if you list several tone strings you may need to store the startup options in a separate file and give Notify the filename.

Storing Options in a File

If the startup options you specify for Notify require more characters than can fit on a single DOS command line, you can store these options in a file and tell Notify the name of the file using the /@ startup option. For example, if you create different tone strings for each of the different

Note	Hertz	Note	Hertz
A	28	F	349
A#/Bb	29	F#/Gb	370
B	31	G	392
C (−3)	33	G#/Ab	415
C#/Db	35	A	440
D	37	A#/Bb	466
D#/Eb	39	B	494
E	41	C (+1)	523
F	44	C#/Db	554
F#/Gb	46	D	587
G	49	D#/Eb	622
G#/Ab	52	E	659
A	55	F	698
A#/Bb	58	F#/Gb	740
B	62	G	784
C (−2)	65	G#/Ab	831
C#/Db	69	A	880
D	73	A#/Bb	932
D#/Eb	78	B	988
E	82	C (+2)	1047
F	87	C#/Db	1109
F#/Gb	92	D	1175
G	98	D#/Eb	1245
G#/Ab	104	E	1319
A	110	F	1397
A#/Bb	117	F#/Gb	1480
B	123	G	1568
C (−1)	131	G#/Ab	1661
C#/Db	139	A	1760
D	147	A#/Bb	1865
D#/Eb	156	B	1976
E	165	C (+3)	2093
F	175	C#/Db	2217
F#/Gb	185	D	2349
G	196	D#/Eb	2489
G#/Ab	208	E	2637
A	220	F	2794
A#/Bb	233	F#/Gb	2960
B	247	G	3136
C (Middle)	262	G#/Ab	3322
C#/Db	277	A	3520
D	294	A#/Bb	3729
D#/Eb	311	B	3951
E	330	C (+4)	4186

Table 11-1.   Table of Tones and Frequencies

Song	Tone Strings
1812 Overture	/B-1,220,2,294,2,330,2,370,2,330,2,294,2,330,2,370,4,294,5,294,5
	(A) (D) (E) (F#) (E) (D) (E) (F#) (D) (D)
Beethoven's 5th	/B-1,196,6,196,6,196,6,156,12,40000,8,175,6,175,6,175,6,147,15
	(G) (G) (G) (E^b) (REST) (F) (F) (F) (D)
C Major Scale	/B-1,262,6,294,2,330,2,349,2,392,2,440,2,494,2,523,6,28,1,28,1
	(C) (D) (E) (F) (G) (A) (B) (C) (A) (A)
Happy Birthday	/B-1,349,10,28,1,349,5,392,15,349,15,466,15,440,30,28,1,28,1
	(F) (A) (F) (G) (F) (B^b) (A) (A) (A)

Table 11-2.   Table of Tone Examples

priorities, this will probably take more characters than DOS allows on a command line, so you could do the following:

1. Using Editor, create a DOS Text file that contains *only* the startup options you want Notify to use. Do not list Notify in the file.

2. Save the file using the name C:\OPTIONS.TXT.

3. From where you load Notify (either the DOS command line or AUTOEXEC.BAT), enter

Notify /@-c:\options.txt

Notify then looks to that file to find the startup options it should use. Notify accepts over 2000 characters from one file.

Using Other Startup Options

Notify has several startup options that let you customize the way Notify runs on your computer. These options (some presented with examples) are as follows:

/@	This specifies a file where Notify's startup options are listed. See "Storing Options in a File" earlier in this chapter. /@-C:\OPTIONS would load the contents of the file named OPTIONS as part of the Notify startup options.
/A	This allows the use of bold and underline attributes in the Notification window.
/Dx	This specifies the display duration for the notification window in seconds. x indicates to which priority this applies. /DH-10 would specify 10 seconds for the display duration of high-priority messages.
/F	This specifies the number of seconds between checks for new messages or events. If your notification is extremely slow, try setting this option to a smaller number. /F-10 instructs Notify to check for new messages or events every 10 seconds.
/NA	This turns off bold and underline display attributes for the contents of the Notify window. If notification messages cause screen display problems on your monitor, this option should correct the problems.
/NBx	This turns off the beeps or tones for messages with the specified priority level. /NBL specifies no beep or tone for low-priority messages.
/NN	This turns off notification for all messages and events. To turn notification back on, see "Changing Options" in this chapter.
/Px	This indicates the pause interval in seconds that Notify should wait before redisplaying the same window. /PA-5 specifies a pause interval of 5 seconds for Appointment Calendar alarm.
/PH	This specifies the path to the Office host to which you are assigned. This tells Notify the location of the USERID .FIL file it must find before it can load. This would be used if the directory containing USERID.FIL is not in your path, or if you have multiple hosts in your path. /PH-F:\OFFICE30 instructs Notify to look in F:\OFFICE30 for the USERID.FIL file.

/TX   This specifies the maximum number of times that Notify should redisplay the same notification window. If you do not clear the notification message before it displays the specified number of times, Notify clears the notification itself. This option is useful if you are away from your computer frequently. Without this option set, Notify displays the notification message indefinitely. /TH-10 causes Notify to redisplay the notification window for high-priority messages a maximum of 10 times.

Changing Options

Once you have loaded Notify, you can still make changes to the options that were set when it was loaded. To change Notify's options, rerun Notify from the DOS command line with the new options that add to or replace existing options. To change an existing option, enter the same option with the new values. This is necessary since Notify holds all options until specifically reset. The only exception is the /NN startup option, which is replaced any time you rerun Notify without the /NN switch listed. With the 6/14/90 version of office you cannot change the user information that Notify gets when it loads initially. For example, if you move to a different com-puter where another user has already logged on and run Notify, Notify keeps her or his user information even after running Notify again.

Repeat Performance

Repeat Performance is a device driver that increases the performance of your computer's keyboard. Using Repeat Performance, you can set the rate at which your keyboard repeats keystrokes and the time delay before a keystroke is repeated. You can also set a type-ahead buffer size; in other words, you can regulate the number of keystrokes that are stored when your computer is not accepting input from the keyboard. Repeat Performance is loaded through your computer's CONFIG.SYS file, which is edited automatically during installation.

Installing Repeat Performance

If you use Office PC, you can install Repeat Performance when you install Office on your computer. Office LAN users can also run the Repeat Performance installation program, RPINSTAL, when they use the SETMEUP program to configure their individual computers. At any time, Office PC or Office LAN users can run RPINSTAL by itself to install Repeat Performance. During the installation of Repeat Performance, you can exit without saving the current options settings by pressing CTRL-C. You must run both RPINSTAL and RP (for making temporary option changes) from the DOS command line. They cannot be run as entries from the Shell menu.

To install Repeat Performance using RPINSTAL, enter **RPIN-STAL** on the DOS command line. If the Office program directory is listed in the DOS path statement, Repeat Performance is loaded. If Repeat Performance does not load, enter the full path to the Office directory. A banner and explanation screen about Repeat Performance displays; press ENTER to continue with the installation. RPINSTAL then steps you through and lets you set each option it provides. At the bottom of the selection screens for each option, there is a test field where you can test the settings you select before actually selecting them.

The first option explained is Repeat Speed. This is the rate at which the keyboard accepts keystrokes. From the explanation screen for Repeat Speed, press ENTER to continue to the selection screen for Repeat Speed and Delay, as shown in Figure 11-1. Use the RIGHT ARROW and LEFT ARROW keys to change the setting for the Repeat Speed from anywhere between 11 characters per second to 1000 characters per second. RPINSTAL displays the default setting of 40 characters per second if you are installing Repeat Performance for the first time. After setting the Repeat rate, press the DOWN ARROW key to move to Delay. This refers to the time delay between when a key is pressed and when that keystroke begins to repeat. You can select a time value from 0.10 seconds to 5 seconds. RPINSTAL defaults to a 0.25 second delay for a new installation. When you are finished setting Repeat Speed and Delay, press F7 to continue. You can also press F1 to cancel any changes and return the options to their default values.

The next screen explains Repeat Performance's Skid Squelch. Skid Squelch prevents extra characters from being entered after a key has been released. As part of Skid Squelch, Repeat Performance automati-

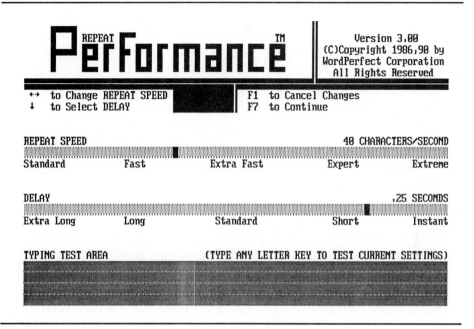

Figure 11-1.   Repeat Speed and Delay selection screen

cally adjusts the repeat rate so it is not more than the current program can handle. This allows Skid Squelch to work even with programs that have slow repeat rates. To continue with the installation, press ENTER.

The explanation screen for the Turbo Button feature is displayed next. This lets you temporarily increase the repeat rate above the value you set with Repeat Speed. This feature is used primarily when large strings of the same character are entered. To move to the Turbo Button selection screen shown in Figure 11-2, press ENTER. On the Turbo Button selection screen, use the LEFT ARROW and RIGHT ARROW keys to change the setting for the turbo repeat rate. This can be any value between 11 and 10,000 characters per second. RPINSTAL displays the default setting of 100 characters per second if this is a new installation. Press the DOWN ARROW key when finished setting the rate to select the key that activates the turbo repeat rate (the Turbo Button). This can be any key; the CTRL key displays as the default. When you are finished with the Turbo Button selection screen, press F7 to continue.

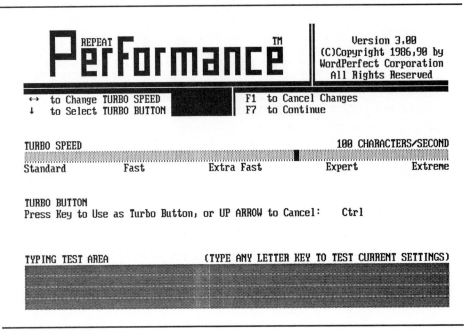

Figure 11-2.   Turbo Button selection screen

The next screen outlines how to use the Quick Entry of Special Characters feature shown in Figure 11-3. This feature lets you repeat any character in the ASCII character set and is especially useful when using ASCII graphics characters. You can type **Y** to experiment with this option. You can also type **N** or press ENTER, which takes you to the Type Ahead Buffer explanation screen. DOS normally only stores 15 keystrokes entered when your computer is performing tasks other than reading the keyboard. This feature lets you enlarge the buffer so more keystrokes can be entered and stored—useful if keystrokes are being "dropped" when you type in several keystrokes at one time. Press ENTER again to move to the screen where you can set the size of the **Type Ahead Buffer** anywhere from 1 to 1000 characters. Remember that the larger the number entered, the more memory Repeat Performance requires.

After you press ENTER, the explanation of the Disable Caps Lock feature displays. Normally, when you press the CAPSLOCK key on your keyboard, any characters entered display in uppercase, but when you use the SHIFT key with the Caps Lock feature turned on, characters

---

Quick Entry of Special Characters

The IBM PC already allows you to enter special characters by holding down the
Alt key and typing a decimal character code on the numeric keypad. Repeat
Performance enhances this feature by allowing these special
characters to be repeated like any other keystroke. This increases the
speed of line drawing, chart fill-in, and other applications which
use special characters.

This feature is activated when you hold down the Alt key and either Shift
key simultaneously, type the decimal character code, and then let up on the Alt
key only. The character will repeat as long as the Shift key is held down.
For example, to draw a double line:

    Hold down the Alt key
    Hold down either Shift key
    Type 205 on the numeric keypad
    Let up on the Alt key, keeping the Shift key depressed
    Wait while the character repeats
    Let up on the Shift key to stop repeating the character

Do you want to experiment with this feature? (Y/N) N

Figure 11-3.   Quick entry of special characters explanation

will display in lowercase. From this screen, you can type **Y** or press ENTER to disable this feature, or type **N** to retain the original function.

After entering a selection, you move to the explanation screen for Tone Frequency and Duration. This refers to the beep your computer makes when an error occurs, input is needed, and so on. You can set the frequency and duration of the beep by pressing ENTER to move to the selection screen for Tone Frequency and Duration, as shown in Figure 11-4. From this screen, press the LEFT ARROW and RIGHT ARROW keys to change the frequency of the beep. RPINSTAL sounds the current setting of the frequency so you can hear what it sounds like. You can press F8 to turn the tone on or off. The frequency can be anywhere from 59 to 5576 hertz, and the default of 880 hertz is displayed for new installations. Press the DOWN ARROW key to change to the Tone Duration setting. Use the LEFT ARROW and RIGHT ARROW keys to set the duration of your computer's beep. While you are setting the tone in Repeat Performance, you can press SPACEBAR to listen to the current setting for the tone. The tone can be from 0.01 seconds to 2.5 seconds, with 0.10 seconds as the default. Press F7 to continue when the Tone Frequency and Duration settings are as you wish.

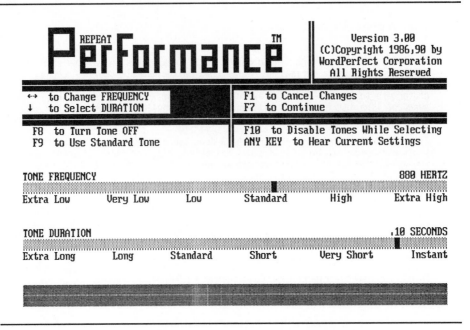

Figure 11-4.   Tone Frequency and Duration selection screen

RPINSTAL now displays a summary screen, as in Figure 11-5, with the settings for all of the options that you have selected. You can type **Y** to have RPINSTAL give you the chance to change each setting, or **N** to confirm the settings and continue. At the next prompt, input the disk or path where RP.EXE and RP.SYS should be installed. Following this, you are also given the chance to install the same settings to multiple disks. Only do this if you are going to use these disks to boot up the machine on which RPINSTAL was run. Finally, RPINSTAL prompts you to complete and return the Office registration card, and then to press ENTER.

After completing an installation, you need to restart your computer to load Repeat Performance and use the options according to the settings you input.

```
Verification of Settings
───────────────────────

You have selected the following settings:

Buffer Size:          200 Characters
Repeat Speed:          40 Characters/Sec
Delay:                .25 Sec
Turbo Repeat Speed:   100 Characters/Sec
Turbo Button:             Ctrl
Shift CapsLock:           LOWER
Tone:                     ON
Tone Frequency:       800 Hz
Tone Duration:        .10 Sec

Do you want to make any changes? (Y/N) N
```

Figure 11-5.   Repeat Performance summary screen

Adjusting RP Settings

At any time, you can change the options you set in Repeat Performance either temporarily or permanently. To make a permanent change to the settings in Repeat Performance, run RPINSTAL again to change the settings. You can also change the settings temporarily by running RP.EXE. Any options set under RP.EXE are only in effect until you restart or reboot your computer.

Changing Options Permanently

To make permanent changes to the options in Repeat Performance, run RPINSTAL as when you initially installed Repeat Performance. If you run RPINSTAL with Repeat Performance installed, the summary screen of Figure 11-5 is displayed first. At this point, you can leave the current settings intact, or edit each of the options. To leave the settings intact, type **N**. RPINSTAL then prompts you for the drive letter on which Repeat Performance should be installed using the current settings. This is an easy way of saving the same Repeat Performance settings to more than one computer.

If you type **Y**, RPINSTAL gives you the choice of editing each option or leaving it intact. From the summary screen, RPINSTAL first displays the current size of the type-ahead buffer, and next displays the setting to reverse the Caps Lock feature. Since the current setting is displayed for these options, you can press ENTER to retain these settings, or you can enter a new setting.

After completing the first two options, RPINSTAL takes you through the Repeat Speed and Delay screen, Turbo Speed and Button screen, and Tone Frequency and Duration screen. Each of these screens displays the current settings for Repeat Performance as the defaults. On each of these screens, you can press F1 to cancel any changes and return to the settings that were in place before you ran RPINSTAL. Pressing F7 saves the current settings on the screen and continues to the next screen.

After you set the options on each of these screens, RPINSTAL again displays a summary screen of the current settings for Repeat Performance. Once again, you can type **Y** to make changes to the settings, or **N** to keep the displayed settings. Typing **Y** returns you to the first option and you can again set each option. If you type **N**, RPINSTAL asks for the drive letter where the current settings should be installed. You can repeat RPINSTAL at any time to change or adjust the settings for Repeat Performance.

Changing Options Temporarily

You can temporarily set options for Repeat Performance by running RP.EXE. These settings are only in effect until you turn off or reboot your computer. You then return to the settings that were in place before you ran RP.EXE.

To set temporary options for Repeat Performance, enter **RP** on the DOS command line. After displaying the banner, RP takes you directly to the Repeat Speed and Delay screen. From the screens under RP, you can exit at any time by pressing F7. You can also move between the options screens by pressing PGDN to move to the next screen, or PGUP to move to the previous screen. As with RPINSTAL, F1 cancels any changes made to the screens and resets the options to the settings in effect when RP was started.

From the Repeat Speed and Delay screen, you can use PGDN to move to the Turbo Speed and Button screen, and then to the Tone Frequency and Duration screen. After completing the temporary settings for these options, press F7 to keep the settings and exit RP. You can run RP any time during a session to set and reset options if necessary. When you restart or reboot your computer, Repeat Performance returns to the settings installed the last time RPINSTAL was run.

Removing Repeat Performance

If you need to remove Repeat Performance from a computer, you can use RPREMOVE.EXE. This might become necessary when installing Repeat Performance to a different computer. This deletes RP.EXE and RP.SYS from your computer, and deletes the entries for them in the CONFIG.SYS file. You can then reinstall Repeat Performance on another computer.

To remove Repeat Performance from your computer, enter **RPRE-MOVE** on the DOS command line. After displaying a banner screen, RPREMOVE warns you that continuing will remove Repeat Performance from your computer. If you want to continue, enter the letter for the disk drive on which Repeat Performance is installed. RPREMOVE then edits the CONFIG.SYS file on the drive and removes the command to load RP.SYS. the RP.EXE file is also removed, since temporary settings for Repeat Performance are no longer needed.

Another way to disable Repeat Performance temporarily is to enter the **RP OFF** command on the DOS command line. This disables Repeat Performance until you restart or reboot the computer, or until you enter the **RP ON** command on the DOS command line to enable Repeat Performance again.

TSR Manager

The TSR Manager, or TSRM, that comes with Office offers an easy way of managing terminate-and-stay-resident (TSR) programs. Using TSRM, you can load and unload multiple TSR programs. TSRM also lets you load TSR's along with an associated program by using a file containing a listing of the TSR's and the program name. Best of all, TSRM allows you to load and unload your TSR's selectively and keep the memory they require free to use with other programs. TSRM does this by removing the TSR from base memory and placing it in expanded memory or on disk until you actively load it into base memory. This is especially valuable when keeping TSR's continually loaded would prevent you from running certain applications due to memory limitations. TSRM is the only Office program that must be run from the Shell menu. If you try to load it from DOS, an error displays telling you TSRM must be run from Shell.

Starting TSRM

If you use the default Shell menus that come with Office, the main Shell menu has a listing for "Other Menu." Press **O** to move to the other menu, and press **T** from the submenu to start TSRM. If you have a different Shell menu, or would like to move TSRM to a different menu, create an entry on the Shell menu with a Program Information screen similar to the one shown in Figure 11-6. For information on creating a Shell program entry, see Chapter 10, "Using Shell."

When using TSRM, you can employ two different screen formats to load and display TSR information. The first is Menu mode. This is TSRM's default startup mode and looks like the screen shown in Figure 11-7. At the top of the menu, there is information about the memory any loaded TSR's may require, and how much memory is available. The menu itself lists the TSR's that you have loaded in the order in which they were loaded. At the bottom of the screen are the TSRM options and the TSRM command line. From the command line, you can execute any DOS command or load a TSR.

The second mode available is Command mode. In Command mode, only the TSRM command line is displayed and resembles a DOS command line, as shown here:

```
(TSRM) T:\OFF30>
```

The TSRM to the left of the prompt indicates that the command line is being run under TSRM and any TSR's that are loaded are loaded under TSRM. You can view a listing of all loaded TSR's while in Command mode by pressing F5 for List Information.

```
                         Program Information
Menu Letter:             T

Menu Description:        TSR Manager

Menu Item Type:          Normal         Pause: NO

Default Directory:

Program Name:            tsrm.exe

Clipboard  Filename:

Macros Names - End of Line:  EOL .SHM  Go to: GOSHELL .SHM  Return: RTSHELL .SHM

Startup Options:

Prompt for startup options? NO    Swap Shell out?          NO

Start resident?          NO        Allow switch anytime?    NO

     Type the letter (A-Z) used to start the program.

                                         (F7 = Exit, F3 = Help)
```

Figure 11-6.   TSRM Program Information screen

```
                         TSR Manager 3.0
Memory Used:         0   Resident Programs   Memory Free:   349424
┌──────────────────────────┬──────────────────────────┐
│                          │                          │
│                          │                          │
│                          │                          │
│                          │                          │
│                          │                          │
│                          │                          │
│                          │                          │
│                          │                          │
│                          │                          │
└──────────────────────────┴──────────────────────────┘
T:\OFF30
Ctrl-F1 Shell; Shift-F3 Switch Mode; F7 Exit;

DOS Command or Hotkey:
```

Figure 11-7.   TSRM menu

Loading TSR's from TSRM

Loading a TSR under TSRM is the same regardless of the current mode. On the TSRM command line, enter the name of the TSR to be loaded and include any required startup options or switches. If you are in Menu mode, the memory requirement for the TSR is displayed next to it in the menu. Once a TSR has been loaded, you can activate it using the same hotkeys you would use if the TSR were started from DOS.

Since TSR's are often used in conjunction with other programs, you can also load TSR's with their associated programs. Examples of this would include a grammar checker loaded with WordPerfect, or a mouse driver loaded with a graphics program. You can do this by creating a DOS Text file listing the TSR's with the main program last in the listing. For example, you could load a mouse driver and Grammatik IV together with WordPerfect, as shown here:

```
MOUSE.COM
G4.EXE
WP.EXE
```

When you start TSR's with programs using a file, you must enter an @ before the filename to indicate to TSRM that it is a file and not an individual TSR or program. TSRM also allows you to switch directly from a program loaded from inside a file to Shell if you mark the program with an asterisk in the file, as with the format shown here:

```
MOUSE.COM
G4.EXE
*WP.EXE
```

Exiting TSRM

To exit TSRM, you must be at the TSRM menu if you are using Menu mode, or at the command line if you are in Command mode. From here, press F7 to exit. If there are TSR's currently resident, TSRM gives you the option of removing all TSR's from memory, or exiting TSRM and leaving the TSR's resident. To remove all loaded TSR's, type **Y**. To exit TSRM and leave the TSR's resident, type **N**. If no TSR's are resident when you press F7, you are returned to the Shell menu without a prompt.

System Administrator Guide

Single Host Installation
Maintaining Office
Using Office Connections

P
A
R
T

T
H
R
E
E

Single Host Installation

Before all network users can take advantage of Office LAN 3.0, it must be properly installed on the network. This chapter explains how to install an Office LAN 3.0 single-host system or convert an Office 2.0 system to an Office LAN 3.0 single-host system. Before you learn the various installation steps, it will help to understand some of the terminology, requirements, and limitations associated with the system administration of Office LAN 3.0.

Introduction to a Single-Host System

When you purchase Office LAN 3.0, you can install and use a single-host system. The single-host system is the most basic and most common Office configuration. The basic building block of an Office system is a *host*—a set of network directories in which Mail and Scheduler keep their information and data files. All Office LAN users are assigned to a host. A host has to be located on the network file server so that all users can access the shared directories. You can have multiple hosts on a single file server. However, if you do, you need to purchase the Word-Perfect Connections package to allow the hosts to communicate. See Chapter 14, "Using Office Connections," for more information on the WordPerfect Connections package. You may want to put multiple hosts on a single file server for security reasons—for example, if you want to separate your corporate employees from all other employees.

When a user is assigned to a host, individual files are created on the network for that user in the host directories. These files are used for sending, receiving, and storing Mail messages and Scheduler items.

Along with the directories, a host has a set of information files containing specific information about the host, its users, and its resources. All users on the host can access these information files, which allows sharing of information.

Requirements for a Single-Host System

In order to set up a single-host system you must meet the following requirements:

- You must have a minimum of 3 to 4 megabytes of free disk space on your network. The actual amount of disk space needed depends on the number of users you are installing on the host. If you have minimal disk space, you will limit the number of mail messages and scheduled events your system can handle.

- Initially, you must be able to create up to eight files for each user you are installing on the host.

- For all Office directories, each user needs to be able to read, write, open, create, and delete files, modify the attributes of an open file, and search a network directory.

Limitations of a Single-Host System

The Office programs themselves do not realistically limit the number of users you can assign to a single host. However, you may be limited by the number of work station attachments your network allows to the file server where the Office directories are located. Since the host directories are on the network, you can only have as many users accessing a host at once as your network allows simultaneous work station attachments to that file server.

Installing Office LAN 3.0

Each package of WordPerfect Office 3.0 includes an installation program (Install) to simplify the initial setup and/or update of Office. The Install program for Office LAN takes you through the steps of creating both an Office directory and an Office administration directory, installing the Office files, and definning the Office host. If you need to convert an Office 2.0 system to Office 3.0, the installation program helps you to convert your 2.0 user and resource Notebook files. It also allows you to convert your 2.0 Mail and Scheduler system. For information on converting an Office 2.0 system to Office 3.0, see "Converting from Office 2.0 to 3.0" later in this chapter.

The Office LAN files are in compressed format on the floppy disks. For this reason, you must use the Install program to install Office 3.0. To run the Install program, insert the floppy disk labeled Office LAN 1 into a floppy drive. Switch to that drive by entering the drive letter followed by a colon, usually **a:**, and then type **install** and press ENTER. Your monitor displays the title screen with an option to continue or exit. Type **Y** to proceed; you should see a menu listing the different installation options, as shown in Figure 12-1.

- *Basic Installation*   While all of the options copy the programs to a specified target directory, the Basic Installation option does this without prompting you to confirm the installation of each program, and is ideal for a first time setup.

- *Custom Installation*   The Custom Installation option prompts you before installing each Office file group. Install lists the name of the file group, such as Shell, and briefly describes what the file group does, so you know if you need to install the specified files. If you type **Y** for Yes, this group of files is installed; if you type **N** for No, they are not. After you type **Y** or **N**, the next file group is displayed. A custom installation is useful if you only want to install certain files, or if you are not familiar with Office and want a description of the programs and files used in Office 3.0.

- *Update from Office 2.0*   Select this option if you are converting your 2.0 system to 3.0. Like Custom Installation, this option prompts you before installing a group of files.

- *Update Office 3.0*   This option is used for interim releases of Office 3.0. It allows you to install only those file groups that you need to update. This option uses the existing directory structure without making modifications.

```
Office LAN Installation Options                    Installation Problems?
                                                       (800)321-3253

1 - Basic Installation            Install all Office 3.0 file groups.

2 - Custom Installation           Install user-selected Office 3.0 file groups.

3 - Update from Office 2.0        Install user-selected Office 3.0 file groups
                                  and convert Office 2.0 system files.

4 - Update Office 3.0             Do not change existing Office 3.0
                                  directories; install Office 3.0 update
                                  file groups (i.e., interim release
                                  installation).

5 - Notes on Connection Server




Selection: 1                                              (F7 Exit)
```

Figure 12-1.   Office LAN installation options

After you select the desired installation type, you'll see an information screen. This screen explains the steps that will be taken during the installation. If you are performing a basic installation, you'll see the screen shown in Figure 12-2. After the information screen displays, type **Y** to continue. If you select Basic Installation, Install asks you to enter where you want the files installed, as illustrated in Figure 12-3. If you select anything other than a basic installation, you are asked for the source directory (where the files should be installed from) as well as the target directory (where you want the files installed).

The Program File Directory is where all of the Office programs and files needed to run Office 3.0 are stored. By default, Install lists *F*:\OFFICE30 as the Program File Directory, where *F* represents the first available network drive. If the directory listed for Program File Directory does not exist, Install will create it. Users need all rights to this directory, except supervisory rights. If you direct the user's tempo-

Basic Installation
There are three steps to the Basic Installation process:

Step 1: Directory Selection
You will be prompted for the drive letters and pathnames of two
directories: a program file directory and a system administration file
directory. The program directory will hold the files necessary to run
Office programs (Mail, Scheduler, Calendar, etc.) and must be accessible
to all users on the network who want to run these programs. The system
administration directory will hold the files and programs necessary to
initialize and maintain Office programs and should only be accessible to
the system administrator(s).

Step 2: File Installation
Once you have specified the Office directories, Basic Installation
decompresses and copies all Office program and system administration file
groups into the directories. (If you do not want to install all file
groups, type n now and select Custom Installation (2)).

Step 3: Mail/Scheduler System (Host) Installation
After the files are installed, you are asked if you want to use the System
Administration Shell menu, which will help you install the Mail/Scheduler
system, also known as a host.

Do you want to continue with this selection? Yes (No)

Figure 12-2.   Basic Installation information screen

Office LAN 3.0 Directory Structure (Basic)   Installation Problems?
                                                        (800)321-3253

    Installing from A:\

1 - Install Program File Directory: F:\OFFICE30\ will be created

2 - Office Admin File Directory: F:\OFFADMIN\ will be created

3 - Install all Office 3.0 modules

```
NOTE: If you do not want to use the suggested
      directories, select the directory options
      and make the desired changes. The
      directories will be created if they do not
      already exist. When you are ready to
      continue, select option 3.
```

Selection: 3   (F7 Exit)

Figure 12-3.   Basic installation directory structure

rary files and setup files to a hard drive or personal network drive, you can restrict the rights to the Program File Directory. See "Startup Options" in the various program chapters in the "Reference Section" (Part Two) for information on the specific startup options. Restricting rights in the program directory increases the security on your network. If you have already installed Office 3.0 and are updating or reinstalling, the Install program lists the current Office 3.0 directory as the Program File Directory.

The Office Admin File Directory stores all the files necessary to build an Office host. Only the system administrator should have rights to this directory. By default, Install lists *F*:\OFFADMIN as the Office Admin File Directory where *F* represents the first available network drive. If the directory listed for Office Admin File Directory does not exist, Install will create it.

Once you enter the correct directories, select the option to begin the actual installation. If you are performing a basic installation, this is option 3, as shown in Figure 12-3. Install then prompts you to input your customer registration number. If you enter your registration number here, all the Office programs will display the registration number on the main help screens. Users can then easily locate the registration number when working with the WordPerfect customer support department. Entering this number is optional, and Install continues when you press ENTER.

If you enter an incorrect registration number or want to add a number later, you can run the Install program again. If you are only running Install to add the registration number, select the Custom Install option. The correct directory entries will be listed and you can continue to the screen that asks for the registration number. After entering the correct registration number, type **N** for No at all prompts that ask if you want to install the specified file groups. The file created when you enter a registration number is called OF{OF}US.LCN.

After you enter the registration number or press ENTER, Install begins copying files. The files on the Office disks are in a compressed format to conserve disk space. This makes it impossible to run any programs from the Office disks without first running Install to restore the files to their normal format. During this process, you are prompted to insert the disks labeled Office LAN 2, 3, 4, 5, and 6 or LAN 2, 3, 4 if you are using 3 1/2-inch disks. If you selected any option other than Basic Installation, Install allows you to install or bypass each of the

Office file groups individually. As the files are copied, a message at the bottom of the screen indicates which file is being installed and to which directory. If you need to abort the installation at any time, you can press F1 for Cancel. Install displays a message indicating that the files may not be completely installed. To ensure that all the files are installed, you need to run the Install program again.

Defining the Office Host

After the files are copied to the correct directories, Office displays the Office LAN 3.0 Host Definition screen shown in Figure 12-4. The information you enter on the Host Definition screen is used to create the HOSTID.NB file—one of the three information files needed before the Office system can function. This screen displays the Host Directory Path followed by six options. The Host Directory Path is the directory you

```
Office LAN 3.0 Host Definition

    Host Directory Path: F:\OFFICE30\

1 - Host Name:

2 - Host File ID:

3 - Administrator Name:

4 - Administrator Phone:

5 - Display Current Host Names

6 - Continue

                   ┌─────────────────────────────────────────────┐
                   │ NOTE:  Select an option and enter the requested host │
                   │        information.  If you have a multiple-host │
                   │        system already in place and need to see what │
                   │        host names are currently being used, select │
                   │        option 5.  When you have entered all the host │
                   │        information, select option 6 to continue. │
                   └─────────────────────────────────────────────┘

Selection: 1                                            (F7 Exit)
```

Figure 12-4.   Office LAN 3.0 Host Definition screen

indicated as the Program Files Directory. As mentioned, a host is a set of Mail and Scheduler directories. For information on the exact structure of an Office host, see "Host Directory Structure" later in this chapter.

The only options you must fill out on the Host Definition menu are 1 and 2. Option 1, Host Name, is the name that identifies the host, and must be no longer than 26 characters including spaces. You can increase the size of the host name to 32 characters by modifying the HOST-ID.NB file. You may use the name of the file server on which you are installing the host, your company name, a department name, or any other name that you choose. The host name can contain any letters of the alphabet, numbers from 0 through 9, a space, a dollar sign, an underscore (_), and ASCII characters from 128 through 155, 157, from 160 through 167, and 225. For information on the ASCII characters, see Appendix B, "ASCII Character Chart." The host name is necessary on both single- and multiple-host system installations. The host name appears before the user's name in the Mail and Scheduler headers, as shown here:

WP Mail – HOST1:DEVINR   Monday, February 24, 1992 9:00 am

The second option, Host File ID, is an identification code of one to three characters. The Host File ID is used to create directories and files and can only contain valid DOS filename characters. ASCII characters 128 and above are not supported, and you cannot use the underscore character (_) as the last value in the Host File ID. If you are installing multiple hosts, the host name and File ID should be unique for each host.

The Administrator Name (option 3) and the Administrator Phone (option 4) are optional. Enter this informaiton if you want your users to have direct access to you for Office problems and complications. This information is displayed on the List Hosts screen in the Mail and Scheduler programs.

If you have already installed other hosts, you can display current host names with option 5. This option lists the names of the hosts you have already defined in the HOSTID.NB file so you do not duplicate the host names.

System Administration Menus

After filling in the necessary information in the Host Definition screen, you can display the System Administration Shell menu. Type **Y** to display the menu shown in Figure 12-5. The System Administration menus help you set up the information files for an Office host. You can access the information to build an Office host from the DOS command line, but the System Administration menus automate this task considerably. The options available on the System Administration menus all use predefined Shell and Editor macros to access the various information. If you ever need to access the System Administration menus to change options after installing Office, change to the Office administration directory and type **offadmin**. OFFADMIN is a batch file that loads the System Administration Shell menus and increases the work space so the macros will execute properly.

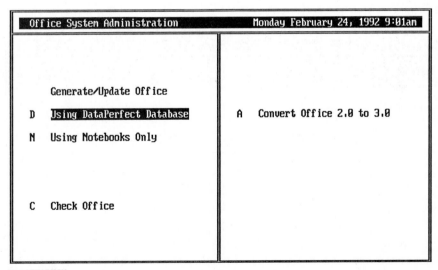

Figure 12-5.   Main Office System Administration menu

Office Information Files

The three information files that the Office host uses are HOSTID.FIL, USERID.FIL, and RESOURCE.FIL. These information files tell the Office system which hosts, users, and resources are valid. Office creates the information files from the corresponding Notebook files HOST-ID.NB, USERID.NB, and RESOURCE.NB.

Hint: The fields in the Notebook files have been set to a default size. If some of your fields are considerably smaller than the default, you can shorten the field size in Notebook; this will greatly speed up the performance of the GENOFF program. For information on decreasing the field sizes, see Chapter 8, "Using Notebook."

The Shell Administration menus help you enter this information. To display the Shell menu that accesses these Notebooks, press **N** for Using Notebooks Only. This displays the Generate Office Using Notebook menu shown in Figure 12-6.

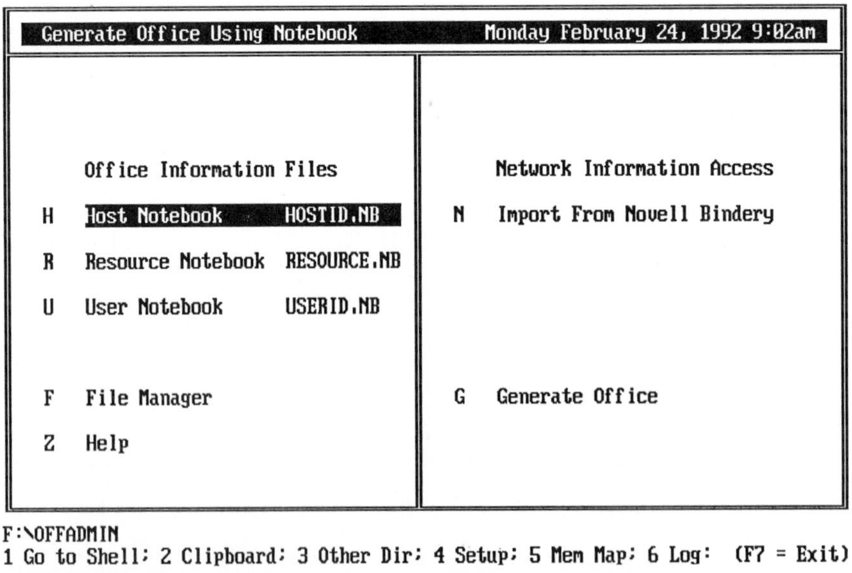

```
┌─────────────────────────────────────────────────────────────────────┐
│ Generate Office Using Notebook        Monday February 24, 1992 9:02am │
├────────────────────────────────────┬──────────────────────────────────┤
│                                    │                                  │
│     Office Information Files       │   Network Information Access      │
│                                    │                                  │
│   H  Host Notebook     HOSTID.NB   │  N   Import From Novell Bindery    │
│                                    │                                  │
│   R  Resource Notebook RESOURCE.NB │                                  │
│                                    │                                  │
│   U  User Notebook     USERID.NB   │                                  │
│                                    │                                  │
│                                    │                                  │
│   F  File Manager                  │  G   Generate Office              │
│                                    │                                  │
│   Z  Help                          │                                  │
│                                    │                                  │
└────────────────────────────────────┴──────────────────────────────────┘
F:\OFFADMIN
1 Go to Shell: 2 Clipboard: 3 Other Dir: 4 Setup: 5 Mem Map: 6 Log:  (F7 = Exit)
```

Figure 12-6.   Generate Office Using Notebook menu

Creating the HOSTID.NB File

You do not have to enter any information in the HOSTID.NB file. The necessary information for your single-host system is automatically inserted in the HOSTID.NB when you enter the information in the Host Definition screen displayed in Figure 12-4. If you want to add hosts later or change the information in the HOSTID.NB, you need to enter the additional host information from the System Administration menu.

Creating the USERID.NB File

The USERID.NB file contains information about all the users on the host. To access USERID.NB, press **U** from the menu. Before you enter Notebook, a prompt asks you if the path and filename are correct. If you have not moved the USERID.NB file since installation, type **Y** for Yes. If you have moved the file, type **N** and enter the correct path. Once you have entered Notebook, press F9 to enter the information for an individual user. Figure 12-7 displays the fields in USERID.NB. If the word "Optional" displays to the right of a field, you don't have to enter any information in that field.

The information you enter in the first three fields—Full Name, Phone, and Department—displays in the List Users screen for Mail and Scheduler. The information displayed in the Notebook List Display is the information that is displayed in the List Users screen for Mail and Scheduler. If you want to change the information that displays in the List Users screen, you can edit the List Display in the USERID.NB file. For example, if you do not want phone numbers displayed in the List Users screen, you can remove the field from the Notebook List Display. For information on editing the List Display, see Chapter 8, "Using Notebook." Of the first three fields, only Full Name is required. The following sections explain the fields in the USERID.NB. After you have entered the information in the fields for each user, press F7 to exit and save USERID.NB.

Full Name

The Full Name field is required. You can enter either the first or last name first. The name you enter first determines the order in which the

```
                    WordPerfect Office User
        Full Name:
            Phone:                                      Optional
       Department:                                      Optional

        Host Name:
      Domain Name:                                      Optional

  Network Login ID:
    Office User ID:                                     Optional
   Unique File ID:     (Max 3 characters)
         Password:                                      Optional

  Group Membership:                                     Optional



  Alias Definition:                                     Optional


Tab Next Field; F2 Search; F7 Exit; F9 Create;         Record 1
```

Figure 12-7.   Fields in the USERID.NB

names are sorted in the List Users screen in Mail and Scheduler. The default field size is 26 characters and can be increased to 32.

Phone

The Phone field is optional. If you list a phone number here, all Mail and Scheduler users will have access to it. If some users do not wish to have a phone number listed, you can selectively enter phone numbers. The default field size is 26 characters.

Department

The Department field is optional. This field is helpful if you need to send a Mail message or schedule an event with a user whose full name you don't remember but whose department you know. This may also help you quickly identify users with similar names if you know what department they are in. The Department field can contain 26 characters.

Host Name

The Host Name field is required. The host name must be the name you entered when you installed the host. Be sure to enter the name exactly as before. The default Host Name field size is 26 characters and can be increased to 32.

Note: If the host name does not match the name you entered on the Host Definition screen, the user will not be installed.

Domain Name

The Domain Name field is optional but is not used on a single-host system.

Network Login ID

The Network Login ID field is required. You must enter the exact Network Login ID of each user. The default field size for the Network Login ID is 26, but it can be increased to 48 if your network uses exceptionally long Login IDs.

Office User ID

The Office User ID field is optional. If your Network Login ID is longer than 32 characters, you must enter an Office User ID. If you enter an Office User ID, each one must be unique for all users on the host. An Office User ID can contain any letters of the alphabet, numbers from 0 through 9, a space, a dollar sign, an underscore (_), and ASCII characters from 128 through 155, 157, from 160 through 167, and 225. For information on the ASCII character, see Appendix B, "ASCII Character Chart."

If your Network Login ID is less than 32 characters and you want the Network Login ID also to be the Office User ID, leave this field blank. Having Login IDs the same as Office User IDs means that users don't need to remember two names. When you generate the Office system using the GENOFF program, you need to indicate whether the Network Login ID equals the Office User ID. For more information on using GENOFF, see the section "Generating Office" later in this chapter. If you do not want the Network Login ID and Office User ID to be the same, you must enter a value in this field.

Unique File ID

Unique File ID field is required. The File ID is one to three characters and must be a valid DOS filename character. ASCII characters 128 and above are not supported, the File ID cannot end with the underscore character (_), and you cannot use a space in the File ID. No two users on the same host can have the same File ID. You can use any valid characters (listed above), but it is usually easiest to use the user's initials. The File ID is attached to many of the Office files. For this reason, it is helpful to use familiar initials for the File ID.

Password

The Password field is optional. If you want to protect the information in each user's Mail and Scheduler programs, you can set a system password on the system level. If you set a password, make sure you set the Password option in the GENOFF options to Yes. If a password is set and passwords are set to Yes in GENOFF, users must enter a password each time they enter the Mail or Scheduler program. If you do not set the Password option to Yes in GENOFF, but have inserted passwords in the USERID.NB, other users who try to access another user's Mail or Scheduler program will be prompted for the password, but the user whose Mail or Scheduler others are trying to access will not. If a user sets an individual password, that password overwrites the system password. A password can be up to 16 characters.

Group Membership

The Group Membership field is optional. Along with individual user information, you can indicate group membership. Creating groups allows you to enter a single group name and send a message or schedule an event for all users in the group. If you have several departments on your Office host, you many want to create a group for each department. You can also create personal groups while in Mail or Scheduler.

    If you enter a group name here, Office creates the group and adds any other users with the same group name to the group when you run GENOFF. These groups become the Global Groups displayed in Mail and Scheduler. If you are entering multiple group names, separate them with a comma; do not use the ENTER key.

Alias Definition

The Alias Definition field is optional for single-host systems.

Creating the USERID.NB with GENUNB

If the host you are installing is on a Novell network, you can use the GENUNB program to extract the information for the USERID.NB from the Novell bindery and insert it into the USERID.NB. This eliminates the need to insert information for each user manually. GENUNB only inserts information in the required fields. GENUB inserts the Network Login ID and also uses this as the Office User ID. GENUNB creates a unique File ID for each user extracted from the bindery. If you want to enter any of the optional information—such as phone, department, password, and group membership—you have to enter this information manually.

Note: You must have supervisory rights to run GENUNB.

To use the GENUNB program from the Generate Office Using Notebook System Administration menu:

1. Press **N** for Import From Novell Bindery.

2. Enter the host name, which must be the name you entered when you installed the host. Be sure you enter the name exactly as before. If the host name does not match the name you entered on the Host Definition screen, the users will not be installed.

3. Type **Y** if the correct path to the USERID.NB is displayed. Type **N** if the correct path is not displayed, and then enter the correct path.

4. Enter a letter for a network drive mapped to the host file server.

At this point, GENUNB extracts the information from the Novell bindery and inserts it into the USERID.NB file. As GENUNB is extracting the information, it briefly displays the name of the user currently being extracted.

If you run GENUNB and information already exists in the USER-ID.NB, GENUNB appends the information for the new users to the existing information in the USERID.NB file. If a user is not found in the bindery and there is a record for him or her in the USERID.NB, this user will be deleted.

GENUNB Startup Options

GENUNB has several startup options you can use to specify certain conditions when running GENUNB. You can enter these options from the DOS command line or on the Program Information screen for the Import From Novell Bindery Shell menu option. To run GENUNB from the command line:

1. Change to the Office Administration directory.

2. Type **GENUNB** *pathname x* where *pathname* is the path to the USERID.NB and *x* is the startup option you want to use.

Here is a list of all GENUNB startup options:

/A	This lists all of the defined hosts as options for running GENUNB.
/B	This allows GENUNB to be run from a batch file.
/G	This deletes all groups entered in USERID.NB, creates groups from those listed in the bindery, and adds designated users to the groups.
/H	This displays the GENUNB help screen, which lists all the available startup options.
/HN-*name*	This lets you specify the host name to insert for new users when using GENUNB in a batch file.
/R	This rebuilds the USERID.NB file from the USERID.FIL file. If users are in the USERID .FIL file but not in the USERID.NB file, this option adds them to the USERID.NB file.
	If you accidentally delete your USERID .NB, this option is extremely useful for restoring the information. This will only work for a Novell network.

Creating the RESOURCE.NB File

If you are scheduling resources such as computers, projectors, and conference rooms with Scheduler, you need to edit the RESOURCE.NB file and create the resources. Remember, a resource is anything other than a user that will be included in a scheduled event.

To access the RESOURCE.NB file, press **R** from the Generate Office Using Notebook menu. Before you enter Notebook, a prompt asks you if the path and filename are correct. If you have not moved RE-SOURCE.NB since installation, type **Y** for Yes. If you have moved the file, type **N** and enter the correct path.

The information displayed in the Notebook List Display—Description, Resource ID, Host Name, and Owner—is what is displayed in the List Resources screen for Scheduler. If you want to change what information displays or the order in which the information displays in the List Resources screen, you can edit the List Display in RESOURCE.NB. For information on editing the List Display, see Chapter 8, "Using Notebook."

Once you have entered Notebook, press F9 to enter the information for an individual resource. Figure 12-8 displays the fields in the RESOURCE.NB. The RESOURCE.NB file is very similar to the USER-ID.NB file. If the word "Optional" displays to the right of a field, you don't have to enter any information in that field.

The following sections explain the fields in the RESOURCE.NB file. After you have entered the information in the fields for each resource, press F7 to exit and save RESOURCE.NB.

```
                         WordPerfect Office Resource

    Resource Description:

              Host Name:
            Domain Name:                                      Optional

            Resource ID:
        Owner's User ID:
         Unique File ID:    (Max 3 characters)
               Password:                                      Optional

       Group Membership:                                      Optional




        Alias Definition:                                     Optional




  Tab Next Field; F2 Search; F7 Exit; F9 Create;             Record 1
```

Figure 12-8.   Fields in the RESOURCE.NB

Resource Description

The first field, Resource Description, is required. You should enter an exact description of the resource. The more information you enter for the description, the easier it is for users to know exactly what they need to schedule. For example, if the resource is a conference room, enter

Conference Room, 1st floor (Capacity 25)

The description you enter here displays in the List Resources screen in Scheduler. You can change the description in RESOURCE.NB without affecting any items that have already been scheduled. The default field size for the Resource Description field is 26 characters, but you can increase it to 32.

Host Name

The Host Name field is required. The host name must be the name you entered when you installed the host. Be sure to enter the name exactly as before. If the host name does not match the name you entered on the Host Definition screen, the resource will not be installed. The default Host Name field size is 26 and can be increased to 32.

Domain Name

The Domain Name is an optional field but is not used on a single-host system.

Resource ID

You must assign a unique Resource ID to each resource. A Resource ID can contain any letters of the alphabet, numbers from 0 through 9, a space, a dollar sign, an underscore (_), and ASCII characters from 128 through 155, 157, from 160 through 167, and 225. For information on the ASCII character, see Appendix B, "ASCII Character Chart." The default Resource ID field size is 26 and may be increased to 32.

Owner's User ID

A resource also needs an owner. The owner's User ID field is required. The owner accepts and rejects events for which a resource is scheduled. Enter the owner's User ID. If you are using Network Login IDs as Office User IDs, enter the owner's Login ID. After entering an owner's User ID, make sure to inform the user that they own that resource.

Unique File ID

Unique File ID is a required field. The File ID is one to three characters and must be a valid DOS filename character. ASCII characters 128 and above are not supported, the File ID cannot end with the underscore character (_), and you cannot use a space in the File ID. Unique means that no two resources on the same host can have the same File ID. You can use any valid characters (listed above), but it is usually easiest to use characters from the resource description. The File ID is attached to many of the Office files. For this reason, it is helpful to use familiar initials for the File ID.

Password

The Password field is optional. If you want to protect the schedule of a resource, you can set a password so that only those who know the password can retrieve the schedule of the resource. If you set a password, make sure you set the Password option in the GENOFF options to Yes. If a password is set and passwords are set to Yes in GENOFF, resource owners must enter a password each time they enter the Mail or Scheduler program. If you do not set the Password option to Yes in GENOFF, but have inserted passwords in the RESOURCE.NB, other users will be prompted for the password, but the owner will not. If the resource owner sets an individual password for the resource, that password overwrites the system password. A password can be up to 16 characters.

Group Membership

The Group Membership field is optional. You can enter group membership if you want several resources to form a Scheduler group. You can then schedule this group for events without having to type the individual resource names. This might be helpful if you have conferences that require the use of a room, a computer, and a projector. They could comprise a group. If you enter a group name here, Office creates the group and adds any other resources that have the same group name to the group when you run GENOFF. These groups become the Global Resource Groups displayed in Scheduler. Users can also create personal resource groups while in Scheduler. If you are entering multiple group names, separate the group names with a comma; do not use the ENTER key.

Alias

The Alias field is optional on a single-host system.

Generating Office

After you have entered all the information in the USERID.NB and RESOURCE.NB files, you are ready to run the Generate Office program, referred to as GENOFF. GENOFF first builds the host directory from the host information you entered during the installation process. After creating the host directory, GENOFF takes the information from HOSTID.NB, USERID.NB, and RESOURCE.NB and creates the information files needed to run Office. These information files are stored in the host directory. The Notebook files remain in the System Administration directory for maximum security.

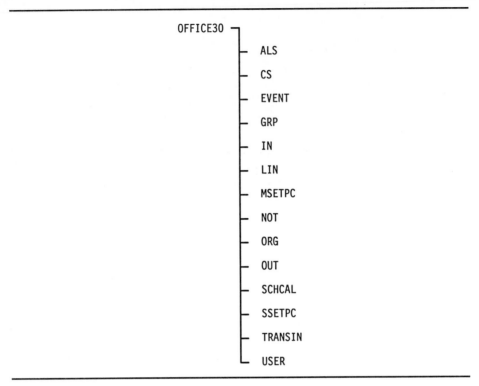

Figure 12-9. Host directory structure

Host Directory Structure

It is helpful to understand the directory structure of a host when installing and using Office. A host directory contains 14 subdirectories, shown in Figure 12-9. These directories can be grouped in the following categories:

Mail Directories

IN	User's IN Files for Mail
OUT	User's OUT files for Mail
LIN	Contains 16 subdirectories where all message files created by Mail are kept
MSETPC	Default location of set files for Mail

Scheduler Directories

USER	User's REQUESTED file for Scheduler
ORG	User's ORGANIZER files for Scheduler
EVENT	Contains all Event files created by Scheduler
SSETPC	Default location of set files for Scheduler
SCHCAL	Scheduler/Appointment Calendar communication files

Shared Directories

GRP	Contains all Group files defined in the USERID.NB and RESOURCE.NB (for Mail and Scheduler)
ALS	System ALIAS files. Named by Unique File ID in the USERID.NB (for Mail and Scheduler)

Notify Directory

NOT	System Notification files. Used when File Polling is set to Y with GENOFF

There are two other directories, TRANSIN and CS. These are only used by the WordPerfect Connections software and do not apply to a single-host system. For information on the WordPerfect Connections package, see Chapter 14, "Using Office Connections." By default, all of these directories are hidden, with the exception of GRP, MSETPC, and SSETPC. Hiding these directories provides maximum security and prevents accidental destruction of the Mail and Scheduler system.

Figure 12-10 further illustrates exactly how these directories are used when you send a Mail message. Figure 12-11 shows how the directories are used when you schedule an event.

Running GENOFF

To run the GENOFF program:

1. Press **G** for Generate Office from the Generate Office Using Notebook menu. The following menu appears:

```
Generate Office

    1 - Generate Using Current Setup Options

    2 - Generate Changing Setup Options

    3 - View Log of Last Generation
```

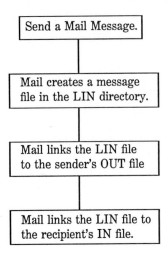

Figure 12-10. Mail message flow chart

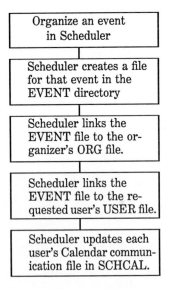

Figure 12-11. Scheduled event flow chart

2. Press **1** for Generate Using Current Setup Options. If this is the first time you have run GENOFF, you will be prompted to input the desired options. If you have already run GENOFF and wish to change the options, press **2** for Generate Changing Setup Options.

3. A directory prompt displays at the bottom of the screen so you can verify that GENOFF is using the correct Notebook files. Type **Y** if the directory is correct, or type **N** and enter the correct directory. GENOFF then builds HOSTID.FIL. The status information displays in the lower window of the screen. If this is the first time you have run GENOFF, a prompt asks you if the host should be created. Type **Y** to create the host.

4. After the HOSTID.FIL is built, GENOFF displays the available GENOFF options, as shown in Figure 12-12. At this point, set the desired options.

Very detailed help screens display on the right-hand side of the screen indicating the function of each option. For more information on the GENOFF options, see the following section, "GENOFF Options."

5. After you have set the options, press **F7** to begin GENOFF.

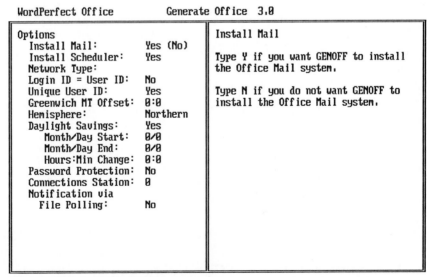

```
WordPerfect Office          Generate Office  3.0

┌─────────────────────────────────┬───────────────────────────────┐
│ Options                         │ Install Mail                  │
│   Install Mail:        Yes (No) │                               │
│   Install Scheduler:   Yes      │ Type Y if you want GENOFF to  │
│   Network Type:                 │ install the Office Mail system.│
│   Login ID = User ID:  No       │                               │
│   Unique User ID:      Yes      │ Type N if you do not want     │
│   Greenwich MT Offset: 0:0      │ GENOFF to install the Office  │
│   Hemisphere:          Northern │ Mail system.                  │
│   Daylight Savings:    Yes      │                               │
│     Month/Day Start:   0/0      │                               │
│     Month/Day End:     0/0      │                               │
│     Hours:Min Change:  0:0      │                               │
│   Password Protection: No       │                               │
│   Connections Station: 0        │                               │
│   Notification via              │                               │
│     File Polling:      No       │                               │
│                                 │                               │
│                                 │                               │
└─────────────────────────────────┴───────────────────────────────┘
Tab Next Option; Shift-Tab Previous Option;
```

Figure 12-12.   GENOFF options

As GENOFF processes the information in the Notebook files, it displays status messages in the bottom window of the screen. When GENOFF finishes creating the information files, a message either indicates any errors that may have occurred, or indicates that the process was completed successfully.

If errors occurred, you can view a log file that indicates exactly what occurred while GENOFF was processing. To access the log file, press **G** for Generate Office from the Generate Office Using Notebook menu and then press **3** for View Log of Last Generation. The GENOFF log file will be retrieved into Editor and you can search for and view any errors that occurred during the generation process. For information on GENOFF error messages and possible solutions, see the section "GENOFF Error Messages" later in this chapter. After viewing the errors, press F7 twice to return to the Generate Office Using Notebook Shell menu.

After you have run GENOFF successfully, the Office system is installed.

GENOFF Options

The first time you run GENOFF, you must specify the options you want GENOFF to use. If you want to change these options, you can choose **G** for Generate Office from the Generate Office Using Notebook menu, and then press **2** for Generate Changing Setup Options.

Install Mail   Type **Y** if you want to create the directories necessary to run the Mail program. Type **N** if you do not want to create these directories.

Install Scheduler   Type **Y** if you want to create the directories necessary to run the Scheduler program. Type **N** if you do not want to create these directories.

Network Type   Indicate the number displayed on the right-hand side of the screen that corresponds to your network type. If your network type is not listed, type **O** for Other.

Login ID = User ID   If you want your Network Login ID to be used as your Office User ID, type **Y** for Yes. If you set this option to Yes, GENOFF runs slightly faster. If you set this option to Yes, and you have entered Office User IDs in the USERID.NB file, GENOFF ignores the Office User IDs.

If you type **N** for Login ID = User ID, you must have an Office User ID for each user in the USERID.NB file.

Note: If you are using Banyan StreetTalk, this option must be set to No. Banyan StreetTalk names include the @ sign, which is not a legal character in User IDs. The StreetTalk name should be entered as the User Login ID in the USERID.NB file. You should enter an optional name for the Office User ID field in the USERID.NB.

Unique User ID   On a single-host system, this option must be set to Yes.

Greenwich MT Offset, Hemisphere, Daylight Savings   These three options are only necessary if you are going to use a wide area network. These options allow you to adjust the times of Mail and Scheduler items according to the recipient's local time. For a single-host system, you can enter the correct information if you want, but this is not necessary.

Password Protection   The Password Protection option lets you specify whether Mail and Scheduler should access a system-level password. If Password Protection is set to Yes and you have entered a password for each user in the USERID.NB, users will be prompted for a password when starting Mail or Scheduler. If a user tries to retrieve another user's Mail or Scheduler, she or he will have to enter the password. If you want someone to access another person's Mail or Scheduler, you should set passwords for the users they want to access and set passwords to Yes.

If Password Protection is set to Yes, but no passwords have been entered in the USERID.NB file, any user can access any other user's Mail and Scheduler. This is the lowest level of security.

If Password Protection is set to No and passwords have not been assigned within the individual user's Mail or Scheduler, no other user can access another user's Mail or Scheduler. This is the highest level of security.

If Password Protection is set to No and individual passwords have been assigned by each user, only users who know the password can access another user's Mail or Scheduler. This is another way that users can access other people's Mail and Scheduler.

If Password Protection is set to No and passwords have been added to USERID.NB, the user does not have to enter a password, but other users who try and access her or his Mail and Scheduler do have to enter a password. This option lets you set passwords for only selected users.

Connection Station   The Connection Station option only applies to multiple-host systems. For a single-host system, this option must be set to 0.

Notification via File Polling   The final GENOFF option lets you choose which method of notification to use. With File Polling, Notify stores notification messages in a file. This file is periodically polled and the notification messages are delivered. With the standard method of notification, a network parameter is set and Notify checks the network for information for that user and then notifies the user. If you are not running NETBIOS, you must set this option to Yes if you want to receive notification of Mail and Scheduler items. If your network does use NETBIOS, you can set this option to Yes if you want to guarantee notification of all Mail and Scheduler items. With File Polling set to Yes, you will receive notification of every Mail and Scheduler item as soon as you log onto the network. For example, if you have been away on vacation for a week, as soon as you log onto the network you are notified of every Mail and Scheduler item that you received while you were gone. In addition, with File Polling you don't lose notification messages that are sent at approximately the same time.

GENOFF Startup Options

GENOFF has several startup options that you can use to specify certain conditions when running GENOFF. If you are running GENOFF from the System Administration menu, you should enter these startup options on the Shell Program Information screen for the Generate Office menu item. You will rarely need to use these options if you are using the System Administration menus provided. If necessary, you can also run GENOFF from the DOS command line. To run GENOFF from the DOS command line:

1. Change to the Office Administration directory.

2. Type **GENOFF/x**, where *x* is the startup option you want to use.

Here is a list of all GENOFF startup options:

/B-*pathname*	Use this option if you are running GENOFF from a batch file. The *pathname* indicates the path to the Notebook files.
/H	This tells GENOFF to display the help screen, which lists all the available startup options. This option can only be used from the DOS command line.
/P	With /P, only the HOSTID.FIL file is generated. This option is useful if you are not using the System Administration menus and you need to run GENUNB to extract the user information from the Novell bindery. Before GENUNB will run, a HOSTID.FIL file must exist.
/S	This displays the GENOFF Setup screen, which allows you to make any necessary changes.
/V-Y	This makes all directories visible—that is, unhides all host directories. By default, only the GRP, MSETPC, and SSETPC directories are not hidden. This option is useful if your network does not support hidden directories. It may also be useful if you need to do extensive troubleshooting.

/V-N   This is the default. It makes the GRP,
                             MSETPC, and SSETPC directories visible
                             and hides the other host directories. In-
                             creases network security and prevents acci-
                             dental damage to the host directories. Use
                             this option to rehide files after using the /V-Y
                             option.

/VF-Y   This causes GENOFF to unhide any newly
                             created file. Does not change the status of
                             existing files. This option is useful for trouble-
                             shooting.

GENOFF Error Messages

While running GENOFF or viewing the GENOFF log, you may see
specific error messages. These error messages appear in a box, followed
by a more specific error description. There are two levels of severity for
these error messages. The first section lists the most severe error
messages along with solutions. The second section lists errors that may
occur, but after they occur you can still run the Office programs.

High Priority Errors

Message:

> CANNOT RENAME .FIL FILE
> FILE MOVED TO *.NB DIRECTORY

This message occurs when GENOFF cannot replace the old USERID-
.FIL or HOSTID.FIL with the newly created file. This usually occurs
when a user is accessing the information contained in one of these files.
For example, a user may be using the List Users screen in Mail or
Scheduler. If GENOFF cannot replace the file after several attempts, it
saves the file in the System Administration directory. The files are saved
under the names HOST_*xxx*.FIL and/or USER_*xxx*.FIL, where *xxx*
is the Host ID for that host. After these files are saved, you can copy
them to your Office program directory.

Message:

SEVERE ERROR- CANNOT CONTINUE

There are four sets of circumstances that may cause this error:

• The "Could NOT Open/Find File" message occurs when GENOFF cannot find or open a file it needs to generate Office. This error usually occurs when you enter the incorrect path to the *.NB files upon starting GENOFF. It may also occur if the *.NB files have been deleted or you do not have rights to the directory in which they are stored. Try running GENOFF again and enter the correct path to the *.NB files. Also check your rights to the directory in which these files are stored.

• The "*.NB Corrupted" message occurs when fields in the Notebook files do not match what GENOFF expects. For example, if you delete or rename a mandatory field in one of the Notebook files, you will need to rename the fields to the original name and then run the Install program. This may also occur if are trying to use your Office 2.0 Notebook files to run GENOFF with instead of your 3.0 files. In addition, this error may occur if the Notebook files are actually corrupted. If this is the case, try retrieving the file into Notebook and changing the text format. For more information on fixing corrupted Notebook files, see Chapter 8, "Using Notebook."

• The "Illegal NB File Format" message indicates that one of the Notebook files is not in 4.2 format. GENOFF only recognizes Notebook files in this format. To correct the problem, retrieve the correct Notebook file and change the file format to 4.2.

• The "Insufficient File Handles" message indicates that GENOFF could not create the necessary temporary files to run the program. Increase the FILES command in your CONFIG.SYS file to 40. You can run the SETMEUP program to do this automatically.

Message:

FIELD/RECORD IS NOT UNIQUE
CANNOT BUILD OUTPUT FILE

This message occurs if you enter duplicate information in fields that require uniqueness within the host. The message lists the Notebook file, the field, and the field contents where the error occurs. GENOFF will not finish if it encounters this error. To correct the problem, edit the necessary field or fields that are not unique and rerun GENOFF.

Secondary GENOFF Error Messages

Message:

> BAD RECORD FOUND-
> DROPPED

This message occurs under two circumstances:

- The "Illegal Character in File ID" message indicates there is an illegal DOS filename character in the File ID field of one of the users, resources, or hosts. This user, resource, or host is invalid until you edit the Notebook, insert a valid character in the record containing the error, and rerun GENOFF.

- The "Illegal Character in User ID" or "Resource ID Field" message tells you there is an illegal character in the Office User ID, Resource ID, or owner's User ID filed in the corresponding Notebook file. Retrieve the file, insert a valid character, and rerun GENOFF.

Message:

> RESOURCE OWNER NOT VALID
> CANNOT BUILD RESOURCE.FIL

This error message indicates that you have entered an invalid owner name in the RESOURCE.NB file. In other words, the name you entered for the owner of a resource cannot be found in the USERID.NB. Make sure the name is spelled correctly and that you have entered it into the USERID.NB. Then run GENOFF again.

Updating Users with *SETMEUP*

Included with Office 3.0 is a program called SETMEUP. This program updates each user's system so she or he can run the Office programs. SETMEUP checks the AUTOEXEC.BAT and CONFIG.SYS files to make sure the specific commands needed to run Office are present. Before the SETMEUP program modifies the AUTOEXEC.BAT or CONFIG.SYS file, it makes backup copies of the users' original files. SETMEUP names the backup files AUTOEXEC.OLD and CONFIG-SYS.OLD.

SETMEUP checks the AUTOEXEC.BAT file to see if the Office 3.0 directory is in the path statement. If it is not found, SETMEUP asks the user if he or she wants to add it to the current path command. SETMEUP also checks for the NOTIFY command. The NOTIFY command allows notification of Mail and Scheduler items. If the command is not found, SETMEUP asks the user if he or she wants to add it to their AUTOEXEC.BAT file. SETMEUP then checks for the CL/I command, which installs Appointment Calendar alarms. If CL/I is not found, SET-MEUP asks the user if he or she wants to add it to his or her AUTOEXEC.BAT file. Finally, SETMEUP checks the AUTOEXEC-.BAT file for the command to start Shell automatically when the user turns on her or his computer. If the command to start Shell is not found, SETMEUP asks the user if she or he wants to add it to the AUTO-EXEC.BAT file.

SETMEUP also checks for specific commands in the CONFIG.SYS file. First it checks whether the FILES command is equal to or greater than 40. If there is no FILES command in the CONFIG.SYS file, SETMEUP automatically adds FILES=40. If a FILES command exists but is less than 40, SETMEUP automatically inserts a new FILES command at the end of the CONFIG.SYS file. (When two identical commands exist in a CONFIG.SYS file, only the last command is in effect.) After checking the FILES command, SETMEUP asks you if you want to install Repeat Performance and add the necessary commands to the CONFIG.SYS file. If you answer Yes to install Repeat Performance, the installation program for Repeat Performance is started and you can enter the desired options. For information on Repeat Performance, see Chapter 11, "Using Notify, Repeat Performance, and TSR Manager."

The SETMEUP program should be run on each user's machine and can be found in the Office 3.0 program directory. The system administrator can run the program on each machine or have each user run the program on her or his individual computer.

Note: If you want each user to run SETMEUP, Appendix A, "LAN User Installation" includes the necessary commands.

To run the SETMEUP program:

1. Change to the Office 3.0 program directory.

2. Enter **SETMEUP** on the DOS command line.

3. Follow the on-screen prompts.

SETMEUP is a useful tool that helps set up individual users on the network.

Creating an Office Environment File

The Office environment file sets certain specifications for all Office users on the network. The Office environment file is like a global setup file for all users. Each time a user enters an Office program, the environment file is read. Any startup options that pertain to that program are used. Startup options that are not used by the program are ignored.

One of the options that would be helpful in the environment file is /NT-x, where x represents your network type. With this option specified, a user will not be prompted for a network type if the USERID.FIL file cannot be found. Another useful option is /PS-*directory*. This option redirects user's setup files to the directory specified. You can create a central directory on the network where all users' setup files are stored and specify that directory with this option. This prevents you from having user setup files in several places, which often causes problems. You could also list a directory on a user's hard drive for the setup files. If you list a directory on the hard drive, such as C:\, the directory must exist for all users. Another useful option in the environment file is /D-*directory*; this option redirects users' temporary files. As with the

/PS option, you can enter a central network drive for all users' temporary files or a directory on a user's hard drive. If you use the /PS and /D options, you can limit the rights the users need in the Office program directory. With these options specified, users only need rights to read, open, and search files and directories.

To create the environment file:

1. Start Editor.

2. Enter the options you want contained in the environment file. You can list the options on a single line separated by a space, or you can list each option on its own line.

3. Press F7.

4. Type **Y** to save the file.

5. Enter the path to the Office program directory followed by **OF{OF}.ENV** for the filename.

6. Type **Y** to exit Editor.

Each time an Office program is started, the program will read the environment file. If a user implements one of the options listed in the environment file on a personal system, the user's options override the options set in the environment file. The environment file is useful for system administrators who want to centralize and standardize several of the options available in Office.

Note: To ensure that no one modifies the environment file, assign a read-only status to the file.

Creating a Default Shell Menu

It is often helpful for all users to start with a standardized Shell menu. If the Shell menu that comes with Office (SHELL.NEW) does not fit your users' needs, you can modify the menu. To modify the SHELL-.NEW menu:

1. From the Office program directory prompt, type **shell**. The default Shell menu appears.

2. Modify the menu to meet your needs. For information on adding, deleting, or editing Shell menu items, see Chapter 10, "Using Shell."

3. Press F7 to exit the Shell menu.

Once you exit the Shell menu for the first time, a new Shell menu file is created. The file is named *XXX*SHELL.FIL, where *XXX* is your File ID. For all users to be able to access this modified Shell menu, you need to rename it SHELL.NEW. The first time a user starts Shell, Shell looks for the SHELL.NEW file. The Shell file with your initials needs to be renamed SHELL.NEW so all users can access this modified menu. To rename the modified Shell menu:

1. Type **fm** at the Shell program directory prompt.

2. Highlight the file named *XXX*SHELL.FIL.

3. Press **3** or **M** for Move/Rename.

4. Enter **SHELL.NEW** for the filename.

5. Press F7 to exit File Manager.

Note: If you want to have a copy of the default Shell menu that is shipped with Office 3.0, you should rename the SHELL.NEW file before you rename your modified Shell menu file to SHELL.NEW.

Once the file is renamed, the modified Shell menu will appear the first time a user starts Shell. Users can then customize their own Shell menus if they want. As soon as you exit Shell for the first time, a *XXX*SHELL.FIL file is created for you.

Single-Host Installation Overview

To aid you in future installation and as an overview of this chapter, these are the general steps for installing a single-host system:

1. Use the Install program to copy the Office program and System Administration files to the selected directory on the network.

2. After the files are copied, enter the Host Definition information.

3. Use the System Administration menus to enter user and resource information in the USERID.NB and RESOURCE.NB Notebook files.

4. Run the GENOFF program to create the corresponding information files from the USERID.NB, RESOURCE.NB, and HOST-ID.NB files.

5. Run the SETMEUP program on each user's computer.

6. Create an Office environment file.

Converting from Office 2.0 to Office 3.0

Each package of WordPerfect Office 3.0 includes an installation program (Install) to simplify the update from Office 2.0 to 3.0. The Install program for Office LAN creates an Office 3.0 directory and an administration directory, installs the Office files, and defines the Office host.

Note: Before converting Office 2.0, create a backup copy of your Office 2.0 files and directories. This ensures that you have a working copy of your system if the conversion does not work properly.

Installing the Office Files

The Office LAN files are in compressed format. For this reason, you must use the Install program to install Office 3.0. To run the Install program, insert the floppy disk labeled Office LAN 1 into a floppy drive. Switch to that drive by entering the drive letter followed by a colon, usually **a:**, and then type **install** and press ENTER. Your monitor displays the title screen with an option to continue or exit. Type **Y** to proceed; you should see a menu listing the different installation options. Press **3** for Update from Office 2.0.

After you select the desired installation type, an information screen displays. This screen explains the steps that will be taken during the installation. You'll see the screen shown in Figure 12-13 when converting from 2.0 to 3.0. After the information screen displays, type **Y** to continue.

You are asked to enter the source directory (where the files should be installed from) as well as the target directories (where you want the files installed).

The Program File Directory is where all of the Office programs and files needed to run Office 3.0 are stored. Do not use your Office 2.0 directories for the target directories. By default, Install lists *F*:\OFFICE30 as the Program File Directory where *F* is the first available network drive. If the directory listed for Program File Directory does not exist, Install will create it. Users need all rights to this

---

```
Update from Office 2.0
There are three steps to the Update from Office 2.0 process:

  Step 1: Directory Selection
  You will be prompted for the drive letters and pathnames of two
  directories:  a program file directory and a system administration file
  directory.  Use two new directories for the program and system
  administration files.  DO NOT use your Office 2.0 directories.

  Step 2: File Installation
  After you specify the Office directory, Update from Office 2.0 displays
  the name and a brief description of each Office file group and asks if
  you want that file group installed.

  Step 3: Mail/Scheduler System Conversion
  After the files are installed, you are asked if you want to use the System
  Administration Shell menu, which will help you convert your Office 2.0
  Mail/Scheduler system to an Office 3.0 Mail/Scheduler system.




Do you want to continue with this selection? Yes  (No)
```

Figure 12-13.   Conversion information screen

directory, except supervisory rights. If you direct the user's temporary files and setup files to a hard drive or personal network drive, you can restrict the rights to this directory. See "Startup Options" in the various program chapters for information on the specific startup options. Restricting rights in the program directory increases the security on your network.

The Office Admin File Directory stores all the files necessary to build an Office host. Only the system administrator should have rights to this directory. By default, Install lists *F*:\OFFADMIN as the Office Admin File Directory where *F* is the first available network drive. If the directory listed for Office Admin File Directory does not exist, Install will create it.

Once you enter the correct directories, press 4 to begin the actual installation. Install then prompts you to input your customer registration number. If you enter your registration number here, all the Office programs will display the registration number on the main help screens. Users can then easily locate the registration number when working with the WordPerfect customer support department. Entering this number is optional, and Install continues when you press ENTER.

If you enter an incorrect registration number or want to add a number later, you can run the Install program again. If you are only running Install to add the registration number, select the Custom Install option. The correct directory entries will be listed and you can continue to the screen that asks for the registration number. After entering the correct registration number, type **N** for No at all the prompts that ask if you want to install the specified file groups. The file that is created when you enter a registration number is called OF{OF}US.LCN.

After you enter the registration number or press ENTER, Install begins copying files. The files on the Office disks are in a compressed format to conserve disk space. This makes it impossible to run any program from the Office disks without first running Install to restore the files to their normal format. During the installation process, a prompt asks if you want to install the specified file group and displays a brief description of the file group. Type **Y** if you want to install the files or **N** if you do not want to install them. As the files are copied, a message at the bottom of the screen indicates which file is being installed and to which directory.

After the selected files are installed, Install checks for any existing Office 2.0 system files that exist in directories in the path. If a system

file exists—such as SHELL.FIL, CALENDAR.FIL, or NOTE-
BOOK.SYS—Install displays a prompt similar to this one:

SHELL.FIL was found in F:\OFFICE20
Do you want to convert this file as part of the update
procedure? Yes (No)

If you type **Y** for Yes, the file will be copied to the Office 3.0 directory. If
you type **N** for No, Office 3.0 will create a new system file when needed.
Install continues to ask if you want to convert these files until it finds all
the 2.0 system files in the directories in your path.

Note: Individual user's Shell, Calendar, and setup files will not be
converted. If your users want to use these files in 3.0, you need to copy
them from the 2.0 directory or directories into the appropriate 3.0
directory or directories.

Defining the Office Host for Conversion

After the files are copied to the correct directories, Office displays the
Office LAN 3.0 Host Definition screen shown in Figure 12-14. The
information you enter on the Host Definition screen is used to create
HOSTID.NB. In Office 2.0, there was no HOSTID.NB file so there is no
host information to convert. The information entered here will create a
new HOSTID.NB to be used with Office 3.0. This is one of the three
information files needed before the Office system can function.

This screen displays the Host Directory Path followed by six op-
tions. The Host Directory Path is the directory you indicated as the
Program Files Directory. As mentioned, a host is a set of Mail and
Scheduler directories. For information on the exact structure of an
Office host, see the section "Host Directory Structure" earlier in this
chapter.

```
Office LAN 3.0 Host Definition

    Host Directory Path: F:\OFFICE30\

1 - Host Name:

2 - Host File ID:

3 - Administrator Name:

4 - Administrator Phone:

5 - Display Current Host Names

6 - Continue

              ┌─────────────────────────────────────────────────┐
              │ NOTE: Select an option and enter the requested host │
              │       information.  If you have a multiple-host      │
              │       system already in place and need to see what   │
              │       host names are currently being used, select    │
              │       option 5.  When you have entered all the host  │
              │       information, select option 6 to continue.      │
              └─────────────────────────────────────────────────┘

Selection: 1                                            (F7 Exit)
```

Figure 12-14.   Office LAN 3.0 Host Definition screen

       The only options you must fill out on the Host Definition menu are 1 and 2. Option 1, Host Name, is the name that identifies the host, and can be no longer than 26 characters including spaces. The host name can contain any letters of the alphabet, numbers from 0 through 9, a space, a dollar sign, an underscore (_), and ASCII characters from 128 through 155, 157, from 160 through 167, and 225. For information on the ASCII characters, see Appendix B, "ASCII Character Chart." The host name is necessary on both single- and multiple-host systems. The host name appears before the user's name in the Mail and Scheduler headers, as shown here:

```
 WP Mail - HOST1:DEVINR                Monday, February 24, 1992  9:00 am
```

The second option, Host File ID, is an identification code of from one to three characters. The Host File ID is used to create directories and files and can only contain valid DOS filename characters. ASCII characters 128 and above are not supported, and you cannot have the underscore character as the last value in the Host File ID. If you are installing multiple hosts, the host name and File ID should be unique.

The Administrator Name (option 3) and the Administrator Phone (option 4) are optional. Enter this information if you want your users to have direct access to you for Office problems and complications. This information is displayed on the List Hosts screen in the Mail and Scheduler programs.

If you are installing several hosts, you can display current host names with option 5. This option lists the names of the hosts you have already defined in the HOSTID.NB file so you do not duplicate the names.

System Administration Menus for Conversion

After filling in the necessary information in the Host Definition screen, you can display the System Administration Shell menu. Type **Y** to display the menu shown in Figure 12-15. The system administration menus help you convert the Office 2.0 information files for an Office host. These menus also give you options for converting your Mail and Scheduler systems. The options available on the system administration menus all use predefined Shell and Editor macros to access the information listed on the Shell menu. If you ever need to access the system administration menus to change options after installing Office, change to the Office administration directory and type **offadmin**. OFFADMIN is a batch file that loads the System Administration Shell menus and increases the work space so the macros will execute properly.

To access the Convert menu from the main System Administrator's menu, press **A** for Convert Office 2.0 to 3.0. The menu shown in Figure 12-16 appears and displays the options for converting.

```
┌──────────────────────────────────────────────────────────────────────┐
│ Office System Administration            Monday February 24, 1992 9:01am│
│ ┌────────────────────────────────────┬───────────────────────────────┐│
│ │                                     │                               ││
│ │                                     │                               ││
│ │       Generate/Update Office        │                               ││
│ │  D  Using DataPerfect Database      │   A   Convert Office 2.0 to 3.0││
│ │                                     │                               ││
│ │  N  Using Notebooks Only            │                               ││
│ │                                     │                               ││
│ │                                     │                               ││
│ │                                     │                               ││
│ │  C  Check Office                    │                               ││
│ │                                     │                               ││
│ │                                     │                               ││
│ └────────────────────────────────────┴───────────────────────────────┘│
└──────────────────────────────────────────────────────────────────────┘
F:\OFFADMIN
1 Go to DOS; 2 Clipboard; 3 Other Dir; 4 Setup; 5 Mem Map; 6 Log:   (F7 = Exit)
```

Figure 12-15.   Main Office System Administration menu

```
┌──────────────────────────────────────────────────────────────────────┐
│ Convert Office 2.0 to 3.0               Monday February 24, 1992 9:13am│
│ ┌────────────────────────────────────┬───────────────────────────────┐│
│ │                                     │                               ││
│ │     Convert Information Files       │     Convert Office System     ││
│ │  R  Convert Resources   RESOURCE.NB │   E   Estimate Resources Required││
│ │                                     │                               ││
│ │  U  Convert Users       USERID.NB   │   M   Convert Mail 2.0 to 3.0 ││
│ │                                     │                               ││
│ │                                     │   S   Convert Scheduler 2.0 to 3.0││
│ │                                     │                               ││
│ │                                     │   V   View Logs of Conversions││
│ │                                     │                               ││
│ │  G  Generate Office                 │                               ││
│ │                                     │                               ││
│ │                                     │                               ││
│ └────────────────────────────────────┴───────────────────────────────┘│
└──────────────────────────────────────────────────────────────────────┘
F:\OFFADMIN
1 Go to Shell; 2 Clipboard; 3 Other Dir; 4 Setup; 5 Mem Map; 6 Log:  (F7 = Exit)
```

Figure 12-16.   Convert Office 2.0 to 3.0 menu

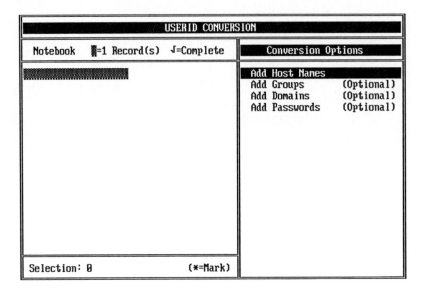

Figure 12-17.   USERID Conversion screen

Converting User Information

The first step in converting is to change the information in the 2.0
USERID.NB file to 3.0 format. To convert the Notebook files:

1. Press **U** for Convert Users.

2. Enter the path to the Office 3.0 USERID.NB file. A brief message indicates that the header information is being checked.

3. Enter the path to the Office 2.0 USERID.NB directory. The
screen shown in Figure 12-17 appears.

4. The right side of the screen lists the conversion options available.
Select the options you want to use in the conversion by marking
them with an asterisk. The first option is mandatory.

• *Add Host Names*   In Office 3.0, Add Host Names is a required field in the USERID.NB. You must add a host name to convert the 2.0 users. The host name must be the name you entered in the Host Definition screen during installation. As the users are converted, the host name you enter here is inserted into the USERID.NB file. As soon as you begin the conversion process, you will be prompted for the host name.

• *Add Groups*   If you want to add global groups, mark the Add Groups option. Before the conversion occurs you are prompted to enter the name of the group or groups you want to create. As each user is converted, a list of group names appears, as shown in Figure 12-18. You can mark the group names in which you want to include the user. Existing 2.0 groups also display, with the word "Current" to the right of the group name.

• *Add Domains*   Domains are not necessary in a single-host configuration so you do not need to mark this option.

• *Add Password*   You can add or change an existing password for each user as the user is being converted to 3.0. If the user had a password in 2.0, you are asked whether you want to replace it. If a password did not exist, you are prompted to enter a password for the user.

5. After marking the desired options, press ENTER to begin the conversion process and follow the on-screen prompts.

As each user is converted, a check mark is placed in the box on the left-hand side of the screen. After all users are converted, you are prompted to replace the current Office 3.0 USERID.NB file. If you have not entered any information in the Office 3.0 USERID.NB, type **Y** to replace the file and save the converted information. If you have already entered new information in the 3.0 USERID.NB file, type **N** so you do not overwrite the new information. After you type **N**, the converted file is saved as USERID.CNV. You can then merge the two files in Notebook to combine the new information with the converted information.

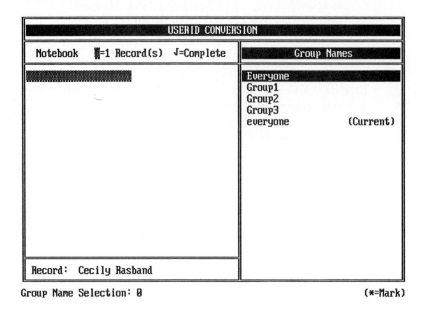

Figure 12-18.   USERID Conversion with Group Names options

The conversion process does not convert any optional fields you may have added to your Notebook in Office 2.0. You can add the optional fields to your 3.0 Notebook manually and enter the desired information.

Converting Resource Information

After converting the 2.0 USERID.NB file, you need to convert your 2.0 RESOURCE.NB file. If you did not use Scheduler resources with 2.0, you do not need to convert this information. If you plan on using resources with 3.0, see the section "Creating the RESOURCE.NB File" earlier in this chapter.

To convert the resource Notebook file:

1. Press **R** for Convert Resources.

2. Enter the path to the Office 3.0 RESOURCE.NB file. A brief message indicates that the header information is being checked.

3. Enter the path to the Office 2.0 RESOURCE.NB directory. The screen shown in Figure 12-19 appears.

4. The right side of the screen lists the conversion options available. Select the options you want to use in the conversion by marking them with an asterisk. The first two options are mandatory.

  • *Add Host Names*   In Office 3.0, Host Name is a required field in the RESOURCE.NB file. You must add a host name to convert the 2.0 resources. The host name must be the name you entered in the Host Definition screen during installation. As the resources are converted, the host name you enter here is inserted into the RESOURCE.NB file. As soon as you begin the conversion process, you will be prompted for the host name.

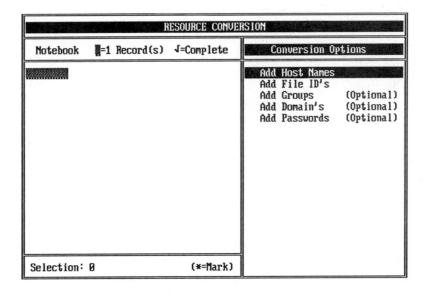

Figure 12-19.   RESOURCE Conversion screen

- *Add File IDs* File IDs are a required field in the RE-SOURCE.NB file. As each resource is converted, a prompt asks you to enter a File ID for the resource. The File ID is from one to three characters and must be a valid DOS filename character. ASCII characters 128 and above are not supported, and the File ID cannot end with the underscore character. No two resources on the same host can have the same File ID. You can use any valid characters (listed above), but it is usually easiest to use characters from the resource description. The File ID is attached to many of the Office files. For this reason, it is helpful to use familiar initials for the File ID.

- *Add Groups* If you want to add global resource groups, mark this option. Before the conversion occurs, you are prompted to enter the name of the group or groups you want to create. As each resource is converted, a list of group names appears. You can mark the group names in which you want to include the resource.

- *Add Domains* Domains are not necessary in a single-host configuration so you do not need to mark this option.

- *Add Password* You can add a password for each resource as the resource is being converted to 3.0. As the resource is being converted, you are prompted to enter a password.

5. After marking the desired options, press ENTER to begin the conversion process and follow the on-screen prompts.

As each resource is converted, a check mark is placed in the box on the left-hand side of the screen. After all the resources are converted, you are prompted to replace the current Office 3.0 RESOURCE.NB file. If you have not entered any information in the Office 3.0 RE-SOURCE.NB file, type **Y** to replace the file and save the converted information. If you have already entered new information in RE-SOURCE.NB, type **N** so you do not overwrite the new information. After you type **N**, the converted file is saved as RESOURCE.CNV. You can then merge the two files in Notebook to combine the new information with the converted information.

The conversion process does not convert any optional fields you may have added to your Notebook in Office 2.0. You can add the optional fields to your 3.0 Notebook manually and enter the desired information.

Running GENOFF

After successfully converting the USERID.NB and RESOURCE.NB files, you need to run the Generate Office program to build the host directory and create the actual HOSTID.FIL, USERID.FIL, and RE-SOURCE.FIL information files. The first thing GENOFF does is build the host directory from the host information you entered during installation. After creating the host directory, GENOFF takes the information from the HOSTID.NB, USERID.NB, and RESOURCE.NB files and creates the information files needed to run Office. These information files are stored in the host directory. The Notebook files remain in the system administration directory for maximum security. For information on the exact directory structure of an Office host, see the section "Host Directory Structure" earlier in this chapter.

To use GENOFF:

1. Press **G** from the Convert Office 2.0 to 3.0 Shell menu. The following menu appears:

```
Generate Office

    1 - Generate Using Current Setup Options

    2 - Generate Changing Setup Options

    3 - View Log of Last Generation
```

2. Press **1** for Generate Using Current Setup Options. If this is the first time you have run GENOFF, you will be prompted to input the desired options. If you have already run GENOFF and wish to change the options, press **2** for Generate Changing Setup Options.

3. A directory prompt displays at the bottom of the screen so you can verify that GENOFF is using the correct Notebook files. Type **Y** if the directory is correct or type **N** and enter the correct directory. GENOFF then builds the HOSTID.FIL. The status information displays in the lower window of the screen. If this is the first time you have run GENOFF, a prompt asks you if the host should be created. Type **Y** to create the host.

4. After the HOSTID.FIL is built, GENOFF displays the available GENOFF options shown in Figure 12-20. At this point, set the desired options.

Very detailed help screens display on the right-hand side of the screen, indicating the function of each option. For more information on the GENOFF options, see "GENOFF Options" earlier in this chapter.

5. After you have set the options, press F7 to begin GENOFF.

As GENOFF processes the information in the Notebook files, it displays status messages in the bottom window of the screen. When GENOFF finishes creating the information files, a message indicates any errors that may have occurred or indicates that the process was completed successfully.

If errors occurred, you can view a log file that indicates exactly what occurred while GENOFF was processing. To access the log file,

```
WordPerfect Office          Generate Office  3.0

 Options                            Install Mail
   Install Mail:         Yes (No)
   Install Scheduler:    Yes        Type Y if you want GENOFF to install
   Network Type:                    the Office Mail system.
   Login ID = User ID:   No
   Unique User ID:       Yes        Type N if you do not want GENOFF to
   Greenwich MT Offset:  0:0        install the Office Mail system.
   Hemisphere:           Northern
   Daylight Savings:     Yes
     Month/Day Start:    0/0
     Month/Day End:      0/0
     Hours:Min Change:   0:0
   Password Protection:  No
   Connections Station:  0
   Notification via
     File Polling:       No



Tab Next Option; Shift-Tab Previous Option;
```

Figure 12-20. GENOFF options

press **G** for Generate Office from the Convert Office 2.0 to 3.0 menu, and then press **3** for View Log of Last Generation. The GENOFF log file is retrieved into Editor and you can search for and view any errors that occurred during the generation process. For information on GENOFF error messages and possible solutions, see "GENOFF Error Messages" earlier in this chapter. After viewing the errors, press F7 twice to return to the Generate Office Using Notebook Shell menu.

After you have run GENOFF successfully, the Office system is installed.

Converting Mail 2.0 and Scheduler 2.0

Along with the Notebook files, the 2.0 Mail and Scheduler systems must be converted. If you do not care if users lose their Mail messages or scheduled events, you do not need to convert these programs. If you did not use the Mail and/or Scheduler programs you do not need to convert the information.

Note: Mail and Scheduler 2.0 cannot communicate with Mail and Scheduler 3.0. If you want all 2.0 Mail messages and scheduled items to appear in the 3.0 system, use the convert utilities.

Before converting the Mail or Scheduler system, make sure that there are no users in the Mail or Scheduler program. To convert the Mail or Scheduler systems:

1. Press **M** for Convert Mail 2.0 to 3.0, or press **S** for Convert Scheduler 2.0 to 3.0.

2. Type **Y** if the correct Office 3.0 directory is displayed, or type **N** and enter the correct directory.

3. Enter the path to 2.0 Mail or Scheduler system.

Before the conversion continues, an estimate is performed to see if you have enough resources to convert. If sufficient resources exist, the conversion continues. If there are not enough resources, the following error message displays:

Estimate shows the convert may fail. Continue anyway? (Y/N)Y

If this error message displays, you should probably continue with the conversion. The Mail Convert and Scheduler Convert overestimate the necessary requirements, and the conversion often completes successfully even if this error message displays. As the conversion process begins, a screen displays status information.

If the conversion fails, you can check the conversion log. To view the log, press **V** from the Shell menu. If a conversion fails, you may want to free up additional space on the network or check the number of directory entries available. You need at least one directory entry for each user and one directory entry for each message that will be converted. After modifying the available space or directory entries, try converting again.

When you run the conversion programs from the menu, the 2.0 system is not destroyed. After making the necessary changes, you can run the convert programs again without any problems.

After you have successfully converted your Office 2.0 system to 3.0, you need to use the SETMEUP program to install the necessary commands on each user's computer to run Office 3.0. For more information on using SETMEUP, see "Updating Users with SETMEUP" earlier in the chapter. You can also create an Office environment file that will help users access global setup options set by the system administrator. For more information on the Office environment file, see "Creating an Office Environment File" earlier in this chapter.

Conversion Overview

To aid you in future conversions and as an overview of this chapter, these are the general steps for converting the Office 2.0 system to the Office 3.0 system:

1. Use the Install program to copy the Office program and System Administration files to the selected directory on the network.

2. After the files are copied, enter the Host Definition information.

3. Use the Convert Office 2.0 to 3.0 System Administration menu to convert the Office 2.0 USERID.NB and RESOURCE.NB files to Office 3.0.

4. Run GENOFF.

5. If necessary, convert the Office 2.0 Mail and Scheduler systems.

6. Run the SETMEUP program on each user's computer.

7. Create an Office environment file.

Troubleshooting

The following list outlines some common error messages users might receive when trying to enter the Mail or Scheduler program after you have installed or converted to Office 3.0. Along with the error message, the cause of the problem is given:

Error Message

Message:

   Access Denied

The user has not been added to the USERID.FIL file. Add the user to the USERID.NB and run GENOFF.

Message:

   Access Denied: Unknown User on *path:\Host name*

There are three sets of circumstances that may cause this error:

   • The user is not found in the current USERID.FIL file. Check the host name for the user in the USERID.NB and run GENOFF.

- The user is accessing the wrong USERID.FIL: check the path displayed with the error message and make sure it is the correct path to the Office program directory.

- The user's name is entered incorrectly in the USERID.NB. Check the file, edit the necessary information, and then run GENOFF.

Message:

Access Denied: Unable to Initialize Mailbox

Mail can't find the IN and/or OUT files for the user. Check whether the files exist. Run GENOFF. Make sure user has rights to the IN and OUT directories.

Message:

XXX, User File Not Found, Contact System Administrator

or

XXX, Organizer File Not Found, Contact System Administrator

This error occurs while entering Scheduler. *XXX* represents the User ID; if either of these files is not found, check whether they exist. Run GENOFF. Make sure user has rights to the USER and ORG directories.

Message:

Corrupted or Missing USERID.FIL

An incorrect path was entered in the HOSTID.NB. Make sure the path specifies the Office Program Directory and not the Office Admin File Directory.

The causes and solutions listed in this section provide the information needed to troubleshoot most errors that occur with the Mail and Scheduler programs on the system level.

Maintaining Office

THIRTEEN

Once you have installed the Office 3.0 system, you may need to add, delete, or edit information for the host, users, and/or resources. The second half of this chapter explains how to maintain the host, user, and resource information files. Besides maintaining the information files, you need to maintain the data files used for Mail and Scheduler. A maintenance program shipped with Office called Check Office, or CHKOFF, maintains and optimizes the Mail and Scheduler programs. Because the Mail and Scheduler files are located on a shared network directory, it is important that only necessary and valid files are stored there. CHKOFF ensures that this occurs. The CHKOFF program also improves the performance and speed of Mail and Scheduler.

Why Run CHKOFF?

The main purpose of the CHKOFF program is to validate Mail and Scheduler data files. If CHKOFF finds files that are no longer needed, it deletes them. For example, if you delete a user from the USERID.NB without running CHKOFF, then IN, OUT, USER, ORG, EVENT, LIN, SCCHAL, and set files for that user remain on the shared network directory and take up extra space. If you delete a user and then run CHKOFF, CHKOFF deletes any files that were only used by that person.

CHKOFF also repairs damaged files. If a user is having problems receiving or displaying Mail messages in her or his In or Out Box or scheduled events in her or his Request or Organized box, you can run CHKOFF with the Rebuild option (see "CHKOFF Options" later in this chapter) to delete and then rebuild all of the links from the LIN and

EVENT files. After you run CHKOFF with the Rebuild option, some of the Mail and Scheduler files may be unrecoverable. In this case, they will be deleted from the user's In, Out, Organized, and/or Request box. The system administrator can view a log of the processes CHKOFF performed and see exactly why the files were deleted.

CHKOFF also lets you specify certain system limits that make maintaining a system more manageable. With CHKOFF, you can delete files larger than a specified size. If you discover that users are attaching very large files and then not deleting them, this option is quite helpful. You can also delete files older than a specified date. This is useful if you have staff members who never delete outdated Mail messages and Scheduler items that take up valuable space on the network. CHKOFF also lets you limit the number of entries a user can have in her or his In, Out, Request, and Organized boxes in Mail and Scheduler. This is helpful if you have limited network space available for Mail and Scheduler files.

When to Run CHKOFF

The frequency with which you should run CHKOFF depends on the number of users and the amount of use Mail and Scheduler receive. To start with, run CHKOFF on a weekly basis. The first few times you run CHKOFF, monitor the CHKOFF log to see how much activity occurs when you run CHKOFF. If CHKOFF is performing few functions, you can reduce the number of times you run it. On the other hand, if CHKOFF is performing many functions and is taking a very long time to run, you may want to run it more frequently. There is no set interval at which you should run CHKOFF. However, the larger the number of users and the amount of use Mail and Scheduler receive, the more often you should run CHKOFF. You should always run CHKOFF after removing users and resources from USERID.NB or RESOURCE.NB. When you remove users, you can free up to seven directory entries for each user. CHKOFF also removes all message and/or event files that only pertain to that user or resource.

If you ever lose information from the Office directories due to a hardware system failure and then need to restore that information, you should run CHKOFF. Running CHKOFF helps get the system back in sync.

It is best to run CHKOFF when the system is not being used. However, you can run any of the CHKOFF options when the system is in use except when using the Rebuild option. When you perform a rebuild, Mail and Scheduler cannot be in use.

How to Run CHKOFF

You can run the CHKOFF program from a DOS prompt or from the System Administration menus that are shipped with Office 3.0. There is no reason you should need to run CHKOFF from DOS, but if you do,

1. Change to the Office Administration directory.

2. Type **chkoff/x,** where x is the option you want to run CHKOFF with. See "CHKOFF Options" for more information about the individual CHKOFF options.

To run CHKOFF from the System Administration menu shipped with Office:

1. Change to the Office Administration directory.

2. Type **offadmin.** The main System Administration menu appears.

3. Press **C** for Check Office to display the Check Office menu shown in Figure 13-1.

4. With the Check Office menu displayed, select the desired option.

CHKOFF Options

When you start CHKOFF from DOS or select Choose CHKOFF Options from the Check Office menu, the following options are available. When these options are run by themselves, CHKOFF only reports

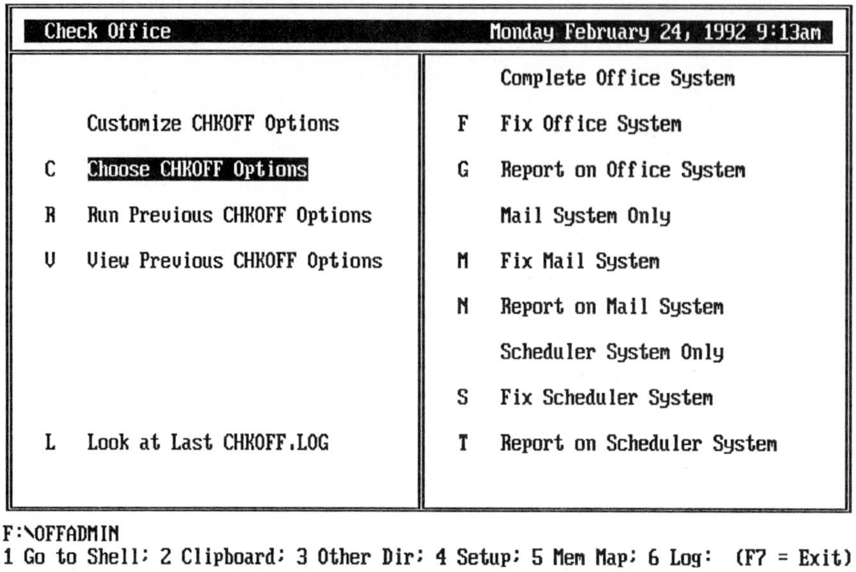

```
┌─────────────────────────────────────────────────────────────────────┐
│ Check Office                           Monday February 24, 1992 9:13am │
├───────────────────────────────────┬───────────────────────────────────┤
│                                   │      Complete Office System        │
│       Customize CHKOFF Options    │  F   Fix Office System             │
│   C   Choose CHKOFF Options       │  G   Report on Office System        │
│   R   Run Previous CHKOFF Options │      Mail System Only               │
│   V   View Previous CHKOFF Options│  M   Fix Mail System               │
│                                   │  N   Report on Mail System          │
│                                   │      Scheduler System Only          │
│                                   │  S   Fix Scheduler System           │
│   L   Look at Last CHKOFF.LOG     │  T   Report on Scheduler System     │
│                                   │                                     │
└───────────────────────────────────┴───────────────────────────────────┘
F:\OFFADMIN
1 Go to Shell; 2 Clipboard; 3 Other Dir; 4 Setup; 5 Mem Map; 6 Log:  (F7 = Exit)
```

Figure 13-1.   Check Office menu

information without performing the functions. If you want these options to perform their various functions, you *must* also include the Fixup option, /F.

/E-*x* or Expired	Deletes Mail messages or scheduled items that are older than the number of days specified by *x*. For scheduled events, *x* must be older than the starting date of the event, not the date the event was scheduled.
/ED-*x* and ES-*x* or Expire Days and Size	Deletes messages or events that are a specified number of days old and larger than a specified size. This option is useful if you are losing a lot of network space with old and large messages.

Both days and size must be met before the message or event is deleted. If you choose this option and do not enter a parameter for one of the options (days or size) the default parameter is used (10 days and 100K). You can use the Expired Days and Size option with the Expired option. These options are independent.

/F or Fixup	Performs the fixes and/or deletions specified with other startup options. Without this option, CHKOFF only reports the condition of the Mail and Scheduler systems.
/HN-*name* or Host Name	Only necessary for multiple-host systems. If you have a multiple-host system, you can run CHKOFF on a single host by specifying the host name after this option.
/I or Information	Shows a screen of statistical information after CHKOFF is run. This information is a summary of the information that is displayed in the CHKOFF log file. The Information option shows information for both a report and fixup. The screen looks similar to the one shown in Figure 13-2.
/K or Kill	Displays and fixes all Mail and Scheduler problems even if they occurred in the last few hours. Without this option, CHKOFF has a grace period of a few hours before it reports or fixes any problems. Normally, you shouldn't use the Kill option because processing may not be complete and Office will naturally correct the problems that would be found. You might want to use this option if you are sure an error occurred recently and you need to fix it immediately.

/L-*x* or Limit	Lets you limit the number of entries each user can have in her or his In and Out Boxes in Mail and in her or his Request and Organized boxes in Scheduler. If you do not use this option, users can have approximately 500 entries in each box.
/M or Mail	Only runs CHKOFF for the Mail system. If you do not use Scheduler, you should use this option.
/O-*filename* or Output	Causes CHKOFF to output information to a log file. The log file is an ASCII text file that gives a detailed account of what CHKOFF did. This information includes problems

```
                          Mail System Information

Users........................11          Hosts........................1

Message statistics:                      Mailbox statistics:
    normal messages............0             users with mail............0
    phone messages.............0          IN box entries:
    forwarded messages.........0             new....................0
    file(s) only...............0             unread.................0
    total number of messages...0             total..................0
                                          OUT box entries:
Distribution statistics:                     total..................0
    to less than 3 users.......0
    to more than 50% of users..0

Event statistics:                        Schedule statistics:
    memos......................0             users with schedules.......0
    appointments...............0          USER entries:
    todo list items............0             new....................0
    total number of events.....0             unread.................0
                                              total..................0
Resources......................9         ORIGINATION entries:
                                              total..................0
```

Figure 13-2.   Information screen for CHKOFF

CHKOFF found, as well as the problems that it fixed. By default, the log is saved to the Office Administration directory under the name CHKOFF.LOG, but you can change the path and filename if you like. You may want to change the filename if a log currently exists by the same name and if it contains valuable information.

/R or
Rebuild

Only use Rebuild if you are having serious problems with the Mail and/or Scheduler systems. These problems may be manifested in error messages when users are trying to access Mail or Scheduler. For example, if a user receives the error message "Access Denied: Unable to Initialize Mailbox" and the user is a valid user with the appropriate rights and the correct files are present in the host directory, you may want to run CHKOFF to clean up any damaged files. If you use the Rebuild option, you cannot have any users in the Mail or Scheduler program. When you use Rebuild, CHKOFF deletes and then rebuilds all USER, ORG, IN, and OUT files. The Rebuild option may take a very long time to run.

/S or
Scheduler

Only runs CHKOFF for the Scheduler system. If you do not use Mail, you should use this option.

/PU-*path* or
User ID Path

Only needed on multiple-host systems. With this option, you can specify the path to the USERID.FIL file.

/V or
Verbose

Shows more detailed information in the log file and on the screen. This option is useful when used in conjunction with the /O and/or /I options.

Check Office Menu Options

The left side of the Check Office menu contains options that let you choose, run, and view selected CHKOFF options, as well as look at the last CHKOFF.LOG file. The right side of the menu includes menu options that run with standardized CHKOFF options. You can run CHKOFF for Complete Office System, for Mail System Only, or for Scheduler System Only. With each of these options, you can fix any problems that CHKOFF detects or just report problems.

Customize CHKOFF Options

If you want to run with specific CHKOFF options, press C for Choose CHKOFF Options. The screen shown in Figure 13-3 appears. Each option has a number that you can select, and you can choose as many options as needed. After selecting an option, you are prompted to input any necessary information. For example, if you select option 1, Expired, you will be prompted for the number of days after which a message should be deleted.

```
                       CHKOFF.EXE Start-Up Options
  #    Name         Options    Description

  1 - Expired                  Show (delete if Fixup set) messages more than xx
                               days old. (Default=30 days)
  2 - Expire Days              Show (delete if Fixup set) messages more than xx
            Size               days old and xx Kbytes. (Default=10 days/100 Kbytes)
  3 - Fixup                    Fix any problems encountered.
  4 - Host Name                Add a Host Name.
  5 - Information              Show Statistical Information.
  6 - Kill                     Show (fix if Fixup set) all problems, even if
                               they occurred within the last few hours.
  7 - Limit                    Show users with mail entries greater than xxx.
  8 - Mail                     Check only the Mail system.
  9 - Output                   Copy the screen to a file. (Default=CHKOFF.LOG)
  R - Rebuild                  Reconstruct all Mail and Scheduler in/out boxes.
                               NOTE: Never use this while the system is in use!
  S - Scheduler                Check only the Scheduler system.
  U - UserID Path              Path to the USERID.FIL file.
  V - Verbose                  Show extra information.


  Selection: 0                              (F9=Run CHKOFF, F7=Exit)
```

Figure 13-3.   CHKOFF options screen

After you have selected the desired options, press F9 to run CHKOFF. If you decide not to run CHKOFF, press F7 to exit and return to the Check Office menu.

If you have run CHKOFF with customized options and later need to run with the same options, you can press **R** for Run Previous CHKOFF Options. This menu item is useful if you establish certain options that your system needs and that never need to be altered.

If you can't remember exactly which option you had set previously, you can select View Previous CHKOFF Options by pressing **V**. You'll see a screen similar to the one shown here:

```
CHKOFF.EXE /E=45/O/I/V
```

After checking the options, you can choose to run CHKOFF with the same options or change them as needed.

Other CHKOFF Menu Options

The menu options on the right side of the Check Office menu let you run CHKOFF without specifying any options. Each of these menu items has certain default options preset for you. The Report options—Report on Office System, Report on Mail System, and Report on Scheduler System—all use the /O, /I, and /V options. The Mail and Scheduler reports use the /M or /S option, respectively, to show only information for that particular system. All of the report options output the information to the log file, show information on the screen, and display detailed information. After selecting one of these options, you should view the log file by pressing **L** for Look at Last CHKOFF.LOG from the Check Office menu. Then you can determine if you need to perform the fixes listed in the log.

If you decide to fix the errors listed in the log, or if you need to run CHKOFF, you can use the Fix options—Fix Office System, Fix Mail System, and Fix Scheduler System—which all use the /O, /I, and /F options. With these options, information is output to a log file, summary information is displayed after CHKOFF completes, and CHKOFF makes all necessary fixes.

After using any of the options from the Check Office menu, you can view the CHKOFF log file that was created. When you view the log from the Check Office menu, a macro is invoked that retrieves the log file into Editor so you can view it easily. To view the last CHKOFF log file:

1. Press **L** for Look at Last CHKOFF.LOG from the Check Office menu.

2. Press ENTER if the correct path to the Office Admin directory displays, or enter the correct path to the Office Admin directory. the

3. Use the arrow keys to move through the file.

After you enter the path, you should see a screen similar to the one shown in Figure 13-4. The actual screen that displays depends on the CHKOFF options selected and the errors and information reported by CHKOFF. If you used any of the Report options on the menu or if you specified the /V option, you will see all the information that displayed as CHKOFF was running. If you used any of the Fix options on the menu or did not specify the /V option, you will see a user list and any errors that occurred or were fixed.

```
information output=chkoff.log verbose

Using:  f:\office30\userid.fil

Verifying information in USERID.FIL

Building the host list
Using:  f:\office30\userid.fil

Verifying information in USERID.FIL

Building the host list

Building the user list

Building the resource list
Start -- checking LIN files for structural integrity
Checking files in F:\OFFICE30\lin\0\
Checking files in F:\OFFICE30\lin\1\
Checking files in F:\OFFICE30\lin\2\
Checking files in F:\OFFICE30\lin\3\
Checking files in F:\OFFICE30\lin\4\
Checking files in F:\OFFICE30\lin\5\
Checking files in F:\OFFICE30\lin\6\
DOS F:\OFFADMIN\CHKOFF.LOG                 File 1  Pg 1  Ln 1      Pos 1
```

Figure 13-4.   Sample CHKOFF log file

4. After viewing the log, press F7 to exit Editor.

5. Type **Y** if you want to save the log file or type **N** if you do not want to save the log file.

6. Type **Y** to exit Editor.

Updating and Maintaining User and Resource Information

At times you may need to add or delete user or resource information from the Office system. For example, if an employee leaves your company, you should delete her or his information. If you hire a new employee, you should add information for the employee in the USE-RID.NB file. You may also need to edit user or resource information. You need to do all the adding, deleting, and editing of users and resources in the USERID.NB or RESOURCE.NB file. After you have added, deleted, or changed the information in these files, you need to run GENOFF to update the USERID.FIL and RESOURCE.FIL information files.

Adding a User or Resource

To add a user to the USERID.NB or a resource to the RESOURCE.NB file:

1. Change to the Office Admin directory.

2. Type **offadmin** to display the main System Administration menu.

3. Press **N** for Using Notebooks Only.

4. Press **U** for User Notebook or press **R** for Resource Notebook.

5. Before you enter the Notebook, a prompt asks you if the path and filename are correct. If the path is correct, type **Y** for Yes. If you have moved the file, type **N** and enter the correct path. If you choose User Notebook, a screen similar to the one shown in Figure 13-5 appears, listing the information in your USERID.NB file. If

Full Name	Department	Phone	Host Name	User ID
Cecily Rasband	Personnel	555-3333	Host1	Cecily
Connie Campbell	Marketing	555-2222	Host1	Connie
Devin Rowley	Marketing	555-5555	Host1	DevinR
Don Rowley	Research	555-1111	Host1	DonR
Earnie Glazener	Research	555-3333	Host1	Earnie
Greg Hall	Marketing	555-4444	Host1	Greg
Jack Cummings	CS	555-5555	Host1	JackC
Lisa Cram	CS	555-2222	Host1	LisaC
Matt Mathisen	Research	555-3333	Host1	MattM
Mike Gibson	Marketing	555-1111	Host1	MikeG
Richard Reid	Research	555-2222	Host1	RichardR

1 Create; 2 Delete; 3 Edit; 4 Options; 5 Name Search: 3   Record 1

Figure 13-5.   Sample USERID.NB List Display

you choose Resource Notebook, a screen similar to the one shown in Figure 13-6 appears, listing the information in your RE-SOURCE.NB file.

6. Press F9 to create a new record.

7. Enter the information for the new user or resource.

8. Repeat steps 6 and 7 until all new users or resources have been added.

9. Press F7 to exit Notebook.

10. Type **Y** twice to save and replace the old USERID.NB or RESOURCE.NB file.

11. Run GENOFF. To run GENOFF from the Generate Office Using Notebook menu, press **G** and select the desired option. For more information on running GENOFF, see "Generating Office" in Chapter 12.

```
Description                      Resource ID   Host Name   Owner
Board Room 1002 - Capacity 55    BR 1002       Host1       Cecily
Board Room 2052 - Capacity 30    BR 2052       Host1       Cecily
Company Car 1                    Car 1         Host1       DonR
Company Car 2                    Car 2         Host1       Greg
Company Jet                      Jet 1         Host1       Connie
Demo Computer 1 - 386/20         Comp 1        Host1       Cecily
Demo Computer 2 - 386SX          Comp 2        Host1       Cecily
Large Screen Monitor             Monitor 1     Host1       Cecily
Overhead Projector               Proj 1        Host1       Cecily




1 Create; 2 Delete; 3 Edit; 4 Options; 5 Name Search: 3          Record 1
```

Figure 13-6.   Sample RESOURCE.NB List Display

If you do not run GENOFF after adding users or resources, the information files will not be updated and the users will not be added to the Office system.

Adding Users with GENUNB

If you are on a Novell network and have added users to the Novell bindery since installing Office, you can use GENUNB to add the additional users to the USERID.NB. This eliminates the need to insert information for each user manually. GENUNB only inserts information in the required fields. It inserts the network Login ID and also uses this as the Office User ID. GENUNB creates a unique File ID for each user extracted from the bindery. If you want to enter any of the optional information—such as phone, department, password, and group membership—you must enter this information manually.

Note: You must have supervisory rights to run GENUNB.

To use the GENUNB program from the Generate Office Using Notebook System Administration menu:

1. Press **N** for Import From Novell bindery.

2. Enter the host name. This must be the same name you entered when you installed the host. Be sure you enter the name exactly as before. If the host name does not match the name you entered on the Host Definition screen, the user will not be installed.

3. Type **Y** if the correct path to the USERID.NB is displayed. Type **N** if the correct path is not displayed, and then enter the correct path.

4. Enter a letter for a network drive mapped to the host file server.

At this point, GENUNB extracts the information from the Novell bindery and inserts it into the USERID.NB file. Once GENUNB updates the USERID.NB file, you need to run GENOFF.

If you run GENUNB and information already exists in the USERID.NB, GENUNB appends the new information to the existing information in the USERID.NB file. If users no longer exist in the bindery, they are deleted from USERID.NB after you run GENUNB.

Deleting a User or Resource

If employees leave the company or resources are no longer available, you need to delete them from the USERID.NB and/or RESOURCE.NB files. To delete a user or resource:

1. Change to the Office Admin directory.

2. Type **offadmin** to display the main System Administration menu.

3. Press **N** for Using Notebooks Only.

4. Press **U** for User Notebook or press **R** for Resource Notebook.

5. Before you enter the Notebook, a prompt asks you if the path and filename are correct. If the path is correct, type **Y** for Yes. If you have moved the file, type **N** and enter the correct path.

6. Use the arrow keys or Name Search to highlight the user or resource you want to delete. If several users or resources need to be deleted, highlight these records and then mark them with an asterisk (*).

7. Press **2** or DEL to delete the records.

8. Type **Y** to confirm the deletion.

9. Press F7 to exit Notebook.

10. Type **Y** twice to save and replace the old USERID.NB or RESOURCE.NB file.

11. Run GENOFF. To run GENOFF from the Generate Office Using Notebook menu, press **G** and select the desired option. For more information on running GENOFF, see "Generating Office" in Chapter 12.

If you do not run GENOFF after deleting users or resources, the information files will not be updated and the users will still be listed as valid users on the List Users screen in Mail and Scheduler.

After deleting users or resources, you should also run CHKOFF. Running CHKOFF deletes the files that belonged to the deleted user or resource, thus freeing up space. See "How to Run CHKOFF" in this chapter for more information.

Editing Users or Resources

If information about a particular user or resource changes, you need to edit the USERID.NB or RESOURCE.NB. For example, if a user's phone number changes, you should update the user's record in the USERID.NB to reflect this change. You may also need to edit the USERID.NB if a user wants to change her or his system password. You may need to change the information in the USERID.NB or RE-SOURCE.NB file if you entered it incorrectly during the initial installation of Office. For example, if you entered the wrong User ID and the user cannot access his or her Mail or Scheduler, you need to edit this information. To edit the USERID.NB or RESOURCE.NB:

1. Change to the Office Admin directory.

2. Type **offadmin** to display the main System Administration menu.

3. Press **N** for Using Notebooks Only.

4. Press **U** for User Notebook or press **R** for Resource Notebook.

5. Before you enter the Notebook, a prompt asks you if the path and filename are correct. If the path is correct, type **Y** for Yes. If you have moved the file, type **N** and enter the correct path.

6. Use the arrow keys or Name Search to highlight the user or resource you want to edit.

7. Press ENTER.

8. Use the TAB key to move to the field you need to edit.

9. Delete the incorrect information and add the new information.

10. Press F7 to return to the List Display.

11. Repeat steps 6 through 9 until all user or resource information is updated.

12. Press F7 to exit Notebook.

13. Type **Y** twice to save and replace the old USERID.NB or RESOURCE.NB file.

14. Run GENOFF. To run GENOFF from the Generate Office Using Notebook menu, press **G** and select the desired option. For more information on running GENOFF, see "Generating Office" in Chapter 12.

If you do not run GENOFF after editing information for users or resources, the information files will not be updated and the changes will not take effect.

Maintenance Summary

Proper maintenance of your Office system helps ensure that information for users and resources is correct and up to date. Regular usage of the

CHKOFF program helps optimize the performance of the Mail and Scheduler systems. This optimization involves

- Deleting unwanted and unneeded files

- Validating all Mail and Scheduler files

- Rebuilding corrupted systems

- Limiting the size and number of Mail and Scheduler items

- Limiting the number of days a Mail or Scheduler item may be kept on the system

Maintaining the Office system is vital for productive and efficient use for all users.

Using Office Connections

If the system you are working with requires more than a single-host directory structure, you need to install multiple hosts and use the WordPerfect Connections package to communicate between the hosts. The WordPerfect Connections package is sold separately from Word-Perfect Office LAN. The basic component of the WordPerfect Connections package is the Connection Server program, which runs from a workstation on the network and completes Mail and Scheduler deliveries between hosts.

You may need more than one host because you have too many users for one file server to accommodate. Office can accommodate over 40,000 users on a single host. With such a large limit, the number of users assigned to one host will probably be limited by the user limits for the network software being used. The number of users you can have on a single host is less than or equal to the number of users that can be attached to a file server at one time. Another reason for multiple hosts is to provide enhanced network security. With multiple hosts, you can assign certain users to a host where all other network users have no access rights, thus increasing the security.

When you use multiple hosts, remember that Mail and Scheduler work the same on each individual host as they do on a single-host system. Each program performs deliveries to other users on the same host without using the Connection Server. However, Mail and Scheduler cannot perform deliveries to users on other hosts unless the Connection Server is installed and running.

This chapter explains how to set up a multiple-host system and a multiple-domain system using the WordPerfect Connections package. It also briefly describes the use of gateways with WordPerfect Office. This chapter is not intended to include every detail about setting up these systems, but rather to explain some of the basic steps for extending your Office system using these different configurations.

Introduction to the Connection Server

Before installing and setting up multiple hosts, you should understand what the Connection Server is and how it performs Mail and Scheduler deliveries between hosts. The Connection Server program is run from a normal network workstation that can access the different file servers where the hosts it is responsible for are located. The Connection Server gets information about the different hosts from the HOSTID.FIL information file. This file is created by GENOFF.EXE from the HOSTID.NB, as explained in Chapter 12, "Single Host Installation." The HOSTID.FIL gives the Connection Server information such as the unique paths to find the different hosts, and what type of connection to use for each host. The logical drive assignments for the computer where the Connection Server is run must be the same as the drive designations used in the HOSTID.NB file.

The connection type specified in the HOSTID.NB file refers to the level of responsibility the Connection Server has for the users on that host. A host can be defined as one of four different connection types in the HOSTID.NB. Only the first connection type, Delivery, will be covered in this section. Transfer, Route, and Gateway connection types will be explained in the section "Installing Multiple Domains" later in this chapter.

For each host with Delivery specified as its connection type in the HOSTID.NB, the Connection Server is directly responsible for routing and delivering Mail and Scheduler items to users on those hosts. The Connection Server does this by cycling through the delivery hosts and repeatedly checking each of them for message files to be delivered to users or routed to other hosts. Together these delivery hosts make up a single domain. A *domain* is the group of delivery hosts for which the Connection Server is responsible. While the Connection Server is responsible for completing the routing of messages between delivery hosts

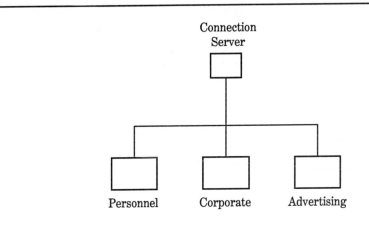

Figure 14-1.   Sample domain

in its domain, it calls application programs, Mail Server (MLS.EXE) and Scheduler Server (SCS.EXE), to complete the distribution to individual users on the hosts.

For example, if the user Tom on the host named Personnel sent a Mail message to Kent on Corporate, as shown in Figure 14-1, the following steps would occur:

1. Mail creates a new file in the LIN directory on host Personnel and places a link in the file for Tom in the Out directory for that LIN file. It also places a copy of the LIN file in the TRANSIN directory on Personnel.

2. During its next polling cycle, the Connection Server finds the new file in the TRANSIN directory on Personnel. From information inside the LIN file, Connection Server finds that the message needs to be routed to host Corporate. It then checks the HOSTID.FIL to find the location of Corporate and copies the LIN file from the TRANSIN directory on Personnel to the TRANSIN directory on Corporate. To minimize the use of network resources, the copy of the LIN file in the TRANSIN directory of Personnel is deleted.

3. The next time the Connection Server checks the TRANSIN directory on Corporate, it finds the copy of the LIN file it placed

there and sees that it is at the end of its route. The Connection Server then copies the file to the correct directory under the Connection Server directory on Corporate and deletes the file from the TRANSIN directory on Corporate. This file has now been queued for processing by the Mail Server application program (MLS.EXE) which the Connection Server starts.

4. After completing its polling cycle, the Connection Server activates the Mail Server, which processes all of the files on each host that the Connection Server has copied into the subdirectories under the CS directory. It finds the copy of the LIN file in a subdirectory under the CS directory on Corporate and moves it to the LIN directory on Corporate. Mail Server then places a link in Kent's IN file to the file in the LIN directory so he can access the message.

5. Next Mail Server sends a status message back to the original sender of the message—in this case Tom on Personnel—telling him that the message was delivered. Depending on the status level set under the transport options for that message, other status messages showing when the recipient opens and deletes the message are also returned to the sender. These status messages change the status displayed on the Information screen when viewed from the Out Box in Mail or the Organized Box in Scheduler. The Connection Server views these status messages as normal messages and uses the same routing method described above. Scheduler also uses the same steps when sending a schedule request to users on other hosts.

Another message type is the one that Mail and Scheduler generate when a message is retracted or an event is deleted by the organizer. These retraction messages remove the original file and all links. The only difference between Mail and Scheduler is that if a Mail message has been read, that message becomes the property of the recipient and a retraction cannot remove it. With Scheduler, if an event has been canceled by the organizer, that event is removed from all recipients' Schedulers.

Installing Office LAN for Multiple Hosts

You install the Office programs on multiple hosts the same way you install them on a single host. For each host, you must run Install to copy the desired Office program files in the correct directory. Carefully consider where to install the hosts and what logical drive designations to use. After the initial installation of the Office program files is complete, Install inputs the path to the directory where the files were installed and a host name you enter into the HOSTID.NB for the Connection Server to use. The logical drive assignments used when installing Office LAN should therefore be the same as those used by Connection Server to access those hosts.

For example, if Install prompts you for the directory in which to place the Office program files and you enter **G:\OFFICE30**, Install places G:\OFFICE30 in the HOSTID.NB along with other host information you specify after completing the Office LAN installation for that host. To make sure that the Connection Server can find the host correctly, G: should have the same logical drive designation for both the computer running the Connection Server and the computer from which Install is run. To meet these conditions, you may have to do some planning before running Install.

When installing multiple hosts, the system administrator should allow only one Office administration directory per domain. A single administration directory is important because the Office information Notebook files—HOSTID.NB, USERID.NB, and RESOURCE.NB— contain information on a domain level. Each time Install is run to place the Office program files on an individual host, you need to enter the same path to the Office Administration directory. This lets Install find the same HOSTID.NB each time it is run and add the information for each host as it is installed.

If you are using new installations of Office to build a domain, you must also create the master USERID.NB and RESOURCE.NB files. These Notebook files need to contain information about every user and resource to be defined in the domain. For users of Novell Netware, the GENUNB.EXE utility program is provided to extract user information from the Novell binderies on the necessary file servers and copy it to the USERID.NB on that file server. The USERID.NB files must be kept specific to each server, since GENUNB removes from the USER-ID.NB users for whom it does not find information in the bindery. These files can then be merged into one master USERID.NB file.

If you are combining existing hosts into a single domain, or combining hosts that have been converted from Office 2.0, you must merge the USERID.NB and RESOURCE.NB files for each of the existing hosts into master files and place the files in the administration directory for the domain. For more information on merging Notebook files, see Chapter 8, "Using Notebook."

After you finish installing the Office program files and creating the Notebook files for the domain, you need to create the Office host directories and information files for each host in the domain. The program that creates the Office information files from the Notebook files and builds the host directory structures, GENOFF.EXE, is run for the entire domain from the domain administration directory. Because GENOFF is run for the entire domain, it only needs to be run once per domain. From the information in the Notebook files, GENOFF finds the location of each host and creates the correct directories and user files for each host. Since GENOFF is run on the domain level, the logical drive designations for the computer used to run GENOFF *must* match those used when running Connection Server and Install. This ensures that GENOFF.EXE builds each host structure on the right file server and volume.

For example, if G:\OFFICE30 is the path in the HOSTID.NB for a host located on the volume labeled VOL1 on the file server Personnel, the computer used to run Install, GENOFF, and Connection Server will have to have G: assigned as the logical drive designation for PERSONNEL/VOL1. This ensures that each of these programs will be working with the same set of network directories.

Installing WordPerfect Connections

Once all of the host directory structures are installed for each of the hosts, the WordPerfect Connections programs must be installed. The Install program for WordPerfect Connections is very similar to Install for Office LAN. It has three different install options, depending on which type of installation you are performing.

As part of the installation, you are asked for directories in which the WordPerfect Connections files should be installed. Each of the installation types requires that you enter the path to the directory in which the WordPerfect Connections program files should be installed, as well as the path to the administration directory for the domain. The directory for the WordPerfect Connections program files should not be one of the directories in which the Office LAN program files are installed. It is recommended that this directory be on the local hard disk drive of the computer that is used to run the Connection Server. Install also needs to know the path to the domain administration directory in order to install an administration database and its accompanying support files, including an administration menu that can be accessed when the OFFADMIN batch file is run. The database that is installed with the WordPerfect Connections package is intended to help manage users on large systems. The database provides verification of uniqueness not available with Notebook files alone. For more information on using the database, see the section "Using the Administrator Database" in this chapter.

Running Install

Before installing WordPerfect Connections, decide which computer to use to run the Connection Server. Since this computer should have a hard disk drive and the WordPerfect Connections program files should be installed on the hard drive, Install should be run from that machine. If you intend to run the Connection Server from a network drive, you can install WordPerfect Connections from any computer.

Once you decide where you want the program files installed, place the disk labeled "WordPerfect Office Connections" for 3 1/2-inch disks or "WordPerfect Office Connections 1" for 5 1/4-inch disks into a disk drive, change to that drive, and type **install**. With the banner screen displayed, Install asks if you want to continue with the installation or quit. To continue, type **Y** or press ENTER. Type **N** to exit the installation and return to DOS. If you choose to continue, Install displays the Options screen, as shown in Figure 14-2. This screen outlines the different installation options available. If this is an initial installation of WordPerfect Connections, press **1** or **B** to select a Basic Installation. With a Basic Installation, all files are installed. If you do not want to copy all of the files, select the option that best fits your needs. The rest of the steps outlined here assume that you are performing a Basic Installation.

After you select Basic Installation, you'll see a screen with information about the steps involved in performing the installation. Type **Y** or

```
1 - Basic Installation          Install all Connection Server file groups,

2 - Custom Installation         Install selected Connection Server file
                                groups,

3 - Update Connection Server    Do not change existing Connection Server
                                directories; install Connection Server
                                update file groups (i.e., interim release
                                installation),
```

```
Selection: 1                                                    (F7 Exit)
```

Figure 14-2.   Install options for the Connection Server

press ENTER to continue with the installation, or type **N** to abort and return to a DOS prompt. When you continue, you'll see the Connection Server Directory Structure screen shown in Figure 14-3. From the Directory Structure screen, you enter the path to the directory in which you want the program files installed. You also enter the path to the domain administration directory. Once you have entered the correct paths in these two fields, press 3 or ENTER to proceed with the installation. Install then prompts you for the registration number of the WordPerfect Connections package being installed. This is optional, and the installation continues after you press ENTER.

Since this is a Basic Installation, Install copies the files from the WordPerfect Connections disk or disks to the correct directories. If you are installing from 5 1/4-inch disks, Install displays a prompt when it is time to change the disk and place the disk labeled "WordPerfect Office Connections 2" in the disk drive. After you complete the installation, a screen containing information about running Install subsequent times displays. You can press any key to exit Install and return to a DOS prompt.

```
Connection Server Directory Structure (Basic)

    Installing from A:\

1 - Install Program File Directory: C:\OFFCS\  will be created

2 - Office Admin File Directory:    F:\OFFADMIN\


3 - Install All Connection Server File Groups


              +-------------------------------------------+
              | NOTE: If you do not want to use the       |
              |       suggested directories, select the   |
              |       directory options and make the      |
              |       desired changes.  The directories   |
              |       will be created if they do not      |
              |       already exist.  When you are ready  |
              |       to continue, select option 3.       |
              +-------------------------------------------+


Selection: 3                                        (F7 Exit)
```

Figure 14-3.   Directory Structure screen

Running Connection Server

Once the Office hosts are in place and the Connection Server software has been installed, you can use the Connection Server to link individual hosts and form a domain. If you are using a dedicated computer to run Connection Server (as is recommended), here are some configuration ideas that may make it easier to use Connection Server.

First, assuming that the computer is dedicated to running the Connection Server, you can add a command to the AUTOEXEC.BAT file for the computer to start the Connection Server each time you boot. You can also save time by creating a virtual disk or RAM drive, if memory permits, where the Connection Server can access at least its application programs such as MLS.EXE and SCS.EXE. To do this, copy the application program files onto the RAM drive before starting the Connection Server, and then use the /PE and /PW startup options listed on the following page. This saves time since the application programs can be loaded directly from memory rather than from disk each time.

Both of these ideas require the use of some of Connection Server's startup options. The following list outlines the options available for Connection Server:

/C-x	Sets the Connection Server polling cycle time in seconds, where x is the number of seconds.
/H	Displays the available startup options for Connection Server.
/LC-x	Indicates the maximum number of log files that can be made.
/LF-*filename*	Lists the name to be used for all log files.
/LHIGH	Sets logging information to the maximum level.
/LLOW	Sets logging information to the minimum level.
/LON	Turns on file logging on startup.
/LS-x	Maximum size limit for the log file, where x represents the number in kilobytes. The default size is 100K.
/PE-*path*	Path to where the application program files are located. Use this option if you are running the application programs from a RAM drive.
/PH-*path*	Path to a HOSTID.FIL used to give Connection Server routing information.
/PL-*path*	Path where the log files should be stored.
/PW-*path*	Path to Connection Server's work directory. Since Connection Server terminates if this directory cannot be accessed, this should be a local drive.
/S	Causes Connection Server to terminate after completing a single polling cycle.

Reattaching Automatically

Since it is not uncommon for a network workstation to lose its logical connection to a file server, the Connection Server provides a way to reattach to a file server automatically. You do this through the use of a DOS Text file similar to a batch file. This file contains the commands necessary for a workstation to establish a logical connection with a file server. Since each host normally has a unique drive designation, there must be a unique file for each host. These files must contain the commands necessary to attach to a file server and create a unique drive designation for each file server and volume the Connection Server needs to access. Because the commands for regaining a logical network connection vary for the different types of network software, you must create these files and place them in the same directory as the application program files.

Whenever the Connection Server receives an error from the network, indicating that it has lost a logical connection to a file server, the Connection Server then looks for these reattachment files in the directory in which the application program files are located. Since each host must have unique reattachment commands, the Connection Server finds the three-character Host ID for the host it can no longer access and searches for a file named CS*XXX*ATT.BAT, where *XXX* is the three-character Host ID for that host. It then executes the commands listed in the file to reestablish its logical connection. If for some reason the reattachment fails, the Connection Server waits for a few minutes and then tries again. This cycle continues until the attachment is successful or the Connection Server is turned off.

Since there is no guarantee which logical connection may be lost, it is important to place copies of any files needed to complete a reattachment on the local drive of the Connection Server. The files should include all utilities needed to complete a logical connection and drive designation to a file server and volume by a workstation.

Troubleshooting

Because the Connection Server provides links between hosts at many points, there are several basic items you can check to troubleshoot any problems with the Connection Server. First, if the Connection Server constantly displays a message notifying you that a certain host is blocked, you can check the following:

• See if the workstation has sufficient rights in the TRANSIN directory. These include rights to read, write, open, create, delete, search, and modify an open file's attributes.

• Make sure the drive designation used by the workstation to access the host is the same as the drive designation in the HOST-ID.NB.

• Make sure there is a HOSTID.FIL information file in the host directory.

These problems account for a large portion of blocked hosts. Another common problem is when the Connection Server terminates almost immediately after you start it and displays an error message indicating that a HOSTID.FIL or applications programs could not be found. These problems can usually be corrected either by running GENOFF.EXE, or by using the /PH-*path* or /PE-*path* startup options to indicate the locations of these files.

A third common problem occurs when the Connection Server setup option in GENOFF.EXE is set to 0, indicating that the Connection Server is not used. If there is no routing of messages or events between hosts, or if there is no communication between Appointment Calendar and Scheduler, check this option under GENOFF to make sure it is set to 1.

Finally, if the Connection Server is unable to complete the transfer of messages to a host, make certain that there is enough disk space available on the file server for the file to be copied to that server. Also, make sure that the Connection Server account does not have memory use restrictions on the file server, and that there are directory entries available.

Installing Multiple Domains

When the number of hosts on one domain becomes too large for one Connection Server to handle, you need to link multiple domains. Linking multiple domains expands the delivery capabilities of your Office installation. The number of hosts one Connection Server can accommodate varies. The number of hosts on one Connection Server depends on the number of concurrent file server attachments one workstation can have, and whether there are multiple hosts installed on a file server. To install multiple domains and link them with the Connection Server, install each domain as outlined in the first section of this chapter, with the hosts inside the domain defined as Delivery connection types in the HOST-ID.NB. You make links to other domains by defining hosts from those domains in the local HOSTID.NB. However, instead of defining them with a Delivery connection type, define hosts from other domains as a Transfer, Route, or Gateway connection type in the HOSTID.NB.

Using Transfer Hosts

A Transfer connection type provides the logical connection to another domain. In other words, the Connection Server for one domain must be able to copy files to the TRANSIN directory on a Transfer host, so it must have a logical drive designated for that host. This also means that if the same host is used as a Transfer host by other domains as well, several Connection Servers need to have logical connections to the file server on which that Transfer host is located.

An example of a Transfer host is shown in Figure 14-4. In this example, there are two separate domains, each with its own HOST-ID.NB. In the HOSTID.NB for Domain 1, Personnel, Corporate, and Advertising are defined with Delivery connection types. To provide a link to Domain 2, Marketing is defined in Domain 1's HOSTID.NB, not as a Delivery host but as a Transfer connection type. Since the Connection Server must have a logical connection to the file server where Marketing is located, the path to get to Marketing is entered in the HOSTID.NB on Domain 1, as shown in Figure 14-5. This is the path used by the Connection Server to copy files to the TRANSIN directory on Marketing.

The link created using a transfer host is a *one-way link*. Messages or events from Domain 1 to Domain 2 are sent to Marketing by the Connection Server in Domain 1, but messages or events cannot be sent back the same way. To create the link back from Domain 2 to Domain 1,

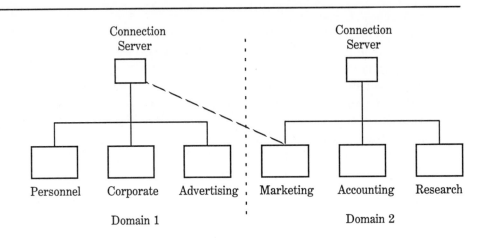

Figure 14-4. Multiple domains with one Transfer host

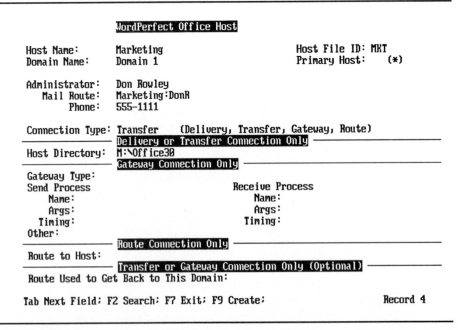

Figure 14-5. Entry in HOSTID.NB for Transfer host

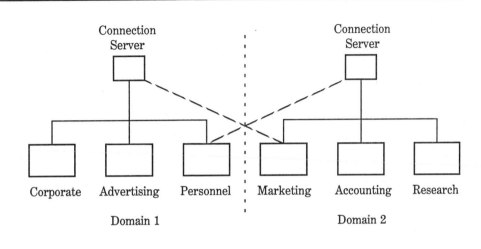

Figure 14-6.   Multiple domains with two Transfer hosts

a host in Domain 1 must be entered as a Transfer connection type in Domain 2's HOSTID.NB. This creates two separate one-way links, as shown in Figure 14-6.

In the HOSTID.NB file, there is a field labeled Primary host. This field is used to designate which host, if any, is the primary host for the domain. A host specified as a primary host does not have any special function until it is used in a multiple-host system. Each time the Connection Server routes a message out of the domain to a Transfer host, the primary host for the local domain is added to the return route for that message. This means that if you specify a primary host, that host should be used as the Transfer host for other domains when they send to the local domain. Conversely, hosts defined as Transfer hosts in the local HOSTID.NB should be primary hosts in their local HOSTID.NB.

Using Route Hosts

Another way to get messages to another domain is to use hosts defined with a Route connection type. Unlike a Transfer connection, a Route

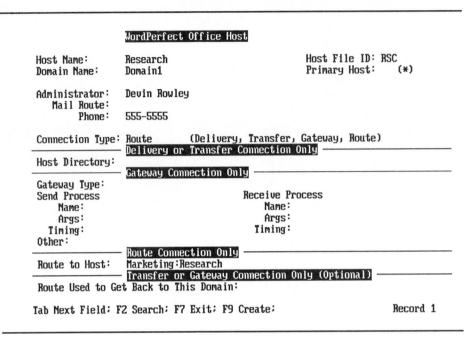

Figure 14-7. Record for Route host in HOSTID.NB

connection type does not require additional logical connections to be made to access that host or domain. A Route connection uses existing logical connections to hop from Connection Server to Connection Server until it arrives at the specified host.

In the example shown in Figure 14-6, the other two hosts in Domain 2—Research and Accounting—could be defined using the Route connection type in Domain 1's HOSTID.NB. For example, the route for Research would be entered in the HOSTID.NB as shown in Figure 14-7.

To deliver a message from a user on the Corporate host in Domain 1 to a user on the Research host in Domain 2, the following steps would occur:

1. When the user on Corporate sends the message, Mail creates a unique message file in a subdirectory of the LIN directory, and places a copy of that file in the TRANSIN directory on Corporate.

2. The Connection Server for Domain 1 finds the file in the TRAN-SIN directory and copies the message file to the TRANSIN directory of Marketing in Domain 2. After the file is successfully copied, it is deleted from the TRANSIN directory on Corporate.

3. The Connection Server for Domain 2 then takes the file from the TRANSIN directory on Marketing, and, using the information from the HOSTID.NB in Domain 2, finds the location of Research and copies the file to the TRANSIN directory on Research. The Connection Server then deletes the file from the TRANSIN directory on Marketing.

4. The next time the Connection Server for Domain 2 checks Research, it finds the file in its TRANSIN directory. The delivery route is completed and the Connection Server places the file in a subdirectory of the CS directory on Research.

5. After completing its cycle, the Connection Server calls the Mail Server application program, MLS.EXE, which moves the file to a subdirectory of the LIN directory on Research, and places links to that file for each of the specified users on the Research host.

After this process is completed, Mail Server sends a status message to the user on Corporate to show that the message was delivered. The return status message is sent to the user using the reverse route that the original message used, with the addition of one more hop. In the preceding example, the return status message follows this route: Research to Marketing, Marketing to Personnel, and Personnel to Corporate. The additional hop from Research to Marketing is added by the Connection Server during the initial delivery to make sure that the return status message leaves the domain from a host that should have a link to other domains.

Using the Default Route Host

Office also allows for a special route host called the *Default Route* host. The Default Route host is defined in the HOSTID.NB and is used when the Connection Server receives a message file that is to be delivered to a host name that it cannot find in HOSTID.FIL. When the host name cannot be found, the message file is routed to the Default Route host. Since all unknown message files use the Default Route, there can only be *one* Default Route host per domain.

To define a Default Route host in the HOSTID.NB, create a record in the HOSTID.NB and define it with a Route connection type. In the Host Name field, enter an asterisk (*). The asterisk acts like the DOS wildcard character; the Connection Server uses it in place of any host name it receives that is not specifically listed in the HOSTID.FIL. In the Route to Host field, enter the name of the Transfer host where you want all unidentifiable messages sent, as shown in Figure 14-8.

The Default Route host eliminates the need to define all global hosts in the local domain's HOSTID.NB. In other words, each HOST-ID.NB only contains Delivery and Transfer hosts along with a single Route host, the Default Route host. This is especially helpful for a system administrator who must maintain a large system. For each domain, the Default Route host only needs to point to the Transfer host in the next domain, and all messages not intended for the local domain are routed to the specified Transfer host.

One disadvantage of the Default Route host is that the Connection Server has a limit on the number of times it moves a file from one host

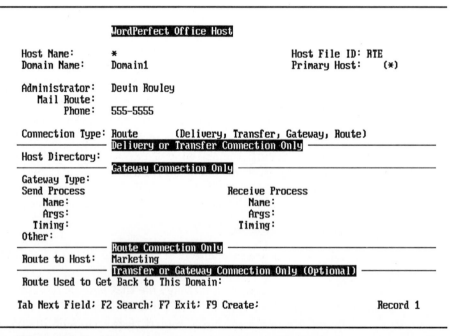

Figure 14-8.   Record for Default Route in HOSTID.NB

to the next. Generally, this is about 12 hops. After 12 hops, the message is considered undeliverable and the Connection Server stops advancing it. With a Default Route host, it is easier to set up endless loops where a message file cannot be routed to the correct domain. Also, if a user enters a host name incorrectly, it would take considerably longer before an undeliverable status was returned, pointing out the mistake. This can also lead to additional traffic for the Connection Server.

Using Gateways

Besides sending Mail and Scheduler files between domains to which the Connection Server has a logical connection, Office 3.0 also supports delivery to remote domains using other transport services. With gateways, you can send messages and files from an office in San Fransisco to an office in New York. Gateways also allow you to connect dissimiliar mail systems. For example, if part of your office uses the WordPerfect Office Mail program and another part of your office uses another non-WordPerfect mail system, you can define a gateway that allows messages to be sent between the two mail programs. These include Message Handling Service (MHS), Easylink, X.400, and Connection Manager, an asynchronous modem communications package created specifically for Office. Office also has gateways to move between different platforms where Office versions 3.0 and later are used, such as MacIntosh, VAX, and UNIX. These gateways support direct connections between the platforms without having to use a separate transport service to complete the link.

A Gateway connection type is defined in the HOSTID.NB—just as Delivery, Transfer, and Route connection types are defined. The HOSTID.NB information window specifically for Gateways, shown here, allows you to define separate application programs and arguments for sending and receiving through a gateway.

```
─────────────────── Gateway Connection Only ───────────────────
Gateway Type:
Send Process                        Receive Process
      Name:                               Name:
      Args:                               Args:
    Timing:                             Timing:
     Other:
```

The Gateway Type field at the top of the window is used to designate the type of gateway this host uses, such as MHS or ASYNC. The Name field under both Send Process and Receive Process gives the Connection Server the name of the application program it needs to call to activate this process. This name is the name of an executable application program that comes with each specific gateway, or a batch file that is used to load the program.

The Args and Timing fields are provided to enter options or variable values specific to a send or receive process. The contents of these fields are passed to the application program listed in the Name field when the Connection Server activates them. The Other field at the bottom of the window lists options, variables, or switches that are not specific to either the send or receive process. This would normally include information such as a directory location for file storage or phone numbers to use as links.

Using the Administrator Database

The administrator database that comes with WordPerfect Connections is intended to help manage a large number of users and resources. The database can verify uniqueness as information is entered in the database, and notify you if there are any conflicts. The first time you use the database, you can select one of two different verification levels: One assumes Office User IDs to be unique in all domains, and the other assumes User IDs are unique only on each individual host. The database also verifies that a resource is assigned to the same host as the user specified as its owner, and that all users and resources are assigned to valid hosts.

Although the database is a useful tool, GENOFF only recognizes Notebook files as valid information files and cannot use information directly from the database. In other words, each time you want to install a user or resource on a host using GENOFF, you must first input that user's or resource's information in the database and then run a report to generate a file in Notebook format that GENOFF can recognize. Also, the GENUNB.EXE utility program that extracts user information from a Novell bindery and inputs it into the USERID.NB can only input information into a Notebook file and not directly into the database. If you are using the database and using GENUNB, the system administrator must import all Notebook information into the database after running GENUNB.

To help minimize these procedures, a separate Office Administration menu is provided with predefined macros to help with the import and export of information to and from the database. To display the menu, select the Using DataPerfect Database entry on the main Office Administration Shell menu. (The DataPerfect version that comes with Office is the run-time version of WordPerfect's DataPerfect database product.) This displays the menu shown in Figure 14-9.

From the Generate Office Using Database menu, there are options for accessing the database for host, user, or resource listings. There are also entries to automate the import of Notebook files into the database and the export of the database to a Notebook file before running GENOFF.EXE. From the Generate Office Using Database menu, you can view the current Notebook files and run GENUNB to extract Novell

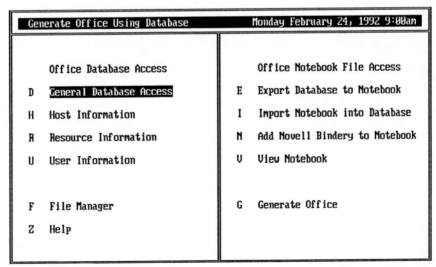

Figure 14-9.   System Administration Database Shell menu

bindery information and place it in the USERID.NB. There is also an entry for running GENOFF to create or update the information files using the current Notebook files.

If you decide to use the database to maintain your Office system, make sure that you become familiar with the basic keystrokes used by DataPerfect to manage the database before trying to create or edit information for an entire domain.

With the WordPerfect Connections package, you can link together multiple Office hosts to create a wide-area communications system. These systems can range from small systems on the same file server to large systems located in different cities. Using WordPerfect Connections and the separate gateway packages also provides links to other transport services so you can correspond with other types of e-mail systems or even different operating systems.

Appendixes

LAN User Installation
ASCII Character Chart
WordPerfect Character Charts
Program File Listing
Predefined Macros
Advanced Macro Commands

P
A
R
T

F
O
U
R

LAN User Installation

Included with Office 3.0 is a program called SETMEUP, which updates each LAN user's personal system so he or she can run the Office programs. SETMEUP checks the AUTOEXEC.BAT and CONFIG.SYS files. If the files do not exist, SETMEUP creates them and inserts the necessary commands to run Office. If the files exist, SETMEUP checks for specific commands needed to run Office. Before the SETMEUP program modifies the AUTOEXEC.BAT or CONFIG.SYS file, it makes backup copies of the user's original files and names these files AUTOEXEC.OLD and CONFIG.OLD.

SETMEUP checks the AUTOEXEC.BAT file to see if the Office 3.0 directory is in the PATH command. If it is, Office programs will load regardless of the directory from which they are started. If the directory is not found in the PATH command or if the PATH command is not found, SETMEUP asks the user if he or she wants to add it to the current PATH command. SETMEUP also checks for the NOTIFY command, which allows users to be notified of Mail and Scheduler items. If the command is not found, SETMEUP asks the user if he or she wants to add NOTIFY to the AUTOEXEC.BAT file. SETMEUP then checks for the CL/I command, which installs Appointment Calendar alarms. Without the CL/I command, users do not receive alarm notification. If CL/I is not found, SETMEUP asks the user if he or she would like to add it to the AUTOEXEC.BAT file. Finally, SETMEUP checks the AUTOEXEC.BAT file for the command to start Shell automatically when the user turns on the computer. If the command to start Shell is not found, SETMEUP asks the user if he or she wants to add it to the AUTOEXEC.BAT file.

SETMEUP also checks for specific commands in the CONFIG.SYS file. First it checks the FILES command, which must be equal to or greater than 40. If there is no FILES command in the CONFIG.SYS file, SETMEUP automatically adds FILES=40. If a FILES command exists but is less than 40, SETMEUP automatically inserts a new

FILES command at the end of the CONFIG.SYS file. (When two copies of the same command exist in a CONFIG.SYS file, only the last command is used.) After checking the FILES command, SETMEUP asks the user if he or she wants to install Repeat Performance and add the necessary commands to the CONFIG.SYS file. If the user answers Yes to install Repeat Performance, the installation program for Repeat Performance is started and the user can enter the desired options. For information on Repeat Performance, see Chapter 11, "Using Notify, Repeat Performance, and TSR Manager."

The SETMEUP program should be run on each user's machine. SETMEUP is an executable file (SETMEUP.EXE) and is installed in the Office Program Directory. The system administrator can run the program on each machine or have each user run the program on his or her individual computer. To run the SETMEUP program:

1. Change to the Office Program Directory.

2. Enter **SETMEUP** on the DOS command line.

3. Type **Y** to continue with the program.

4. Follow the on-screen prompts.

The SETMEUP program is a useful tool that helps users set up individual workstations to work properly with Office 3.0.

ASCII Character Chart

Decimal Value	Hexadecimal Value	Control Character	Character
0	00	NUL	Null
1	01	SOH	☺
2	02	STX	☻
3	03	ETX	♥
4	04	EOT	♦
5	05	ENQ	♣
6	06	ACK	♠
7	07	BEL	Beep
8	08	BS	◘
9	09	HT	Tab
10	0A	LF	Line-feed
11	0B	VT	Cursor home
12	0C	FF	Form-feed
13	0D	CR	Enter
14	0E	SO	♫
15	0F	SI	☼
16	10	DLE	►
17	11	DC1	◄
18	12	DC2	↕
19	13	DC3	‼
20	14	DC4	¶
21	15	NAK	§

Decimal Value	Hexadecimal Value	Control Character	Character
22	16	SYN	▬
23	17	ETB	↕
24	18	CAN	↑
25	19	EM	↓
26	1A	SUB	→
27	1B	ESC	←
28	1C	FS	Cursor right
29	1D	GS	Cursor left
30	1E	RS	Cursor up
31	1F	US	Cursor down
32	20	SP	Space
33	21		!
34	22		"
35	23		#
36	24		$
37	25		%
38	26		&
39	27		'
40	28		(
41	29		)
42	2A		*
43	2B		+
44	2C		,
45	2D		-
46	2E		.
47	2F		/
48	30		0
49	31		1
50	32		2

Decimal Value	Hexadecimal Value	Control Character	Character
51	33		3
52	34		4
53	35		5
54	36		6
55	37		7
56	38		8
57	39		9
58	3A		:
59	3B		;
60	3C		<
61	3D		=
62	3E		>
63	3F		?
64	40		@
65	41		A
66	42		B
67	43		C
68	44		D
69	45		E
70	46		F
71	47		G
72	48		H
73	49		I
74	4A		J
75	4B		K
76	4C		L
77	4D		M
78	4E		N
79	4F		O

Decimal Value	Hexadecimal Value	Control Character	Character
80	50		P
81	51		Q
82	52		R
83	53		S
84	54		T
85	55		U
86	56		V
87	57		W
88	58		X
89	59		Y
90	5A		Z
91	5B		[
92	5C		\
93	5D		]
94	5E		^
95	5F		—
96	60		`
97	61		a
98	62		b
99	63		c
100	64		d
101	65		e
102	66		f
103	67		g
104	68		h
105	69		i
106	6A		j
107	6B		k
108	6C		l

Decimal Value	Hexadecimal Value	Control Character	Character
109	6D		m
110	6E		n
111	6F		o
112	70		p
113	71		q
114	72		r
115	73		s
116	74		t
117	75		u
118	76		v
119	77		w
120	78		x
121	79		y
122	7A		z
123	7B		{
124	7C		¦
125	7D		}
126	7E		~
127	7F	DEL	⌂
128	80		Ç
129	81		ü
130	82		é
131	83		â
132	84		ä
133	85		à
134	86		å
135	87		ç
136	88		ê
137	89		ë

Decimal Value	Hexadecimal Value	Control Character	Character
138	8A		è
139	8B		ï
140	8C		î
141	8D		ì
142	8E		Ä
143	8F		Å
144	90		É
145	91		æ
146	92		Æ
147	93		ô
148	94		ö
149	95		ò
150	96		û
151	97		ù
152	98		ÿ
153	99		Ö
154	9A		Ü
155	9B		¢
156	9C		£
157	9D		¥
158	9E		Pt
159	9F		ƒ
160	A0		á
161	A1		í
162	A2		ó
163	A3		ú
164	A4		ñ
165	A5		Ñ
166	A6		ª

Decimal Value	Hexadecimal Value	Control Character	Character
167	A7		º
168	A8		¿
169	A9		⌐
170	AA		¬
171	AB		½
172	AC		¼
173	AD		¡
174	AE		«
175	AF		»
176	B0		░
177	B1		▒
178	B2		▓
179	B3		│
180	B4		┤
181	B5		╡
182	B6		╢
183	B7		╖
184	B8		╕
185	B9		╣
186	BA		║
187	BB		╗
188	BC		╝
189	BD		╜
190	BE		╛
191	BF		┐
192	C0		└
193	C1		┴
194	C2		┬
195	C3		├

Decimal Value	Hexadecimal Value	Control Character	Character
196	C4		—
197	C5		+
198	C6		╞
199	C7		╟
200	C8		╚
201	C9		╔
202	CA		╩
203	CB		╦
204	CC		╠
205	CD		═
206	CE		╬
207	CF		╧
208	D0		╨
209	D1		╤
210	D2		╥
211	D3		╙
212	D4		╘
213	D5		╒
214	D6		╓
215	D7		╫
216	D8		╪
217	D9		┘
218	DA		┌
219	DB		█
220	DC		▄
221	DD		▌
222	DE		▐
223	DF		▀
224	E0		α
225	E1		β

Decimal Value	Hexadecimal Value	Control Character	Character
226	E2		Γ
227	E3		π
228	E4		Σ
229	E5		σ
230	E6		μ
231	E7		τ
232	E8		ϕ
233	E9		Θ
234	EA		Ω
235	EB		δ
236	EC		∞
237	ED		$\varnothing$
238	EE		ϵ
239	EF		$\cap$
240	F0		$\equiv$
241	F1		$\pm$
242	F2		$\geq$
243	F3		$\leq$
244	F4		$\lceil$
245	F5		$\rfloor$
246	F6		$\div$
247	F7		$\approx$
248	F8		$\circ$
249	F9		$\bullet$
250	FA		$\cdot$
251	FB		$\sqrt{}$
252	FC		η
253	FD		^{2}
254	FE		∎
255	FF		(blank)

WordPerfect Character Charts

The characters listed here can only be used in Editor and Notebook. Note that the ability to display and print these characters is entirely dependent on your printer and graphics card.

These character charts are reprinted by permission. Copyright© 1985, 1990 WordPerfect Corporation. All rights reserved.

WordPerfect ASCII Set

Character Set: 0
Contains: ASCII space through tilde (decimal 32 through 126)

```
           0 1 2 3 4 5 6 7 8 9 0 1 2 3 4 5 6 7 8 9 0 1 2 3 4 5 6 7 8 9
   0
  30             !  "  #  $  %  &  '  (  )  *  +  ,  -  .  /  0  1  2  3  4  5  6  7  8  9  :  ;
  60    <  =  >  ?  @  A  B  C  D  E  F  G  H  I  J  K  L  M  N  O  P  Q  R  S  T  U  V  W  X  Y
  90    Z  [  \  ]  ^  _  `  a  b  c  d  e  f  g  h  i  j  k  l  m  n  o  p  q  r  s  t  u  v  w
 120    x  y  z  {  |  }  ~
```

Multinational 1

Character Set: 1
Contains: Common multinational characters and diacriticals

	0	1	2	3	4	5	6	7	8	9	1 0	1	2	3	4	5	6	7	8	9	2 0	1	2	3	4	5	6	7	8	9
0	`	´	ˆ	˜	¯	/	˘	˙	˝	˚	˛	,	.	ˇ	—	¯	˘	ß	ı	ȷ	Á	á	Â	â
30	Ä	ä	À	à	Å	å	Æ	æ	Ç	ç	É	é	Ê	ê	Ë	ë	È	è	Í	í	Î	î	Ï	ï	Ì	ì	Ñ	ñ	Ó	ó
60	Ô	ô	Ö	ö	Ò	ò	Ú	ú	Û	û	Ü	ü	Ù	ù	Ý	ÿ	Ã	ã	Đ	đ	Ø	ø	Õ	õ	Ý	ý	Ð	ð	Þ	þ
90	Ă	ă	Ā	ā	Ą	ą	Ć	ć	Č	č	Ĉ	ĉ	Ċ	ċ	Ď	ď	Ě	ě	Ė	ė	Ē	ē	Ę	ę	Ğ	ğ	Ğ	ğ	Ğ	ğ
120	Ģ	ģ	Ĝ	ĝ	Ġ	ġ	Ĥ	ĥ	Ħ	ħ	İ	i	Ī	ī	Į	į	Ĩ	ĩ	Ĳ	ĳ	Ĵ	ĵ	Ķ	ķ	Ĺ	ĺ	Ľ	ľ	Ļ	ļ
150	Ŀ	ŀ	Ł	ł	Ń	ń	Ň	ň	Ň	ň	Ņ	ņ	Ő	ő	Ō	ō	Œ	œ	Ŕ	ŕ	Ř	ř	Ŗ	ŗ	Ś	ś	Š	š	Ş	ş
180	Ŝ	ŝ	Ť	ť	Ţ	ţ	Ŧ	ŧ	Ŭ	ŭ	Ű	ű	Ū	ū	Ų	ų	Ů	ů	Ũ	ũ	Ŵ	ŵ	Ŷ	ŷ	Ź	ź	Ž	ž	Ż	ż
210	Ŋ	ŋ	Ď	ď	Ĺ	ĺ	Ñ	ñ	Ř	ř	Š	š	Ť	ť	Ŷ	ŷ	Ỳ	ỳ	Ď	ď	Ơ	ơ	Ư	ư

Multinational 2

Character Set: 2
Contains: Rarely used noncapitalizable multinational characters and diacriticals

	0	1	2	3	4	5	6	7	8	9	1 0	1	2	3	4	5	6	7	8	9	2 0	1	2	3	4	5	6	7	8	9
0	.	°	°	´	ˏ	=	˗	K	˻	ʲ	ˈ	ˊ	ˏ	ˎ	ˌ	ˍ	ˏ	˝	ˋ	ˏ	ʟ	ɛ	ʄ	˘	˘	˙	˙	¨

Box Drawing

Character Set: 3
Contains: All double and single box-drawing characters

	0	1	2	3	4	5	6	7	8	9	1 0	1	2	3	4	5	6	7	8	9	2 0	1	2	3	4	5	6	7	8	9
0	░	█	▌	▐	▀	▄	▬	▬	─	│	┐	┘	└	┌	├	┤	┴	┬	┼	═	║	╗	╝	╚	╔	╠	╣	╩	╦	╬
30	┌	┐	└	┘	├	┤	┴	┬	┼	╒	╓	╕	╖	╘	╙	╛	╜	╞	╟	╡	╢	╤	╥	╧	╨	╪	╫	│	║
60	├	┝	┞	┟	┠	┡	┢	┣	┤	┥	┦	┧	┨	┩	┪	┫	┬	┭	┮	┯	┰	┱	┲	┳	┴	┵	┶	┷	┸

Typographic Symbols

Character Set: 4
Contains: Common typographic symbols not found in ASCII

	0	1	2	3	4	5	6	7	8	9	**1**0	1	2	3	4	5	6	7	8	9	**2**0	1	2	3	4	5	6	7	8	9
0	●	○	■	•	▪	,	¶	§	¡	¿	«	»	£	¥	₧	ƒ	ª	º	½	¼	¢	²	ⁿ	®	©	¤	¾	³	´	·
30	"	"	"	–	—	‹	›	○	□	†	‡	TM	SM	℞	●	○	■	▪	□	□	–	ff	ffi	ffl	fi	fl	…	$	₣	₢
60	₠	£	,	„	⅓	⅔	⅛	⅜	⅝	⅞	Ⓢ	℗	©	‰	‱	‰	№	—	'	H_T	F_F	C_R	L_F	N_L	Y_T

Iconic Symbols

Character Set: 5
Contains: Rarely used "picture" (icon) symbols

	0	1	2	3	4	5	6	7	8	9	**1**0	1	2	3	4	5	6	7	8	9	**2**0	1	2	3	4	5	6	7	8	9
0	♥	♦	♣	♠	♂	♀	☿	☺	◗	♪	♫	■	△	‼	√	☼	⌐	∟	□	◙	↵	☞	☜	✔	□	⊠	☹	#	♭	♮
30	☊	⏀	♒	₵	⌐

Math/Scientific

Character Set: 6
Contains: Non-extensible, non-oversized math/scientific characters not found in ASCII set

	0	1	2	3	4	5	6	7	8	9	**1**0	1	2	3	4	5	6	7	8	9	**2**0	1	2	3	4	5	6	7	8	9
0	−	±	∓	≤	≥	∝	/	/	\	÷	+	|	⟨	⟩	∼	≈	≡	∈	∩	‖	Σ	∞	¬	→	←	↑	↓	↔	↕	▶	◀	▲
30	▼	·	·	∘	•	Å	˙	μ	−	×	∫	Π	∓	∇	∂	′	″	‾	ℯ	ℓ	ℏ	ℑ	ℜ	℘	⇄	↰	⇒	⇐	⇑	⇓
60	⇔	⇕	↗	↘	↖	↙	∪	⊂	⊃	⊆	⊇	϶	∅	⌈	⌉	⌊	⌋	≪	≫	∠	⊗	⊕	⊖	⊙	⊕	∧	∨	⋎	⊤	⊥
90	⌢	⊢	⊣	□	■	◇	◆	⟦	⟧	≠	≢	∴	∵	∷	¢	ℒ	ℭ	∍	℘	○	△	◇	⋆	‴	Ц	≗	≐	<	≤	>
120	≥	∃	∀	⋘	⋙	⫣	⊊	⊋	⊓	⊔	⊏	⊑	⊊	⊐	⊒	⊒	△	▽	◁	▷	⋈	⌣	⌢	○	→	↤	↦	←	←
150	→	⇀	⇌	↼	↑	↑	↓	↓	⇈	⇊	∪	∩	⊂	⊃	◎	⊛	⊝	⊙	℧	△	◁	◁	▷	△	▽	∔	≓	≒	⇌	≍
180	⊨	≙	∤	∣	|	★	≼	≴	≽	≵	≮	⊀	≺	≻	⊁	⋠	⋡	⊄	⊅	⊈	⊉	⊔	⊓	⊔	⊐	⋉	⋊	⋇	∗	ℨ	∉
210	⊘	ℰ	ℐ	ℑ	ℕ	ℝ	₂	└	∃	⋯	…	⋮	⋱	⋰	−	+	−	=	∗	/	∥	⫼	ℋ	℘

Math/Scientific Extension

Character Set: 7
Contains: Extensible and oversized math/scientific characters

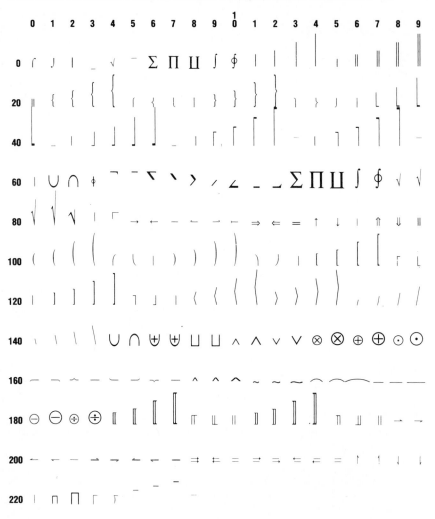

Greek

Character Set: 8
Contains: Full Greek character set for ancient and modern applications

	0	1	2	3	4	5	6	7	8	9	0	1	2	3	4	5	6	7	8	9	0	1	2	3	4	5	6	7	8	9
0	Α	α	Β	β	Β	θ	Γ	γ	Δ	δ	Ε	ε	Ζ	ζ	Η	η	Θ	θ	Ι	ι	Κ	κ	Λ	λ	Μ	μ	Ν	ν	Ξ	ξ
30	Ο	ο	Π	π	Ρ	ρ	Σ	σ	Σ	ς	Τ	τ	Υ	υ	Φ	φ	Χ	χ	Ψ	ψ	Ω	ω	ά	έ	ή	ί	ï	ó	ύ	ü
60	ώ	ε	ϑ	ϰ	ϖ	ρ	ϒ	φ	ω	;	·	¨	ˉ	ˊ	ˋ	˜	˘	˙	ˏ	ˇ	ˌ	˘	ˉ	ˊ	ˋ	˜	˘	˙	ˏ	ˇ
90	ʼ	ʽ	ˮ	ˮ	ˮ	ˮ	ˮ	ˮ	ᾶ	ὰ	ά	ᾳ	ᾷ	ᾱ	ᾰ	ᾶ	ᾶ	ᾳ	ᾳ	ᾳ	ᾴ	ᾲ	ᾶ	ᾷ	ᾳ	ᾳ	ᾴ	ᾲ	ἐ	ἑ	ἒ	ἓ
120	ἔ	ἕ	ἠ	ἡ	ᾖ	ᾗ	ᾐ	ᾑ	ᾒ	ᾓ	ᾔ	ᾕ	ἢ	ἣ	ἤ	ἥ	ἦ	ἧ	ᾖ	ᾗ	ᾐ	ᾑ	ᾒ	ἰ	ἱ	ἲ	ἳ	ἴ	ἵ
150	ἶ	ἷ	ἶ	ἷ	ἰ	ὸ	ὀ	ὁ	ὂ	ὃ	ὄ	ὅ	ὐ	ὑ	ὒ	ὓ	ὔ	ὕ	ὖ	ὗ	ῠ	ῡ	ὼ	ῶ	ῳ	ῴ	ῲ	ῶ
180	ὠ	ὡ	ὢ	ὣ	ὤ	ὥ	ὦ	ὧ	ᾠ	ᾡ	ᾢ	ᾣ	ᾤ	ᾥ	ᾦ	ᾧ	ʼ	,	ϛ	Ϝ	ϙ	ϡ	Ἀ	Ἁ	Ἐ	Ἑ	Ἰ	Ὁ	Ὑ	Ὡ

Hebrew

Character Set: 9
Contains: Hebrew characters

	0	1	2	3	4	5	6	7	8	9	0	1	2	3	4	5	6	7	8	9	0	1	2	3	4	5	6	7	8	9
0	כ	ב	ב	א	ג	ד	ה	ה	ו	ז	ח	ט	י	ך	כ	ל	כ	מ	ם	נ	ן	ס	ע	פ	ף	פ	צ	ק	ר	ש
30	ש	ת	ּ	ֻ	ַ	ֵ	ֶ	ֹ	ִ	ֿ	׳

Cyrillic

Character Set: 10
Contains: Full Cyrillic character set for ancient and modern applications

	0	1	2	3	4	5	6	7	8	9	0	1	2	3	4	5	6	7	8	9	0	1	2	3	4	5	6	7	8	9
0	А	а	Б	б	В	в	Г	г	Д	д	Е	е	Ё	ё	Ж	ж	З	з	И	и	Й	й	К	к	Л	л	М	м	Н	н
30	О	о	П	п	Р	р	С	с	Т	т	У	у	Ф	Х	х	Ц	ц	Ч	ч	Ш	ш	Щ	щ	Ъ	ъ	Ы	ы	ь	Ь
60	Э	э	Ю	ю	Я	я	Ґ	г	Ђ	ђ	Ѓ	ѓ	Є	є	Ѕ	ѕ	І	і	Ї	ї	Ј	ј	Љ	љ	Њ	њ	Ћ	ћ	Ќ	ќ
90	ў	ў	Џ	џ	Ћ	ь	Ѳ	ѳ	Ѵ	ѵ	Җ	җ

Japanese

Character Set: 11
Contains: Hiragana and Katakana characters

	0	1	2	3	4	5	6	7	8	9	**1**0	1	2	3	4	5	6	7	8	9	**2**0	1	2	3	4	5	6	7	8	9
0	あ	い	う	え	お	っ	や	ゆ	よ		ゕ	ゖ	あ	い	う	え	お	か	き	く	け	こ	が	ぎ	ぐ	げ	ご	さ	し	す
30	せ	そ	ざ	じ	ず	ぜ	ぞ	た	ち	つ	て	と	だ	ぢ	づ	で	ど	な	に	ぬ	ね	の	は	ひ	ふ	へ	ほ	ば	び	ぶ
60	べ	ぼ	ぱ	ぴ	ぷ	ぺ	ぽ	ま	み	む	め	も	や	ゆ	よ	ら	り	る	れ	ろ	わ	を	ん	〔	〕	〖	〗	「	」	『
90	』	．	。	、	、	゛	〃	ー	゛	゜	ア	イ	ウ	エ	オ	ッ	ャ	ュ	ョ	ヴ	ヵ	ヶ	ア	イ	ウ	エ	オ	カ	キ	ク
120	ケ	コ	ガ	ギ	グ	ゲ	ゴ	サ	シ	ス	セ	ソ	ザ	ジ	ズ	ゼ	ゾ	タ	チ	ツ	テ	ト	ダ	ヂ	ヅ	デ	ド	ナ	ニ	ヌ
150	ネ	ノ	ハ	ヒ	フ	ヘ	ホ	バ	ビ	ブ	ベ	ボ	パ	ピ	プ	ペ	ポ	マ	ミ	ム	メ	モ	ヤ	ユ	ヨ	ラ	リ	ル	レ	ロ
180	ワ	ヲ	ン	ヽ	ヾ																									

User-Defined

Character Set: 12
Contains: 255 user-definable characters

Program Files

This appendix lists all of the files that are shipped with WordPerfect Office as well as the files that are created when using WordPerfect Office. Each section lists the filename along with a description of the file.

Office 3.0 Files

When you install Office 3.0, the following files are installed to the Office Program Directory. These files are shipped on the WordPerfect Office disks and you can only access them by running the Install program to decompress the files. The first column lists the filename. The second column lists the program that uses the files. If the program file lists Miscellaneous, the file is used in several programs or is a utility file. The third column gives a brief description of the file.

Note: The files marked with an asterisk in the Description column may not be shipped with versions of Office 3.0 dated after 6/14/90.

Filename	Program	Description
CALC.EXE	Calculator	Calculator program file
CALC.HLP	Calculator	Calculator help file
CL.EXE	Appointment Calendar	Calendar program file
CL.HLP	Appointment Calendar	Calendar help file

Filename	Program	Description
CURSOR.COM	Miscellaneous	Utility used to change the appearance of the cursor in all programs.
ED.EXE	Editor	Editor program file
ED.HLP	Editor	Editor help file
ED.MRS	Editor	Macro resource file for Editor macros.
EDHELP.1	Editor	Template file for creating a user-defined help screen for Editor.
FIXBIOS.COM	Miscellaneous	Run from DOS to correct problems with some incompatible ROM BIOS versions.
FM.EXE	File Manager	File Manager program file
FM.HLP	File Manager	File Manager help file
INSTALL.INF	Miscellaneous	Install information file created during the installation procedure. Used if Install is run again.
[LAN] ML.EXE	Mail	Mail program file
[LAN] ML.HLP	Mail	Mail help file
NB.EXE	Notebook	Notebook program file
NB.HLP	Notebook	Notebook help file
NOTEBOOK.NEW	Notebook	Notebook setup file used when no setup file is found.
[LAN] NOTIFY.EXE	Notify	Notification program that notifies users of Mail messages and Scheduler events.
OFF_APPL.NB	Miscellaneous	Notebook file that lists all predefined macros shipped with Office 3.0 and shipped on the Supplemental macro disk. The Notebook file lists the name of the macro along with useful information for running the macros.

Filename	Program	Description
OF{OF}US.LCN	Miscellaneous	Office license file used to display your registration number in each program's main help screen. This file is in an encrypted format and cannot be edited.
README.PC	Miscellaneous	Lists changes and enhancements not currently documented in the manual for Office PC.
LAN README.LAN	Miscellaneous	Lists changes and enhancements not currently documented in the manual for Office LAN.
README.PRD	Miscellaneous	*Lists information about printer drivers shipped with Office 3.0.
README.W30	Miscellaneous	*Lists information about running Office 3.0 with Microsoft Windows 3.0.
RP.EXE	Repeat Performance	Repeat Performance program file.
RP.SYS	Repeat Performance	Repeat Performance system device file.
RPINSTALL.EXE	Repeat Performance	Repeat Performance installation program.
RPREMOVE.EXE	Repeat Performance	Repeat Performance remove program.
LAN SC.ERR	Scheduler	Scheduler error message file
LAN SC.EXE	Scheduler	Scheduler program file
LAN SC.HLP	Scheduler	Scheduler help file
SETMEUP.EXE	Miscellaneous	User installation program that modifies AUTOEXEC.BAT file and CONFIG.SYS file.
SH.MRS	Shell and Editor	Macro resource file for Shell macros.
SHELL.EXE	Shell	Shell program file

Filename	Program	Description
SHELL.NEW	Shell	Default Shell menu shipped with Office 3.0.
SHELL.OVL	Shell	Shell program overlay file. SHELL.EXE and SHELL.OVL must be the same date for Shell to run properly.
SHELLDOS.COM	Shell	Utility that allows some non-WordPerfect products to return to Shell while the program is still resident in memory. This file is automatically executed when needed.
SHMCNV.EXE	Shell	Converts 2.0 Shell macros to 3.0 format.
SUBSHELL.MNU	Shell	Sample Shell submenu shipped with Office.
TSRM.EXE	TSR Manager	Program file for TSR Manager
WP.LRS	Notebook	Language resource file used for Notebook sorting sequences and date display.
WPOPTR.EXE	WPOPTR	WordPerfect Office Printer definition program file used to edit or add printer drivers for Office 3.0.
*.NB	Notebook	Predefined sample Notebook files
*.PIF	Miscellaneous	Program information files needed to run WordPerfect Office under Microsoft Windows 2.11 or later.
*.PRD	Appointment Calendar, Editor, Mail, Notebook, and Scheduler	Printer definition files

Macro Files

Along with the files listed previously, several macro files are shipped with Office 3.0. These macros are used with the predefined macros discussed in Appendix E.

Filename	Description
*.EDM	Predefined Editor macro files
*.PRI	WordPerfect 5.1 primary merge files used with the predefined macros.
*.SHM	Predefined Shell macro files
*.WPK	Predefined WordPerfect 5.1 keyboard files used with the predefined macros.
*.WPM	Predefined WordPerfect macros used with the predefined macros.
RHYMER.TSR	Used with the sample Shell submenu that starts WordPerfect with Rhymer.

Learn Files

Office also has learning files. If these files were installed during the installation process, they are located in a subdirectory called LEARN off of the main Office Program Directory. These files are used in conjunction with the WordPerfect Office 3.0 Workbook.

Filename	Description
ADVSALES.LRN	WordPerfect text file
ART.CAL	Sample Calendar file
ART.NB	Sample Notebook file
ASHSALES.PLN	PlanPerfect file
COUNCIL.DAT	DataPerfect file
COUNCIL.IND	DataPerfect file

Filename	Description
COUNCIL.STR	DataPerfect file
COUNCIL.TOD	DataPerfect file
COUNCIL.TXX	DataPerfect file

Setup Files

The following is a list of setup files used by the WordPerfect Office programs. The first column lists the program name; the second column lists the setup filename if you are using Office PC, and the third column lists the setup filename if you are using Office LAN. Throughout this section, *XXX* represents your WordPerfect Office File ID.

Program Name	PC	LAN LAN
Calendar	CALENDAR.FIL	*XXX*CAL.FIL
Editor	{ED}ED.SET	*XXX*}ED.SET
File Manager	{FM}FM.SYS	*XXX*}FM.SYS
Mail		*XXX* (This file is stored in the MSETPC subdirectory)
Notebook	NOTEBOOK.SYS	*XXX*_NB.SYS
Scheduler		*XXX* (This file is stored in the SSETPC subdirectory)
Shell	SHELL.FIL	*XXX*SHELL.FIL

Backup Files

Calendar, Editor, and Notebook allow you to set backup options to protect against accidental loss of files. The following files are created when you use the backup feature.

Program	Filename	Description
Calendar	*.BK!	Calendar backup file. The * represents the name of the Calendar file.
Calendar	*.ARC	Calendar archive file used to store information that is a specified number of days old. The * represents the name of the Calendar file.
Editor	*.BK!	Original backup file. The * represents the name of the original file. With Original Backup on, the original (unedited) version of the file is saved each time you save and replace a file on disk.
Editor	*}ED.BK?	Timed backup file. The * represents {ED if you are using Office PC or your Office File ID if you are using Office LAN. The ? represents the number of the editing screen on which the file was created.
Notebook	*}NB.BK	Notebook backup file. The * represents {NB if you are using Office PC or your Office File ID if you are using Office LAN.

Temporary Files

The following temporary files are created in the respective programs. Normally these files are automatically deleted when the program is exited properly. If a user has one of these files in a directory, check the date of the file. If the date is not today's date, the file can probably be deleted. The first column lists the name of the file on Office PC; the second column list the name of the file on Office LAN. The third column gives a brief description of the file.

PC	LAN [LAN]	Description
Appointment Calendar		
{CL}.VMF	XXXCAL.VMF	Calendar overflow file
{CL}.PRT	XXXCAL.PRT	Print queue file
Editor		
}ED{ED1.EDT	XXX{ED1.EDT	Top virtual filename, the 1 represents the current editing window.
}ED{ED1.EDB	XXX{ED1.EDB	Bottom virtual filename, the 1 represents the current editing window.
}ED{ED.EDC	XXX{ED.EDC	Check file
}ED{ED1.EDD	XXX{ED1.EDD	Deleted text filename, the 1 represents the current editing window.
}ED{ED.EDR	XXX{ED.EDR	Default range file
}ED{ED.EDS	XXX{ED.EDS	Space file
{ED}ED.	XXX{ED}.	Restart filename used with /1 startup option.
{ED}ED.EDM	XXX}ED.EDM	Temporary macro file
{ED}XX.EDQ	XXX}XX.EDQ	Temporary print queue

Note: With the 6/14/90 release of Office 3.0 all french brackets used the form of {ED}ED. Versions released after 6/14/90 use the form indicated in the examples above, }ED{ED.

PC	LAN [LAN]	Description
File Manager		
LF_}FM{1.DIR	XXX}FM{1.DIR	Created when the number of entries in the first directory listing exceeds 102.

PC	LAN LAN	Description
File Manager		
LF _ }FM{2.DIR	*XXX*}FM{2.DIR	Created when the number of entries in the second directory listing exceeds 102.
	DIR{FM}.TRE	Tree scan file for non-network drives, stored in the root directory.
	XXX{FM}*Y*.TRE	Tree scan file for network drives, where *Y* represents the network drive letter. These are stored where the FM setup file is located.
Mail		
	*XXX*ML{*Y*.TMP	*XXX* represents the user's File ID and *Y* represents the process that creates the temporary file. The following processes create temporary files, the boldfaced letter represents the variable that is placed in the *Y* value in the temporary filename: **A**ccess, **L**ook, **P**rint, and, **S**tatus (viewing the information screen). Temporary files are also created when the To: line is expanded to more than 1K. These files follow the same format, but the *Y* is replaced with **A** for the Primary Copy type, **B** for the Blind Copy type, and **C** for the Carbon Copy type.

PC	LAN LAN	Description
Notebook		
{NB}NB.NBT	*XXX*}NB.NBT	Top virtual file
{NB}NB.NBB	*XXX*}NB.NBB	Bottom virtual file
{NB}NB.CHK	*XXX*}NB.CHK	Check date of top virtual file.
{NB}NB.SPC	*XXX*}NB.SPC	4K file of extra space
{NB}NB.PFX	*XXX*}NB.PFX	Stores 5.0 prefix information.
{NB}NB.SRT	*XXX*}NB.SRT	Sort file template
{NB}NB.DIR	*XXX*}NB.DIR	Created when the number of entries in List Files exceeds 92.
Scheduler		
	XXX{SC}.VRT	Internal database virtual file.
Shell		
SHL{LIB}.VMF	*XXX*{LIB}.VMF	This is a Clipboard temporary file. Created when the information in the Clipboard exceeds the allocated amount of memory for the Clipboard.
SHL*.SAV	*XXX**.SAV	Stores a memory image of everything swapped to disk on the main Shell menu. The * represents a unique character sequence. This file appears if you go into List Files when the information is swapped to disk. This file also appears if the system crashes when information is swapped to disk.

PC	LAN LAN	Description
SHL*Y.SAB	XXX*Y.SAB	Stores a memory image of a submenu which has been swapped to disk. The Y represents the level of the submenu, with B being the first submenu level. The * represents a unique character sequence. This file appears if you go into List Files when the information is swapped to disk. This file also appears if the system crashes when information is swapped to disk.
SHL*.S?V	XXX*.S?V	Stores a memory image of everything to disk in a submenu. The ? represents B, C, D, and so on, which is the level of the submenu that created the temporary file.

Predefined Macros

Shipped with Office are several predefined Shell and Editor macros. You can use these macros to enhance the performance of many of the Office programs and to integrate the capabilities of these programs. When you install Office, the macros are installed in the OFFICE30 directory. You can move the macros to their own directory if you want. If you move the macros, make sure you indicate the macro directory on the Shell Setup menu. Along with the Shell and Editor macros are several WordPerfect macros; these can be stored with the other Office macros or in your WordPerfect macro directory. If you experience memory problems or unusual termination problems while trying to run the macros, you may need to increase your Shell workspace. See Chapter 10, "Using Shell," for information about increasing your workspace. The Office predefined macros are grouped into four categories: program integration macros, accelerator macros, worklog macros and bookmark macros. This appendix lists each macro by name according to its category. If any special requirements are needed to run the macro, they are listed in a "Requirements" section. There is a brief description of the macro, followed by detailed instructions for using it. Many of these macros use several other macros and files to perform their functions; the additional files needed to run the macro are listed under the title "Other Files Needed."

Note: The macros described in this appendix may differ slightly with each release of Office. If the keystrokes outlined in this appendix do not correspond with the macro you are using, follow the on-screen prompts and use the on-line help to find the specific keystrokes and instructions for the macro you wish to use.

Program Integration Macros

The program integration macros let you perform functions that you can normally only perform from within a certain program from any program running under Shell. For example, without a program integration macro, memos, appointments, and to-do items can only be added from within the Appointment Calendar program. With a program integration macro, these items can be added from any program running under Shell.

ALTSHFTA.SHM

Description

The ALTSHFTA macro lets you create memos, appointments, or to-do items from any program that allows you to go to Shell, including the main Shell screen. This eliminates the need to load the Appointment Calendar each time you need to enter one of these items. For example, if you are writing a letter in WordPerfect and remember a certain task you need to do, you can use this macro to enter the to-do item in your calendar without exiting WordPerfect and interrupting the task at hand.

Using the ALTSHFTA Shell Macro

1. From any screen that allows you to go to Shell, press ALT-SHIFT-A.

2. Press **1** or **M** for Memo, **2** or **A** for Appointment, or **3** or **T** for To-Do.

3. Enter the date, in *mm-dd-yy* format, on which you want the entry added.

4. Follow the on-screen prompts in the lower-left corner of your screen for the selected option.

If you selected Memo, simply type the text of the memo and press F7. If you selected Appointment, enter the starting and ending times at the prompt. If you want to view the existing appointments in your calendar before entering the appointment, press ENTER to see the appointments for the selected day. Once the appointments appear, enter the starting and ending times. Next, enter the text of the appointment and press F7. If you selected To-Do, enter the priority for the to-do item. If you are not sure what priorities exist for the selected day, press ENTER to view that day's to-do items. Once the to-do items appear, type in the desired priority, enter the text of the to-do item, and press F7.

When you enter a memo, appointment, or to-do item, a portion of the Calendar screen appears on the screen and may temporarily over-write the original screen contents. The date for which you are entering the item appears on the left side of the screen, and the current date and time appear in the upper-right corner of the screen. The right-hand side of the screen displays the window for which you are entering the item. If you are entering an appointment, a screen similar to the one shown in Figure E-1 appears. Once you press F7 to exit, the original screen is restored.

Other Files Needed

SHELL.EXE	ALTSHFA1.SHM
SHELL.OVL	FINDPROG.SHM
CL.EXE	RETURN.SHM

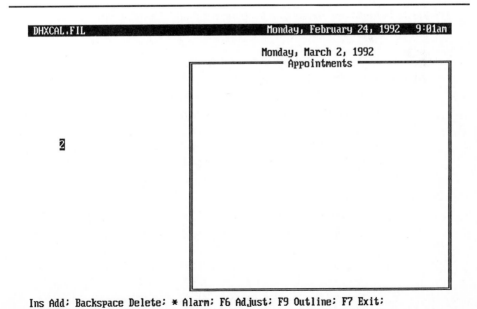

Figure E-1.   ALTSHFTA Shell macro Appointments window

ALTSHFTD.SHM

Requirements

You must have WordPerfect 5.1 to use this macro.

Description

The ALTSHFTD macro integrates features of Notebook and Word-Perfect 5.1 to create memos, letters, and itineraries. The macro takes information from the ADDRESS.NB Notebook file and inserts it into a memo, letter, or itinerary form in WordPerfect 5.1. If you do not want to use the information in the ADDRESS.NB file or do not have an AD-DRESS.NB file, you can insert the information manually from the keyboard.

Using the ALTSHFTD Shell Macro

1. From WordPerfect 5.1, press ALT-SHIFT-D. The menu shown in Figure E-2 appears.

2. Select the desired options and make the necessary changes. The Document Name option refers to the text you want to insert into the body of the document. You do not have to enter any information for this option. The Author option is the name of the person who will sign the letter or the name of the person the memo is from. If you are using Office LAN, your User ID is automatically inserted for that option. The information for the Author's Title option is inserted below the name in the letter. The Document Type option lets you select from Memo, Letter, or Itinerary. The Information Source option lets you select whether the information should be taken from the ADDRESS.NB file or from information input from the keyboard.

```
Create Document

    1 - Create Document

Options

    2 - Document Name
    3 - Author                Drh
    4 - Author's Title
    5 - Document Type         Memo
    6 - Information Source     Form Fill-in




    Selection: 0
```

Figure E-2.   ALTSHFTD.SHM menu

3. After the desired options are selected, press **1** or **C** to create the document. If you are using the Merge from NB option, the macro retrieves the file in Notebook and asks you to mark the appropriate records. You can mark several records if the item needs to go to several different people. If you are using the Form Fill-in option, the macro prompts you for the needed information. After entering the information, press ENTER to continue.

4. Once the document is created, you can enter any additional information. You can also make any editing or formatting changes before saving or printing the file.

Figure E-3 shows a sample memo created with the macro, and Figure E-4 shows a sample itinerary.

MEMORANDUM

To: Mary Melby

From: Carolyn Delco

Date: July 25, 1991

Subject: Employee Retreat

The employee retreat is scheduled for August 20-21. We will be holding a meeting on August 1st to make the final preparations. The theme of the retreat is "Team Work".

Please bring ideas for activities, classes, along with any suggestions you have for the keynote speaker. You will be responsible for conducting the activities and coordinating the facilities. Ramon Curtis will be contacting you regarding the facilities available to us at the conference center.

I look forward to working with you and know this will be a very successful employee retreat.

Figure E-3.   Sample memo created with the ALTSHFTD Shell macro

---

ITINERARY

July 25, 1991

Name: Curtis Ramon

Dates of Trip: From August 31 to September 5

Destination: England

Purpose: Secure account with English distributors

Cost Estimate: $3,000.00

Schedule

Names and Addresses

Figure E-4.   Sample itinerary created with the ALTSHFTD Shell macro

Other Files Needed

SHELL.EXE
SHELL.OVL
WP.EXE (5.1)
WP.FIL
NB.EXE
ALTSHFTD.WPM
ED{NB}.SHM
ADDRESS.NB

ALTSHFTM.SHM

Description

The ALTSHFTM macro lists several of the Shell macros available with Office and allows you to view help screens and execute macros from this menu. This macro gives you an idea of the macros available and their capabilities. This macro is also useful if you cannot remember the name of a particular macro. You can execute this macro and then execute any of the other macros listed on the menu.

Using the ALTSHFTM Shell Macro

1. From any program running under Shell, press ALT-SHIFT-M. The menu shown in Figure E-5 appears.

2. From the menu, you can press **1** or **X** to execute the macro, **2** or **S** and enter the name or part of the name of the macro you want to find, or **3**, **L**, or F3 to look at the help screen for the macro.

3. To exit the Shell Macro List, press F7.

Note: Some macros listed on the Shell Macro List are only shipped on the Supplemental Macro disk. If you execute a macro and receive a message that says the macro cannot be found or may be on another disk, the macro is probably on the Supplemental Macro disk. The help screens for all of the macros indicate which disks the macros are

```
                       Shell Macro List
Macro      Description            Macro      Description

ALTSHFTA   Appointment Calendar   ALTSHFTD   Create WorPerfect Documents
ALTSHFTX   Execute a Macro        AUTOSC     Auto-Scheduling
CALC       Pop-Up Calculator      CUT        Cut Macro to the Clipboard
DIAL       Dial a Number          MAIL       Mail the current text
PRINT      Print from CL, SC or NB QUICK     Send a Quick Mail Message
REPORT51   Worklog Report         SAVE       Save the Phone Message
SPELL      Spell check the text   WORKLOG    Worklog Client/Project Info




1 Execute; 2 Search; 3 Look; 3                    (F3=Help, F7=Exit)
```

Figure E-5.   ALTSHFTM Shell macro menu

shipped on: PC, LAN, or Supplemental. You can order the Supplemental
Macro disk by calling WordPerfect Orders at (801) 225-5000.

Other Files Needed

SHELL.EXE
SHELL.OVL
ALTSHFM2.SHM
ALTSHFM3.SHM
MMAINHLP.SHM
MMHLPM.SHM
ASAHLP.SHM
ASDHLP.SHM
ASXHLP.SHM
AUTOHLP.SHM

DIAL.SHM

Requirements

You must have a modem attached to your computer.

Description

The DIAL macro dials a phone number on the current line from any program that allows you to go to Shell. The macro uses the Notebook Dial feature to dial the number. This macro is especially useful if you are reading a phone message in Mail and want to return the call. The macro does not recognize spaces as valid characters in the phone number.

Using the DIAL Shell Macro

1. Position the cursor on the first number of the phone number.

Note: If you are running this macro from the Phone Message screen in Mail, you do not have to position the cursor on the phone number line.

2. Press ALT-SHIFT-F10 and enter **DIAL**.

3. The number displays at the bottom of the screen, as shown here:

Is *xxx-xxxx* Correct? (Y/N) **Y**

Type **Y** if the number is correct or **N** if it is not. If the number is not correct, move the cursor to the correct phone number and press ENTER. You can also press INS and type in the correct number.

Other Files Needed

SHELL.EXE
SHELL.OVL
DIAL1.SHM
SCRN.SHM
RETURN.SHM
DIALHLP.SHM

MAIL.SHM

LAN Description

The MAIL macro lets you send the current text on the screen as a Mail message. If you are in WordPerfect, Editor, or Notebook, the text is sent as an attached file. If the text on the screen is not saved, the macro prompts you to enter a filename. If the text is saved and has been modified, the file is resaved. If you are in any other text editing screen, such as Calculator or Scheduler, the text is saved to the Clipboard and inserted into the Message window. This macro automates the task of creating and sending Mail messages from existing text.

Using the MAIL Shell Macro

1. From the screen containing the text you want to send in the Mail message, press ALT-SHIFT-F10 and enter **MAIL**.

2. Enter the User ID of the person to whom you want to send the message as well as the subject of the message. If the text is from a program other than WordPerfect, Editor, or Notebook, the text is inserted in the Message window. If the text is from WordPerfect or Editor, the full pathname and filename are inserted into the Files window.

3. Press F7 to send the Mail message, exit the Message screen, and return to the original program.

Other Files Needed

SHELL.EXE
SHELL.OVL
ML.EXE
MAIL1.SHM
FILENAME.SHM
FINDPROG.SHM

PRINT.SHM

Requirements

The printed format uses the WordPerfect 5.1 Tables feature, so you must have WordPerfect 5.1 to use this macro.

Description

The PRINT macro lets you print information from Calendar, Scheduler, and Notebook in an organized and presentable form. From Notebook, the PRINT macro prints all the information displayed on the List Display screen in a WordPerfect 5.1 table. From Calendar or Scheduler, you can print the day, week, month, or year in a variety of formats, including a day timer format. When using the day, week, or month format, information is taken from the Memo, Appointments, and To-Do List window and inserted in a WordPerfect 5.1 table.

Using the PRINT Shell Macro in Notebook

1. Enter the Notebook program and retrieve the desired file.

2. Press ALT-SHIFT-F10 and enter **PRINT** to invoke the macro, which saves the information to the Clipboard and enters WordPerfect 5.1. The macro then creates a primary merge file for the Notebook file. If you have run the macro with that file before, the existing primary merge file is used. If you have not, a new primary file is created.

3. From the menu shown in Figure E-6, select the desired options. The printed file will look similar to that shown in Figure E-7.

```
Print: Print/Save

        1 - Print
        2 - Save
        3 - Append
        4 - Edit

Options

        D - Document Name    ADDRESS.DOC

Print Job

        Page(s)              1-1
```

Figure E-6.   PRINT Shell macro Notebook print options

TEST.NB

First	Last	Work	Home	Company
Chris	Clason	226-3318	226-5400	Spouse Inc.
Derek	Marsh	287-2300	289-9021	Visallia School District
Iola	Haney	297-7900	674-7392	Medical Lab. Inc.
John	Joseph	299-6400	298-7676	JJ Attorney at Law
Jonna	Betts	299-FORMS	297-9876	Forms Plus
Julie	Marsh	287-7892	289-9021	MAD
Michael	Johnson	555-5527	555-8564	International Widget
Richard	Allen	298-8600	298-8626	EG Hutton
Richard	Brooks	298-7899	298-7676	Security International
Sandra	Jean	222-KITES	223-3456	Pismo Kites

Figure E-7.   Sample Notebook file printed with the PRINT Shell macro

Note: With the 6/14/90 release, the macro only works correctly if the field names in the List Display are one word long. You cannot have any leading or trailing spaces in the field names.

Using the PRINT Shell Macro in Calendar and Scheduler

The steps for creating a printed form are the same for both Scheduler and Calendar. These steps use Calendar as the example:

1. Enter the Appointment Calendar program.

2. Move to the desired day, week, month, or year.

3. Press ALT-SHIFT-F10 and enter **PRINT** to invoke the macro. The following menu appears:

```
Print

    1 - Print/Save
    2 - Duration       Day
    3 - Format         3 1/2" x 6 1/2" Organizer (Portrait)
```

4. Select **2** or **D** for Duration and select the desired option.

5. Select **3** or **F** for Format, highlight the format in which you want the Calendar printed, and press **1** or **S** to select the format. The formats that appear on this menu depend upon the duration you selected in step 4. Table E-1 lists the available formats for the

	Day	Week	Month	Year
8 1/2″ by 11″ Portrait		X	X	
8 1/2″ by 11″ Landscape		X	X	
5 1/2″ by 8 1/2″ Portrait	X	X	X	
5 1/2″ by 8 1/2″ Landscape	X	X	X	X
3 1/2″ by 6 1/2″ Portrait	X	X	X	

Table E-1.   Calendar and Scheduler Print Formats Available with the PRINT Shell Macro

various durations. Examples of several of the formats are included at the end of this section.

6. Press **1** or **P** for Print/Save.

After you select Print/Save, the information from the Calendar is retrieved into WordPerfect 5.1 and merged into a table. During this process, several messages flash on the bottom of the screen. Unless you receive an error message that terminates the macro, do not worry about the information flashing on the screen. The process of merging the Calendar information into a table may take some time, depending on the amount of information being merged and the speed of your computer. After the file has been merged, the following menu appears:

```
Print: Print/Save

    1 - Print
    2 - Save
    3 - Append
    4 - Edit

Options

    D - Document Name    CL_MONTH.DOC
    I - Side             Front

Print Job

    Page(s)              1-16
```

Before printing the Calendar file, you should press **4** or **E** for Edit to see how the file looks. This macro is designed to print on laser printers, but you can modify the codes to allow other printers to print properly. If you are using a laser printer with fonts that range from 6 to 14 points, you will need to make very few modifications. In order to fit the different types of information on the page, several font codes are used in the document. Table E-2 lists the ideal font sizes for the different

	Small (3 1/2″ by 6 1/2″ only) Calendars	Large Calendars
Initial Document Font	8pt	10pt
Fine	not used	6pt
Small	6pt	8pt
Large	10pt	12pt
Very Large	12pt	14pt

Table E-2.   Fonts Used When Printing Calendars

attributes used with the macro. The information in the table indicates what kind of modifications you may need to make to the document before printing. If your printer does not have all of these fonts, you can increase the size of the various cells to accommodate the text. See your WordPerfect 5.1 manual for information on editing tables.

If you want to save the document, press **2** or **S** for Save. The document is saved with the name listed for option D, Document Name. You can change the name of the merged Calendar file with this option. Press **D** and enter the new name; you can also include a full path with the filename. To append the information you have just merged to another Calendar file, press **3** or **A**. This option is useful if you want to keep a master merged Calendar file, but only want to merge a few weeks or months at a time.

If you are printing your Calendar with any of the Organizer formats, you need to use the Side option to indicate on what side you want to print. By default, the macro displays Front when you first enter the Print: Print/Save menu. After the front side is printed, the macro returns you to the Print: Print/Save menu and lists Back for the Side option. If you are printing double-sided calendars, you need to reinsert the paper into the printer after the first side is printed. If you are printing the landscape form of the Organizer calendar, place the printed pages in the printer with the printed side face down. The top of the printed pages must face the same way they came out of the printer. If you are printing the portrait form of the Organizer format, the top of the printed pages must face the printer. Because different printers handle orientation differently, you may need to modify the steps for printing double-sided calendars. If your printer jams trying to print the second side, try using a heavier paper. Also, if you are having difficulties, you may just want to print the pages on one side and then use a duplex copy machine to make double-sided calendars.

To get perfect results, you may need to take some time modifying the primery file(s) used by the PRINT macro. However, once this macro is functioning properly, you can print personalized professional-looking calendars. Figure E-8 shows an example of the Year calendar for 1992. Figure E-9 shows a portrait 8 1/2″ by 11″ Month calendar. The Organizer formats fit in the standard day-timer notebooks. Figure E-10 shows one day using the larger 5 1/2″ by 8 1/2″ portrait Organizer format. Figure E-11 shows one day of a blank 3 1/2″ by 6 1/2″ Organizer format. Both the Organizer formats can fold in half to fit into a notebook organizer. (All art in Figures E-8 through E-11 has been reduced to fit text pages.)

1992

January

Su	Mo	Tu	We	Th	Fr	Sa
1	2	3	4	5	6	7
8	9	10	11	12	13	14
15	16	17	18	19	20	21
22	23	24	25	26	27	28
29						

February

Su	Mo	Tu	We	Th	Fr	Sa
1	2	3	4	5	6	7
8	9	10	11	12	13	14
15	16	17	18	19	20	21
22	23	24	25	26	27	28
29	30	31				

March

Su	Mo	Tu	We	Th	Fr	Sa
			1	2	3	4
5	6	7	8	9	10	11
12	13	14	15	16	17	18
19	20	21	22	23	24	25
26	27	28	29	30		

April

Su	Mo	Tu	We	Th	Fr	Sa
					1	2
3	4	5	6	7	8	9
10	11	12	13	14	15	16
17	18	19	20	21	22	23
24	25	26	27	28	29	30

May

Su	Mo	Tu	We	Th	Fr	Sa
	1	2	3	4	5	6
7	8	9	10	11	12	13
14	15	16	17	18	19	20
21	22	23	24	25	26	27
28	29	30				

June

Su	Mo	Tu	We	Th	Fr	Sa
			1	2	3	4
5	6	7	8	9	10	11
12	13	14	15	16	17	18
19	20	21	22	23	24	25
26	27	28	29	30	31	

July

Su	Mo	Tu	We	Th	Fr	Sa
						1
2	3	4	5	6	7	8
9	10	11	12	13	14	15
16	17	18	19	20	21	22
23	24	25	26	27	28	29

August

Su	Mo	Tu	We	Th	Fr	Sa
		1	2	3	4	5
6	7	8	9	10	11	12
13	14	15	16	17	18	19
20	21	22	23	24	25	26
27	28	29	30			

September

Su	Mo	Tu	We	Th	Fr	Sa
				1	2	3
4	5	6	7	8	9	10
11	12	13	14	15	16	17
18	19	20	21	22	23	24
25	26	27	28	29	30	31

October

Su	Mo	Tu	We	Th	Fr	Sa
1	2	3	4	5	6	7
8	9	10	11	12	13	14
15	16	17	18	19	20	21
22	23	24	25	26	27	28
29	30					

November

Su	Mo	Tu	We	Th	Fr	Sa
		1	2	3	4	5
6	7	8	9	10	11	12
13	14	15	16	17	18	19
20	21	22	23	24	25	26
27	28	29	30	31		

December

Su	Mo	Tu	We	Th	Fr	Sa
					1	2
3	4	5	6	7	8	9
10	11	12	13	14	15	16
17	18	19	20	21	22	23
24	25	26	27	28	29	30

Figure E-8.   Year calendar printed with the PRINT Shell macro

Other Files Needed

SHELL.EXE
SHELL.OVL
CL.EXE
WP.EXE (5.1)
WP.FIL
NB.EXE
SC.EXE
OFF_APPL.PRI
CL_PDDL.PRI
CL_PDDP.PRI
CL_PDPP.PRI
CL_PMDOP.PRI
CL_PMDEL.PRI

JANUARY
S M T W T F S
            1 2 3 4
5 6 7 8 9 10 11
12 13 14 15 16 17 18
19 20 21 22 23 24 25
26 27 28 29 30 31

FEBRUARY
1992

MARCH
S M T W T F S
1 2 3 4 5 6 7
8 9 10 11 12 13 14
15 16 17 18 19 20 21
22 23 24 25 26 27 28
29 30 31

SUN	MON	TUE	WED	THU	FRI	SAT
						1
2	3	4	5	6	7	8
9	10	11	12	13 1 Take salad to department luncheon	14 Valentine's Day PAYDAY!	15
16	17 President's Day	18	19	20	21	22 Brook's Birthday
23	24 9:00am Doctor's Appointment	25	26	27	28 PAYDAY!	29

Figure E-9.   Month calendar printed with the PRINT Shell macro

Saturday,
February 22, 1992

Things To Do	Appointments
1 Buy present for Brooks 2 Prepare agenda for Committee meeting	9:00am Interview with Sandra Jean 10:00am 12:00n Lunch with Paul 1:00pm 2:00pm Committee Meeting 4:00pm

Memos
Brook's Birthday

Figure E-10.   5 1/2″ by 8 1/2″ Organizer format printed with the PRINT Shell macro *(continued on next page)*

Saturday, February 22, 1992

Daily Log
7 am
8 am
9 am
10 am
11 am
12 pm
1 pm
2 pm
3 pm
4 pm
5 pm
6 pm

Expenses	

Figure E-10.   5 1/2″ by 8 1/2″ Organizer format printed with the PPRINT Shell macro

Sunday,
February 23,
1992

FEBRUARY
S M T W T F S
                     1
2   3   4   5   6   7   8
9 10 11 12 13 14 15
16 17 18 19 20 21 22
23 24 25 26 27 28 29

Friday, February 21, 1992

Things To Do	Appointments

Memos

Daily Log

8 am	
9 am	
10 am	
11 am	
12 pm	
1 pm	
2 pm	
3 pm	
4 pm	
5 pm	

Expenses	

Figure E-11.   3 1/2″ by 6 1/2″ Organizer format printed with the PRINT Shell macro

SAVE.SHM

LAN Description

The SAVE Shell macro lets you save the current information in a Mail Phone Message screen to the ADDRESS.NB, CONTACT.NB, or MESSAGE.NB sample Notebook file. These Notebook files are shipped with Office. For the macro to work properly, the Notebook Record and List Displays must be in the form originally sent with Office. This macro is useful if you need to add information to one of these files without retyping it all. If you use it with the MESSAGE.NB file, you can use the macro to produce a type of phone log.

Note: In the first release of Office (6/14/90), this macro was called MSG.SHM.

Using the SAVE Shell Macro

1. From the Mail Phone Message Read screen, press ALT-SHIFT-F10 and enter **SAVE**. The macro begins saving information to the Clipboard. A menu appears at the bottom of the screen listing the three different Notebook files.

2. Press **1** or **A** to select ADDRESS.NB, press **2** or **C** to select CONTACT.NB, or press **3** or **M** to select MESSAGE.NB. The information is retrieved into the specified Notebook file. If you select ADDRESS.NB, the name, company, and phone number are inserted into the Notebook file. If you select CONTACT.NB, the name, phone, company, and date and time of the phone call are inserted into the Notebook file. If you select MESSAGE.NB, all of the information from the Mail Phone Message Read screen is entered into the Notebook file.

3. After the information is inserted into the appropriate Notebook file, type **Y** if you want to edit the record and then press F7 to return to the Mail program when the editing is completed. If you do not want to edit the record, type **N** to return to the Mail program.

Other Files Needed

SHELL.EXE
SHELL.OVL
ML.EXE
NB.EXE
SAVEHLP.SHM
MSG2.SHM
ADDRESS.NB
CONTACT.NB
MESSAGE.NB

SPELL.SHM

Requirements

You must have WordPerfect 5.1 to use the SPELL macro. Later versions of Office may support this macro with WordPerfect 5.0. The text that you are spell checking cannot be over 6K.

Description

The SPELL macro uses WordPerfect to spell check the current text on the screen while in any text editing window that allows you to go to Shell. If you are not in a text editing mode, such as the Notebook List Display, the macro displays an error message. Because none of the Office programs have spell checking capabilities, this macro is very useful. For example, if you are in the Mail Send screen and have entered a message, you can spell check the contents of the message, thus avoiding the humiliation of sending a misspelled Mail message to 100 people.

Using the SPELL Shell Macro

1. From any text editing screen, press ALT-SHIFT-F10 and enter **SPELL**. The information is copied to the Clipboard and retrieved into WordPerfect. Once the information is in WordPerfect, spell checking begins.

2. During the spell checking process, follow the prompts at the bottom of the screen to correct any errors that are detected.

After the text has been spell checked, the macro automatically returns you to the program from which you executed the macro and inserts the revised text.

Other Files Needed

    SHELL.EXE
    SHELL.OVL
    ML.EXE
    WP.EXE
    SPELLHLP.SHM
    FINDPROG.SHM
    MAIL_MSG.SHM (created)

Accelerator Macros

Accelerator macros speed up the performance of many routine and daily tasks. These macros also provide shortcuts for performing many tasks.

AUTOSC.SHM

LAN **Description**

The AUTOSC Shell macro automates the task of scheduling meetings that occur on a regular basis. For example, if your company has a board meeting every Monday morning, you can use the AUTOSC macro to schedule this meeting automatically for a certain number of weeks. The macro can schedule monthly, biweekly, weekly, and daily events. The information from the Schedule screen is copied and used to schedule the event the specified number of times. If you are scheduling a monthly, biweekly, or weekly event, the macro schedules the event for the same day of the week. The macro prompts you to confirm any events that fall on a weekend before scheduling the event.

Using the AUTOSC Shell Macro

You must start the AUTOSC macro from the Scheduler Schedule screen and you must enter information in the People and Event fields. If the information does not exist or if you start the macro from the wrong screen, you'll receive an error message.

1. From the Schedule screen, press ALT-SHIFT-F10 and then enter **AUTOSC.**

2. Select **1** or **M** for Monthly, **2** or **B** for Bi-Weekly, **3** or **W** for Weekly, or **4** or **D** for Daily from the menu at the bottom of the screen.

3. Enter the number of months, number of times, weeks, or days for which you want the event scheduled.

After you enter the desired number, the macro displays a message at the bottom of the screen indicating which event it is currently scheduling. After the events are scheduled, the macro returns you to the main Scheduler screen.

Other Files Needed

SC.EXE
SHELL.EXE
SHELL.OVL
AUTOSC1.SHM
AUTOHLP.SHM
SCRN.SHM

ALTS.EDM

Description

The ALTS macro matches pairs of letters. The macro finds matches for the following characters: [ ], { }, ( ), < >, " ", and ' '. This macro is designed for programmers and only works in the DOS Editing mode in Editor.

Using the ALTS Editor Macro

1. Position the cursor on one of the characters for which you want to find a match, and press ALT-S.

The ALTS macro scans the text and moves the cursor to the matching character. If you want to block the information between two of the characters, turn block on (ALT-F4) before executing the macro. After executing the macro, you can perform a function on the blocked text, such as saving, moving, or deleting the text within the matched characters.

Other Files Needed

ED.EXE
ALTSHLP.EDM

ALTT.EDM

Description

The ALTT macro transposes the letter, character, or code at the cursor with the letter, character, or code to the left of the cursor. For example, if you enter **teh**, you could place the cursor on the "h," execute the macro, and the word would appear as "the." This macro also works in macro editing modes.

Using the ALTT Editor Macro

1. Place the cursor on the letter, character, or code furthest to the right that you want to transpose.

2. Press ALT-T and the information is transposed.

Other Files Needed

ED.EXE
ALTTHLP.EDM

ALTU.EDM

Description

The ALTU macro capitalizes the first letter of the word on which the cursor is resting. The first character of the word must be a letter from A to Z.

Using the ALTU Editor Macro

1. Place the cursor anywhere on the word you want to capitalize.

2. Press ALT-U. The first letter is capitalized and the cursor moves to the next word.

Other Files Needed

ED.EXE
ALTUHLP.EDM

Worklog Macros

The two Worklog macros shipped with Office help to simplify and automate the Shell Worklog feature.

WORKLOG.SHM

Requirements

You must specify a worklog filename in the Work Logging Setup menu. To verify that the file is specified, from the main Shell menu press **4** for Setup, **2** for Options, and then **4** or **L** for Work Log Setup. If a filename is not specified on the first line, enter the a full path followed by **WORKLOG.NB**.

Description

The WORKLOG macro automates the task of turning worklogging on and off and changing the currently active worklog information.

Using the WORKLOG Shell Macro

1. From any screen that allows you to go to Shell, including the Worklogging screen, press ALT-SHIFT-F10 and enter **WORKLOG**.

2. Select the desired option from the menu at the bottom of the screen. The menu is similar to the one shown here:

1 Change Project/Client; 2 Turn Worklogging On (or Off): 1

If you choose option 1 to Change the Project/Client information, the macro retrieves the CLIENT.NB file into Notebook where you select the Project/Client to which you want to change. If the CLIENT.NB file is not in the default Notebook directory, the macro prompts you to enter the correct path and filename.

Note: If there is a file currently active in Notebook, you are prompted to save or clear the current file.

To select a new Project/Client, highlight the desired selection and press F7. The information selected from the CLIENT.NB file is used as the current worklogging information. For this macro to work most effectively, you need to input all possible worklogging Project/Client information in the CLIENT.NB Notebook file.

If you choose option 2 to turn worklogging off, the worklogging feature is turned off and the current worklog information is output to the WORKLOG.NB file for future use. If you choose option 2 to turn worklogging on, worklogging becomes active. When turned on, the worklogging feature uses the current Project/Client and User information in the Work Logging screen. If there is no information entered in the Work Logging screen, the macro only records the starting date and time, the number of hours spent on the project, and the number of keystrokes used.

Other Files Needed

SHELL.EXE
SHELL.OVL
NB.EXE
WLOGHLP.SHM
WLSELECT.SHM
FINDPROG.SHM
CLIENT.NB

REPORT51.SHM

Requirements

The printed format of the worklog report uses the WordPerfect 5.1 Tables feature, so you must have WordPerfect 5.1 to use this macro. In addition, records must exist in your WORKLOG.NB file.

Description

The REPORT51 Shell macro lets you create a printed report for a Worklog Summary or a Project Summary. With a Worklog Summary, you select the records from the WORKLOG.NB that you want in the printed report. Figure E-12 shows an example of a printed Worklog Summary. The information is taken from the WORKLOG.NB file and merged into a WordPerfect 5.1 table. At the far right, the report lists the hours spent on each project, and at the bottom right corner, the report lists the total number of hours spent on all projects listed. This report is ideal for tracking certain projects and calculating the number of hours spent on each project.

A Project Summary is similar to the Worklog Summary, but it creates a report for a specific project or client. After invoking the macro and selecting Project Summary, you are prompted for the name of the Client ID for which you want to create a report. Information is extracted from all the records containing the specified Client ID and merged into a WordPerfect 5.1 table. Figure E-13 shows a sample Project Summary. The global project information is listed at the top of the table and the specific worklog records are listed within the table. A

Worklog Summary
Wednesday, June 27, 1991, 3:33pm
to
Monday, July 16, 1991, 1:07pm

Date:	1991/06/27 15:35		**Hours:**	1.02

User ID:	John Cressall	**User Type:**	Attorney
Client/Proj:	Haney	**Client Type:**	Deed
Started:	Wednesday, June 27, 1991, 3:33pm	**Ended:**	Wednesday, June 27, 1991, 4:35pm

Comment:

Date:	1991/07/12 14:30		**Hours:**	2.00

User ID:	Richard Cressall	**User Type:**	Accountant
Client/Proj:	Melby	**Client Type:**	Financial Folio
Started:	Thursday, July 12, 1990, 2:30pm	**Ended:**	Thursday, July 12, 1990, 4:30pm

Comment:

Date:	1991/07/12 15:18		**Hours:**	3.01

User ID:	John Cressall	**User Type:**	Attorney
Client/Proj:	Marsh vs. City of Visallia	**Client Type:**	Closing Arguments
Started:	Thursday, July 12, 1991, 3:18pm	**Ended:**	Thursday, July 12, 1991, 6:18pm

Comment:

Date:	1991/07/16 11:07		**Hours:**	2.03

User ID:	Sandra	**User Type:**	Executive Secretary
Client/Proj:	Conference	**Client Type:**	Training Material
Started:	Monday, July 16, 1991, 11:05am	**Ended:**	Monday, July 16, 1991, 1:07pm

Comment:
Training seminar outline, handouts, name tags

Total Hours   8.06

Figure E-12.   Sample Worklog Summary Report printed with the REPORT51 Shell macro

Project Summary

Client/Project: Conference   User ID: Christopher
Client Type: Promotional Ad   User Type: Marketing Rep

Date/Time Started	Date/Time Ended	Hours	Comments
Wednesday, June 27, 1991, 3:30pm	Wednesday, June 27, 1991, 7:30pm	4.00	
Thursday, July 12, 1991, 2:30pm	Thursday, July 12, 1991, 4:31pm	2.01	
Monday, July 16, 1991, 11:05am	Monday, July 16, 1991, 1:07pm	2.03	Training seminar outline, handouts, name tags
Wednesday, July 18, 1991, 11:07am	Wednesday, July 18, 1991, 1:10pm	2.05	
	Total Hours	10.09	

Figure E-13.   Sample Project Summary Report printed with the REPORT51 Shell macro

column in the middle of the table lists the hours spent on each project, with the total displaying at the bottom of the table. With releases of Office after 6/14/90, if you have projects that have the same Client ID but do not have the same client type, you can have the macro generate a report that includes all projects regardless of the client type or you can generate a report specific to a client type.

Using the REPORT51 Shell Macro

To create a Worklog Summary Report:

1. Press ALT-SHIFT-F10 and enter **REPORT51**. The macro retrieves the WORKLOG.NB file into Notebook. If the WORKLOG.NB file is not in the default Notebook directory, the macro prompts you to enter the correct path and filename.

Note: If there is a file currently active in Notebook, you are prompted to save or clear the current file.

2. Press **1** or **W** to select Worklog Summary.

3. Highlight the record you want to include in the report and type an asterisk (*). Repeat this step until all the records you want in the report are marked.

4. Press F7 to continue. The macro merges the information into a 5.1 table and displays a Print menu.

5. From the menu, you can choose to print, save, append, edit, or change the document name. Select the desired option(s).

To create a Worklog Project Report:

1. Press ALT-SHIFT-F10 and enter **REPORT51**. The macro retrieves the WORKLOG.NB file into Notebook. If the WORKLOG.NB file is not in the default Notebook directory, the macro prompts you to enter the correct path and filename.

Note: If there is a file currently active in Notebook, you are prompted to save or clear the current file.

2. Press **2** or **J** to select Project Summary.

3. Press **1** or **C** to select Client ID only, or press **2** or **T** to select Client ID and Type.

4. Enter the Client ID. If you selected option 2, Client ID and Type, enter the client type as well. The macro merges the information into a 5.1 table and displays a Print menu.

5. From the menu, you can choose to print, save, append, edit, or change the document name. Select the desired option.

If the reports do not print correctly, you can modify the primary file to fit the specifications of your printer. The primary files used for these reports are LOGRPRTS.PRI and LOGRPRTJ.PRI.

Other Files Needed

SHELL.EXE
SHELL.OVL
NB.EXE
WP.EXE
WP.FIL
RPT51HLP.SHM
FINDPROG.SHM
ED{NB}.SHM
WORKLOG.NB
LOGRPRTS.PRI
LOGRPRTJ.PRI

Bookmark Editor Macros

The Bookmark Editor macros are a programming tool that insert place markers to help you locate a breaking point while programming. The four different Bookmark macros insert marks, find marks, list marks, and remove marks. With these macros, you can improve your efficiency and productivity while programming.

ALTM.EDM

Description

The ALTM macro inserts a bookmark at the current cursor position. If the text is in a macro editing mode, the mark is inserted as a comment. If the text is in DOS Text mode, the mark is inserted as a remark (REM). You can insert up to nine marks. Marks are inserted in numeric order and may be inserted in any open Editor file or macro. Marks should not be saved with a file.

Using the ALTM Editor Macro

1. Position the cursor where you want to insert the mark and press ALT-M. Figure E-14 shows a file with Marks inserted.

Other Files Needed

ED.EXE
ALTMHLP.EDM
MARK_UPD.EDM

```
{Screen Copy}{;}{MARK-1}~{Home}{Up}{;}{MARK-2}~{Home}{Left}{Enter}
{;}{MARK-3}~{Home}{Down}{;}{MARK-4}~{Home}{Right}{Enter}
a
```

SHM C:\OFF30\ED_FILES\ALTSHFTC.SHM   Mac 1 Ln 2   Pos 37

Figure E-14.   Macro file showing bookmarks

ALTF.EDM

Description

The ALTF Editor macro finds existing marks in documents. You can search for a specific mark number, any mark in the currently displayed file or macro, or any mark in any active file or macro.

Using the ALTF Editor Macro

1. From Editor, press ALT-F.

2. If necessary, press the UP ARROW or DOWN ARROW key to change the search direction.

3. Type the number of the mark you want to find, type an asterisk (*) to find the next mark in the currently displayed file or macro, or type an # to search all active Editor files or macros for a mark.

After you enter the desired selection, the cursor moves to a mark if one is found.

Other Files Needed

    ED.EXE
    ALTFHLP.EDM

ALTL.EDM

Description

The ALTL Editor macro lists all the marks in the currently active files or macros. While listing the marks, you can search for a specific mark or delete a mark.

Using the ALTL Editor Macro

1. From Editor, press ALT-L. A screen similar to the one shown in Figure E-15 appears. The screen lists the mark number, the text, the macro or filename where the mark occurs, the number of the active macro or file window, and the line number on which the mark occurs.

2. Press **1** or **F** to Find the mark and move to the mark, press **2** or **R** to remove the mark, or press **3** or **H** and enter the mark number to highlight the desired mark quickly.

Other Files Needed

ED.EXE
ALTLHLP.EDM
ALTR.EDM
ALTF.EDM

```
                         Current File/Macro Marks
   Mark #    Text                               Mac Name     Mac #  Line #

   {MARK 1}  (Cannot Display Macro Commands)    ALTL.EDM       9     15
   {MARK 2}  (Cannot Display Macro Commands)    ALTM.EDM       2     16
   {MARK 3}  (Cannot Display Macro Commands)    ALTSHFTV.SHM   3     2
   {MARK 4}  (Cannot Display Macro Commands)    MACRO1.EDM     4     2
   {MARK 5}  (Cannot Display Macro Commands)    MACRO2.EDM     5     2
   {MARK 6}  (Cannot Display Macro Commands)    MACRO3.SHM     6     42




 1 Find; 2 Remove; 3 Highlight Mark #: 1               (F3=Help, F7=Exit)
 DOS C:\OFF30\ED_FILES\DLAST.FIL        File 1  Pg 1  Ln 1      Pos 1
```

Figure E-15.   Bookmark listing

ALTR.EDM

Description

The ALTR Editor macro removes existing marks in documents. You can remove a specific mark number, all marks in the currently displayed file or macro, or all marks in any active file or macro.

Using the ALTR Editor Macro

1. From Editor, press ALT-R.

2. Enter the number of the mark to remove a single mark, enter an asterisk (*) to remove all marks from the currently displayed file or macro, or enter an exclamation point (!) to remove all marks from all active files or macros.

Advanced Macro Commands

The Shell and Editor programs that come with Office 3.0 can execute advanced macros using many of the same commands as WordPerfect 5.0 and later. Many of these commands require extra parameters that you can specify at the command, or by using the contents of a variable. Most commands also require a tilde (~) to designate parameters at the end of the command.

    The following list outlines the available macro commands, and indicates which Office programs can use the commands in their macros. It also displays some brief examples of the macros. Some of the commands can be used in conjunction with several other commands, but the examples may only show ways to use the commands individually. For detailed examples of the macro commands, you can view the predefined macros that ship with Office 3.0.

Macro Command	Macro Type	Command Description	Example
{;}Comment~	EDM SHM	All text or commands between the command and the tilde are ignored during execution	{;} This is a comment in a macro~

Macro Command	Macro Type	Command Description	Example

{ALT-*n*}	EDM	Executes a macro, or assigns or reads the contents of a variable	{LABEL}Repeat~
			 {CHAR}Z~Replace Y/N~
			 {CASE}
			   {ALT-Z}~
			   Y~Continue~
			   y~Continue~
			   N~Stop~
			   n~Stop~
			   {OTHERWISE}~
			   Repeat~ ~

{Alt-Shft-*n*}	SHM	Executes a macro, or assigns or reads the contents of a variable	{TEXT}1~Input the first name:~ {IF}"{Alt-Shft-1}" ="Bob"~ {GO}Continue~
{ASSIGN} *variable*~ *value*~	EDM SHM	Assigns a value or expression to a variable	{ASSIGN}Num~2~ {ASSIGN}Name~Bob~
{BELL}	EDM SHM	Computer will beep during macro execution	{BELL}
{BREAK}	EDM SHM	Breaks out of the current loop structure, nested macro, or subroutine	{ON ERROR}{BREAK}~ {ON CANCEL}{BREAK}~

{CALL}*label*~	EDM SHM	Moves macro execution to the routine named *label*	{IF}"{VARIABLE}One~"
			 ="Y"~
			   {CALL}Start~
			 {ELSE}
			   {CALL}Finish~
			 {END IF}

{CANCEL OFF}	EDM SHM	Disables the Cancel function (F1) for macro execution, but not for editing	{CANCEL OFF}

Macro Command	Macro Type	Command Description	Example
{CANCEL ON}	EDM SHM	Enables the Cancel function (F1)	{CANCEL ON}
{CASE} *condition* ~ *case1* ~ *label1* ~ ... *casen* ~ *labeln* ~ ~	EDM SHM	Transfers macro execution to the label whose case equals the condition. {CASE} does not require a {RETURN} after execution	{LABEL}Repeat ~ {CASE}{VARIABLE} V1 ~ ~ 1 ~ Start ~ Y ~ Start ~ y ~ Start ~ ~ 2 ~ Finish ~ N ~ Finish ~ n ~ Finish ~ {OTHERWISE} ~ Repeat ~ ~
{CASE CALL} *condition* ~ *case1* ~ *label1* ~ ... *casen* ~ *labeln* ~ ~	EDM SHM	Transfers macro execution to the label whose case equals the condition. {CASE CALL} requires a {RETURN} following execution of the subroutine. Execution resumes after the {CASE CALL} command	{LABEL}Repeat ~ {CASE CALL} {VARIABLE}V2 ~ ~ 1 ~ SubRtn1 ~ 2 ~ SubRtn2 ~ 3 ~ SubRtn3 ~ {OTHERWISE} ~ Repeat ~ ~ {LABEL} NextRoutine ~
{CHAIN} *macro* ~	EDM SHM	Indicates the name of the macro to execute upon completion of the current macro	{CHAIN} NextMacro ~

Macro Command	Macro Type	Command Description	Example
{CHAR} *variable* ~ *prompt* ~	EDM SHM	Displays the specified prompt and stores the next keystroke in the variable listed	{CHAR}Input ~ Is this correct? ~
{Ctrl-Alt-*n*}	SHM	Executes the program assigned to letter *n* on the Shell menu	{Ctrl-Alt-W}
{Ctrl-Alt-Shft-*n*}	SHM	Returns the Ctrl-Alt-Shft-*n* keystroke to the present application	{Ctrl-Alt-Shft-P}
{Ctrl-PgUp}	SHM	Invokes the Shell Macro Ctrl-PgUp menu	{Ctrl-PgUp}
{Ctrl-Shft-*n*}	SHM	Returns the Ctrl-Shft-*n* keystroke to the present application	{Ctrl-Shft-L}
{DISPLAY OFF}	EDM SHM	Macro execution does not echo to the display	{DISPLAY OFF}
{DISPLAY ON}	EDM SHM	Enables macros echo to the display during execution	{DISPLAY ON}

Macro Command	Macro Type	Command Description	Example
{ELSE}	EDM SHM	Provides an optional alternative routine if the conditions for the {IF} and {IF EXISTS} commands are not met	{IF}{VARIABLE} Cost~ <25~ {CALL}TooLittle~ {ELSE} {CALL}TooMuch~ {END IF}
{END FOR}	EDM SHM	Marks the end of loops using the {FOR} and {FOR EACH} commands	{FOR}Num~1~10~1~ {CALL}Increment~ {END FOR}
{END IF}	EDM SHM	Marks the end of conditional routines using the {IF} and {IF EXISTS} commands	{IF}{VARIABLE} Cost~ <25~ {CALL}TooLittle~ {ELSE} {CALL}TooMuch~ {END IF}
{END WHILE}	EDM SHM	Marks the end of a loop using the {WHILE} command	{WHILE}{VARIABLE} V1~ <20~ {CALL}Build~ {END WHILE}
{EXEC ADD} *letter~ parameters~*	SHM	Executes the program assigned to the listed letter on the Shell menu. The parameters are passed to the program after any parameters on the Startup Options line in the Program Information screen	{EXEC ADD}e~/b/w-50~ {EXEC ADD}m~/u-dhx~

Macro Command	Macro Type	Command Description	Example
{EXEC DOS} *program~parameters~*	SHM	Executes the named program or command from the DOS command line and passes it the listed parameters	{EXEC DOS} FORMAT ~a:~
{EXEC RPL} *letter~parameters~*	SHM	Executes the program assigned to the listed letter on the Shell menu. The parameters passed to the program replace any parameters on the Startup Options line in the Program Information screen	{EXEC RPL}e~/b/w-50~ {EXEC RPL}m~/u-dhx~
{FILE EXISTS} *filename~*	SHM	Searches the directories in the current DOS path to find the specified file	{IF} {FILE EXISTS}S.BAT~~ {EXEC DOS}S.BAT~ {ELSE} {PROMPT} This file does not exist.~ {END IF}
{FIND PROG} *program~*	SHM	Returns the letter in the current Shell menu assigned to the specified program	{ASSIGN}1~{FIND PROG} SC.EXE~~{EXEC ADD} {Alt-Shft-1}~/u-a~

Macro Command	Macro Type	Command Description	Example
{FOR}*variable~* *start~stop~step~*	EDM SHM	Executes the routine following the {FOR} command until the start value is incremented by the step value to equal or exceed the stop value	{FOR}Num~1~10~1~ {CALL}Increment~ {END FOR}
{FOR EACH}*variable~* *value~...valuen~~*	EDM SHM	Assigns (sequentially) each value listed to the named variable and executes the routine following the {FOR EACH} command	{FOR EACH}Name~ Joe~Bob~Don~~ {CALL}NameWrite~ {END FOR}
{GET CURSOR} *col~row~*	SHM	Stores the current column and row position of the curosor in the named variables	{GET CURSOR}C1~R1~
{GO}*label~*	EDM SHM	Continues execution of the macro at the point of the named label	{GO}Start~
{IF}*condition~*	EDM SHM	Conditionally executes commands following the {IF} statement, depending on the state of the specified condition	{IF} "{VARIABLE} Name~" ="Harold"~ {CALL}Write~ {END IF}

Macro Command	Macro Type	Command Description	Example
{IF EXISTS} *variable* ~	EDM SHM	If the specified variable has been assigned a value, the commands following the {IF EXISTS} command are executed	{IF EXISTS}Num~ {CALL}NumErase~ {ELSE} {ASSIGN}Num~25~ {END IF}
{IN MEMORY} *letter* ~	SHM	Returns a 1 or true if the program assigned to the specified letter on the current Shell menu is loaded into memory. If not, returns a 0 or false	{IF}{IN MEMORY}m~ {CALL}Send~ {ELSE} {EXEC ADD}m~ {CALL}Send~ {ENDIF}
{INPUT} *message* ~	EDM	Displays the listed message and pauses. Execution continues when ENTER is pressed	{INPUT}Write your Mail message and press ENTER when finished~
{KBSTAT} *value* ~	SHM	Clears or sets the Lock keys on the keyboard	{KBSTAT}48~ *See* {PROG SYSTEM} *for explanation of values*

Macro Command	Macro Type	Command Description	Example
{KTON}*key*~	EDM SHM	Returns a converted value for any keystroke. Dividing the value by 256 returns the Word-Perfect character set the key belongs in as the quotient, and the character number as the remainder	{CHAR}kstrk~Press Any Character~ {ASSIGN}kval~{KTON} {VARIABLE}kstrk~ ~
{LABEL}*label*~	EDM SHM	Designates a specified point in a macro, normally the beginning of a subroutine	{LABEL}Start~
{LEN}*variable*~	EDM SHM	Returns the number of characters assigned to a specified variable	{TEXT}Date~Enter Today's Date: ~ {ASSIGN}Num~ {LEN}Date~
{LOOK}*variable*~	EDM SHM	Stores any existing keystrokes in the keyboard buffer to the specified variable. If there are no keystrokes, the variable is cleared	{LOOK}Start~

Macro Command	Macro Type	Command Description	Example
{MENU DESC} *letter*~	SHM	Displays the Shell menu description listed for the program assigned to the specified letter on the Shell menu	{MENU DESC}a~
{MID}*variable*~ *offset*~ *count*~	EDM SHM	Returns the string inside the specified variable, beginning at the offset and using the count to move to the end of the string	{ASSIGN}First~ {MID}Name~1~10~~
{NEST} *macro*~	EDM SHM	Executes the specified macro. After execution, control returns to the parent macro	{NEST}CallNew~
{NEXT}	EDM SHM	Returns execution to the start of a loop using the next set of loop conditions	{NEXT}
{NOTK} *number*~	EDM SHM	Returns a character for a converted keystroke number. The character is found in the WordPerfect character set by dividing the value by 256 to find the set, and using the remainder as the character number	{NTOK}32791~

Macro Command	Macro Type	Command Description	Example
{ON CANCEL} *command*~	EDM SHM	Performs the specified command if Cancel (F1) is pressed during execution	{ON CANCEL}{BREAK}~
{ON ERROR} *command*~	EDM SHM	Performs the specified command if an error occurs during execution	{ON ERROR} {CALL}ErrMessage~ ~
{ON NOT FOUND} *command*~	EDM SHM	Performs the specified if a search fails during execution	{ON NOT FOUND}
{OTHERWISE}	EDM SHM	As the last case in a {CASE} or {CASE CALL} command, any conditions not being met execute the commands listed here	{LABEL}Repeat~ {CHAR}Z~Replace Y/N~ {CASE}{ALT-Z}~ Y~Continue~ y~Continue~ N~Stop~ n~Stop~ {OTHERWISE}~ Repeat~ ~
{PAUSE}	EDM SHM	Suspends macro execution until ENTER is pressed	{PAUSE}
{PAUSE KEY}*key*~	EDM SHM	Suspends macro execution until the specified key is pressed	{PAUSE} {CANCEL}~
{PROG SYSTEM} *variable*~	SHM	Returns a value signifying the current state of the specified feature or option	{PROG SYSTEM}CYear~
{PROMPT} *message*~	EDM SHM	Displays the specified message	{PROMPT}This is a prompt~

Macro Command	Macro Type	Command Description	Example
{PUT CURSOR} *col~row~*	SHM	Positions the cursor on the column and row position specified	{PUT CURSOR} 5~5~
{QUIT}	EDM SHM	Exits the macro and returns to the current application	{QUIT}
{RESTART}	EDM SHM	Exits a macro from a nested macro at the completion of the nested macro's execution	{RESTART}
{RESTORE SCREEN}	SHM	Restores the screen that was displayed the last time {SAVE SCREEN} was executed	{RESTORE SCREEN}
{RETURN}	EDM SHM	Marks the end of a macro, nested macro, or a {CASE} or {CASE CALL} command	{RETURN}
{RETURN CANCEL}	EDM SHM	Returns a Cancel command to the next higher level of execution	{RETURN CANCEL}
{RETURN ERROR}	EDM SHM	Returns an error to the next higher level of execution	{RETURN ERROR}

Macro Command	Macro Type	Command Description	Example
{RETURN NOT FOUND}	EDM SHM	Returns a search not found condition to the next higher level of execution	{RETURN NOT FOUND}
{SAVE SCREEN} *upper-left-col*~ *upper-left-row*~ *lower-right-col*~ *lower-right-row*~	SHM	Saves the contents of the screen inside the specified column and row boundaries	{SCREEN SAVE} 4~4~22~22~
{Screen Copy}	SHM	Begins Shell's Screen Copy. The same as using ALT-SHIFT-MINUS	{Home}{Home}{Up} {Screen Copy} {Home}{Down} {Home}{Right}
{Screen Retrieve}	SHM	Retrieves the current contents of Shell's Clipboard to the current cursor position. The same as ALT-SHIFT-+I	{Screen Retrieve}
{SHELL MACRO} *macro*~	EDM	Executes the specified Shell macro	{SHELL MACRO} CutPaste~
{SHELL SYSTEM} *variable*~	SHM	Returns the value of the specified Shell system variable	{SHELL SYSTEM}EMM~
{SPEED} *increment*~	EDM SHM	Pauses macro execution between commands by intervals of the increment multiplied by 1/100 of a second	{SPEED}100~

Macro Command	Macro Type	Command Description	Example
{PUT CURSOR}			
{STATE}	EDM SHM	Returns a value reflecting the current state of the application	{ASSIGN}2~ {STATE}~
{STATUS PROMPT} *prompt~*	EDM	Displays the specified prompt on the status line	{STATUS PROMPT} This Prompt Displays on the Status Line~
{STEP OFF}	EDM SHM	Disables single-step macro execution	{STEP OFF}
{STEP ON}	EDM SHM	Enables single-step macro execution — normally for troubleshooting macros	{STEP ON}
{SYSTEM} *variable~*	EDM	Returns the current state of the specified system variable	{SYSTEM}Path~
{TEXT} *variable~* *prompt~*	EDM SHM	Displays the specified prompt and then assigns characters from the keyboard to the variable until ENTER is pressed	{TEXT}Name~ Enter Your Full Name~
{VARIABLE} *variable~*	EDM SHM	Displays or executes the current contents of the specified variable	{IF}"{VARIABLE}One~" = "{VARIABLE}Two~"~ {PROMPT}These are equal~

Macro Command	Macro Command Type	Command Description	Example
{WAIT} *increment*~	EDM SHM	Delays execution of commands by the value of the increment multiplied by 1/10 of a second	{WAIT}10~
{WHILE} *condition*~	EDM SHM	Performs a loop, executing the commands that follow the {WHILE} command until the condition is not true	{WHILE} {VARIABLE}Num~ <10~ {CALL}Increment~ {ENDWHILE}

{PROG SYSTEM} Command Values

The {PROG SYSTEM} macro command returns values indicating options or settings in the current application. When using {PROG SYSTEM}, you can use the number to the left of each variable, or the variable name itself.

Program Variables for Appointment Calendar

System Variable	Possible Returned Values
(1) NAME	Returns the filename and extension of the current Appointment Calendar file
(2) DAY	Returns the current DOS day of the month. The range is from 1 to 31
(3) MONTH	Returns the current DOS month. The range is from 1 to 12
(4) YEAR	Returns the current DOS year
(5) WEEKDAY	Returns the current DOS weekday. The range is Sunday through Saturday

(6) CDAY	Returns the day of the month currently highlighted on the Calendar. The range is from 1 to 31
(7) CMONTH	Returns the month on which the cursor is currently positioned. The range is from 1 to 12
(8) CYEAR	Returns the year on which the cursor is currently positioned
(9) CWEEKDAY	Returns the weekday on which the cursor is currently positioned. The range is from Sunday through Saturday

Program Variables for Calculator

System Variable	*Possible Returned Values*
(1) NVAL	Returns the current value of the repeating variable n
(2) FIX	Returns the current number of fixed digits to display following the decimal point
(3) BASE	Returns the decimal value of the current numbering system: 2, 8, 10, or 16
(4) TRIGMODE	Returns 0 if the current trigonometric mode is radians, and 1 if the current mode is degrees

Program Variables for Editor

System Variable	*Possible Returned Values*
(1) DOCUMENT	Returns the status of the document in the editing screen. A 1 means the document has been edited and 256 means the editing screen is blank
(2) LEFT	Returns the value of the character or command to the immediate left of the cursor
(3) LINE	Returns the line number of the current line on the page
(4) ALINE	Returns the absolute line number of the current line in the document

(5) NAME	Returns the filename and extension of the current document
(6) MODE	Returns the current mode of Editor set with TEXT IN/OUT or by defaulting to a retrieved file
(7) PAGE	Returns the number of the current page in the document
(8) PATH	Returns the path, including a trailing back-slash (\\), of the current document
(9) POS	Returns the position of the cursor on the current line
(10) RIGHT	Returns the value of the character or command to the immediate right of the cursor
(11) SHELLVER	Returns a value to calculate the current version of Shell. This value divided by 256 gives the major version number. The remainder indicates the minor version number
(12) PRINT	Returns a 0 if not currently printing, and 1 if currently executing a print command
(13) EXT	Returns the filename extension of the current document in uppercase
(14) FILE	Returns the number of the current document in Editor. The range is 1 to 9

Program Variables for File Manager

System Variable	*Possible Returned Values*
(1) NAME	Returns the name, in uppercase, of the file or directory that is currently highlighted; no extension is included
(2) EXTENSION	Returns the extension for the file or directory that is currently highlighted
(3) FILES	Returns the number of files currently listed
(4) MARKS	Returns the current number of marked files
(5) DIRECTORY	Returns the directory that is currently displayed

(6) PATTERN	Returns the filename pattern used for the current listing
(7) SORTMODE	Returns the current sorting method used in the file listing. 1 is by Filename, 2 is by Extension, 4 is by Date and Time, and 8 is by Size
(8) REPLACE	Returns 0 to indicate that confirm is off, and 1 to indicate that confirm is on
(9) AFTER	Returns the date used for the "From" display under Select Files
(10) BEFORE	Returns the date used for the "Before" display under Select Files
(11) USED	Returns the number of bytes of storage space currently in use on the current disk
(12) FREE	Returns the number of bytes of storage space currently unused on the current disk
(13) DRIVE	Returns the uppercase letter used to designate the current drive
(14) MARKED	Returns 0 to mean that the currently highlighted file is not marked, and returns 1 to mean the file is marked

Program Variables for Mail

System Variable	*Possible Returned Values*
(1) INBOX	Returns the total number of messages in the In Box
(2) OUTBOX	Returns the total number of messages in the Out Box
(3) UNREAD	Returns the total number of unread messages in the In Box
(4) ITEMS	Returns the number of attachments to the current message
(5) USERID	Returns the Office User ID for the current user

(6) READ	Returns a 0 if the current message is unread, and a 1 if the message has been read
(7) FIELD	Returns the field number in which the cursor is located for any of the editing screens. If the cursor is not in an editing screen, a 0 returns

Program Variables for Notebook

System Variable	*Possible Returned Values*
(1) FIELD	From the Record Display, returns the name of the currently highlighted field
(2) PORT	Returns the number of the COM port to be used for dialing
(3) TOTAL	After moving to the bottom of the List Display, returns the total number of records in the file
(4) MARKS	Returns the total number of records that have been marked
(5) NAME	Returns the name of the current Notebook file
(6) MARKED	Returns 0 if the current record is not marked, and 1 if the record is marked
(7) RECORD	Returns the number of the current record in the file
(8) PATH	Returns the path, including a trailing backslash (\), of the current Notebook file
(9) DOCUMENT	Returns 0 if the current file has not been modified, 1 if the file has been modified, and 256 if the file is blank

Program Variables for Scheduler

System Variable	*Possible Returned Values*
(1) REQUESTED	Returns the total number of events in the Requested box

(2) ORGANIZED	Returns the total number of events in the Organized box
(3) PENDING	Returns the total number of events in the Requested box that have a pending status
(4) USERID	Returns the User ID or Resource ID for the current user or resource
(5) USERTYPE	Returns 0 for a user, and 1 for a resource
(6) DAY	Returns the current DOS day of the month. The range is from 1 to 31
(7) MONTH	Returns the current DOS month. The range is from 1 to 12
(8) YEAR	Returns the current DOS year
(9) WEEKDAY	Returns the current DOS weekday. The range is Sunday through Saturday
(10) CDAY	Returns the day of the month that is currently highlighted. The range is from 1 to 31
(11) CMONTH	Returns the month on which the cursor is currently positioned. The range is from 1 to 12
(12) CYEAR	Returns the year on which the cursor is currently positioned
(13) CWEEKDAY	Returns the weekday on which the cursor is currently positioned. The range is Sunday through Saturday
(14) FIELD	Returns the field on which the cursor is currently located on the Schedule, Search, and Group screens. The value returned indicates the field number on the screen

{SHELL SYSTEM} Command Values

You can use the {SHELL SYSTEM} macro commands to return values indicating the current state of Shell, or resources that Shell is aware of. When using {SHELL SYSTEM}, you can use the number to the left of the variable, or the variable name itself.

Shell System Variables

System Variable	*Possible Returned Values*
(1) STATE	Current state of Shell. Possible values:
	1 Shell is active
	2 Macro Definition mode
	4 Macro Execution mode
	8 Work Log is defined
	16 Data is present in Clipboard
	32 Clipboard cut is active
	256 Executing DOS command or batch file
	512 Current program not run from under Shell. This includes batch files run from the Shell menu
	1024 At DOS command line under Shell
(2) MENULTR	Returns the letter assigned to the current active program on the Shell menu
(3) MENUNAME	Returns the Shell menu description for the current active program
(4) PROGNAME	Returns the program name
(5) SWAP	Returns 1 if enough expanded memory is free to complete a swap, 2 if there is enough free disk space, and 4 if swapping is enabled
(6) MENULEV	Returns the menu level of the current Shell menu. 0 is for the main menu, 1 for first level submenu, 2 for second level submenu, and so on
(7) CLIPBOARD	Returns the following values for different content formats:
	0 WordPerfect 4.2 or DOS text
	1 WordPerfect 4.2 merge file
	2 WordPerfect 5.*x* text
	3 WordPerfect 5.*x* merge file
	4 Graphics or binary file

(8) CURDIR	Returns the path to the current default DOS directory
(9) WORKLOG	Returns the following values for the Work-log status: 1 Client logging on or off 2 Program logging on or off 4 Timed backup on or off 8 Timer
(10) LOGNAME	Returns the path to the Work Log notebook
(11) PROJECT	Returns the Project name in the current Work Log notebook
(12) PROJECTID	Returns the Project ID name in the current Work Log notebook
(13) USER	Returns the user name for the current Work Log notebook
(14) USERJOB	Returns the user job type name in the current Work Log notebook
(15) MACRODIR	Returns the path to the Global Macro directory for Shell
(16) MEMORY	Returns the number of bytes of free memory available
(17) EMM	Returns the status of available expanded memory
(18) DISK1	Returns the number of bytes available on disk 1 using /O or /V
(19) DISK2	Returns the number of bytes available on disk 2 using /O or /V
(20) PATH	Returns the path to the current active application
(21) PROG	Returns the name of the current executed program

(22) KBSTAT	Returns the current status of the keyboard using the following values:

1	Right SHIFT key is pressed
2	Left SHIFT key is pressed
4	CTRL key is pressed
8	ALT key is pressed
16	SCROLL LOCK is on
32	NUM LOCK is on
64	CAPS LOCK is on
128	Insert mode is enabled

(23) DEFDIR	Returns the default directory listed for the current active application.

{SYSTEM} Command Values

You can use the {SYSTEM} macro command to return values indicating the current state of Editor, or information about the current document in Editor. When using {SYSTEM}, you can use the number to the left of the variable, or the variable name itself.

System Variables

System Variable	*Possible Returned Values*
(1) DOCUMENT	Returns the status of the document in the editing screen. A 1 means the document has been edited and 256 means the editing screen is blank
(2) LEFT	Returns the value of the character or command to the immediate left of the cursor
(3) LINE	Returns the line number of the current line on the page
(4) ALINE	Returns the absolute line number of the current line in the document
(5) NAME	Returns the filename and extension of the current document

(6) MODE	Returns the current mode of Editor set with TEXT IN/OUT or by defaulting to a retrieved file
(7) PAGE	Returns the number of the current page in the document
(8) PATH	Returns the path, including a trailing backslash (\), of the current document
(9) POS	Returns the position of the cursor on the current line
(10) RIGHT	Returns the value of the character or command to the immediate right of the cursor
(11) SHELLVER	Returns a value to calculate the current version of Shell. This value divided by 256 gives the major version number. The remainder indicates the minor version number
(12) PRINT	Returns 0 if not currently printing, and 1 if currently executing a print command
(13) EXT	Returns the filename extension, in uppercase, of the current document
(14) FILE	Returns the number of the current document in Editor. The range is 1 to 9

{STATE} Command Values

The following values are returned when you use the {STATE} macro command, which senses the environment state for the current application.

State Values for Appointment Calendar

Value	State of Appointment Calendar
1	The cursor is located in the Memo window
2	The cursor is located in the Appointments window
4	The cursor is located in the To-Do window

8	The Financial Functions screen is displayed
32	The Setup menu is displayed
64	The Print menu is displayed
128	The Color Setup menu is displayed
256	A help screen is displayed
512	Edit windows are in Typeover mode
1024	Paused waiting for user input
4096	The current file has been modified
8192	The Auto-Date screen is displayed
32768	Cannot swap to Shell

State Values for Calculator

Value	*State of Calculator*
1	The Main screen is displayed
2	The Scientific Functions screen is displayed
4	The Programmer Functions screen is displayed
8	The Financial Functions screen is displayed
16	The Statistical Functions screen is displayed
128	The Color Setup menu is displayed
256	A help screen is displayed
1024	Paused for user input
2048	The tape is turned on
4096	The tape is full
32768	Cannot swap to Shell

State Values for Editors

Value	*State of Editor*
1	Edit screen 1 is displayed
2	Edit screen 2 is displayed
4	The cursor is located in the main editing screen
16	Editor is in Macro Definition mode
32	Editor is in Macro Execution mode

128	Block definition is turned on
256	The Editor is in Typeover mode
512	The Reveal Codes function is active
1024	A Yes/No prompt is displayed
32768	Cannot swap to Shell

State Values for File Manager

Value	*State of File Manager*
1	The Main screen is displayed
2	The Look function is active
4	The Select Files menu is displayed
8	The Progam Launch screen is displayed
16	The Setup menu is displayed
256	A help screen is displayed
512	The Name Search function is active
1024	Paused for user input
2048	The File Listing contains marked files
4096	Confirm Replace is enabled
8192	File Listing is using Date limits
32768	Cannot swap to Shell

State Values for Mail

Value	*State of Mail*
1	The Main screen is displayed
2	The Read screen is displayed
4	The Information screen is displayed
8	The Group screen is displayed
16	The Send screen is displayed
32	The Phone Message screen is displayed
64	The Look function is active
128	The Color Setup menu is displayed
256	A help screen is displayed

512	The Edit screen is in Typeover mode
1024	A Yes/No prompt is displayed
2048	The displayed list has marked items
4096	One of the List Display functions is active
8192	The Temporary Send Options menu is displayed
16384	The cursor is located in the In Box
32768	Cannot swap to Shell

State Values for Notebook

Value	State of Notebook
1	The List Display screen is displayed
2	The Record Display screen is displayed
4	The List Files screen is displayed
8	The Merge screen is displayed
32	The Print Options menu is displayed
64	The Options for Current Notebook menu is displayed
128	The Color Setup menu is displayed
256	A help screen is displayed
512	Typeover mode is active in the Record Display
1024	Paused for user input
2048	In the current listing, items have been marked
4096	The current file has been modified
16384	Executing a dial-up
32768	Cannot swap to Shell

State Values for Scheduler

Value	State of Scheduler
1	The Month screen is displayed
2	The cursor is located in the Day window on the Month screen
4	The Schedule screen is displayed
8	The Week screen is displayed

16	The Busy screen is displayed
32	The Setup menu is displayed
64	The Print menu is displayed
128	The Color Setup menu is displayed
256	A help screen is displayed
1024	Paused for user input
2048	Items are marked on the current list
4096	One of the List Display functions is active
8192	The Search screen is displayed
16384	The Events screen is displayed
32768	Cannot swap to Shell
65536	The Look function is active
131072	The Export Option screen is displayed
262144	The Group screen is displayed

State Values for Shell

Value	*State of Shell*
1	At the DOS command line
2	The Clipboard menu is displayed
4	The Setup screen is displayed
8	The Memory Map screen is displayed
16	The Work Log screen is displayed
256	A help screen is displayed
1024	Paused for user input
4096	A password is set on the current Shell menu file
8192	Can go to DOS

Programs are identified by boldface; keystrokes are shown in italics.

The manuscript for this book was prepared and submitted to Osborne/McGraw-Hill in electronic form. The acquisitions editor for this project was Roger Stewart, the associate editor was Laurie Beaulieu, the technical reviewer was E. A. Glazener, and and the project editor was Janis Paris.

Text design by Judy Wohlfrom and Peter Hancik, using Baskerville for text body and Swiss boldface for display.

Cover art by Bay Graphics Design, Inc. Color separation and cover supplier, Phoenix Color Corporation. Screens produced with InSet, from InSet Systems, Inc. Book printed and bound by R.R. Donnelley & Sons Company, Crawfordsville, Indiana.

Calculator 3.0 Template

	F1	F2	F3	F4	F5	F6	F7	F8	F9	F10
Ctrl	Shell	Memory Clear								
Shift	Clear All	Memory Recall								
Alt										
Key	Clear Entry	Memory Store	Help	Scientific	Tape	Programmer	Exit	Financial	Colors	Statistics

(cut here)

Appointment Calendar 3.0 Template

	F1	F2	F3	F4	F5	F6	F7	F8	F9	F10
Ctrl	Shell		Screen/Update	Move	File Format		Print	Setup Options		Retrieve
Shift	Setup Options	← Search	Switch		Date					
Alt										
Key	Cancel	→ Search	Help	Copy		Adjust/Bold	Exit	Underline	Outline	Save

(cut here)

WordPerfect Office: The Complete Reference

File Manager 3.0 Template

	F1	F2	F3	F4	F5	F6	F7	F8	F9	F10
Ctrl	Shell		Screen Mode		Mark/Unmark All		Print (PL)	Select Files	Execute (PL)	
Shift	Setup	← Search	Switch	Block						
Alt			Hex Dump							
Key	Cancel	→ Search	Help	Copy	Find Files	Edit (PL)	Exit	Windows		

Editor 3.0 Template

	F1	F2	F3	F4	F5	F6	F7	F8	F9	F10
Ctrl	Shell	Wrap	Screen	Move	Text In/Out	Macro Def	Print	Options	Top	Function/Mac Def
Shift	Setup	← Search	Switch	Append	Date	Dup Line			Middle	Retrieve
Alt	Null	Replace	Codes	Block		Copy Line			Bottom	Macro
Key	Cancel	→ Search	Help	Copy	List Files	Dup Word	Exit	Switch	Block	Save

Notebook 3.0 Template

	F1	F2	F3	F4	F5	F6	F7	F8	F9	F10
Ctrl	Shell	↓ Search & Mark	Line Draw						Sort	
Shift	Setup	↓ Search	Switch	Manual Dial	Date		Print	Options	Middle	Retrieve
Alt		↑ Search & Mark			Mark/Unmark All					
Key	Cancel	→ Search	Help	Dial	List Files	Bold	Exit	Underline	Create Record	Save

Mail 3.0 Template

	F1	F2	F3	F4	F5	F6	F7	F8	F9	F10
Ctrl	Shell		Screen Update							
Shift	Setup	↓ Search	Switch		Date Format		Print	Options		Retrieve
Alt				Block	Mark/Unmark All					
Key	Cancel	→ Search	Help		List	Bold	Exit	Underline	Send	Save

(cut here)

WordPerfect Office: The Complete Reference

Scheduler 3.0 Template

	F1	F2	F3	F4	F5	F6	F7	F8	F9	F10
Ctrl	Shell		Screen		Export		Print	Schedule Options		Retrieve
Shift	Setup		Switch		Date					
Alt			Busy						Schedule	
Key	Cancel	Search	Help		List	Bold	Exit	Underline		Save